PEACE MOVEMENTS
WORLDWIDE

Recent Titles in Contemporary Psychology

Preventing Teen Violence: A Guide for Parents and Professionals
Sherri N. McCarthy and Claudio Simon Hutz

Making Enemies: Humiliation and International Conflict
Evelin Lindner

Collateral Damage: The Psychological Consequences of America's War on Terrorism
Paul R. Kimmel and Chris E. Stout, editors

Terror in the Promised Land: Inside the Anguish of the Israeli-Palestinian Conflict
Judy Kuriansky, editor

Trauma Psychology, Volumes 1 and 2
Elizabeth Carll, editor

Beyond Bullets and Bombs: Grassroots Peace Building between Israelis and Palestinians
Judy Kuriansky, editor

Who Benefits from Global Violence and War: Uncovering a Destructive System
Marc Pilisuk with Jennifer Achord Rountree

Right Brain/Left Brain Leadership: Shifting Style for Maximum Impact
Mary Lou Décosterd

Creating Young Martyrs: Conditions That Make Dying in a Terrorist Attack Seem Like a Good Idea
Alice LoCicero and Samuel J. Sinclair

Emotion and Conflict: How Human Rights Can Dignify Emotion and Help Us Wage Good Conflict
Evelin Lindner

Emotional Exorcism: Expelling the Psychological Demons That Make Us Relapse
Holly A. Hunt, Ph.D.

Gender, Humiliation, and Global Security: Dignifying Relationships from Love, Sex, and Parenthood to World Affairs
Evelin Lindner

PEACE MOVEMENTS WORLDWIDE

Volume 2: Players and Practices in Resistance to War

Marc Pilisuk and Michael N. Nagler, Editors

CONTEMPORARY PSYCHOLOGY
Chris E. Stout, Series Editor

PRAEGER

AN IMPRINT OF ABC-CLIO, LLC
Santa Barbara, California • Denver, Colorado • Oxford, England

Library of Congress Cataloging-in-Publication Data

Peace movements worldwide / Marc Pilisuk and Michael N. Nagler, editors.
    p. cm. — (Contemporary psychology)
    Includes bibliographical references and index.
    ISBN 978-0-313-36478-5 (hard copy : alk. paper) — ISBN 978-0-313-36479-2 (e-book) — ISBN 978-0-313-36480-8 (vol. 1 hard copy : alk. paper) — ISBN 978-0-313-36481-5 (vol. 1 e-book) — ISBN 978-0-313-36482-2 (vol. 2 hard copy : alk. paper) — ISBN 978-0-313-36483-9 (vol. 2 e-book) — ISBN 978-0-313-36484-6 (vol. 3 hard copy : alk. paper) — ISBN 978-0-313-36485-3 (vol. 3 e-book)
    1. Peace movements 2. Peace movements—History. I. Pilisuk, Marc. II. Nagler, Michael N.
    JZ5574.P44   2011
    303.6'6—dc22   2010037446

ISBN: 978-0-313-36478-5
EISBN: 978-0-313-36479-2

15   14   13   12   11   1   2   3   4   5

This book is also available on the World Wide Web as an eBook.
Visit www.abc-clio.com for details.

Praeger
An Imprint of ABC-CLIO, LLC

ABC-CLIO, LLC
130 Cremona Drive, P.O. Box 1911
Santa Barbara, California 93116-1911

This book is printed on acid-free paper ∞

Manufactured in the United States of America

CONTENTS

ACKNOWLEDGMENTS

The three volumes of this book were invited by our publisher who saw, as we do, the value in an overview, as far as it was possible to take one, of the peace movement as a whole. First Debora Carvalko and then Lindsay Claire and Denise Stanley have been immensely supportive throughout. We soon found that the task of inviting, identifying, and editing selections from academics, officials, and activists from the varied aspects of the search for peace was a challenge to our time and organizational talents. To all of our contributors, some world renowned, all busy, we extend our thanks and appreciation for working with us, sometimes on short notice, to include their chapters. We remain amazed and grateful for the work for peace described in their contributions and the courage and persistence of the people they write about. The Metta Center for Nonviolence receives a special thanks for providing us with a welcoming place to meet.

This collection could never have seen the light of day without the dedicated involvement of a number of people. Gianina Pellegrini spent long hours beyond the few for which she was compensated to keep us on task, to communicate respectfully to hundreds of people through thousands of messages. She edited manuscripts, recruited other graduate students from Saybrook University to help, organized tasks and meetings, volunteered to write two articles on her own that we truly needed, fell behind in her own studies but never despaired or lost a chance to encourage others. Chris Johnnidis of the Metta Center provided initial help in setting up an interactive filing system. The project got a boost when Gianina spread the word at Saybrook University. Saybrook deserves thanks for finding some of the most talented and dedicated students anywhere. Rebecca Norlander provided endless hours of editing, evaluating, and reformatting articles and is a co-author of an article. Angel Ryono likewise helped write, edit, and find authors to fill gaps, and is a co-author of two articles. Other students whose generous help included becoming chapter authors. They are: Nikolas Larrow-Roberts, Rev. José M. Tirado, Ellen Gaddy, and Melissa Anderson-Hinn. Two other colleagues, Mitch Hall and Daniel Adamski, saw enough in the project to pitch in with major editing tasks and went on to be co-authors of chapters. Many others whom we were not able to include in the anthology helped us tremendously, sharing their specific expert knowledge and contacts to help us frame the task. These include Donna Nassor, Sandy Olleges, Kevin Bales, Curt Wand, Glen Martin, Byron Belitsos, Ethel Tobach, Douglass Fry, Ahmed Afzaal, Susan McKay, Joel Federman, Gail Ervin, Dan Christie, Jeff Pilisuk, and Josanne Korkinen.

Marc wants to express appreciation for the inspiration of two mentors, Anatol Rapaport and Kenneth Boulding; of his parents, who always valued peace and justice; and to his wife, Phyllis, who tolerated his sleep-deprived state for close to a year understanding what he was trying to do. He thanks Michael Nagler for being a partner whose knowledge and belief in the peace movement are just amazing.

Michael wants to thank the staff at the Metta Center for giving him the space and the encouragement to see this task through; his friends and colleagues in the peace movement for stepping up with translation (Matthias Zeumer), ideas, and other contributions; Marc Pilisuk for inviting him on board in the first place; and above all his mentor and guide, Sri Eknath Easwaran of the Blue Mountain Center of Meditation, for showing him his life's path and never losing faith that he would follow it to the end.

SET INTRODUCTION

The only thing we can, and therefore must control, is the imagery in our
own mind.

—Epictetus

We humans have great abilities to create images, and with them, to build a
significant part of our reality, and therefore to nurture or to destroy our
species and its surroundings. We have used these abilities creatively but not
always kindly, or wisely. As our science and technologies have made it possible to appreciate how our lives are part of one global world, they have also
provided us with the means to destroy Earth's capacity to support life. The
peace movement that is growing throughout the world gives recognition
and power to the first side of the balance, reacting against violence and war,
raising aloft a higher vision of harmony and peace. It provides us with a living history of the strength of people, of communities and tribes—and sometimes of governments—to create social institutions and ideas that give
peace its chance to grow. It is in the search for peace, for a way to live in
harmony with each other and with the natural order that we seem to come
most alive and closest to the meaning of our existence on this earth. The
peace movement is likely the only undertaking that holds out a promise that
the remarkable experiment of life can go on.

We consider peace to include both the absence of unnecessary violence
and the pursuit of a world that offers deep contentment with the process of

life. We feel some dismay as we look at paths taken by humans toward large-scale violence. But the destruction and suffering we find are not the whole story. There is another and far more hopeful story, partly old, partly new, and partly yet to be written.

Peace connotes a world with harmony among people and between people and their environment. It is surely not a world without anger or one without conflict. But it is a world in which the fulfillment of human needs can occur without inflicting preventable violence and human beings can grow closer to one another in spirit, which, as Augustine said, is the ultimate purpose and underlying desire of our very nature (see Volume 1, Chapter 2). Like science, which has a capacity for change as new evidence emerges, the pursuit of peace is an ongoing process in which its adherents can and do learn from the past and continually make new discoveries. Like democracy, the pursuit of peace does not always produce a better world right away, but that pursuit unquestionably has the capacity to bring correctives into the directions of our evolution as a species. The peace movement is an exciting and empowering wave of worldwide change that can harness the power of each of us, individually and collectively, for love and for life.

There are many books about peace. In the three volumes of this anthology we have chosen not to be an encyclopedia of the efforts for peace,[1] or a history of worldwide efforts to realize it,[2] nor for that matter a celebration of a hopeful future. Rather we have tried to present a mosaic that gives due recognition to the obstacles to be overcome while sampling the amazing creativity of what has been and is being done to overcome them. The doers are scientists and poets, professors and peasant women, intergovernmental agencies and community art projects, soldiers and pacifists, environmentalists and defenders of human rights. Rather than force a rigid analysis on how all their efforts combine we have tried mainly to let the voices be heard.

Volume 1 focuses on different ways people have looked at peace—to construct a theory of its nature and possibilities. We present a framework for peace studies set forth by Johan Galtung, who more than anyone living deserves to be considered the founder of the field (peace entered academic discourse as a discrete subject only very recently), and we go on to writings that examine the deeper meanings of peace. The ubiquity of human aggression and violence leads some to the despairing conclusion that we are inherently warlike. We report on the new perspectives in biology, anthropology, and psychology that paint a different picture of what humans are or are not constrained to do by our nature, and take issue with the prevalent concept that we are "wired" to fight—or even to cooperate—which implies a determinism that is denied by science and common experience. Because world peace will require some transformative changes in the way we view ourselves and our world, a section is devoted to the issue of human identity and the culture of peace. We look at the contribution of organized religion to the quest for peace. (Spirituality, as somewhat distinct from organized religion, and other broad topics are handled in Volume 3.) Volume 1 ends with chapters taking a hard look at the magnitude of change required for peace and the institutional, particularly economic and monetary forces, that need to be transformed if peace is to reign.

Volume 2 looks at what is being done in response to war and other forms of violent conflict. Moving along the chain of causality, we cite efforts to prevent mass killing by monitoring and controlling weapons that in some cases are capable not only of ending lives needlessly but of obliterating life as we know it, as well as the ongoing efforts to expose corporate beneficiaries of war and to invest instead in enterprises that promote human and environmental health. Then we examine the aftermath of violence—the trauma, the scars, and the all-important processes of reconciliation and healing. We end Volume 2 with accounts of select national and regional movements, the world over, that have grown in opposition to war.

Volume 3 is the proactive and constructive complement to the anti-war movements described in Volume 2. Here we illustrate efforts at building a peaceful world and its cultural infrastructure through peace education and through reform of a media that at present does little to counter those powerful forces that promote a culture of violence and even instigate incidents of mass violence. We sample some highly creative ways that peace is being built at levels from courageous individuals to developing villages and on to international treaties and institutions. Then we examine, with examples, the process by which people can experience transformative change on a personal level that empowers participation in building a peaceful world.

When "peace" is taken in its full meaning, when one backs out from the simple cessation of one armed conflict or another to begin to sense the preconditions, the "dispositions" (as Erasmus says) that produced the outcome of conflict and its cessation, one begins to realize that the search for peace is almost coterminous with the evolution of human consciousness, of our destiny. Such a discussion obviously cannot be covered even in an anthology of this size. What one can do, and what we have tried to do, is sketch out a picture reasonably faithful to the variety, the intensity, and the unquenchable audacity of the men and women who have taken up this struggle from above (through law and policy), from below (from grassroots to civil society), and most characteristic of the present, from within (through personal transformation). For this goal, many have lain down their very lives. We come away from our survey of all this activity, dedication, and sacrifice with a combined sense of awe and inspiration.

At the end of the day, it is this inspiration that we wish to share with you. For as various writers in all three volumes have noted, all the ingredients for an evolutionary step forward toward this as-yet unrealized world are in place—some of them have been for some time. What is missing is the overview, the sense of the big picture, and the confidence in the heart of each one of us that we can make a difference. This we can do even in face of the apparently never-to-be-dislodged juggernaut of war: the mindset, the dehumanizing training, the institutions, the frightening technology. In face of that enormity, a countering awareness has arisen of the unquenchable drive for peace and what *it* has brought into being. The art, science, and practice of peace are having impacts on human understanding, institutions, and behaviors that are indispensable—if not for the courage to get engaged, at least for our sanity. But we hope for more; we hope you will come away from this set of books with re-fired determination to join this struggle, and a slightly sharper sense of where to make your best contribution. Nothing would please us more.

NOTES

1. Lazlo and Yoo, 1986; Kurtz and Turpin, 1999; Powers and Vogele, 1997.

2. Among many examples, see Chatfield and Kleidman, 1992; Chatfield, 1973; Beales, 1971; and http://www.peacehistorysociety.org/. For conscientious objection worldwide, see the works of historian Peter Brock.

Introduction to Volume 2

In this volume of *Peace Movements Worldwide* we deal with the antithesis of peace: the mass violence typically associated with war. Peace movements have arisen because of the unspeakable damage that war inflicts. We include efforts to prevent war through the control and abolition of weapons, to resist the human participation in the killing that war brings, and to heal the devastating consequences of violence. The volume ends with a sampling of peace movements that have grown in various parts of the world as expressions of a very human desire to oblige war makers to let us live in peace.

The social realities we have created commit and justify violence. We create enemies to punish or to destroy. We recall history by recounting and glorifying military victories. We leave many of our species destitute but use deadly force to control their dissent. Our resources are drained by a culture of violence.

The magnitude of the damage in violent conflicts reflects the ingenuity humans have applied to create ever more effective tools of destruction. Some of the most deadly have been used, some not, at least not yet. The most deadly so far are nuclear weapons. Those who work on them have created a secret society with elements of a cult[1] and a scientific and technocratic language that distances themselves from the human consequences of their work.[2] Yet such consequences defy our capacity for recognition of their horror. Explosion of a single megaton weapon creates a crater 300 feet deep and 1200 feet in diameter. The surface fireball radiates three times the light and heat of that same area on the surface of the sun. In less than 12 seconds a blast of compressed air destroys every structure within three miles. Winds of 250 mph propel debris that kills 50 percent of the people in the area, all before the spread of death from massive firestorms and radiation.

A disturbing trend has been to design nuclear weapons that blur the line between their claimed use as a deterrent and their actual use in combat. A similar trend has occurred in the use of chemical and biological weapons, the banning of which has not prevented their stockpiling or their use in defoliating land, contaminating crops, and destroying both wild and domesticated animals. Chemicals such as depleted uranium and white phosphorous add to the damage from incendiary weapons.

Landmines and antipersonnel weapons provide a special challenge since they are developed to kill and maim unsuspecting people and vehicles and they continue to do so long after hostilities have ceased. A significant part of the energy of the peace movement has aimed to bring about an end to the reliance on weapons of all types as a means for settling conflicts.

Some of the most courageous work in the movement for peace is seen in efforts to protect people caught in the violence of war. The proportion of civilian to military casualties has grown in every war since World War II and civilian casualties now greatly exceed those of soldiers. They are more than numbers: They are children who have lost a parent or a limb; hungry and scared families huddled helplessly awaiting the return of soldiers or bombs that have already devastated their lives. And the movements to resist further violence have reflected the best in courage and compassion that human beings have shown. Unarmed peace brigades have provided shields of protection. Women's groups, such as those in a coalition of Christian and Muslim women in Liberia have massively but nonviolently forced back both government and opposing warlord factions to bring an end to unprincipled rampages of killing and rape. Rescue workers and doctors have beaten a path to bring food, water, and medicines to help victims survive and resist.

Resistance has grown against the military perpetrators of violence, the specialized training programs that teach military leaders to control, intimidate, and eliminate adversaries. This resistance aims at those who do the dirty work of protecting corporate and military empires. The often clandestine intelligence agency support for those who inflict violence has been met by whistle-blowers and by groups set up to be watchdogs to expose such activities. The School of the Americas Watch is one such group. Another group of dissident psychologists has organized to resist the misuse of their field in assisting programs of torture. Resistance has spread to contractors who supply both mercenaries and the infrastructure to feed and house armies and to those who sell weapons and profit from the arms trade.

Soldiers through history have risen up against their officers and the national policies that have sent them with a promise of glory into a situation of hell. It takes enormous courage for a soldier to break ranks from the disciplined institution that demands their sacrifices and nurtures their loyalty to one another. But many have and their voices speak strongly because their experience has been direct.

The trauma involved in war has effects that linger long after the formal cessation of hostilities. This is widespread among soldiers and particularly severe among those who have engaged in killing. Healing the wounds becomes important to restore their lives but also to prevent the internalized and lasting fear and anger from generating more violence. All of the victims need healing: people who have lost a family member to murder; victims of torture; thousands of people who have survived a genocidal conflict and must now live among their former enemies; the children who have known no life other than being a child soldier; and those—mostly women—who have spent their lives forced into slavery. All need to be a part of recovery from violence.

Finally in this volume we sample the peace movements around the world that have grown to give voice to ordinary people taking on the extraordinary task of opposing war and all forms of unnecessary violence.

NOTES

1. Gusterson, 1998.
2. Cohn, 1987.

PART I

PREVENTION

What has made the devastation wrought by war so great over the past 100 years is the development of ever more "sophisticated" weapons. Much human ingenuity has been devoted to their invention, development, and use. The most deadly so far are nuclear weapons. Their damage from blast, firestorm, and radiation is so great that a single bomb destroyed most of Hiroshima. Thousands of such weapons, each many times more destructive than the first ones used, are in to be found in Russian and U.S. stockpiles. They are now in the arsenal of many nations and are continuing to proliferate and to be used in threats.

The atomic bombs dropped on Hiroshima and Nagasaki produced the greatest immediate mass death from individual weapons yet known. One 20-megaton bomb exploded on the surface of Columbus Circle in New York would produce a hole where 20 city blocks had been, a hole deep enough to hide a 20-story building. All brick and wood frame houses within 7.7 miles would be completely destroyed. The blast waves would carry through the entire underground subway system. Up to 15 miles from ground zero, flying debris propelled by displacement effects would cause more casualties. There would be 200,000 separate fires ignited, producing a firestorm with temperatures up to 1,500 degrees F. and wind velocities to 150 miles per hour. The infrastructure of food and water supplies, roads, medical services, fuel for transportation, and electric power would be destroyed. And radiation damages that destroy and deform living things would continue for 240,000 years.[1] Such bombs, and others still more destructive, are contained in the warheads of missiles, many of them capable of delivering multiple warheads from a single launch.

The massive industry of weapons development, trade, and sales (beyond nuclear weapons) has also been the cause of massive deaths. Marc Pilisuk describes the history and status of efforts to control weapons and to achieve disarmament.

Attempts to control nuclear weapons, to prevent proliferation, and to work toward their abolition have been a goal of peace seekers since they were discovered. Alice Slater, New York director of the Nuclear Age Peace Foundation and a founder of the Abolition 2000 coalition to ban nuclear weapons, describes the history and current status of these efforts and the prospects for the future. In addition to the international presence and pressure of the nuclear disarmament coalition, powerful community groups have arisen around each nuclear weapons facility. Some like Tri Valley Citizens Against a Radioactive Environment have dominated environmental impact hearings, debunked denials of health risks, and sued the Livermore National Weapons Laboratories. The horror of contemplating the use of nuclear bombs has been a force causing people to shy away from the problem. Dedicated scientists and others have fortunately kept the issue before us. Daniel Ellsberg, famous for his exposure of the Pentagon Papers, which helped to unravel what was being concealed about the Vietnam War, reports a personal history of his life-long commitment to help us all overcome the denial that leaves nuclear policy to others and jeopardizes our common future.

Among weapons, landmines have stood out as having a particularly deadly pattern. They are designed to disable people and vehicles without warning. They make no distinction between soldiers or civilians and children are particularly vulnerable. After hostilities cease, soldiers may turn in their rifles, but landmines continue to kill people and farm animals and to make farmland unusable. Nobel Laureate Jody Williams and colleague Stephen Goose describe a process for dealing with the consequences of landmines and for abolishing their use. The amazing "Ottawa process" provides a model for the effective mobilization of various nongovernmental and citizens groups to gain a foothold in the official processes of government and inter-government organizations and offers an example of citizen diplomacy for the cause of peace.

Weapons are produced, with few exceptions, by giant corporations whose personnel and lobbying efforts are extensive in the halls of governments. Their market is largely dependent on the degree to which governments act as guarantors for corporate interests in other countries. These often concealed corporate actors are part of the machinery of war. Gianina Pellegrini provides an account of the work of groups, surely a part of the peace movement, to expose corporations involved in destructive processes, and to hold them accountable. Finally, there are opportunities to vote with one's money for peace, justice, and sustainability. This occurs in consumer choice in support of particular products but also in capital investments. Tessie Petion and Steven Lydenberg provide an account of the intentions and accomplishments of socially responsible investing through the eyes of one of its pioneering investment houses.

Weapons, it has been said, do not cause killing; people do. But weapons make killing an easy choice and make possible killing people in numbers that could never be justified for any cause. They have become powerful parts of our culture and our economy. Prevention of war requires their control and elimination. In a larger sense, the prevention of mass violence involves more than putting a lid on weapons, more than identifying the weapon profiteers, more even than investing more wisely into nonviolent enterprises. Prevention of mass violence will need changes in culture, in judicial accountability, and in the vitality of resistance and of peace building. Nonetheless, reducing weapons and facing their corporate benefactors are absolutely necessary steps to prevent exorbitant loss of life.

—Marc Pilisuk and Michael N. Nagler

NOTE

1. Scientists Committee for Radiation Information, 1962.

CHAPTER 1

SHEDDING THE TOOLS OF DESTRUCTION: THE DISARMAMENT EFFORT

Marc Pilisuk

Both the ability to fight wars and the extent of their destruction depend on weapons. Production of military weapons reached record levels in the first decade of the 21st century. Worldwide sales and transfer agreements exceed $37 billion in a typical year. Despite some changes in the types of arms transfers since the Cold War era, weapon sales continue to be concentrated in developing nations.[1] This extensive global market in weapons provides the tools by which ethno-political wars are being fought.[2] In the aftermath of such costly bloodletting, people, and their governing officials, often reflect on whether the weapons used have produced suffering that might well have been avoided and whether the actual presence of such weapons presents a threat of future use. The responses have been varied.

The hawkish response has been to create an overwhelming superiority of weapons to deter potential enemies, a path that has not historically been successful. Disarmament is another response. It has more than one meaning. History provides numerous examples in which disarmament referred to the winning side forcing elimination of weapons in the conquered countries. classical antiquity, the Romans tried to disarm Carthage, their long-rival. Following Napoleon's military victories, France placed limits up size of the Prussian and Austrian military. In the 20th century, the treaty ending World War I placed limits on the German army and navy. The intent, during a period of deep English/German rivalry over the oil needed to fuel industrial growth, was to prevent Germany's military from posing a serious threat. At the end of World War II, both Germany and Japan were disarmed. After more than 60 years, both countries still observe limitations on their armed forces and neither country has tried to reassert power by developing nuclear weapons. The reverse of enforced disarmament by countries with victorious military establishments has also occurred. For example, Tsar Nicholas II of Russia, in 1898 called for the Hague Conference to meet to prevent wealthier powers from modernizing their armed forces.[3]

CONTROLLING AND LIMITING WEAPONS

The doves have promoted more multi-party alternatives for attaining arms control and disarmament. The suggestions reflect a spectrum from partial to complete elimination of weapons, from phased reductions of certain weapon categories to immediately enforced elimination, and from unilateral to multilateral efforts—the latter often requiring provisions for inspection and enforcement.

Disarmament is not synonymous with *arms control.* Agreements among nation states to limit or to reduce particular weapons occur in a pragmatic context. This context does not address an anarchic international community in which autonomous nation states are assumed to compete for interests as defined by their governments. Within this mindset, military might is considered a tool to pursue national interests and protect against aggression by other states. The advent of highly destructive biochemical and nuclear weapons has made the costs of waging all-out war incommensurate with any possible gains. Arms control does not aim to eliminate the competitive assumptions that drive nation states, or even to eliminate violent conflict. The goals are better understood as promoting international stability and reducing the likelihood of war. Additional goals are to reduce the costs of weapons and to limit the damage that follows violent conflict, in a sense permitting the military system to continue, with some limitations on its capacity for destruction. Governments consider arms control a part of their security policy. The U.S. Congress, for example, established the Arms Control and Disarmament Agency (ACDA) in 1961 to provide an institution for dealing with arms control issues.[4]

Arms control examples date back to 12th-century Europe when the ⌐rch sought to ban crossbows in warfare among Christians. That ⌐pt did not succeed and crossbows remained in use throughout Europe. ⌐ontrol negotiations were prominent during the 20th century. After

World War I, the major naval powers undertook a serious effort to negotiate their relative levels of naval force. The Washington Conference (1921 to 1922) and the London Conference (1930) succeeded for a time in limiting naval arms. League of Nations efforts to advance international disarmament culminated in the Geneva Conference (1932 to 1934) where a distinction was made between "offensive" and "defensive" weapons with the intention to get rid of the offensive ones. That is a difficult line to draw since perceptions of intention play a major role. In what psychologists have called the *attribution error*, armaments held by an opponent are typically viewed as indicators of aggressive intent, while one's own arms are seen as a defensive response to a situation presented by others. During the 1930s the Western democracies felt threatened by the rise of Japanese, German, and Italian imperialism, and this important effort at arms control was aborted.[5]

Successful stories of disarming the borders between neighboring states include the Rush-Bagot Agreement (1817), which led to demilitarization of the U.S.–Canada border. This illustrates the way disarmament between modern nations can be achieved and the European Union (EU) has moved in this direction. Such agreements do not actually call for nations to reduce their weapons or the size of their armies. However, they affirm a nonmilitary and cooperative relationship among the parties.[6]

THE PURSUIT OF DISARMAMENT

General disarmament addresses a more far-reaching goal for a world in which competing states no longer have the responsibility to promote their own security in an international environment in which might makes right. The image of disarmament is of a world in which conflicts still occur but clear rules preclude use of lethal weapons to resolve them. It prescribes a world with enforceable restrictions in place against the massing of armaments and soldiers along with universal openness for early detection of violations. Disarmament calls for the support of institutions like the International Court of Justice that would be called on in a dispute to make binding judgments and for available police capacities to monitor outbreaks of violence.

In the present climate, nations are unlikely to disarm voluntarily. Realistically, their leaders would consider such actions suicidal, at least until other nations also renounce war and armaments. Moreover, disarmament has a psychological-cultural component. It requires not only laws and official agencies but also a willingness of people to respect those laws and institutions and to consider the goal of pursuing peace by peaceful means to be a universal value on which the survival of life depends. Hence, disarmament is often considered a long-range goal associated with transforming the international political environment and ending the law of the jungle among nations by establishing some form of world government or an effective system of collective security.[7]

The ideal of a world banning access to highly destructive weapons often runs into the argument that weapons are needed to prevent another Adolf Hitler or similarly obsessed leader from dominating the world. The claim is that there will always be such enemies and that disarming would give an upper hand to rulers with evil intent. The answers to this are complex. Risks under disarmament may be greatly reduced by enforceable and universal agreements. Our willingness to undertake such limited risks makes sense only in comparison to the risks incurred by allowing the current and costly patchwork efforts at security to grow worse as the number of parties with access to weapons of mass destruction increases. Moreover, using weapons to deter enemies leaves untouched the basic reasons why violent conflicts occur. To address these concerns, the world will need to deal with gross inequality and exploitation of people and the habitats that sustain them. We will need to address the scarcity of education about effective forms of nonviolent resolution of conflict. These forms include ways to convert potential enemies rather than to confront them and to augment the scant resources now offered for those committed to building cultures of peace. When resources are devoted to preparing for war, we continue a caste of military and corporate professionals whose life work is to find enemies and to fight them.

One early example of arms limitation began in Japan in the mid-1600s and lasted for more than 200 years. The Japanese successfully renounced the use of firearms. During this long period of self-imposed restriction, the sword remained the dominant weapon. This ban changed only in the mid-19th century after outside powers threatened intervention in Japanese affairs. The end of Japan's isolation within the international political system also brought this experiment in disarmament to an end.[8]

In the Western world during the 19th century, disarmament advocates believed that wars occurred because of the competition in armaments among major powers. World War I was precipitated by an assassination of one leader but was rapidly escalated by the involvement of heavily armed states. In a frequently quoted statement, Great Britain's foreign secretary, Sir Edward Grey (1906 to 1916), observed, "The enormous growth of armaments in Europe, the sense of insecurity and fear caused by them—it was these that made war inevitable." This theory of the cause of violent conflicts had policy implications. Disarmament, it was thought, could provide a way to reduce international tension and to prevent war. With the goal of promoting a humane international order, President Woodrow Wilson advocated disarmament as part of his Fourteen Points program. The call for disarmament was not followed and the failure of other powers to disarm after World War I was offered as an excuse by the Hitler regime for rearmament of Germany in the 1930s.[9]

BANS ON SELECTED CATEGORIES OF WEAPONS

Attempts to ban particular types of weapons have had some success. The horrible consequences of poison gas in World War I led, in 1925, to acceptance of the Geneva Protocol. Eventually 132 nations signed the Protocol banning the use of chemical and "bacteriological" weapons.[10] A conference held in Paris, in 1989, to strengthen the Protocol was followed by creation of a UN forum for discussion of disarmament issues. These deliberations led to the Chemical Weapons Convention (CWC) adopted by the UN General Assembly and signed in 1993 by 130 countries.[11] The CWC finally went into force in April 1997. The Organization for the Prohibition of Chemical Weapons, the treaty's implementing organization, came into operation one month later. Each signatory nation agrees, under the treaty, never "to develop, produce, otherwise acquire, stockpile or retain chemical weapons." It agrees not to use or prepare to use chemical weapons (CW) and not to assist others in acting against any of the prohibitions of the convention. Chemical weapons control also requires states to destroy any CW in their possession, to destroy any of their own CW abandoned on the territory of another state, and to dismantle their CW production facilities.[12] One problem, however, in restricting the use of chemical weapons is that the range of products produced is great and most research and production activity is done secretly.[13]

One particularly insidious source of death and disability comes from antipersonnel landmines. Their destructiveness continues long after actual combat has ended. Soldiers typically turn in their guns when peace returns but landmines do not recognize a cease-fire. They cannot be aimed but lie dormant until the detonating mechanism is triggered by an unsuspecting person or animal, killing or injuring civilians, soldiers, peacekeepers, and aid workers alike. Children are particularly susceptible. Over the past decades, hundreds of thousands of landmine deaths and injuries have occurred. An estimated 15,000 to 20,000 new casualties are caused by landmines and unexploded ordnances each year, some 1,500 new casualties each month. The numbers are underestimates since some countries with landmine problems, such as Myanmar (Burma), India, and Pakistan, do not provide public information on the casualties.[14]

One hundred fifty-four countries have signed the 1997 Convention on the Prohibition of the Use, Stockpiling, Production, and Transfer of Anti-Personnel Mines and on Their Destruction. Forty countries, including

Russia, China, and the United States, have not signed. Some antipersonnel landmines from earlier conflicts still claim victims in many parts of the world. Though improved in recent years, the situation remains a global crisis. Antipersonnel landmines are still being planted and minefields dating back decades continue to claim innocent victims. Extensive stockpiles of these weapons remain in warehouses around the world and a few countries still produce them.[15]

CONTROL OVER NUCLEAR WEAPONS

The era of atomic weapons begun with the end of World War II added a further incentive for advocates of disarmament. Many prominent thinkers supported efforts to "ban the bomb," even if this entailed starting with unilateral disarmament. Nuclear disarmament became for many a moral imperative for the stakes at risk seemed nothing less than the extinction of the human species. Movies and television popularized an apocalyptic image, helping to garner new support for the disarmament movement.

Leaders of the superpowers gave considerable attention to arms control during the period of the Cold War. A relaxation of tensions in superpower relations, or détente, coincided with several important arms control agreements. The first round of Strategic Arms Limitation Talks (SALT) was concluded in 1972, the Intermediate Nuclear Forces (INF) agreement in 1987, and by Strategic Arms Reduction Talks (START) in 1991. Some policy analysts concluded that arms control could play a useful (if limited) role in helping to manage the uncertainty of their armament competitions among rival states. A different view by some advocates of disarmament was that arms control was a subterfuge on the part of the leaders of the major powers to frustrate genuine disarmament. The Soviet Union sometimes urged disarmament as a way of causing domestic political embarrassment for the governments of the United States and other NATO countries. Moreover, both superpowers could well have been accused of using the nuclear weapons agreements as a way to make the world safe for wars of domination that used military threats, economic pressures, political assassinations, and conventional weapons in their attempt to create allies in the polarized world of the Cold War.[16]

AFTER THE COLD WAR

After the Cold War, attempts to limit the spread of nuclear weapons and ballistic missiles, and to eliminate the use of chemical and biological agents as weapons of mass destruction, emerged as important policy concerns. Paradoxically, disarmament has even been used as a justification for resorting to war. The coalition that fought Iraq in 1991, for instance, aimed not only at restoring Kuwait as an independent, sovereign state, but also at eliminating Iraq's ability to manufacture and use nuclear, chemical, and biological weapons. The prospect for a major war in northeast Asia was brought on by North Korea's desire to build a nuclear arsenal and the determination of the United States and South Korea to prevent this. The conflict illustrated a common attempt to further international disarmament on a selective basis. A neo-liberal world order could therefore entail the paradox of fighting wars for the sake of disarming particular nations. Hence the plea of disarmament advocates that weapons themselves cause war, might come to have a new, more ominous meaning. Weapons might be justified as instruments for disarming other countries by attacking them.[17]

The UN deserves credit for whatever progress toward disarmament has occurred. UN responsibility falls on the First Committee of the UN General Assembly (a committee of the whole), which is responsible for disarmament and security matters. All 191 member states are included and hundreds of matters are discussed. The UN Disarmament Commission meets in New York once, sometimes twice, each year to work on the agenda proposed by the First Committee for talks in the Conference on Disarmament. Resolutions are passed by a majority vote or by a two-thirds majority for issues deemed important.[18]

The UN Conference on Disarmament (CD), with 66 current members, is a more specialized body. It meets in Geneva to produce multilateral agreements, and is the only group with authority both to set its own agenda and to negotiate actual treaties. The CD takes into account recommendations from the UN General Assembly, and submits annual reports to the General Assembly. Progress has been slow but any progress is remarkable given the wide differences among members on what should be discussed. Some nations refuse to participate in discussions limiting one type of weapon or the weapons in one particular geographic area unless weapons threats from other sources are also on the table for consideration. For example, Egypt has urged Arab states not to consider the Chemical Weapons Treaty until Israel signs the Nuclear Proliferation Treaty. The United States might want to mobilize international support for disarming what it considers "rogue states." Others will only agree to such discussion if they include attention to the weapons within the United States that are seen as a threat to other nations. The United States opposed any negotiating mandate on general nuclear disarmament, while China opposed negotiating a fissile material cut-off treaty in the absence of negotiations on general nuclear disarmament.[19]

In 2005, the UN disarmament agenda set forth the following priorities: cessation of the nuclear arms race and nuclear disarmament, prevention of nuclear war, including prevention of an arms race in outer space, effective international arrangements to ensure non-nuclear weapon states that they would be protected against the use, or threat of use, of nuclear weapons (negative security assurances), new types of weapons of mass destruction, radiological weapons, comprehensive programs of disarmament, transparency in armaments, and landmines.[20] Although talks always provide greater basis for hope than belligerent proclamations, little significant progress was achieved on any of the items. To understand why is important to place the issues of disarmament in a larger, economic, political, and psychosocial context.

PROFITS AND THE WEAPONS MARKET

Weapons are sold throughout the world and sales are highly profitable. Small arms transfers involve independent entrepreneurs and arms brokers who engage in weapons transfers to armed groups and even to repressive governments that are under UN arms embargoes. One well-known arms broker, Victor Bout, has been implicated in violating UN arms embargoes in Angola, Liberia, Sierra Leone, and the Democratic Republic of Congo. The armed groups wreak havoc on innocent civilians. Yet Bout, along with many other dealers, remains free to traffic arms to abusers of human rights, all outside the purview of international regulations. In just one example, arms brokers were reported to have shipped 3,117 surplus assault rifles from Nicaragua to Panama. These weapons, however, were diverted to Colombia's paramilitary group, Autodefensas Unidas de Colombia (AUC). This occurred at the time the AUC was accused of killing thousands of civilians and was on the U.S. Department of State list of terrorist organizations.[21]

Both U.S. and international efforts have tried to curtail such transfers. The U.S. government adopted a law on arms brokering in 1996. The law restricts a range of activities including transporting and financing. It requires arms brokers both to register and to apply for a license for each activity. The law was used to prosecute a British citizen who was attempting to sell shoulder-fired missiles in the United States to a group intending to use the missiles to shoot down a commercial airliner. Many governments, however, have very weak laws or none at all on the arms market. Irish law, for example, does not restrict weapons supplies from foreign countries. Ireland was unable, therefore, to prosecute an arms broker who was reportedly involved in efforts to supply 50 tanks from Ukraine to the Sudanese military. In January 2004, the European Union strengthened its arms embargo on Sudan out of concern for its ongoing civil war. The U.S. law cannot be truly effective until similar laws are adopted and enforced by other states. In the 14 years since the adoption of the law, the United States has only prosecuted five individuals. Recognizing the importance of small arms in abuses of human rights, Amnesty International has called for an international agreement to prevent such transfers to governments and groups with consistent records of gross human rights violations.[22]

DISARMAMENT WITH WEAPONS OF MASS DESTRUCTION

Development of weapons of mass destruction has been occurring with little public awareness. The Cold War is long past. One might have expected that the United States would be a leader in the effort to fulfill its 30-year-old promise, stated in Article VI of the Nuclear Non-Proliferation Treaty, "to pursue negotiations in good faith on effective measures relating to cessation of the nuclear arms race at an early date and to nuclear disarmament." But the dramatic change in the past decade has come only in the words used to describe U.S. nuclear and missile development programs. In actual fact, efforts to produce new, high-technology weapons have increased.[23] The Department of Energy's nuclear weapons research facilities at Livermore, Los Alamos, and Sandia continue this highly classified research. Hidden from view they are advocates for the research and development needed to enter a new era of expansion in nuclear weapons. Among such projects, the National Ignition Facility will house a laser 40 times more powerful than any yet in existence and will have nuclear weapon applications. Space-based laser weapons are viewed as a means to destroy chemical or biological weapons that might threaten the United States.

The matter not examined should be of great concern. Are the threats significant? Might they be better prevented by establishing peaceful economic and social relations with other countries? Are the exorbitant costs worthwhile given the dubious feasibility of such weapons? Surely the space lasers will lead to proliferation of nuclear weapons and surely they will interfere with international hopes for the United States to ratify and abide by the Comprehensive Test Ban Treaty. The United States is clearly not living up to its promise to reduce nuclear weapons capabilities and more nations are developing nuclear weapons and the missiles to deliver them. The video game image of an endless scientific competition to have missiles with nuclear warheads dodging ballistic defense systems may have appeal to armchair military strategists and to defense contractors. But pursuing this activity will make progress toward the elimination of nuclear arsenals impossible and guarantees indefinite continuation of nuclear weapons development.

The costs of such activity have been great. The activity has produced serious consequences to the environment and to human health.[24] Weapons produced by superpowers have created incentives for other countries to develop their own arsenals. Espionage activities have been designed to capture weapons secrets. Secrecy has led to the cover-up of dangerous consequences from research and testing. The diversion of public funds from needed programs in health, education, housing, and renewable energy development—all of which produce more employment for the same money—has been a regrettable part of history. Funding for the small amounts needed for peacekeeping activities that should provide greater security has suffered. Now, after the end of the Cold War when the United States has no credible military adversaries, it will indeed be tragic if the opportunity to end preparedness for nuclear war is lost.

A costly policy of unending weapons development can only exist because the weapons laboratories operate in relative secrecy. They employ bright scientists and furnish them with unmatched equipment and facilities. They provide lucrative contracts to defense industries, which in turn provide extensive consultation to government. The world's most destructive weapons are conceived, justified, funded, and developed behind closed doors.[25]

THE UNITED STATES AND DISARMAMENT

In the liberal democracies of the industrially developed world, organizations promoting disarmament retain some clout in the domestic political arena. A current view holds that modern liberal democracies can achieve effective disarmament among themselves, because they seem less prone to make war on one another. The spread of democracy, then, conceivably advances the cause of disarmament.[26] The U.S. government has been the primary proponent of the theory that democracies are not sources of aggression. However, its own record has been of providing military support for either democracies or dictatorial police states depending only on the favorability of their policies to corporate economic interests.[27] An alternate theory is that the powerful nation state is itself the obstacle to ridding the world of destructive weapons.

Nation states are not well designed for disarmament. Some operate in the old model as vehicles for expanding the interests of rulers. More recently nations exist as the vassals for large corporate interests.[28] Even those nations professing to do what is best for their own citizens find the lure of weapons to be great; hence the cautiousness about agreements that might weaken military power. Genuine progress toward disarmament will likely require the development of some form of world government with the ability to police limits on weapons and with the moral authority to require mediated or judicial resolution of conflicts. But intermediate steps can buy time and citizen involvement makes this possible. Groups like Peace Action have helped to highlight the impacts of weapons policies on local communities. The Nongovernmental Organization (NGO) Committee on Disarmament, Peace, and Security has provided services and facilities to hundreds of citizen's groups concerned with disarmament and related activities of the UN helping to ensure that people not in government can weigh in on international disarmament issues.

The United States as the remaining superpower is particularly important for any progress toward disarmament but the record is not promising. After two world wars, European nations were ready to forgo weapons and policies that had created such devastation. The animosity of governments in capitalist economies to the communist experiment in the Soviet Union remained but primarily as a battle to prevent the colonized world from developing socialist governments and controlling their own resources. The United States as the first atomic power assumed this role of containment primarily through military superiority. The United States dismissed offers by Stalin and later by Khrushchev to permit unification of Germany in exchange for substantial mutual reductions and controls in armaments[29] and the United States won the competition to become the most heavily armed state.[30]

Between World War II and the end of 20th century the United States led 73 military interventions throughout the world, almost double the total from the preceding 55-year period.[31] If we include all covert operations in which casualties occurred the figure rises to 196.[32] The Pentagon has an ever-expanding empire of over 6,000 domestic bases, and 725 overseas. The United States spends more for defense than the next 45 highest-spending countries in the world combined, accounts for 48 percent of the world's total military spending—5.8 times more than China—98.6 times more than Iran.[33]

U.S. policy has often been guided by an assumption that interests, defined by the United States, take precedence over international agreements. This has occurred first in matters that might constrain U.S. military activities. In 2001, the United States withdrew from a major arms control accord, the 1972 Antiballistic Missile Treaty. Also in 2001 the United States walked out of a conference to discuss adding on-site inspectors to strengthen the 1972 Biological and Toxic Weapons Convention, which was ratified by 144 nations including the United States.[34] Meanwhile, U.S. preparations to use chemical and biological weapons at Fort Dietrich and other sites have been extensive.[35] The United States was the only nation to oppose the UN Agreement to Curb the International Flow of Illicit Small Arms. The Land Mine Treaty (banning mines) was signed in 1997 by 122 nations but the United States refused to sign, along with Russia, China, India, Pakistan, Iran, Iraq, Vietnam, Egypt, and Turkey. Again in 2001 the United States refused to join 123 nations pledged to ban the use and production of anti-personnel bombs.[36]

PREPAREDNESS FOR WAR HAS BEEN COSTLY

The United States spent $10.5 trillion dollars on the military during the Cold War.[37] The nuclear powers of that time spent an estimated $8 trillion on their nuclear weapons.[38] If current annual U.S. expenditures for such weapons were instead invested into global life-saving measures the result could have covered *all* of the following: the elimination of starvation and malnutrition, basic shelter for every family, universal health care, the control of AIDS, relief for displaced refugees, and the removal of landmines.[39] The United States poured more than $1 billion per week into the Iraq war that could otherwise have been spent on health care, schools, and infrastructure at home. One might think this would raise the demand for a conversion from weapons spending in the direction of disarmament. However, the dollars are not evaporated. They go largely to contractors, specialized not only in the production of weapons but also in the marketing of strategies in which such weapons appear to be needed and to the support of officials sharing their views.

U.S. plans for the future are no more promising than the record of the past. These involve nuclear weapons and their use in outer space.[40] The National Missile Defense proposal (previously referred to as "Star Wars") poses the greatest threat to the erosion of existing arms control agreements. In preparation for the transition to the use of space for warfare, the Air Force science and technology community has doubled its commitments in "space only" technologies from 13 percent in FY 1999 to 32 percent by FY 2005. This activity jeopardizes the modest stability afforded by the Anti-Ballistic Missile (ABM) Treaty. Yet major lobbies for the defense industries, such as the Missile Defense Advocacy Alliance, provide constant pressure for continued development of space weapons. According to a scientific panel convened by the National Resources Defense Council, the G. W. Bush team assumed that nuclear weapons will be part of U.S. military forces at least for the next 50 years. Plans are in place for extensive and expensive programs to modernize existing weapons, including a new intercontinental ballistic missile (ICBM) to be operational in 2020 and a new heavy bomber in 2040. In addition, the Pentagon has drafted contingency plans for the use of nuclear weapons against at least seven countries, naming not only the "axis of evil" (Iraq, Iran, and North Korea) but also Russia, China, Libya, and Syria. The Pentagon has also launched research and testing programs for a missile defense system. Although technically dubious, the large program has been viewed by other nations with alarm as a signal that the United States is working toward being able to attack other nations with the security that it could intercept missiles sent in retaliation. Such planning has the obvious consequence of provoking other nations to develop their own arsenals, a process already taking place. Russia and China have responded with plans for new or updated development for nuclear weapons. Without enforceable controls, nuclear weapons technology is spreading.[41]

Disarmament is more than a set of formal agreements. It is also a commitment to a vision of the world as a place where mutual cooperation can provide more of what is important to all parties than violent conflict. The reliance on weapons to provide security has been outmoded by technology. The threatened use of force typically begets retaliatory force. Retribution continues a cycle of animosity and violence. Conversely, a proposal for graduated reciprocation in tension reduction (GRIT) suggests that a series of small unilateral moves toward conciliation, announced in advance, are likely to be gradually reciprocated and move the adversaries to more trustful and less threatening relations.[42] A period of thaw in the Cold War included a speech in 1961 by President Kennedy calling for a reappraisal of the Cold War, for new modes of cooperation, and for suspending nuclear weapons tests in the atmosphere. The Union of Soviet Socialist Republics (USSR) broadcast the Kennedy speech intact and Premier Khrushchev responded with a conciliatory speech. The USSR stopped production of strategic bombers and removed objections to the presence of UN observers in Yemen. The United States then removed objections to restoration of the full recognition of the Hungarian delegation to the UN. A limited nuclear weapons test ban was signed. The Soviet foreign minister Gromyko called for a nonaggression treaty between NATO and the Warsaw Pact. Kennedy called for joint efforts to "explore the stars together." Direct flights were scheduled between Moscow and New York. The United States agreed to the sale of wheat to the USSR. Gromyko called for a pact outlawing nuclear weapons in outer space. Kennedy responded favorably and an agreement was reached on the exchange of captured spies.[43] Studies in the laboratory provide confirming evidence that humans in conflict situations can use the GRIT strategy to reduce the distrust that keeps them armed and start a process toward mutually beneficial disarmament.[44] To appreciate why such a conciliatory strategy is not more actively pursued it is important to examine the stakes of powerful decision makers. The perceived short-term benefits to certain beneficiaries of war often dominate the policy process. The small group obsessed with weapons development and with military support for corporate expansion is unduly influencing a dangerous direction for American policy.[45] It is a policy that blurs the lines of reality between video game dueling and the actual domination of space by lethal weapons. The public has not been told this story and has not been asked if this should be the national direction. The survival of the planet will require progress toward disarmament. Public demand for, and involvement in, a culture of peace appears necessary if leaders are to respond to the challenge to convert our swords into ploughshares and study war no more.

NOTES

1. Shanker, 2005.
2. Renner, 1998.
3. Towle, 1997.
4. Institute for Defense and Disarmament Studies, 2005.
5. Maurer, 2005.
6. Institute for Defense and Disarmament Studies, 2005.
7. Myrdal, 1982; Institute for Defense and Disarmament Studies, 2005.
8. Maurer, 2005.
9. Hyde, 1988; Institute for Defense and Disarmament Studies, 2005.
10. UNIDC, 2005.
11. OPCW, 2005.
12. UNIDC, 2005
13. Barnaby, 1999.
14. International Campaign, 2005a.
15. International Campaign, 2005; Human Rights Watch, 2003.
16. UNIDC, 2005.
17. Maurer, 2005.
18. United Nations Department for Disarmament Affairs, 1988.
19. Etzioni, 1967.
20. UNIDC, 2005.
21. Amnesty International, 2010.
22. Multilateral Arms Regulation and Disarmament Agreements, 2005.
23. See Chapter 2 by Alice Slater.
24. Bertell, 2004; Boly, 1989; 1990.
25. Pilisuk, 1999.
26. Maurer, 2005.
27. Chomsky, 2004; Pilisuk and Zazzi, 2006.
28. Korten, 1998; Johnson, 2004; Pilisuk, 2001.
29. Potyarkin and Kortunov, 1986.
30. Chomsky, 2004.
31. Grossman, 1999; Blum, 2004.
32. Ferraro, 2005.
33. Peace Action.
34. Du Boff, 2001.
35. Barnaby, 1999.
36. Du Boff, 2001.
37. Markusen and Yukdin, 1992.
38. Sivard, 1996.
39. Gabel, 1997.
40. Carroll, 2008.
41. Roche, 2002.

42. Osgood, 1962.
43. Etzioni, 1967.
44. Pilisuk and Skolnick, 1968; Pilisuk, 1984; Pilisuk, 2001.
45. Pilisuk and Zazzi, 2006.

CHAPTER 2

Nuclear Disarmament: The Path Forward, Obstacles, and Opportunities

Alice Slater

Despite the fall of the Berlin Wall and the end of the Cold War, nearly 20 years ago, and more than 50 years of movement building and dedicated leadership to ban the bomb, the world still faces the nuclear sword of Damocles President Kennedy hoped to avert when, under enormous public pressure, he promoted and passed the first nuclear arms control measure, the 1963 Partial Test Ban Treaty. Sadly, that treaty merely banned atmospheric nuclear tests, sending the toxic explosions underground where the arms race, driven by the nuclear weapon laboratories, continued to escalate between the United States and the Soviet Union. Over the years, the nuclear arms race was interrupted by a number of successful arms reductions campaigns, eliminating certain classes of weapons like the MX missile, and most recently the nuclear bunker-buster earth penetrator. But these reductions took place without an ongoing commitment to nuclear abolition and without questioning the whole premise of U.S. foreign policy and the expanded national security state that threatened the very foundations of our democracy itself.

With the election of President Barack Obama, there are new opportunities to pursue a genuine end to the nuclear scourge. Recent calls by former

Cold War leaders Henry Kissinger, George Shultz, Sam Nunn, and William Perry for the United States to make new commitments for the elimination of nuclear weapons[1] have been echoed by Obama during his presidential campaign in which he stated that "I will seek a goal of a world without nuclear weapons."[2] But to move forward, we need to be cognizant of what has gone before: the offers on the table that were spurned over the years by the United States; the damaging effects of U.S. plans to dominate and control the military use of space on prospects for reaching agreement with Russia and China on nuclear abolition; the effect on the U.S.-Russian relationship of NATO expansion; and plans to base missile and radar bases on Russia's border in the Czech Republic and Poland that Russia views as provocative and threatening to its national security. Equally important to achieving the goal of nuclear abolition is the need to address the frightening explosion of nuclear proliferation. Corporate spin-masters promote so-called peaceful nuclear technology with deadly bomb-making material metastasizing in reactors around the world creating new nations to be targeted for preemptive war by an unchecked imperial United States; however, it is manifestly apparent that a genuine commitment to nuclear disarmament requires a worldwide phase-out of nuclear power and support for clean, safe, sustainable energy.

BACKGROUND

Today there are still more than 26,000 nuclear weapons on our planet—25,000 of them in the United States and Russia—with thousands of bombs in those countries poised at hair trigger alert and ready to fire in minutes—and arsenals numbering in the hundreds in the United Kingdom, France, China, and Israel and stockpiles of less than 100 warheads in India, Pakistan, and North Korea. Plans from the Bush administration to rebuild the entire nuclear weapons complex and to replace the existing U.S. nuclear arsenal with brand new hydrogen bombs, so-called reliable replacement warheads, have yet to be rejected by the new Obama administration. Indeed, the Obama administration's holdover defense secretary, Robert Gates, made a prominent speech in October 2008, shortly after his appointment was announced, emphasizing the need for the refurbished weapons complex under the Bush plan and the new "safe" replacement warhead, saying, "Try as we might and hope as we will, the power of nuclear weapons and their impact is a genie that cannot be put back in the battle at least for a very long time."[3]

We've been pushing our luck for over 60 years since the first and only two atomic bombs to be used in war obliterated Hiroshima and Nagasaki on August 6 and August 9, 1945, killing more than 214,000 people in the initial days, and causing numerous cases of cancers, mutations, and birth defects in their radioactive aftermath, new incidences of which are still being documented today. During these tragic years of the nuclear age, every site worldwide, involved in the mining, milling, production, and fabrication of uranium, for either war or for "peace," has left a lethal legacy of radioactive waste, illness, and damage to our very genetic heritage. Nuclear bombs and reactor-created plutonium stays toxic for more than 250,000 years and we still haven't figured out how to safely contain it.

Citizens have been mobilizing for nuclear disarmament for more than 50 years. Prominent international scientists led by Bertrand Russell and Albert Einstein, formed the Pugwash Association of scientists, which met in Pugwash, Nova Scotia, to address nuclear disarmament subsequent to the call of the Russell-Einstein manifesto in 1955. They warned that:

> The general public, and even many men in positions of authority, have not realized what would be involved in a war with nuclear bombs. The general public still thinks in terms of the obliteration of cities. . . . but the best authorities are unanimous in saying that a war with H-bombs might possibly put an end to the human race. It is feared that if many H-bombs are used there will be universal death, sudden only for a minority, but for the majority a slow torture of disease and disintegration.

They concluded that:

> In view of the fact that in any future world war nuclear weapons will certainly be employed, and that such weapons threaten the continued existence of mankind, we urge the governments of the world to realize, and to acknowledge publicly, that their purpose cannot be furthered by a world war, and we urge them, consequently, to find peaceful means for the settlement of all matters of dispute between them.[4]

In the early 1950s, children were trained to "duck and cover" in ludicrous school drills where they were instructed to "duck" under their desks and "cover" their heads with their hands as their teachers told them that these futile exercises would help them avoid injury from a nuclear bomb attack.[5] Underground bomb shelters were designated as a part of a Civil Defense plan against nuclear attack, and there are still government fact sheets and information available to the public on how to build a fall out shelter in case of nuclear attack.[6] The Committee for a Sane Nuclear Policy (SANE) was launched in the United States in 1957, driven by citizens' fears of radioactive fallout from atmospheric nuclear testing and burgeoning nuclear arsenals in the United States and the Soviet Union. In a series of advertisements signed by prominent Americans including Eleanor Roosevelt, Martin Luther King, Albert Schweitzer, and its founder, Norman Cousins, SANE launched an urgent plea to end nuclear testing, engendering thousands of public responses that resulted in the first nuclear testing moratorium.[7]

In 1958, St. Louis dental associations, organized by Dr. Barry Commoner, reported that radioactive fallout from above ground nuclear tests had led to statistically significant geometric increases in radioactive carcinogenic strontium-90 levels in children's teeth between 1945 and the early 1960s, raising public awareness of the painful price we were paying for our nuclear folly.[8] The Cuban Missile Crisis in 1961, a terrifying series of events that might have led to a nuclear attack on the U.S. mainland by Soviet missiles planted in Cuba, added to the pressure on President Kennedy to ultimately ratchet down the nuclear arms race, which unfortunately only resulted in a Partial Test Ban Treaty. Nuclear testing went underground and for our Dr. Strangeloves in the weapons labs it was business as usual as they continued to design ever more lethal nuclear weapons.

Global stockpiles of nuclear bombs have been declining from a peak of 70,000 warheads in 1986, but it was the enactment of the Anti-Ballistic Missile Treaty (ABM) in 1972 that provided an opening for a series of verified arms control agreements—Strategic Arms Limitation Talks (SALT) I, II; Strategic Arms Reduction Talks (START) I, II—that put successively lower caps on the numbers of long-range "strategic" nuclear warheads in the U.S. and Russian arsenals. (The START agreements do not address short-range "tactical" nuclear weapons, such as the estimated 150 to 240 tactical nuclear weapons currently deployed in five NATO states—Belgium, Germany, Italy, the Netherlands, and Turkey[9]—or inactive and retired warheads built for weapons systems now withdrawn from operational service.)

The ABM Treaty was enacted to prevent an ever spiraling nuclear arms race. The two Cold War adversaries agreed that the deployment of a missile shield would only provoke the other side to build more nuclear-armed missiles to overcome the shield. The 1993 START II agreement, ratified by Congress in 1996, limited each side to 3,500 long-range missiles and was ratified by Russia in April 2000. The Russia's Duma delayed its approval because of a series of provocative actions by the United States—the expansion of NATO up to the Russian border, the unauthorized bombing of Iraq, the bombing of Yugoslavia without Security Council sanction—each event occurring on the eve of an anticipated Duma vote on the treaty.[10] At the time Russia ratified START II it also ratified the Comprehensive Test Ban Treaty (CTBT), which went down to ignominious defeat in the U.S. Senate as our nuclear weapons scientists gave testimony against its passage, despite Clinton's deal-sweetener to buy their support for an end to underground nuclear explosions with a "stockpile stewardship" program.

This benign-sounding "stewardship" program funded our weapons design-
ers with billions of dollars each year from the time full-scale underground
testing ended. It enabled the weapons labs to develop new nuclear weapons
with computer-simulated virtual reality testing coupled with so-called sub-
critical nuclear tests in which plutonium is shattered in tunnels 1,000 feet
below the desert floor at the Nevada test site, without causing a "critical"
chain reaction. We've detonated over 24 "sub-critical" tests,[11] under both
Clinton and Bush. For 2009, Bush proposed that Congress fund the weapons
labs at $6.6 billion for research, design, testing, and nuclear weapons activities,
with a total budget of some $54 billion for nuclear weapons.[12] Plans to replace
the entire U.S. nuclear arsenal with "reliable replacement warheads," and
reconfiguring a new bomb-making complex, fail to account for the estimated
hundreds of billions of dollars that will be needed in our continuous struggle
to contain the enormous waste and toxic contamination across America,
plaguing our nation since the Manhattan Project began.[13] To his credit, President Obama, during his campaign, said he would revisit these issues, although
his holdover appointment of Defense Secretary Gates would seem to undercut
any efforts to halt the new weapons work planned at the laboratories.

Interestingly, in Eisenhower's famous farewell address, in which he
warned the country of the military-industrial complex, in a little noted aside,
he also cautioned, presciently, against the abuse of science, warning that:

> [I]n holding scientific research and discovery in respect, as we should,
> we must also be alert to the equal and opposite danger that public policy
> could itself become the captive of a scientific-technological elite. It is the
> task of statesmanship to mold, to balance, and to integrate these and
> other forces, new and old, within the principles of our democratic
> system—ever aiming toward the supreme goals of our free society.[14]

Can there be any doubt that the "scientific-technological" elite at Los Alamos and Livermore Laboratories have been driving the nuclear arms race,
squandering lost opportunities for nuclear disarmament since the end of
the Cold War, and developing new untested weapons designs that create
the need for more tests which are then used as an excuse to block U.S. ratification of the Test Ban Treaty? The intertwining of those interests Eisenhower warned about is manifested in the unholy relationship that the
Regents of the University of California hold with the nations' nuclear weapons laboratories. The Regents are responsible for managing and overseeing
the laboratories, placing them in a clearly equivocal moral position. Over
the years, students have organized to protest this unsavory relationship
between academia and lethal weapons development, and have worked to
focus public attention on that untenable relationship.[15]

In 2000, Putin announced on the ratification of START II and the CTBT
in Russia, that he would like to begin START III talks and reduce the long-
range missiles from 3,500 to 1,500 or even 1,000 instead of the original levels contemplated for START III of 2,500 warheads.[16] This forward-looking
proposal was accompanied by a stern caveat that all Russian offers would be
off the table, including the START II ratification, if the United States proceeded with plans to build a National Missile Defense (NMD) in violation
of the ABM Treaty. Astoundingly, U.S. diplomatic "talking points" leaked
by Russia to the *Bulletin of the Atomic Scientists* revealed that the Clinton
Administration was urging the Russians that they had nothing to fear from
our proposed NMD as long as they kept 2,500 weapons in their arsenal at
launch-on-warning, hair-trigger alert. Despite Putin's offer to cut to 1,500
warheads, or even less, the United States assured Russia that with 2,500
warheads Russia would be able to overcome the U.S. NMD shield and
deliver an "annihilating counterattack."[17]

Bush came into office and simply withdrew from the ABM Treaty in order
to pursue U.S. plans "to dominate and control the military use of space, to protect U.S. interests and investments," as set forth in the U.S. Space Command's
Vision 2020 mission statement and in the Rumsfeld Commission report of
2000.[18] He negotiated the Strategic Offensive Reduction Treaty (SORT) with
Putin, in 2002,[19] but compared to previous U.S.-Russia nuclear reduction treaties it fell far short. The treaty limits deployed strategic warheads to between
1,700 and 2,200, but it has no provisions for verification, no timeline for implementation, and it allows each side to take its weapons out of storage on the
first day of 2013. SORT does not call for the elimination of any warheads or
delivery vehicles and does not include short-range tactical weapons. It's a "sort
of" treaty. Meanwhile, Putin declared in 2002 that he would not be bound by
the START II agreement, because of the U.S. abrogation of the ABM Treaty.[20]

Bush offered to engage in negotiations for a treaty to regulate a cut-off in
producing nuclear materials for weapons, but was unwilling to have any verification or monitoring provisions for the treaty, rendering the U.S. proposal
worthless. Most egregiously, from 2005 to 2008, at the United Nations, the
United States has been the only country in the whole world to vote against a
resolution to ban weapons in space. In 2006, Russia argued that if all states
observe a prohibition on space weaponization, there will be no arms race.
Russia and China submitted a draft treaty for a space ban in 2007 and 2008,
which the United States rejected out of hand, characterizing it as "a diplomatic ploy by the two nations to gain a military advantage."[21] Barack Obama
has publicly stated he is against the weaponization of space, so a shift in U.S.
policy on space would provide an enormous opportunity to move forward,
paving the way for progress on nuclear disarmament. It remains to be seen

what the Obama administration will do about the provocative missile and radar bases planned in the Czech Republic and Poland that threaten to derail any progress on nuclear abolition between the United States and Russia. Together they possess more than 95 percent of the world's nuclear bombs. For nuclear disarmament to occur, the United States and Russia must first reach agreement to make deep cuts in their own arsenals before other countries would be willing to join in final negotiations for the total elimination of all nuclear weapons.

THE LEGAL BASIS FOR NUCLEAR ABOLITION

There are 187 nations that signed the 1970 Non-Proliferation Treaty (NPT) in which a deal was struck that the five nuclear weapons states—the United States, Russia, United Kingdom, France, and China—would give up their nuclear weapons in return for a promise from the other nations not to acquire them. India refused to agree to this arrangement, arguing that it was discriminatory and that the better course would be to negotiate for all nations to abolish nuclear weapons. Pakistan and Israel, following India's lead, also refused to sign. North Korea has since withdrawn. The NPT required that there be a review and extension conference 25 years later, and in 1995 the five nuclear powers, who had promised to give up their weapons, pressured the rest of the world to extend the NPT indefinitely. To secure the indefinite extension, the nuclear weapons states pledged in 1995 to work for the "ultimate" elimination of nuclear weapons, to negotiate a Comprehensive Test Ban Treaty (CTBT), a Fissile Material Cut-Off Treaty (FMCT) for weapons purposes, a Middle East zone free of weapons of mass destruction, and to have a "strengthened" review process every five years, with interim meetings to prepare for the five-year reviews.

Civil Society turned up in force at the 1995 NPT Review and Extension Conference to hold the nuclear weapons states to their promises in Article VI of the treaty to make good faith efforts for nuclear disarmament. When it became apparent that there was no commitment to actually eliminating nuclear weapons, more than 65 Non-Governmental Organizations (NGOs), in a basement room at the UN, drafted an Abolition Statement calling for a treaty to eliminate nuclear weapons, as part of an 11-point plan, to be completed by the year 2000.[22] They recognized the "inextricable link" between nuclear weapons and nuclear power and called for the establishment of an International Sustainable Energy Agency and the phase out of nuclear power. The statement was faxed out all over the world and by the end of the four-week NPT meeting, more than 600 NGOs had signed on and the Abolition 2000 Network was formed.

In 1996, in an unprecedented break with the rules of consensus at the Commission on Disarmament in Geneva, the CTBT was brought to the UN General Assembly for signatures over India's objections that there was no provision in the treaty to preclude the continued computer-simulated virtual reality testing of nuclear weapons or ban underground "sub-critical" tests.[23] Thus it wasn't comprehensive and it didn't ban tests. And less than two years after the CTBT was signed, India went overtly nuclear, arguing that it didn't want to be left behind while the current nuclear powers reserved the right to use advanced technology to develop new weapons without full-scale underground tests. Pakistan followed swiftly on India's heels to join the nuclear club.

In 1996, a global Civil Society campaign resulted in a decision by the International Court of Justice (ICJ) to grant a request from the General Assembly to issue an Advisory Opinion on the legality of the threat or use of nuclear weapons. The 14 judges voted unanimously that under the NPT "there exists an obligation to pursue in good faith and bring to a conclusion negotiations leading to nuclear disarmament in all its aspects under strict and effective international control."

In May 2000 the NPT had its first five-year review after the 1995 extension conference. The New Agenda Coalition (NAC), formed in 1998, with eight nations—Ireland, South Africa, Mexico, Sweden, Brazil, New Zealand, and Egypt (Slovenia, eager to join NATO, dropped out under U.S. pressure)—had begun lobbying other nations to press the nuclear powers for more progress on disarmament in UN meetings. Together with Civil Society, particularly the Abolition 2000 Network, which had produced a Model Nuclear Weapons Convention, Costa Rica introduced NAC guidelines into the General Assembly.[24] The NAC had a major impact on the NPT Review as the nuclear weapons states committed to "an unequivocal undertaking by the nuclear-weapon states to accomplish the total elimination of their nuclear arsenals."

The final statement of the NPT Review further asserts that "the total elimination of nuclear weapons is the only absolute guarantee against the use or threat of use of nuclear weapons." Additional pledges were made for practical steps to demonstrate compliance with the NPT including:

- Further unilateral disarmament.
- Increased transparency by the nuclear weapons states of their arsenals.
- Further reduction of nonstrategic nuclear weapons (those with a shorter range).
- Concrete measures to further reduce the operational status of nuclear weapons systems.
- A diminishing role for nuclear weapons in security policies (providing a basis for challenging the nuclear doctrines of the nuclear weapons

states and NATO that continue to promote reliance on nuclear weapons as the "cornerstone" of their security).
- The engagement as soon as appropriate of all the nuclear weapons states in the process leading to the total elimination of nuclear weapons.
- The early entry into force and full implementation of START II and the conclusion of START III while preserving and strengthening the ABM Treaty as a cornerstone of strategic stability.

These new NPT commitments were made by Clinton on May 19, 2000, as the weapons laboratories continued to perform sub-critical tests at Nevada and to lobby for a new earth-penetrating bunker-busting nuclear weapons and more "usable" nuclear weapons, and as Star Wars proceeded in full swing with Administration lawyers making frivolous arguments about the meaning of the restrictions in the ABM Treaty, which Clinton appeared to be violating.[25] At the close of the NPT, both Russia and China took exception to the final document without actually blocking consensus, warning that if the ABM Treaty were to be abrogated, the promises made could not be fulfilled. China said none of the steps above would succeed unless a treaty to maintain space for peaceful uses was phased in simultaneously.

The next review of the NPT in 2005 was a disaster as the Bush Administration haggled over the agenda for two weeks of the four-week meeting, objecting to any mention of the promises made by the United States at the 2000 NPT review for "an unequivocal commitment to the total elimination of nuclear weapons," and the other incremental steps including maintaining the ABM Treaty and ratifying the CTBT. The meeting broke up without any agreement on new steps for nuclear disarmament, while at the time a brutal war was being waged on Iraq based on the false assertions that Iraq had weapons of mass destruction and threatened the world with a "mushroom cloud," and a new drumbeat of hostilities was sounded against Iran and North Korea over the issue of nuclear proliferation.

THE FAUSTIAN BARGAIN IN THE NPT FOR CIVILIAN NUCLEAR POWER

One of the ironies of the NPT is that to secure the promise of the non-nuclear weapons states not to acquire nuclear weapons, the nuclear weapons states promised them an "inalienable right" to the "peaceful uses" of nuclear technology, enabling the very nuclear weapons proliferation the treaty is designed to prevent. The drafters of the CTBT were well aware that by having a nuclear reactor, a nation had been given the keys to a bomb factory when they required the signatures of 44 "nuclear-capable" nations to be included in any effort to ban nuclear tests, regardless of whether they proclaimed any intention to develop weapons.[26] And former Central Intelligence Agency (CIA) director George Tenet said, "The difference between producing low-enriched uranium and weapons-capable high-enriched uranium is only a matter of time and intent, not technology."[27]

There are now 440 "peaceful" reactors in 31 countries[28]—all producing deadly bomb materials with 272 research reactors in 56 countries, some producing highly enriched uranium.[29] There are about 270,000 tons of irradiated fuel containing plutonium and other radioactive elements in storage, much of it at reactor sites. The waste is currently increasing by about 12,000 tons each year.[30] There are 500 tons of weapons usable plutonium already separated out of reactor waste and 1,000 tons of highly enriched uranium making about 1.5 million kilograms of weapons usable fissile materials. It takes only 5 kilograms of plutonium or 17 kilograms of highly enriched uranium to make one nuclear bomb.[31] The Bush Administration had plans to build 50 more reactors by 2020[32]; there are now 34 new nuclear reactors under construction in 11 countries[33]—to churn out more irradiated waste on tap for bomb-making, with no known solution to safely containing the tons of nuclear waste that will be generated over the unimaginable 250,000 years it will continue to threaten life on earth.[34] New projects are under way to mine uranium on every continent, mostly on indigenous lands, where first peoples have suffered inordinately from radiation poisoning.

Yet countless studies report higher incidences of birth defects, cancer, and genetic mutations in every situation where nuclear technology is employed—whether for war or for "peace." A National Research Council (NRC) 2005 study reported that exposure to X-rays and gamma rays, even at low-dose levels, can cause cancer. The committee defined "low-dose" as a range from near zero up to about 10 times that from a CT scan. "There appears to be no threshold below which exposure can be viewed as harmless," said NRC panelist, Herbert Abrams, professor emeritus of radiology at Stanford and Harvard universities.[35] Tens of thousands of tons of nuclear waste accumulate at civilian reactors with no solution for its storage, releasing toxic doses of radioactive waste into our air, water, and soil and contaminating our planet and its inhabitants for hundreds of thousands of years.

What does it take for a country to be willing to inflict the toxic assault of nuclear waste on its own people in light of the lessons we have learned during the past 60 years of the nuclear age? One delegate at the disastrous 2005 Non-Proliferation Treaty Review shared, quite frankly, at an NGO panel that his country was unwilling to forgo its "inalienable right" under the treaty because their scientists wouldn't want to be left behind in state-of-the-art knowledge. They need to play in the major leagues of science with the big boys. So despite the promise of clean, safe, abundant energy from the sun, the wind, the tides, many non-nuclear weapons states have underscored their equal rights to the dark fruits of nuclear technology. Will this kind of scientific machismo, which has created so many gruesome chapters in world history, be supported at the expense of the health of so many people and of the very survival of our biosphere? Will we satisfy our scientists' dangerous thirst for knowledge and status despite the obvious possibility that the peaceful nuclear reactor can readily be converted to a bomb factory?

The industry-dominated International Atomic Energy Agency (IAEA) has been instrumental in covering up the disastrous health effects of the Chernobyl tragedy, understating the number of deaths by attributing only 56 deaths directly to the accident as of 2004.[36] This was a whitewash of health studies performed by Russia and the Ukraine, which estimated thousands of deaths and tens of thousands who suffered thyroid cancer and leukemia as a result of the accident.[37] This cover-up was no doubt due to the collusive agreement between the IAEA and the World Health Organization (WHO), which under its terms provides that if either of the organizations initiates any program or activity in which the other has or may have a substantial interest, the first party shall consult with the other with a view to adjusting the matter by mutual agreement.[38] Thus, our scientists and researchers at the WHO are required to have their work vetted by the industry's champion for "peaceful" nuclear technology, the IAEA. For example, WHO abandoned its 1961 research agenda on human health effects of food irradiation, ceding to the IAEA responsibility for researching its safety. The IAEA is leading a global campaign to further the legalization, and consumer acceptance of irradiated foods. "We must confer with experts in the various fields of advertising and psychology to put the public at ease," one IAEA report states, also recommending that the process "should not be required on the label."[39] Yet, the NRC study, stating that there is no safe dose of radiation, clearly justified the public's rational fear of radiation. Today, in the face of catastrophic climate change, we now see the nuclear industry devoting its resources to public relations campaigns perpetuating the myth that the toxic technology is "clean" and "safe."[40]

CONTROLLING THE FUEL CYCLE

IAEA Director, Mohammed ElBaradei has stated:

We just cannot continue business as usual that every country can build its own factories for separating plutonium or enriching uranium. Then we are really talking about 30, 40 countries sitting on the fence with a nuclear weapons capability that could be converted into a nuclear weapon in a matter of months.[41]

The current flurry of negotiations and the move to try to control the production of the civilian nuclear fuel cycle in one central place, as proposed by El Baradei, would be futile. It would create just another discriminatory aspect of the NPT, with a new class of "haves" and "have-nots" under the treaty, as was done with those permitted to have nuclear weapons and those who are not. Now it is proposed that some nations be permitted to make their own nuclear fuel, while others, such as Iran, would be precluded from doing so. And in the wake of the stern warnings to Iran, and the referral of the issue to the Security Council, which has provoked Iran to begin reprocessing of nuclear fuel under its "inalienable" right, the United States has incomprehensibly announced its Global Nuclear Energy Partnership (GNEP). The GNEP is designed to control the spread of nuclear materials in which "supplier" nations would manufacture nuclear fuel rods, ship them to other countries—by rail, road, and sea—to use in their reactors and then take back the irradiated fuel and reprocess it, breaking a 30-year ban in the United States on turning irradiated reactor fuel into weapons-grade material, first instituted by Presidents Carter and Ford.[42]

Brazil, too, recently got into the action, firing up its own major uranium enrichment plant while we were warning Iran that such action would be viewed as hostile. And six new Arab nations—Egypt, Algeria, Saudi Arabia, Morocco, Tunisia, and the United Arab Emirates—have announced their intention to develop "peaceful" nuclear technology, in what appears to be an attempt to acquire civilian nuclear capacity before the dominant industrial nations succeed in putting the nuclear fuel cycle and access to materials under their exclusive control.[43] Further undermining the integrity of the NPT bargain, the United States made a deal with India in 2008 to supply it with "peaceful" nuclear technology, even though the NPT prohibits any sharing of nuclear technology with nations who have not signed the treaty.[44]

Trying to control the reprocessing and distribution of nuclear fuel would be going down the same path we've been on for the past 50 some-odd years for nuclear arms control. There is no more likelihood that France, Japan, or the United States, for example, will surrender control of nuclear materials production, any more than the nuclear powers have surrendered control of atom bombs. We would have a long drawn-out contentious effort to establish a discriminatory regime—when, instead, we could be expending our energy and intellectual treasure on shifting the energy paradigm to make nuclear, fossil, and industrial biofuels obsolete.

It is time for the IAEA to give up its dual mission in nuclear technology. While the Agency plays an indispensable role in inspecting and verifying compliance with nuclear disarmament agreements, it should not continue to act with a manifest conflict of interest in promoting the commercial interests of the nuclear industry.

HARBINGERS OF CHANGE: TIME TO END THE NUCLEAR AGE

- In June 2008, 69 members of the European Parliament from 19 countries signed a call to negotiate a nuclear weapons convention based on the draft Abolition 2000 Model Nuclear Weapons Convention[45] submitted to the UN, now updated and being promoted by the International Campaign to Abolish Nuclear Weapons (ICAN) spearheaded by the International Physicians for the Prevention of Nuclear War.
- The U.S. Conference of Mayors, responding to a call from the Mayors for Peace, led by the Mayors of Hiroshima and Nagasaki, endorsed a call for negotiations on a Nuclear Weapons Convention to begin in 2010, with complete nuclear disarmament by 2020.[46]
- A new campaign, Global Zero, launched in December 2008, has organized more than 100 world leaders calling for "a legally binding verifiable agreement, including all nations, to eliminate nuclear weapons by a date certain."[47] Congresswoman Lynne Woolsey's House Resolution 68 calls on the United States to enter into negotiations to abolish nuclear weapons.[48]
- In October 2008, UN Secretary-General Ban-ki Moon put forward a five-point proposal to get nuclear disarmament back on track by renewing a general call on nuclear weapons states to meet their nuclear disarmament obligations, and by encouraging nuclear weapons states to negotiate "a nuclear-weapons convention, backed by a strong system of verification."[49]
- Germany has convened a series of meetings this year resulting in 51 nations cooperating to initiative an International Renewable Energy Agency (IRENA).[50] Just as the Comprehensive Test Ban has rendered inoperative Article V of the NPT, which provided a right to "peaceful" nuclear explosions, the establishment of IRENA would supersede Article IV and the "inalienable right" to "peaceful" nuclear technology, providing a benign, non-proliferating substitute of safe, clean, abundant energy that will help turn the world from strife and resource wars.
- Congressman Ed Markey has proposed a resolution, HR 5529, for the United States to support and participate with IRENA.[51]
- Public opinion supports nuclear disarmament. A 2007 poll, jointly conducted by the University of Maryland and Russia's Levada Center, shows large majorities in both Russia and America in favor of eliminating nuclear weapons.[52]

The current crisis over Iran's intentions to exercise its legal "inalienable right" to "peaceful" nuclear technology presents an opportunity for new American leadership to negotiate an end to the nuclear age. Rather than pursuing a lethal path of preemptive war, a new U.S. administration, riding on the shifting currents of world opinion that point to new common understanding that nuclear abolition is an idea whose time has come, could seize this moment and move to finally end the nuclear scourge.

NEXT STEPS FOR U.S. LEADERSHIP FOR NUCLEAR DISARMAMENT

- Take the Russians up on their offer to cut our arsenals to 1,000 warheads and then take China up on its offer calling for all the other nuclear weapons states (United Kingdom, France, Israel, India, Pakistan, North Korea) to negotiate a treaty for the elimination of all nuclear weapons.
- De-alert all nuclear weapons.
- Commit to never be the first to use a nuclear weapon. (Only China has this policy.)
- Cut all funding for new nuclear weapons research and substitute a passive custodial program for maintenance of the arsenal during dismantlement.
- Close the Nevada test site just as France and China have closed theirs in the South Pacific and Gobi Desert.
- Bring all U.S. nuclear warheads back from Europe and abandon NATO policy to rely on nuclear weapons for its security.
- Take up Russia and China's offer for negotiations to maintain the peaceful use of space for all time.
- Stop any further nuclearization and militarization of space.
- Support negotiations for a missile ban treaty.
- Institute a moratorium on uranium mining.
- Call for a global phase out of nuclear power and join Germany's initiative to fund and establish IRENA to promote the use of clean, safe energy.
- Support global efforts for the reallocation of worldwide subsidies of $250 billion to nuclear, fossil, and industrial biomass fuels for clean, safe, sustainable solar, wind, geothermal, and marine energy, and work for the reallocation of $40 billion of U.S. subsidies and tax breaks now supporting unsustainable energy resources to be applied to clean, safe energy.
- Reallocate the resources saved to redress the environmental devastation and human suffering caused by nuclear mining, milling, production, and testing, which have been disproportionately borne by the world's indigenous peoples.
- Provide adequate resources to address the toxic legacy of the nuclear age.

NOTES

1. Shultz et al., 2008.
2. Obama, April 2008.
3. Gates, 2008.
4. Albert Einstein, Bertrand Russell and others.
5. "Duck and Cover," 1950.
6. "Cold War Relics or Tomorrow's Family Life-Savers?" 2005.
7. Stassen and Wittner, 2007.
8. Radiation and Public Health The RPHP, 2003.
9. Kristensen, 2009.
10. Sokov, 2000.
11. "Urge Congress to Cease and Desist on Subcritical Testing." August 28, 2006.
12. Cabasso, 2008.
13. Schwartz, 1998.
14. Eisenhower, 1961.
15. Paddock, 2007.
16. Arms Control Association, 2002.
17. Missile Defense and the ABM Treaty, 2002.
18. Vision for 2010.
19. Treaty on Strategic Offensive Reductions, 2003.
20. Slater, 2008.
21. Ibid.
22. Weiss, 2007.
23. Indian Embassy, 1999.
24. Securing our Survival, 2007.
25. Spring, 1999.
26. CTBTO Preparatory Commission for the Comprehensive Nuclear Test Ban Treaty.
27. Tenet, 2004; Broad and Sanger, 2004.
28. Power Reactor Information System, (PRIS), 2010.
29. NTI, 2009.
30. World Nuclear Association, 2009.
31. International Panel on Fissile Materials, 2007.
32. Galbraith, 2010.
33. World Nuclear Association, 2010.
34. Basic Physics of Nuclear Medicine, n.d.
35. Daniel, 2005.
36. World Nuclear Association, 2010.
37. Greenpeace, 2006.
38. Bertell, 2004.
39. Public Citizen, 2002.
40. Farsetta, 2008.
41. El Baradei, 2005.
42. Edwards, 2006.
43. Beeston, 2006.

44. Pan and Bajoria, 2008.
45. Securing Our Survival, 2007.
46. Akiba, 2009.
47. Global Zero, 2010.
48. International Renewable Energy Agency (IRENA), 2008.
49. Ki-Moon, 2008.
50. International Renewable Energy Agency (IRENA), 2008.
51. Ibid.
52. WorldPublicOpinion.org, 2007.

CHAPTER 3

HIROSHIMA DAY: AMERICA HAS BEEN ASLEEP AT THE WHEEL FOR 64 YEARS

Daniel Ellsberg

It was a hot August day in Detroit. I was standing on a street corner downtown, looking at the front page of the *Detroit News* in a news rack. I remember a streetcar rattling by on the tracks as I read the headline: A single American bomb had destroyed a Japanese city.

I thought: "We got it first. And we used it. On a city."

I had a sense of dread, a feeling that something very ominous for humanity had just happened. A feeling, new to me as an American, at 14, that my country might have made a terrible mistake. I was glad when the war ended nine days later, but it didn't make me think that my first reaction on August 6 was wrong.

Unlike nearly everyone else outside the Manhattan Project, my first awareness of the challenges of the nuclear era had occurred—and my attitudes toward the advent of nuclear weaponry had formed—some nine months earlier than those headlines, and in a crucially different context.

It was in a ninth-grade social studies class, in the fall of 1944, and our teacher, Bradley Patterson, was discussing a concept that was familiar then in sociology—William F. Ogburn's notion of "cultural lag." The idea was

---

A similar version of this article originally appeared at Truthdig.com. For more of Daniel Ellsberg's work, visit his blog: www.ellsberg.net.

that the development of technology regularly moved much further and faster in human social-historical evolution than other aspects of culture: our institutions of government, our values, habits, our understanding of society and ourselves. Indeed, the very notion of "progress" referred mainly to technology. What "lagged" behind, what developed more slowly or not at all in social adaptation to new technology was everything that bore on our ability to control and direct technology and the use of technology to dominate other humans.

To illustrate this, Mr. Patterson posed a potential advance in technology that might be realized soon. It was possible now, he told us, to conceive of a bomb made of U-235, an isotope of uranium, which would have an explosive power 1,000 times greater than the largest bombs currently being used in the war. German scientists in late 1938 had discovered that uranium could be split by nuclear fission, releasing immense amounts of energy.

Several popular articles about the possibility of atomic bombs and specifically U-235 bombs appeared during the war in magazines like *The Saturday Evening Post*. None of these represented leaks from the Manhattan Project, whose very existence was top secret. In every case they had been inspired by earlier articles on the subject that had been published freely in 1939 and 1940, before scientific self-censorship and then formal classification had set in. Patterson had come across one of these wartime articles. He brought the potential development to us as an example of one more possible leap by science and technology ahead of our social institutions.

Suppose, then, that one nation, or several, chose to explore the possibility of making this into a bomb, and succeeded. What would be the probable implications of this for humanity? How would it be used, by humans and states as they were today? Would it be, on balance, bad or good for the world? Would it be a force for peace, for example, or for destruction? We were to write a short essay on this due within a week. As I remember, everyone in the class had arrived at much the same judgment.

The existence of such a bomb, we each concluded, would be bad news for humanity. Humans could not handle such a destructive force. People could not control it, safely, appropriately. The power would be abused: used dangerously and destructively, with terrible consequences; evidenced by the allies' bombing of German cities and the earlier German attempts to destroy Rotterdam and London. Civilization, perhaps our species, would be in danger of a collapse from which it would never fully recover.

As I recall, this conclusion didn't depend mainly on who had the bomb, or how many had it, or who got it first. And to the best of my memory, we in the class weren't addressing it as something that might come so soon as to bear on the outcome of the ongoing war. It seemed likely in the way the case was presented to us that the Germans would get it first, since they had done the original science. But we didn't base our negative assessment on the idea that this would necessarily be a Nazi or German bomb. It would be a bad development, on balance, even if democratic countries got it first.

It was months before I thought of the issues again. I remember the moment when I did, I can still see and feel the scene and recall my thoughts, described above, as I read the headline on August 6.

I remember that I was uneasy about the tone in President Truman's voice on the radio as he exulted over our success in the race for the bomb and its effectiveness against Japan. I generally admired Truman, then and later, but in hearing his announcements I was put off by the lack of concern in his voice, the absence of a sense of tragedy, of desperation or fear for the future. It seemed to me that this was a decision best made in anguish; and both Truman's manner and the tone of the official communiqués made unmistakably clear that this hadn't been the case.

Which meant for me that our leaders didn't have the picture, didn't grasp the significance of the precedent they had set and the sinister implications for the future. And that evident unawareness was itself scary. I believed that something ominous had happened; that it was bad for humanity that the bomb was feasible, and that its use would have bad long-term consequences, whether or not those negatives were balanced or even outweighed by short-run benefits.

Looking back, it seems clear to me my reactions then were right.

Moreover, reflecting on two related themes that have run through my life since then—intense abhorrence of nuclear weapons, and more generally of killing women and children—I've come to suspect that I've conflated in my emotional memory two events less than a year apart: Hiroshima and a catastrophe that visited my own family 11 months later.

On the Fourth of July, 1946, driving on a hot afternoon on a flat, straight road through the cornfields of Iowa, on the way from Detroit to visit our relatives in Denver, my father fell asleep at the wheel and went off the road long enough to hit a sidewall over a culvert that sheared off the right side of the car, killing my mother and sister.

My father's nose was broken and his forehead was cut. When a highway patrol car came by, he was wandering by the wreckage, bleeding and dazed. I was inside, in a coma from a concussion, with a large gash on the left side of my forehead. I had been sitting on the floor next to the back seat, on a suitcase covered with a blanket, with my head just behind the driver's seat. When the car hit the wall, my head was thrown against a metal fixture on the back of the driver's seat, knocking me out and opening up a large trian-gular flap of flesh on my forehead. I was in coma for 36 hours. My legs had been stretched out in front of me across the car and my right leg was broken just above the knee.

My father had been a highway engineer in Nebraska. He said that highway walls should never have been flush with the road like that, and later laws tended to ban that placement. This one took off the side of the car where my mother and sister were sitting. It was amazing that anyone had survived.

Looking back now at what I drew from reading the Pentagon Papers later and from my citizen's activism since then, I think I saw in the events of August 1945 and July 1946, unconsciously, a common message. I loved my father, and I respected Truman. But you couldn't rely entirely on a trusted authority to protect you and your family from disaster. Some vigilance was called for, to awaken them if need be, or warn others. They could be asleep at the wheel, heading for a wall or a cliff.

I sensed almost right away, in August 1945 as Hiroshima and Nagasaki were incinerated, that such feelings—about our president, and our bomb—separated me from nearly everyone around me, from my parents and friends and from most other Americans. These were thoughts to be kept to myself. They were not to be mentioned. They could only sound unpatriotic.

Before that day perhaps no one in the public outside our class—no one else outside the Manhattan Project (and very few inside it)—had spent a week, as we had, or even a day thinking about the impact of such a weapon on the long-term prospects for humanity.

And we were set apart from our fellow Americans in another important way. Perhaps no others outside the project or our class ever had occasion to think about the bomb without the strongly biasing positive associations that accompanied their first awareness in August 1945 of its very possibility: that it was "our" weapon, an instrument of American democracy developed to deter a Nazi bomb, pursued by two presidents, a war-winning weapon and a necessary one—so it was claimed and almost universally believed—to end the war without a costly invasion of Japan.

For nearly all other Americans, whatever dread they may have felt about the long-run future of the bomb (and there was more expression of this in elite media than most people remembered later) was offset at the time and ever afterward by a powerful aura of its legitimacy, and its almost miraculous potential for good that had already been realized. For a great many Americans still, the Hiroshima and Nagasaki bombs are regarded above all with gratitude, for having saved their own lives or the lives of their husbands, brothers, fathers, or grandfathers, which would otherwise have been at risk in the invasion of Japan. For these Americans and many others, the bomb was not so much an instrument of massacre as a kind of savior, a protector of precious lives.

Most Americans ever since have seen the destruction of the populations of Hiroshima and Nagasaki as necessary and effective—as constituting just means, in effect just terrorism, under the supposed circumstances—thus legitimating, in their eyes, the second and third largest single-day massacres in history. (The largest, also by the U.S. Army Air Corps, was the firebombing of Tokyo five months before on the night of March 9, which burned alive or suffocated 80,000 to 120,000 civilians. Most of the very few Americans who are aware of this event at all accept it, too, as appropriate in wartime.)

To regard those acts as definitely other than criminal and immoral, as most Americans do, is to believe that anything—anything—can be legitimate means: at worst, a necessary, lesser, evil. At the very least we can say that it is done by Americans, on the order of a president, during wartime. Indeed, we are the only country in the world that believes it won a war by bombing—specifically by bombing cities with weapons of mass destruction—and believes that it was fully rightful in doing so. It is a dangerous state of mind.

Even if the premises of these justifications had been realistic (after years of study I'm convinced, along with many scholars, they were not; but I'm not addressing that here), the consequences of such beliefs for subsequent policy making were bound to be fateful. They underlie the American government and public's ready acceptance ever since of basing our security on readiness to carry out threats of mass annihilation by nuclear weapons, and the belief by many officials and elites still today that abolition of these weapons is not only infeasible but undesirable.

By contrast, given a few days' reflection in the summer of 1945 before a presidential fait accompli was framed in that fashion, you didn't have to be a moral prodigy to arrive at the sense of foreboding we all had in Mr. Patterson's class. It was as easily available to 13-year-old ninth-graders as it was to many Manhattan Project scientists, who also had the opportunity to form their judgments before the bomb was used.

But the scientists knew something else that was unknown to the public and even to most high-level decision makers. They knew that the atomic bombs, the uranium and plutonium fission bombs they were preparing, were only the precursors to far more powerful explosives, almost surely including a thermonuclear fusion bomb, later called the hydrogen bomb, or H-bomb. That weapon—of which we eventually came to have tens of thousands—could have an explosive yield much greater than the fission bombs needed to trigger it. A thousand times greater.

Moreover, most of the scientists who focused on the long-run implications of nuclear weapons, after the surrender of Germany in May 1945, belatedly believed that using the bomb against Japan would make international control of the weapon very unlikely. In turn that would make inevitable a desperate arms race, which would soon expose the United States to adversaries' uncontrolled possession of thermonuclear weapons, so that, as the scientists said in a pre-attack petition to the president, "the cities of the United States as well as the cities of other nations will be in continuous danger of sudden annihilation." (In this they were proved correct.) They cautioned the president—on both moral grounds and considerations of long-run survival of civilization—against beginning this process by using the bomb against Japan even if its use might shorten the war.

But their petition was sent "through channels" and was deliberately held back by Gen. Leslie Groves, director of the Manhattan Project. It never got to the president, or even to Secretary of War Henry Stimson until after the bomb had been dropped. There is no record that the scientists' concerns about the future and their judgment of a nuclear attack's impact on it were ever made known to President Truman before or after his decisions. Still less was made known to the American public.

At the end of the war the scientists' petition and their reasoning were reclassified secret to keep it from public knowledge, and its existence was unknown for more than a decade. Several Manhattan Project scientists later expressed regret that they had earlier deferred to the demands of the secrecy managers—for fear of losing their clearances and positions, and perhaps facing prosecution—and had collaborated in maintaining public ignorance on this most vital of issues.

One of them—Eugene Rabinowitch, who after the war founded and edited the *Bulletin of the Atomic Scientists* (with its Doomsday Clock)—had, in fact, after the German surrender in May, actively considered breaking ranks and alerting the American public to the existence of the bomb, the plans for using it against Japan, and the scientists' views both of the moral issues and the long-term dangers of doing so.

He first reported this in a letter to the *New York Times* published on June 28, 1971. It was the day I submitted to arrest at the federal courthouse in Boston; for the preceding 13 days my wife and I had been underground eluding the FBI while distributing the Pentagon Papers to 17 newspapers after injunctions had halted publication in the *Times* and *the Washington Post*. The Rabinowitch letter began by saying it was "the revelation by *the Times* of the Pentagon history of U.S. intervention in Vietnam, despite its classification as 'secret,'" that led him now to reveal:

> Before the atom bomb-drops on Hiroshima and Nagasaki, I had spent sleepless nights thinking that I should reveal to the American people, perhaps through a reputable news organ, the fateful act—the first introduction of atomic weapons—which the U.S. Government planned to

carry out without consultation with its people. Twenty-five years later, I feel I would have been right if I had done so.[1]

I didn't see this the morning it was published, because I was getting myself arrested and arraigned, for doing what Rabinowitch wishes he had done in 1945, and I wish I had done in 1964. I first came across this extraordinary confession by a would-be whistle-blower (I don't know another term like it) in *Hiroshima in America: Fifty Years of Denial* by Robert Jay Lifton and Greg Mitchell.[2]

Rereading Rabinowitch's statement, still with some astonishment, I agree with him. He was right to consider it, and he would have been right if he had done it. He would have faced prosecution and prison then (as I did at the time his letter was published), but he would have been more than justified, as a citizen and as a human being, in informing the American public and burdening them with shared responsibility for the fateful decision.

Some of the same scientists faced a comparable challenge four years after Hiroshima, addressing the possible development of an even more terrible weapon, more fraught with possible danger to human survival: the hydrogen bomb. This time some who had urged use of the atom bomb against Japan (dissenting from the petitioners above) recommended against even development and testing of the new proposal, in view of its "extreme dangers to mankind." "Let it be clearly realized," they said, "that this is a super weapon; it is in a totally different category from an atomic bomb"[3]

I learned much later, knowledge of the secret possibility was not completely limited to government scientists. A few others—my father, it turns out, was one—knew of this prospect before it had received the stamp of presidential approval and had become an American government project. And once again, under those conditions of prior knowledge (denied as before to the public), to grasp the moral and long-run dangers you didn't have to be a nuclear physicist. My father was not.

Some background is needed here. My father, Harry Ellsberg, was a structural engineer. He worked for Albert Kahn in Detroit, the "Arsenal of Democracy." At the start of World War II, he was the chief structural engineer in charge of designing the Ford Willow Run plant, a factory to make B-24 Liberator bombers for the Air Corps.

Dad was proud that it was the world's largest industrial building under one roof. It put together bombers the way Ford produced cars, on an assembly line a mile-and-a-quarter long.

Once, my father took me out to Willow Run to see the line in operation. For as far as I could see, the huge metal bodies of planes were moving along tracks as workers riveted and installed parts. But as Dad had explained to me, three-quarters of a mile along, the bodies were moved off the tracks onto a circular turntable that rotated them 90 degrees; then they were moved back on track for the last half mile of the L. Finally, the planes were rolled out the hangar doors at the end of the factory—one every hour: It took 59 minutes on the line to build a plane with its 100,000 parts from start to finish—filled with gas and flown out to war.

It was an exciting sight for a 13-year-old. I was proud of my father. His next wartime job was to design a still larger airplane engine factory—again the world's largest plant under one roof—the Dodge Chicago plant, which made all the engines for B-29s.

When the war ended, Dad accepted an offer to oversee the buildup of the plutonium production facilities at Hanford, Washington. That project was being run by General Electric under contract with the Atomic Energy Commission. To take the job of chief structural engineer on the project, Dad moved from the engineering firm of Albert Kahn, where he had worked for years, to what became Giffels & Rossetti. Later he told me that engineering firm had the largest volume of construction contracts in the world at that time, and his project was the world's largest. I grew up hearing these superlatives.

The Hanford project gave my father his first really good salary. But while I was away as a sophomore at Harvard, he left his job with Giffels & Rossetti, for reasons I never learned at the time. He was out of work for almost a year. Then he went back as chief structural engineer for the whole firm. Almost 30 years later, in 1978, when my father was 89, I happened to ask him why he had left Giffels & Rossetti. His answer startled me. He said, "Because they wanted me to help build the H-bomb."

This was a breathtaking statement for me to hear in 1978. I was in full-time active opposition to the deployment of the neutron bomb, which was a small H-bomb, that President Jimmy Carter was proposing to send to Europe. The N-bomb had a killing radius from its output of neutrons that was much wider than its radius of destruction by blast. Optimally, an air-burst N-bomb would have little fallout and it would not destroy structures, equipment, or vehicles, but its neutrons would kill the humans either outside or within buildings or tanks. The Soviets mocked it as "a capitalist weapon" that destroyed people but not property, but they tested such a weapon, too, as did other countries.

I had opposed developing or testing that concept for almost 20 years, since it was first described to me by my friend and colleague at the RAND Corp., Sam Cohen, who liked to be known as the "father of the neutron bomb." I feared that, as a "small" weapon with limited and seemingly controllable lethal effects, it would be seen as usable in warfare, making the United States the first to use it and "limited nuclear war" more likely. It would be the match that would set off an exchange of the much larger dirty weapons that were the bulk of our arsenal and were all that the Soviets then had.

In the year of this conversation with Dad, I was arrested four times blocking the railroad tracks at the Rocky Flats Nuclear Weapons Production Facility, which produced all the plutonium triggers for H-bombs and was going to produce the plutonium cores for neutron bombs. One of these arrests was on Nagasaki Day, August 9. The triggers produced at Rocky Flats were, in effect, the nuclear components of A-bombs, plutonium fission bombs of the type that had destroyed Nagasaki on that date in 1945.

Every one of our many thousands of H-bombs, the thermonuclear fusion bombs that arm our strategic forces, requires a Nagasaki-type A-bomb as its detonator. (I doubt that one American in 100 knows that simple fact, and thus has a clear understanding of the difference between A- and H-bombs, or of the reality of the thermonuclear arsenals of the past 50 years.)

Our popular image of nuclear war—from the familiar pictures of the devastation of Nagasaki and Hiroshima—is grotesquely misleading. Those pictures show us only what happens to humans and buildings when they are hit by what is now just the detonating cap for a modern nuclear weapon.

The plutonium for these weapons came from Hanford and from the Savannah River Site in Georgia and was machined into weapons components at Rocky Flats, in Colorado. Allen Ginsberg and I, with many others, blockaded the entrances to the plant on August 9, 1978, to interrupt business as usual on the anniversary of the day a plutonium bomb had killed 58,000 humans (about 100,000 had died by the end of 1945).

I had never heard before of any connection of my father with the H-bomb. He wasn't particularly wired in to my anti-nuclear work or to any of my activism since the Vietnam War had ended. I asked him what he meant by his comment about leaving Giffels & Rossetti.

"They wanted me to be in charge of designing a big plant that would be producing material for an H-bomb." He said that DuPont, which had built the Hanford Site, was to have the contract from the Atomic Energy Commission. That would have been for the Savannah River Site. I asked him when this was. He replied, "Late 1949."

I told him, "You must have the date wrong. You couldn't have heard about the hydrogen bomb then, it's too early." I'd just been reading about that in Herb York's then-recent book, *The Advisors*. The General Advisory Committee (GAC) of the Atomic Energy Commission (AEC)—chaired by Robert Oppenheimer and including James Conant, Enrico Fermi, and Isidor Rabi—were considering that fall whether or not to launch a crash program for an H-bomb. That was the "super weapon" referred to earlier. They had advised strongly against it, but President Truman overruled them.

"Truman didn't make the decision to go ahead till January 1950. Meanwhile the whole thing was super-secret. You couldn't have heard about it in 1949."

My father said, "Well, somebody had to design the plant if they were going to go ahead. I was the logical person. I was in charge of the structural engineering of the whole project at Hanford after the war. I had a Q clearance."

That was the first I'd ever heard that he'd had a Q clearance—an AEC clearance for nuclear weapons design and stockpile data. I'd had that clearance myself in the Pentagon—along with close to a dozen other special clearances above top-secret—after I left the RAND Corp. for the Defense Department in 1964. It was news to me that my father had had a clearance, but it made sense that he would have needed one for Hanford.

I said, "So you're telling me that you would have been one of the only people in the country, outside the GAC, who knew we were considering building the H-bomb in 1949?"

He said, "I suppose so. Anyway, I know it was late 1949, because that's when I quit."

"Why did you quit?"

"I didn't want to make an H-bomb. Why, that thing was going to be 1,000 times more powerful than the A-bomb!"

The first explosion of a true H-bomb, five years later, had 1,000 times the explosive power of the Hiroshima blast. At 15 megatons—the equivalent of 15 million tons of high explosive—it was over 1 million times more powerful than the largest conventional bombs of World War II. That one bomb had almost eight times the explosive force of all the bombs we dropped in that war: more than all the explosions in all the wars in human history. In 1961, the Soviets tested a 58-megaton H-bomb.

My father went on: "I hadn't wanted to work on the A-bomb, either. But then Einstein seemed to think that we needed it, and it made sense to me that we had to have it against the Russians. So I took the job, but I never felt good about it.

He said, "There was another thing about it that I couldn't stand. Building these things generated a lot of radioactive waste. I wasn't responsible for designing the containers for the waste, but I knew they were bound to leak eventually. That stuff was deadly forever. It was radioactive for 24,000 years."

There were tears in his eyes. He said huskily, "I couldn't stand the thought that I was working on a project that was poisoning parts of my own country forever, and that might make parts of it uninhabitable for thousands of years."

I thought over what he'd said; then I asked him if anyone else working with him had had misgivings. He didn't know.

"Were you the only one who quit?" He said yes. He was leaving the best job he'd ever had, and he didn't have any other to turn to. He lived on savings for a while and did some consulting.

I thought about Oppenheimer and Conant—both of whom had recommended dropping the atomic bomb on Hiroshima—and Fermi and Rabi, who had, that same month Dad was resigning, expressed internally their opposition to development of the superbomb in the most extreme terms possible: It was potentially "a weapon of genocide . . . carries much further than the atomic bomb itself the policy of exterminating civilian populations . . . whose power of destruction is essentially unlimited . . . a threat to the future of the human race which is intolerable . . . a danger to humanity as a whole . . . necessarily an evil thing considered in any light."[4]

Not one of these men risked his clearance by sharing his anxieties and the basis for them with the American public. Oppenheimer and Conant considered resigning their advisory positions when the president went ahead against their advice. But they were persuaded by Dean Acheson not to quit at that time, lest that draw public attention to their expert judgment that the president's course fatally endangered humanity.

I asked my father what had made him feel so strongly, to act in a way that nobody else had done. He said, "You did."

That didn't make any sense. I said, "What do you mean? We didn't discuss this at all. I didn't know anything about it."

Dad said, "It was earlier. I remember you came home with a book one day, and you were crying. It was about Hiroshima. You said, 'Dad, you've got to read this. It's the worst thing I've ever read.'" I said that must have been John Hersey's book, *Hiroshima*.[5] (I read it when it came out as a book. I was in the hospital when it filled *The New Yorker* in August 1946.) I didn't remember giving it to him.

"Yes. Well, I read it, and you were right. That's when I started to feel bad about working on an atomic bomb project. And then when they said they wanted me to work on a hydrogen bomb, it was too much for me. I thought it was time for me to get out."

I asked if he had told his bosses why he was quitting. He said he told some people, not others. The ones he told seemed to understand his feelings. In fact, in less than a year, the head of the firm called to say that they wanted him to come back as chief structural engineer for the whole firm. They were dropping the DuPont contract (they didn't say why), so he wouldn't have to have anything to do with the AEC or bomb-making. He stayed with them till he retired.

I said, finally, "Dad, how come you never said anything about it?"

My father said, "Oh, I couldn't tell any of this to my family. You weren't cleared."

Well, I finally got my clearances, a decade after my father gave his up. And for some years, they were my undoing, though they turned out to be useful in the end. A decade later they allowed me to read the Pentagon Papers and to keep them in my "Top Secret" safe at the RAND Corp., from which I eventually delivered them to the Senate Foreign Relations Committee and later to 19 newspapers.

We have long needed and lacked the equivalent of the Pentagon Papers on the subject of nuclear policies and preparations, nuclear threats, and decision making—above all in the United States and Russia but also in the other nuclear-weapons states. I deeply regret that I did not make known to Congress, the American public, and the world the extensive documentation of persistent and still-unknown nuclear dangers that was available to me 40 to 50 years ago as a consultant to and official in the executive branch working on nuclear war plans, command, control, and nuclear crises. Those in nuclear-weapons states who are in a position now to do more than I did then to alert their countries and the world to fatally reckless secret policies should take warning from my and others' earlier inaction: and do better.

That I had high-level access and played such a role in nuclear planning is, of course, deeply ironic in view of my personal history. My feelings of revulsion and foreboding about nuclear weapons had not changed an iota since 1945, and they have never left me. Since I was 14, the overriding objective of my life has been to prevent the occurrence of nuclear war.

There was a close analogy with the Manhattan Project. Its scientists—most of whom hoped the bomb would never be used for anything but as a threat to deter Germany—were driven by a plausible but mistaken fear that the Nazis were racing them. Actually the Nazis had rejected the pursuit of the atomic bomb on practical grounds in June 1942, just as the Manhattan Project was beginning. Similarly, I was one of many in the late 1950s who were misled and recruited into the nuclear arms race by exaggerated, and in this case deliberately manipulated, fears of Soviet intentions and crash efforts.

Precisely because I received clearances and was exposed to top-secret intelligence estimates, in particular from the Air Force, I, along with my colleagues at the RAND Corp., came to be preoccupied with the urgency of averting nuclear war by deterring a Soviet surprise attack that would exploit an alleged "missile gap." That supposed dangerous U.S. inferiority was exactly as unfounded in reality as the fear of the Nazi crash bomb program had been, or, to pick a more recent example, as concern over Saddam Hussein's supposed weapons of mass destruction (WMD) and nuclear pursuit in 2003.

Countering an illusory threat, I and my colleagues distracted ourselves and helped distract others from dealing with real dangers posed by the mutual and spreading possession of nuclear weapons—dangers that we were helping make worse—and from real opportunities to make the world more secure. Unintentionally, yet inexcusably, we made our country and the world less safe.

Eventually the Soviets did emulate us in creating a world-threatening nuclear capability on hair-trigger alert. That still exists; Russian nuclear posture and policies continue, along with ours, to endanger our countries, civilization, and much of life itself. But the persistent reality has been that the nuclear arms race has been driven primarily by American initiatives and policies and that every major American decision in this 64-year-old nuclear era has been accompanied by unwarranted concealment, deliberate obfuscation, and official and public delusions.

I have believed for a long time that official secrecy and deceptions about our nuclear weapons posture and policies and their possible consequences have threatened the survival of the human species. To understand the urgency of radical changes in our nuclear policies that may truly move the world toward abolition of nuclear weapons, we need a new understanding of the real history of the nuclear age.

Using the new opportunities offered by the Internet—drawing attention to newly declassified documents and to some realities still concealed—I plan over the next year, before the 65th anniversary of Hiroshima, to do my part in unveiling this hidden history.

NOTES

1. Rabinowitch, 1971.
2. Lifton and Mitchell, 1995.
3. York, 1976.
4. Ibid.
5. Hersey, 1946.

CHAPTER 4

CITIZEN DIPLOMACY AND THE OTTAWA PROCESS IN BANNING LANDMINES: A LASTING MODEL?

Jody Williams and Stephen D. Goose

When six nongovernmental organizations (NGOs) came together in October 1992 to form an International Campaign to Ban Landmines, every government that we met with at that time—without exception—viewed the young campaign as a quixotic effort doomed to failure.[1] Most people around the world—except, of course, those in countries contaminated by landmines—were completely unaware of the humanitarian problems caused by this weapon. Yet within the short span of five years, conventional wisdom about humanitarian law and arms control negotiations was turned on its head as the 1997 Mine Ban Treaty was born. For the first time in history, a weapon widely used for many decades was banned.

The process that evolved—commonly referred to as the "Ottawa Process"—gave the promise of a new dimension in diplomacy—"citizen diplomacy"—and generated hope for its wider applicability.

This chapter is taken from chapter 11 of the book, *Banning Landmines: Disarmament, Citizen Diplomacy, and Human Security*, edited by Jody Williams, Stephen Goose, and Mary Wareham (Rowman & Littlefield Publishers, Inc., 2008). The original chapter benefited significantly from the early input of Dr. David Atwood, Executive Director, Quaker UN Office (QUNO), Geneva.

In awarding the 1997 Nobel Peace Prize to the International Campaign to Ban Landmines (ICBL) and its coordinator, Jody Williams, the Nobel Committee highlighted the ICBL's role in both the process and the treaty, stating that the campaign had been able to "express and mediate a broad range of popular commitment in an unprecedented way. With the governments of several small and medium-sized countries taking the issue up . . . this work has grown into a convincing example of an effective policy for peace." It concluded, "As a model for similar processes in the future, it could prove to be of decisive importance to the international effort for disarmament and peace."

There clearly was reason for such hope. The mine ban movement demonstrated that it is possible for NGOs to put an issue—even one with international security implications—on the international agenda, provoke urgent actions by governments and others, and serve as the driving force behind change. It showed that civil society can wield great power in the post–Cold War world. Moreover, the mine ban movement demonstrated the power of partnerships by achieving rapid success internationally through common and coordinated action by NGOs, like-minded governments, and other key actors such as UN agencies and the International Committee of the Red Cross (ICRC). It showed that that change is most likely to be effected through concerted action. The mine ban movement also demonstrated that it is possible for small and medium-sized countries, acting in concert with civil society, to provide global leadership and achieve major diplomatic results, even in the face of opposition from bigger powers. It showed that it is possible to work outside of traditional diplomatic forums, practices, and methods.

Yet, for many states, citizen diplomacy was simply unacceptable. Involving civil society actors in treaty negotiations added too many unpredictable and uncontrollable elements to diplomatic processes forged over centuries.[2]

Apart from those who actively wished to see the model fail, there were— and still are—some observers who believed that it would not be possible to replicate the mine ban experience. This view holds that the Ottawa Process only succeeded because of the confluence of a variety of factors, such as the particular timing (in terms of world affairs); the skill and audacity of a handful of key government officials and representatives of nongovernmental and international organizations; the reality of the limited military utility of antipersonnel mines and the limited economic stake involved; and the fact that the campaign had to focus only on a single weapon and had the advantages of an easy-to-grasp message with highly emotional content.

How has the model stood up in the 13 years since the Mine Ban Treaty was signed by 122 nations in two triumphant days at the end of 1997? What have its strengths and weaknesses been? What lessons from and aspects of the model have been applied by NGOs in their work on other issues? Has the Ottawa Process model proven to be of "decisive importance" as hoped by the Nobel Committee—or of any meaningful importance at all? Is there a future for such a model of campaigning and diplomacy, particularly in the post–9/11 world?

We will look first at lessons learned from the campaigning side of the model, and then at the diplomatic side, before considering the applicability of the model to other issues.

THE CAMPAIGNING MODEL[3]

The NGOs of the International Campaign to Ban Landmines have been the engine behind the Ottawa Process that resulted in the Mine Ban Treaty. The work of the members of the ICBL in the movement to ban antipersonnel mines has been held up by many as a quintessential example of global citizen diplomacy.

Following are the key campaigning lessons that we identify, which also can be seen to constitute key elements of the model: organizing skills; a flexible coalition structure; strong leadership and committed workers; action plans and deadlines, with outcome-oriented conferences; communication skills; follow-up and follow-through; expertise and documentation; clear and simple articulation of goals and messages; use of multiple fora to promote the message; a focus on the human cost; inclusivity and diversity, yet speaking with one voice; and, finally, recognition that international context and timing matter.

- *Know how to organize.* A positive mythology often invoked about NGOs is that they are selfless and tireless, and that they inherently "know how to campaign." Nothing could be further from the truth. The reality is that the typical members of many NGO coalitions, including research and advocacy organizations and even grassroots organizations, usually do not have skills and experience in large-scale organizing. There is often little understanding of coalition-building and how to work successfully in coalition. Campaigners may have in-depth understanding of their issue, but if they can't work together effectively that expertise may prove of little value. Without a firm grasp of these fundamentals, it can be extremely difficult to campaign successfully.[4]
- *Maintain a flexible structure.* We are convinced that the ICBL's informal and loose structure has been one of its major strengths.[5] The lack of centralization was a conscious decision. Each NGO has to find a way to participate in making the campaign work. This helps to ensure that the ICBL belongs to all of its members, and that these members have to be active in the process to achieve the campaign's goals. There is no bureaucratic structure that either dictates to members how they

should contribute to the campaign or does the work for them. ICBL members have met regularly to strategize and plan joint actions, but each NGO and national campaign has been free to carry out whatever aspects of the work best fit its individual mandate, political culture, and circumstances.

- *Enlist leaders and committed workers.* Successful coalitions will naturally be large and diverse, but experience shows that most operate on the extensive work of a committed and dedicated few, supported by the many. Most organizations cannot devote full-time staff to coalition efforts, but it is essential that there be a core of people working full-time. With diverse coalitions, strong and effective leadership provided by a handful of organizations and individuals is essential. The leadership of the ICBL has been and continues to be those who choose to step up to the plate and follow up their words of commitment with concrete and consistent action.

- *Always have an action plan and deadlines, with outcome-oriented meetings.* The Ottawa Process can be characterized as an ongoing series of international, regional, and national conferences and meetings, both NGO and diplomatic. Although it is easy, and perhaps usually correct, to criticize costly get-togethers, in the case of the mine ban movement, face-to-face contact is carefully planned with concrete objectives in mind, with the intention of one meeting building on another, and most importantly, with an action plan emerging in which various actors took responsibility for specific tasks to move the ban forward. Deadlines are essential to spurring action.

- *Provide communication, communication, and more communication.* Clear and consistent communication is an irreplaceable element of success. Information is power and it is absolutely key that information is shared throughout a coalition. In the early days of the campaign, individual members gained strength by being able to speak with authority about what was happening everywhere to eliminate the problem. Sharing the successes and failures of the work empowered all organizations and lessened the possibility of isolation of any one. Because of strong communication, the ICBL often has known of developments before governments, which made the ICBL a focal point of information for governments and NGOs alike.

- *Follow up and then follow through.* While there are always plenty of good ideas about what needs to be done, the difficulty is implementing those ideas. Follow-up and follow-through are what make the difference. Holding individuals and NGOs accountable for commitments has worked in the ICBL; when commitments have been broken, other campaigners have quickly stepped in and filled the void. A large measure of the trust that governments have for the ICBL has been the result of its consistency in following up and following through on its words with actions.

- *Provide expertise and documentation.* The founding members of the ICBL were NGOs engaged in clearing mines, putting prosthetics on victims, and documenting the impact of mines on civilians. NGOs carried out a concerted research agenda, and published informational materials extensively and distributed them widely to governments as well as the public. They provided comprehensive materials on the impact of landmines around the world, on global mine production, trade, stocks, and use, as well as sophisticated legal analysis; all of which were powerful tools for advocacy. Since the treaty entered into force in 1999, the ICBL has further expanded this role through its Landmine Monitor initiative, the first time that NGOs have come together in a sustained, systematic, and coordinated fashion to monitor and report on the implementation of an international disarmament or humanitarian law treaty.
- *Articulate goals and messages clearly and simply.* The importance of clear, concise, and consistent articulation of goals and messages is hard to overstate. This is true not only with respect to the overarching goals of a campaign, coalition, or movement, but also for each phase, conference, or event. While it is necessary to demonstrate expertise and an understanding of complexities and subtleties, for campaigning purposes simple and direct is always better.
- *Focus on the human cost.* Much of the success of the ICBL has been due to keeping the international focus on the human beings who have suffered because of landmines—the humanitarian aspects of the issue, not the arms control or security aspects. This has been crucial not only in influencing public opinion, but also in influencing governments.
- *Use as many fora as possible to promote the message.* Though it seems obvious, few take advantage of the many opportunities available internationally to get an issue on the agenda and language in final statements and declarations and resolutions to support their cause. It can take considerable effort to do this, first to identify the fora, and then to do the necessary advocacy to bear fruit, but with every success, new audiences are reached.
- *Be inclusive, be diverse, yet speak with one voice.* The ICBL has always ascribed to the big tent theory. To join, it was only necessary for an NGO to inform the coordinator that it shared and endorsed the campaign's call for a total ban on antipersonnel mines, as well as increased resources for mine clearance and victim assistance programs. No dues, no requirements, no restrictions. The big tent had built-in diversity almost from the start, because so many different countries, as well as so many different fields, sectors, and interest groups were affected by mines. The ICBL Advisory Board, which includes representatives from mine-affected states, organizations involved in mine clearance and victim assistance programs, as well as human rights, humanitarian aid, and religious organizations. There have been occasional tensions in the campaign, but

the general principle has been, and remains, that leadership positions should go only to those willing and able to bear the burden of the work, and not just be names on letterhead.

Beyond the sheer numbers of NGOs and individuals involved in the ban movement, there have been other benefits when one can speak as a coalition on behalf of many. Often, even when pursuing similar objectives as NGOs, governments have traditionally been reluctant to deal with NGOs as partners, or to permit their meaningful participation in diplomatic meetings, in no small part because of the fear of being overwhelmed by numbers and diverse views. In that respect, the ability of the ICBL to serve as a banner for nearly every NGO working on the issue, and to speak authoritatively with one voice, has served the movement very well. The campaign has been able to have a seat at the table, with virtually the same status as states, during the Ottawa Process diplomatic meetings and since. It would not have been possible to achieve this status with a larger number of NGOs each working independently and perhaps in competition.

- *Recognize that international context and timing do matter.* The changing global situation in the late 1980s and early 1990s was a critical factor in the development of the movement to ban landmines. With the end of the Cold War governments, NGOs began to look at war and peace issues differently, and many governments were no longer as constrained in their possible responses to issues of global humanitarian and security concern. Many NGOs were looking for new issues in which to become engaged. Increased attention was being devoted to conventional, as opposed to nuclear, weapons at the same time that the impact of anti-personnel landmines was reaching a crescendo, due to widespread and increasing use from the mid-1960s forward. In the global political context the ban movement emerged and achieved dramatic success.

THE DIPLOMATIC MODEL

NGO campaigning has been an important part of the success of the mine ban movement, but many other factors have contributed. Perhaps the most notable feature of the "new diplomacy" has been the partnership formed between key governments and civil society to achieve common humanitarian aims. Other vital elements have been meaningful and consistent: NGO involvement; leadership by small and mid-sized states; and a willingness to operate outside the UN system when necessary, including rejection of consensus rules. These elements have been sustained since the signing of the treaty in what might be called the Mine Ban Treaty Process.

Without the close cooperation of NGOs (primarily through the ICBL), governments, the ICRC, and UN agencies, there is little question that the Mine Ban Treaty would not have come into existence in 1997, and it would not have been so effectively universalized and implemented in the past decade. The mine ban movement certainly was not the first where civil society lobbied for change and governments responded positively.[6] But it has likely been unique in the level of closeness, openness, and cooperation of the partnership, and the degree to which it has been sustained over so many years.

Historically, NGOs and governments have often seen each other as adversaries, not colleagues—and in many cases rightly so. And at first many in the NGO mine ban community worried that governments were going to "hijack" the issue to undermine a ban. But a relationship of trust among the relatively small "core group" of governments (most notably Canada, Norway, Austria, and South Africa) and ICBL leadership quickly developed and has been maintained and expanded over the years.[7]

The willingness of certain governments and individuals in those governments to engage in nontraditional diplomacy and to take risks (to say nothing of their dedication and talent) has been crucial to the success of the Mine Ban Treaty Process. Small and mid-sized states have provided such leadership in the face of opposition from bigger states.

Not all campaigners have been comfortable, however, with such close collaboration with governments. Some believe that it is more reflective of NGO cooptation by governments than partnership and are wary of the relationship. Others have been outspokenly critical of the cooperation, considering it a "sellout." They hold a belief that the proper role of NGOs is always that of opposition and as opposition. At the same time, not all governments share the same degree of enthusiasm for the partnership either and the relative informality of treaty-related meetings has caught more than one diplomat off-guard.[8] And despite the long-standing partnership and the joint efforts to advance treaty compliance through "cooperation" rather than coercion, at times there have been serious strains in the partnership when NGOs have differed with governments in interpretation of some of the treaty's obligations—in particular those related to its arms control aspects.

So at times, what has been the great strength of the mine ban movement—the civil society–government partnership—has almost paradoxically been problematic. When the partners cannot or will not recognize and accept differing rights and responsibilities of each other, it can be quite difficult to navigate those waters and maintain the cooperative nature of the process that has resulted in such continued momentum in the work to eliminate landmines.

IS THE MODEL APPLICABLE TO OTHER ISSUES?

A number of governments showed great vision and leadership in recognizing that "normal" diplomacy was not adequate to tackle the mine problem.

Yet, even as some governments were anxious to apply the landmine model to other issues, others were trying to make sure that the process was understood to be "unique to the landmine issue" and not precedent setting in multilateral diplomacy—particularly in arms control or other security-related issues.

In the past 10 years, there have been campaigning and coalition efforts that demonstrate both the applicability and nonapplicability of the landmine campaign experience. Among those that most closely resemble the ICBL and Ottawa Process model are the efforts on the International Criminal Court, child soldiers, cluster munitions, and the Disability Rights Convention. Those that have not taken much from the model include small arms and light weapons, blood diamonds, global poverty, and "human security." We will look more closely at one example from each category.

The International Criminal Court

The successful negotiation of the Rome Statute in July 1998 creating the International Criminal Court (ICC) came quickly on the heels of the Mine Ban Treaty success. Various aspects of that effort recall the work of the landmine ban movement, with governments and NGOs pressing for the creation of an international criminal court—a goal harkening back to the Nuremberg Trials after World War II.

As with landmines, a coalition of NGOs came together to lobby for a court, and like-minded governments came together to press for a diplomatic meeting on the subject. When it was decided in the latter part of 1997 that a diplomatic conference would be held in Rome in mid-1998, both governmental and NGO activities took on increased urgency and NGOs pressed the governments to agree to fundamental elements of the court.

As Don Hubert succinctly describes in comparing the ICC work with that of the landmine movement, there were many similarities.[9] The expertise offered by NGOs was first rate, especially on substantive legal issues related to an international criminal court. The NGO Coalition produced newsletters daily, as had the ICBL in the Oslo negotiations. NGOs were given observer status, and individual NGO representatives were on a number of government delegations. Although the Rome Conference was a UN negotiating session, rules of procedure were somewhat like those used in Oslo for the Mine Ban Treaty—issues could be decided by a two-thirds majority vote and were not held hostage to consensus. As with the Mine Ban Treaty and ICBL, the NGO Coalition for the ICC undertook a ratification campaign to help ensure that the Rome Statute became international law as quickly as possible and it continues to work to ensure the Court is functioning effectively.

In one notable difference, the United States exhibited fevered opposition to the ICC and aggressively sought to undermine it. The United States did not sign the Mine Ban Treaty, but rarely openly attacked it, and, with some exceptions, did not make serious efforts to dissuade other countries from joining.

Small Arms and Light Weapons

Although the many problems related to the proliferation of small arms and light weapons have been documented for years, it was not until 1998 that NGOs came together to form a new network, the International Action Network on Small Arms (IANSA). The NGOs in the network wanted to try to enhance cooperation and communication as they pressed governments to take action to deal with the problem.

When IANSA was being formed, some among its leadership felt the ICBL as a model was overly centralized and dominated by NGOs from the North. IANSA instead focused its work on the regional level, with regional coordinators. The leadership body was deemed the "Facilitation Committee," rather than a steering or coordination committee. There was no central focal point to develop common messages and there were no global spokespeople. As one participant in the work put it, this structure led to "paralization" with little coordination and no one to make decisions. The network appeared consumed with form and structure, rather than substance. Matters improved after 2001, when IANSA built a secretariat based in London, but some actively involved still describe the network as a whole as very inefficient.[10]

Although NGOs were not exactly clear on what shape their work on small arms and light weapons should take, many governments were clear that they wanted any work on the issue to be carried out under the auspices of the UN. Even though there was cooperative work between NGOs and governments in the lead up to a 2001 conference on the "Illicit Trade in Small Arms and Light Weapons in All its Aspects," that conference was carried out within the UN, consensus ruled, and NGOs were largely kept outside of the deliberations—as the ICBL had been during the early days of the Convention on Conventional Weapons (CCW) Review Process through 1996.

The outcome of the 2001 conference was a "Program of Action" to take steps to deal with SALW and which would lead to another conference in 2006. Although cooperative work between NGOs and governments increased in those five years, and NGO representatives were included on some government delegations at the 2006 Conference, IANSA and other NGOs acting on their own behalf were still not permitted meaningful participation in that meeting. As one SALW campaigner wrote, "It is a frequent refrain amongst small arms diplomats and government officials that 'we' must keep the global process on small arms control within the UN. This constant referencing of the specter of the Ottawa Process and the success of people-centered campaigning in the late 1990s has certainly had a negative influence on the imagination of government officials."[11]

Growing civil society pressure helped bring about the encouraging adoption of a UN General Assembly resolution in December 2006 in support of an Arms Trade Treaty, with 153 governments voting in favor.[12] The resolution requested the UN secretary-general "to seek the views of Member States on creating a legally binding instrument and to establish a group of governmental experts, commencing in 2008, to examine the feasibility, scope, and draft parameters of such an instrument."[13] As work unfolds around the Arms Trade Treaty, it remains to be seen how governments and NGOs will interact in the process.

The Convention on Conventional Weapons

Developments in the Convention on Conventional Weapons (CCW) forum also provide an interesting gauge of the impact of the mine ban movement model. The failure of the CCW to deal adequately with antipersonnel mines during deliberations from 1993 to 1996 as part of its first Review Conference led to Canada's call for an outside process aimed at a ban on the weapon. Those were extremely frustrating years for NGOs on the diplomatic front, as they were blocked from participation in all sessions except the rare plenary meetings.

In the wake of the Mine Ban Treaty experience, the situation in the CCW, in many respects, changed significantly, and for the better. At the Second and Third Review Conferences in 2001 and 2006, respectively, and in the working meetings in between and since (carried out under the banner of "Groups of Governmental Experts"), NGOs have rarely been excluded from participation. They have not only made statements during plenary meetings, but have had the opportunity to intervene and respond on a regular basis during deliberations, and more notably have been asked to give presentations on a wide range of subjects.

Most importantly, during the development of what became CCW Protocol V on explosive remnants of war from 2001 to 2003, there was extensive consultation and cooperation—though largely behind the scenes—among NGOs, the ICRC, and some key governments, especially the Netherlands, which took the lead on the protocol. Without the backdrop of the mine ban experience, and the relationships and working methods formed during that process, it is unlikely that Protocol V would have come into being.

Without question, the CCW has evolved in a positive way as a result of the Ottawa Process. It is interesting to note that this has not occurred in the other quintessential security forum based in Geneva, the Conference on Disarmament (CD). And it is likely not a coincidence that the CD has not been able to accomplish anything over the past decade, struggling even to agree on an agenda or work program.

But, as discouraging as it is to acknowledge, things have not changed in a fundamental way in the CCW. This is true even though only 15 of the CCW's 102 members are not party to the Mine Ban Treaty. Although mostly the same people are in the room, the atmosphere and the way of doing business stand in stark contrast to Mine Ban Treaty meetings.[14] This is due in large part to the fact that decisions—such as they are—are made by consensus among governments, ensuring minimal change, implemented at a snail's pace, if at all. This undermined the potential of the protocol on explosive remnants of war, which in the end was watered down to the point that it contains few binding obligations and is more of a voluntary regime. The notion of a joint sense of commitment to humanitarian aims seems inevitably to lose out in the CCW to narrowly defined assertions of national security interests.

CONCLUSION: ENDURING PARTNERSHIPS TAKE CONSTANT WORK

What does the future hold? The Ottawa Process happened in a post–Cold War, but pre–9/11 world, where both civil society and governments felt there was room for new multilateral efforts and perhaps even new ways to consider "security." But after the terrorist attacks of 9/11 and the "war on terrorism" and all that has come with it, creative thinking about security and multilateralism has a much more perilous future.

It is not in the least bit surprising that many—perhaps even most—governments would want to return to the known, controllable, and comfortable world of traditional negotiations, closed to civil society, particularly in relation to arms control, disarmament, and security issues. It is fair to say that some have worked to ensure that the Ottawa Process was an anomaly and not a precedent.

What is surprising is that, in some instances, even prominent pro–Ottawa Process states seem reluctant to apply the model to other issues. Some glaring examples have been the lack of NGO-government cooperation in the "human security" endeavor and the desire of so many states to cling to the CCW to deal with cluster munitions, despite the Oslo Process launched in 2007.

Key nations of the mine ban movement, emboldened by the success of the Ottawa Process, launched the Human Security Network at a meeting of Foreign Ministers held in Oslo on May 21, 1999. And although there is much debate on the merits of a "human security framework," the initiative has not gained significant traction and momentum in large part because it has been almost entirely government-driven with minimal inclusion of civil society. Given that the founders of the Network are the same governments that worked side by side with NGOs—and continue to do so to this day—to ensure the success of the Mine Ban Treaty, it is difficult not to wonder about their broader commitment to inclusion of civil society in dealing with global issues.

The world has benefited from the partnership between government and civil society that resulted in the Mine Ban Treaty. In this globalized world, transnational civil society has a role to play in finding solutions to our common problems. But it will be up to civil society to ensure that the Ottawa Process model does endure. If the partnership is to grow and develop and be applied to resolve many issues in the world, it will be up to civil society to press harder and more consistently, based on a clear understanding of what works and what does not.

One helpful step, perhaps at the initiative of the ICBL given its pioneering role, would be to bring NGOs and different coalitions and campaigns together in various configurations to share what they have learned and to identify what still needs to be learned to ensure that the voice of civil society is heard on issues that affect our individual and collective human security. Such discussions would benefit at an early stage from input from "like-minded" government allies who share the vision of new frameworks of security, developed and put into practice through a partnership of governments, civil society, NGOs, and international organizations.

NOTES

1. The six NGOs were Handicap International (France), Medico International (Germany), Mines Advisory Group (UK), Physicians for Human Rights (USA), the Vietnam Veterans of America Foundation (USA), and the host of the meeting in New York, Human Rights Watch (USA). One of the more memorable dismissals of the campaign came from then-Minister of Foreign Affairs of Australia, Gareth Evans, who in 1995 described the call for a ban on landmines as "hopelessly utopian." Questions without Notice, Australian Senate, June 1, 1995.

2. As used by the Centre for Civil Society of the London School of Economics, "Civil society refers to the arena of uncoerced collective action around shared interests, purposes, and values. In theory, its institutional forms are distinct from those of

the state, family, and market, though in practice, the boundaries between state, civil society, family, and market are often complex, blurred, and negotiated. Civil society commonly embraces a diversity of spaces, actors, and institutional forms, varying in their degree of formality, autonomy, and power. Civil societies are often populated by organizations such as registered charities, development nongovernmental organizations, community groups, women's organizations, faith-based organizations, professional associations, trade unions, self-help groups, social movements, business associations, coalitions and advocacy groups." See Centre for Civil Society of the London School of Economics, "What Is Civil Society?" http://www.lse.ac.uk/collections/CCS/what_is _civil_society.htm.

3. This section draws on earlier writing by the authors, including Williams, 2000; Goose and Williams, 2004.

4. The ICBL has produced educational materials and carried out workshops on how to organize national campaigns, prepare for major conferences, interact with the media, and other aspects of international campaigning work. In addition to advancing the work to ban landmines, these skills can be used by campaigners in many ways and in other work for social change.

5. Indeed, the ICBL was not even a legally registered entity until after it received the Nobel Peace Prize at the end of 1997. There has never been a secretariat or central office of the ICBL, and until 1998, no "ICBL" employees or joint ICBL budget. Various NGOs in essence seconded (and provided funding for) individuals to work on the campaign.

6. For a fascinating example, see Hoschild, 2005.

7. Given the success of the Ottawa Process and the Mine Ban Treaty, few now recognize or acknowledge the risks involved to both sides as we ventured into that partnership and worked to ensure the success of the "rogue" negotiating process of the Mine Ban Treaty. There were many times when we were not at all certain of the outcome and felt we were working with "smoke and mirrors," convinced that the fragile process could collapse at any moment. Had the process fallen apart, it no doubt would have had a chilling effect on any future civil society, government partnerships, and dampened any governmental "thinking outside the box" in trying to find new solutions to global problems.

8. One example that still causes amusement in the retelling is when a new diplomat replaced his predecessor and apparently had not been fully briefed about the informal nature of meetings. The president of a session had given the floor to Steve Goose, calling him by his first name only, who then spoke about the ICBL position on some aspect of the treaty. Subsequent speakers kept on referring to "Steve" and finally the new diplomat was called on and in quite apparent frustration started his remarks with "And who IS this *Steve?*" Many in the room could not stifle their laughter—which likely added to the diplomat's discomfort.

9. Hubert, 2000.

10. NGOs that are part of both the ICBL and IANSA have often complained to the authors about the inability of IANSA to fully engage its members and make them feel like important, contributing stakeholders.

11. E-mail from Felicity Hill, anti-nuclear activist, in response to questions from the authors and after discussion with SALW activist Cate Buchannan, August 9, 2006.

12. Twenty-four nations abstained from the vote and the United States was the only country to vote against the resolution. For more information see IANSA Web site at: http://www.iansa.org/un/2006/GAvote.htm; also Arieff, 2006. See also "Arms Trade Treaty: A Nobel Peace Laureates' Initiative," http://www.armstrade-treaty.com/.

13. UN Department of Public Information, 2006.

14. For an interesting analysis, see Cave, 2006.

CHAPTER 5

Bringing the Corporate Role in Global Violence to Daylight

Gianina Pellegrini

Long before President Eisenhower's prophetic warning in 1961 about a military-industrial complex, Major General Smedly Butler noted in 1933, "War is just a racket. A racket is best described, I believe, as something that is not what it seems to the majority of people. Only a small inside group knows what it is about. It is conducted for the benefit of the very few at the expense of the masses."[1] Butler went on to document the wars fought to extend corporate markets, the exorbitant profits in war contracts, and the casualties to soldiers.

Today, war continues to be "just a racket" and the inside players consist primarily of government officials and corporate executives. The military-industrial complex has expanded significantly and poses a severe threat to humans and the environment. Multinational corporations have established a mutually dependent relationship with government forces. This relationship relies almost entirely on the profits from war. Corporate executives transfer in and out of government positions, promoting war and the industries that supply military weapons and equipment. This major force in the business of destruction continues in part because its operations are unseen. There are, however, several important groups that watch them closely and provide the possibility to bring daylight to a major obstacle to peace.

This chapter focuses on two, and surely not the only two, multimillion-dollar corporations that epitomize the military-industrial complex and the organizations that have mobilized to stop them. General Electric and Bechtel Corporation have profited from war since the beginning of World War II and today continue to be top United States defense contractors. Not-for-profit organizations such as Corporate Accountability and CorpWatch expose the revolving relationship between corporations and the government and how such relationships threaten the world. Since engaging in war relies directly on the corporations that supply military weapons and equipment, one method of establishing peace is to stop the military contractors that manufacture and provide the necessary supplies to engage in war.

GENERAL ELECTRIC

General Electric (GE), one of the world's most diverse companies, has a long-standing reputation as a consumer and commercial industry, involved in the design and production of lightbulbs, household appliances, locomotives, plastics, aircraft engines, and medical equipment.[2] Often hidden from public view is GE's primary profit-making business as a military contractor, involved in the design, development, and production of military weapons and equipment. GE's business as a military contractor peaked during World War II, when it became the first U.S. producer of jet engines and quickly transitioned into the production and operation of nuclear reactors.[3]

During World War II, GE was involved in the highly secret Manhattan Project to develop the first atomic bombs. The plutonium used for the bombs was manufactured at the Department of Energy's Hanford Nuclear Reservation in Richland, Washington, that had been built and operated by General Electric. GE's early involvement in nuclear research and development gave them a leading role in the production of nuclear reactors, nuclear propulsion, and nuclear weapons.[4] The production of military equipment and nuclear weapons proved to be a highly profitable business. GE's profits tripled during World War II and pushed GE into a billion-dollar company. GE's military production expanded so rapidly that in 1942, *Fortune* magazine referred to GE's headquarters as "the nerve center of one of the world's largest and most complex war machines."[5]

By 1986, GE maintained primary U.S. government contracts on the Minuteman, Trident, and MX Missiles, Trident nuclear submarines, B-1 and Stealth Bombers, and military radar and satellite systems.[6] Today, General Electric continues to be one of the world's largest military contractors. GE and its many subsidiaries continue to contract with the U.S. government for the manufacturing of military weapons, equipment, and the production of nuclear energy. Since 2003, GE and its subsidiaries have been awarded military defense contracts with the U.S. government valuing over

$7 billion. In March 2009, the General Electric Company Aircraft Engines Business Group was awarded a $438 million contract to produce engines for the U.S. Navy.[7]

Many current contracts awarded to General Electric are for work in the Middle East, including extensive involvement in post-war Iraq and Afghanistan. In April 2003, GE Energy Rentals Inc., a division of GE Power Systems, was contracted to provide electrical generators to the U.S. military in Iraq and a contract worth over $5 million from the U.S. Army Engineer District to provide gas services in Afghanistan, primarily at the Bagram and Kandahar airbases.[8]

GE: Bringing Good Things to Life

For decades General Electric's marketing pitch has been: "we bring good things to life." Yet, the company's long involvement in the production of military equipment and nuclear bombs has caused irreversible damage and destruction to humans and the environment. The full extent of the damage cannot be quantified because the destruction goes far beyond the damage caused by the detonation of bombs or the use of other military weapons. Although incapable of accepting full responsibility for the consequences of their actions, GE is responsible for contaminating the environment and destroying lives during the production of nuclear weapons.[9]

General Electric constructed the Hanford Nuclear Reservation in Washington State in 1943 and operated the facility for 18 years as a part of America's weapons program. As mentioned, this facility produced the plutonium used in the first atomic bombs. Beginning in 1949, General Electric, in collaboration with the U.S. Department of Energy, participated in a secret experiment called the "Green Run" where radioactive material was deliberately released in the air to see how far downwind the material would travel. It was reported that one cloud of radioactive material drifted 400 miles to the California–Oregon border. The amount of radiation carried by this one cloud is estimated to be thousands of times higher than radiation emitted at Three Mile Island.[10] By 1978, two-thirds of the most dangerous nuclear waste in the United States had accumulated at the Hanford Plant. *INFACT* newsletter reported the Hanford Nuclear Reservation as "the most contaminated of all the U.S. weapons complexes and one of the most toxic places on earth."[11]

In 1990, 40 years after the first release, the Department of Energy informed the public for the first time that toxic contaminants had been intentionally released into the air and the Columbia River from the Hanford plant. The Department of Energy admitted that the amount of radiation released at the Hanford Nuclear Weapons facility in the 1940s and 1950s was significant enough to cause cancer and up to 35,000 residents of Washington, Oregon, and Idaho were exposed to heavy doses of radiation.[12] The "down-winders" from the Hanford Plant were exposed to twice as much radiation as those at Chernobyl. A stretch of road near and down wind from the Hanford site, labeled as "Death Mile," reflects the human damage of GE's release of radioactive material: Of the 28 houses along Death Mile, 27 homes had incidents of cancer, early heart diseases, or handicapped children. Livestock also suffered severe deformities and birth defects following the release.[13] To this day, GE has refused to acknowledge any responsibility for the release and the subsequent human health and environmental damage it caused.[14]

In addition to the release of radioactivity into the air, GE is also responsible for dumping millions of gallons of radioactive materials on the ground and into trenches and ponds. The toxic waste subsequently accumulated in the Columbia River, which is the most radioactive river in the world.[15] And if intentionally polluting the earth and water did not cause enough damage to human life, information disclosed in 1986 revealed that the United States and General Electric conducted nuclear experiments on human subjects. One of the most appalling experiments was performed on prison inmates in Walla Walla, Washington (near Hanford), in 1963. Without fully disclosing the risks associated with the experiment, 64 male prisoners had their scrotums and testes irradiated to determine the effects of radiation on human reproductive organs.[16] As GE boasted their ability to "bring good things to life" with their production of medical equipment and household appliances, the company simultaneously and knowingly threatened the lives of thousands of people.

GE operated many nuclear production facilities in the latter half of the 20th century that contributed to the destruction of the environment and loss of human life. Some examples include the Pinellas plant, the Knolls Atomic Power Laboratory, and Hudson Falls and Fort Edward facilities in upstate New York. GE operated the Pinellas, Florida, plant from 1956 to 1992 for the U.S. Department of Energy (then called the Atomic Energy Commission). The trigger mechanism for every U.S. warhead was produced at the Pinellas plant during the time GE operated the facility. The grounds surrounding the plant were contaminated with toxic chemicals and radioactive tritium, contaminating the groundwater and surrounding land. As a direct result, Pinellas County had the highest cancer rates in the country during the time the facility was operated by GE.[17]

The Knolls Atomic Power Laboratory, built in 1946 and operated by GE until 1991, was the location for the design of nuclear reactors for the U.S. Navy. GE's 40-year involvement in secret work on submarine reactors left radioactive residue in the soil, on buildings, and in the Mohawk River. GE knowingly built an employee parking lot on a site with a radioactive contamination level 110 times higher than state safety levels, exposing their own workers to high levels of plutonium. Two months after General Electric sold the facility to the U.S. government for $1, the reports of the contamination were made public. The Department of Energy is still attempting to clean up the toxic site.[18]

From approximately 1947 to 1977, the General Electric Company operated the Hudson Falls and Fort Edward facilities in upstate New York. During this time, GE was responsible for discharging as much as 1.3 million pounds of polychlorinated biphenyls (PCBs) into the Hudson River. PCBs are considered to be probable human carcinogens and are linked to a number of health problems, including low birth weight, thyroid disease, immune disorders, and developmental diseases. Under supervision from the U.S. Environmental Protection Agency (EPA), GE is now responsible for dredging and removing the PCB-contaminated sediment along the 200-mile stretch of the Hudson River, a project expected to cost $460 million. GE began the cleanup of the Hudson River in early 2009 and it is expected to take 30 years to complete.[19]

The EPA has labeled the Hudson River the nation's largest Superfund site. A Superfund site is "an uncontrolled or abandoned place where hazardous waste is located."[20] General Electric is reported as the #1 Superfund polluter, bearing at least partial responsibility for the cleanup of 87 active Superfund toxic waste sites around the United States.[21] GE has a long reputation of misconduct affecting the health and safety of humans and the environment. In 2002, the Project on Government Oversight released a study of misconduct by the top 43 government contractors and GE ranked at the top of the repeat offenders list. At this time, GE had 63 instances of actual or alleged misconduct since 1990 that resulted in almost $1 billion in fines, judgments, and out-of-court settlements. GE's reported acts of misconduct include environmental violations, fraud in dealings with the government and consumers, workplace safety violations, and employment discrimination.[22] In multiple instances, General Electric has failed to bring good things to life.

BECHTEL CORPORATION

Founded in 1898, family-owned Bechtel Corporation is the largest contractor in the United States and is actively involved in multiple construction projects worldwide. As one of the world's largest engineering and construction firms, Bechtel Group, Inc., comprises 19 known joint-venture companies and numerous subsidiaries with investments in water, nuclear, energy, and infrastructure projects. Bechtel Group develops, manages, engineers, builds, and operates telecommunication projects, water systems, petroleum and chemical plants, pipelines, nuclear power plants, mining and metal projects, and civil infrastructure projects.[23] Bechtel is well known for its construction of the Hoover Dam, the San Francisco Bay Bridge, the Alaska pipeline, nuclear reactors in Qinshan, China, and oil refineries in Zambia. The company was responsible for the cleanup of the Chernobyl nuclear power plant and is currently one of the primary contractors responsible for the cleanup of the Hanford Nuclear Reservation. Bechtel companies sign new contracts around the world on a daily basis and have worked on over 20,000 contracts in 140 different countries.[24]

Bechtel companies have contracted with multiple U.S. government departments, including the Department of Energy; EPA; U.S. Navy, Air Force, and Army Corps of Engineers; Defense Nuclear Agency; Defense Threat Reduction Agency; and the U.S. Agency for International Development (USAID).[25] Bechtel has positioned itself to be at the forefront of nuclear construction since the dawn of the nuclear age. In 1951, Bechtel built the world's first nuclear reactor in the United States that was reportedly designed to generate electrical power. Bechtel then built the first Indian nuclear plant at Tarapur, which is now the largest nuclear facility in Asia. The construction of the nuclear plant allowed for the detonation of India's first atomic bomb using plutonium produced by the Tarapur reactor. The construction of this facility not only initiated a nuclear arms race in South Asia, the plant also experienced major leaks, resulting in severe radiation exposure throughout the surrounding areas.[26]

One of Bechtel's most important programs, Bechtel Nevada, manages the Nevada test site, an outdoor laboratory larger than the state of Rhode Island, which conducts defense-related nuclear experiments and national security experiments for the National Security Administration (NSA). In conjunction with the Nevada test site was Bechtel's construction of the "doomsday town" in the Nevada desert, a town specifically built to measure the damage a nuclear weapon would have on a typical American town. Bechtel Nevada works on projects for the Defense Threat Reduction Agency, NASA, the Nuclear Regulatory Commission, and the U.S. Air Force, Army, and Navy.[27]

In 2007, the Department of Energy awarded Bechtel the contract to operate the Lawrence Livermore National Laboratory which, among other national security projects, designs and produces nuclear warheads used by the U.S. military. Bechtel, through various partnerships, is now in control of the bulk of the U.S. nuclear weapons facilities, including the Los Alamos National Laboratory, Savannah River Site, Hanford Site, Pantex Plant, Y-12 National Security Complex, and the Nevada Test Site.[28] Bechtel has a long history of constructing and managing chemical and nuclear power plants, many of which are now experiencing leaks or are not in compliance with current safety regulations.[29] Ironically, Bechtel has been awarded many of the contracts to decommission and/or clean up the same nuclear development facilities they constructed in the 1950s. Not only did Bechtel profit during operation of these plants but it also now profits from being contracted to clean up the toxic mess it left behind.

Bechtel's Involvement in War

Today, the majority of Bechtel's profits derive from oil, gas, chemicals, and most often U.S. government contracts. From 1990 to 2002, Bechtel National Inc., which handles all U.S. government contracts, received over 2,000 contracts worth more than $11.7 billion for work in Iraq and Afghanistan.[30] Bechtel Groups have played a prominent role in the construction of highways, airports, and other infrastructures throughout the Middle East since World War II. During World War II, Bechtel companies were responsible for the construction and expansion of oil refineries in Bahrain and Saudi Arabia and later built a pipeline from Saudi Arabia to Jordan. In 1950, Bechtel built a pipeline from Iraq's northern oilfields in Kirkuk to Syria. Bechtel associates are closely connected with well-known company executives in the Arab world, including the Bin Laden Construction firm.[31]

Bechtel profited greatly from the most recent war in Iraq. In a secret, undemocratic process, Bechtel received a request to bid on the reconstruction of Iraq before the actual invasion even began.[32] The U.S. government awarded several multimillion-dollar contracts to Bechtel for the reconstruction of Iraq's infrastructure, including schools, roads, water, and wastewater systems. When awarded the contracts (worth $680 million) to rebuild Iraq's infrastructure, Tom Hash, president of Bechtel National said, "Bechtel is honored to have been asked to help bring humanitarian assistance, economic recovery, and infrastructure reconstruction to the Iraqi people."[33] What Tom Hash does not report, though, is that the "humanitarian assistance" spans far beyond basic infrastructure: Bechtel is also heavily involved in building the lethal weapons that perpetuated the war and subsequent destruction of Iraq. Bechtel Plant Machinery is responsible for the production of military weapons and equipment. Since 2006, Bechtel Plant Machinery has been awarded contracts to produce military equipment valuing more than $2 billion.[34]

Bechtel has an extensive history profiting from war: the company has engaged in numerous business ventures that coincidentally took place in resource-rich parts of the world. A prime example is Bechtel's investments in the Democratic Republic of the Congo. Bechtel was involved in classified and supragovernmental *black* projects in the Congo leading up to and during the first Congo War of 1996 to 1997. In 1996, Bechtel commissioned and paid for NASA satellite studies of the country to develop detailed maps of the region's mineral deposits. The maps were considered to be the most comprehensive mineralogical and geographical data ever assembled. The company provided these maps to the Alliance of Democratic Forces for the Liberation of Congo-Zaire (AFDL), who where responsible for ousting President Mobuto Sese Seko and bringing Laurent Kabila into power. Bechtel International, Inc., executive Robert Stewart established a very close relationship with Kabila and acted as an advisor to him before and during his presidency.[35]

Bechtel in Bolivia

Bechtel presents an image concerned about the environment and humanity. The Bechtel Web site boasts their commitment to environmental excellence and protection stating that "each of [their] projects, whether a power plant, a refinery, a new road, or a telecommunications facility, has the potential to affect people, animals, plants, and the land. [And their] goal always is to protect the environment during a project, and to build in safeguards that will keep protecting it long after the project is complete."[36] What the company fails to reveal is its long history of environmental destruction and absolute disregard for human rights. Bechtel has for decades profited at the expense of people and the environment.

One of the most notable examples of Bechtel's disregard for humanity is their role in the privatization of water in Bolivia. In the late 1990s, the World Bank forced Bolivia to privatize the public water system of its third largest city, Cochabamba, by threatening to withhold debt relief and other development assistance if they did not comply. Bechtel was granted a 40-year lease to take over Cochabamba's water through a subsidiary called Aguas Del Tunari. Within weeks of Bechtel taking over the water supply, the cost of local water was increased to such a rate that many residents were unable to pay. The local minimum wage in Bolivia was at the time approximately $60 a month and many were forced to pay $20 a month, 25 percent of their total income, for local water.[37]

In response to the water price increase, residents of Cochabamba began protesting Bechtel. The Bolivian government enforced martial law in an attempt to stop the protests and remain in good relations with Bechtel and their agreement with the World Bank. The social unrest and the response of the Bolivian government resulted in hundreds injured, one death, and multiple arrests. The Bolivian government was unable to stop the social unrest. In 2000, only 8 months after Bechtel arrived in Bolivia, the Cochabamba citizen coalition known as *La Coordinadora*, along with less organized protesters within Bolivia and internationally, forced Bechtel to withdraw from the country.[38]

Eighteen months after withdrawing from Bolivia, Bechtel and its co-investor, Abengoa of Spain, filed a $50 million lawsuit against the Bolivian government to compensate for its investments (estimated at less than $1 million) and lost future profits. The lawsuit, brought before the International Center for Settlement of Investment Disputes (ICSID), operated by the World Bank, was protested by Bolivian "Water Warriors" and supporters in the United States. The lawsuit was eventually dropped in 2006 in response to Bolivian and U.S. anti-Bechtel protests and Bechtel's fear of bad publicity. Bechtel settled the dispute with a payment of approximately 30 cents.[39]

THE CORPORATE-GOVERNMENT REVOLVING DOOR

It is by no strange coincidence that the weapon manufacturing corporations are the same companies hired to clean up the destruction produced by the use of these weapons. An undeniable relationship exists between corporate executives and government officials. The Military-Industrial Complex is sustained by a revolving door that transports executives to and from government and corporate offices. General Electric and Bechtel Corporation have frequently utilized this revolving door and have influenced government policy for decades.

In 1956, GE ran the Technical Military Planning Operation (TEMPO) "think tank" described by its director, Thomas Paine, as a "go between for the military community and the industrial community."[40] Paine then served as a NASA Administrator from 1968 to 1970 and resigned under charges that he had rigged bidding procedures to guarantee a contract for GE. After resignation from NASA, he became GE's Vice President. Former Secretaries of Defense Thomas Gates and Neil McElroy helped write the 1968 Republican National Platform that called for the development of the B-1 Bomber and the Trident Submarines: the billion-dollar contracts for each were awarded to General Electric. Gates and McElroy later became Directors of GE.[41] From 1977 to 1982, GE hired 120 mid- to high-level Pentagon employees and 12 GE employees moved to mid- to high-level positions in the Pentagon.[42]

David C. Jones was the Chair of the Joint Chiefs of Staff from 1978 to 1982. In 1986 he became a part of GE's board while simultaneously sitting on the Star Wars Advisory Panel. Before joining GE in 1993, Kenneth V. Meyer, a vice president of GE Aircraft Engines, was a major general in the U.S. Air Force and served as director of Air Force contracting at the Pentagon and chief of staff for Air Force Systems Command.[43]

Francis S. Blake, a former senior vice president at GE, served as deputy secretary of energy from May 2001 until he resigned in April 2002. He played a key role in the formation of President Bush's controversial national energy plan, but resigned after less than a year on the job. He attracted criticism for holding a series of policy meetings that were dominated by energy industry representatives. Prior to joining GE in 1991, Blake had been general counsel at the Environmental Protection Agency during the final three years of the Reagan administration and, prior to that, deputy counsel to former Vice President George Bush and deputy counsel to the Presidential Task Force on Regulatory Relief.[44]

Bechtel has similar connections with the U.S. government. Bechtel's relationship with the CIA began in the 1940s when the company built a major pipeline through Saudi Arabia. Bechtel quickly established a strong presence in the Middle East and developed close relationships with highly influential governments and companies in this region. The Central Intelligence Agency (CIA) utilized Bechtel's intelligence of the region to influence political and economic developments.[45]

In the early part of the 20th century, Stephen D. Bechtel partnered with John A. McCone, who became Eisenhower's chairman of the Atomic Energy Commission and later became chief of the CIA under Presidents John F. Kennedy and Lyndon Johnson. In the 1970s Bechtel hired a number of government officials to help with its expanding international operations, including the former Secretary of Health, Education, and Welfare Casper Weinberger, Atomic Energy Commission chief executive Robert Hollingsworth, and former ambassador to Turkey and Saudi Arabia, Parker T. Hart.[46]

Most notably, George P. Shultz, Treasury Secretary under President Nixon, was hired in 1974 as Bechtel's executive vice president. In 1982, Shultz was appointed secretary of state by President Ronald Reagan.[47] In 1983, Shultz sent Middle East peace envoy Donald Rumsfeld on a special mission to Iraq to meet with Saddam Hussein to negotiate Bechtel's bid on the construction of an oil pipeline from Iraq to the Jordanian port of Aqaba. After retiring from the State Department in 1989, Shultz rejoined Bechtel as a member of its board of directors.[48] These same players have been involved in more recent reconstruction efforts in Iraq. In 2003, Defense Secretary Donald Rumsfeld appointed Pentagon official Jay Garner to oversee Iraq's reconstruction. Garner met with Bechtel's Terry Valenzano in Iraq to devise a plan for the reconstruction. Also in 2003, Riley Bechtel was sworn in as a member of President Bush's Export Council to advise the government on how to create markets for American companies overseas.[49]

In 1998, Bechtel hired former Marine four-star general Jack Sheehan as senior vice president responsible for project operations in Europe, Africa, the Middle East, and Southwest Asia. Sheehan also sits on the Defense Policy Board, a Pentagon-appointed board that advises the President on war and defense issues.[50] Additional former government officials hired by Bechtel include Charles Redman, former ambassador to Sweden and Germany and special envoy to Haiti and Yugoslavia, and now-deceased Richard Helms, former CIA director and ambassador to Iran.[51]

Former Bechtel employees have also relocated to the government sector as service providers or consultants. In 2001, former Bechtel Energy Resources President Ross J. Connelly became chief operating officer for the Overseas Private Investment Corporation (OPIC), which provides financing insurance for U.S. companies operating internationally. In 2002, Daniel Chao, Bechtel senior vice president of Bechtel Enterprises Holdings, Inc., was appointed to the U.S. Export-Import Bank advisory board. Former Bechtel chief executive officer (CEO) Stephen D. Bechtel also sat on its advisory committee from 1969 to 1972 and former Vice President John L Moore headed the advisory board from 1977 to 1982. The Export-Import Bank provides loans and other financial support for U.S. companies working internationally. It is no surprise that many of the countries that obtained loans from Export-Import Bank later hired Bechtel companies for construction projects.[52]

In 1998, the Clinton administration appointed former president of Bechtel's Civil Global Industry Unit, Bob Baxter, to the President's Commission on Critical Infrastructure Protection and appointed former Bechtel Technology and Consulting manger Larry Papy to the Panel on Energy Research and Development of the President's Council of Advisers on Science and Technology in 1997.[53]

Corporations like General Electric and Bechtel also spend millions of dollars toward lobbying and campaigning. According to the Center for Responsive Politics, a nonpartisan Washington-based group that tracks campaign finances, Bechtel Groups and its employees have been among the biggest political donors in the construction industry. The company and its workers contributed at least $446,000 to federal candidates and party committees in the 2008 election. General Electric is also deeply invested in campaign and lobbying efforts due to their diverse business ventures: From 2006 to 2008, GE contributed over $2 million to federal candidates and political parties.[54]

CAMPAIGN TO STOP CORPORATE INFLUENCE ON GOVERNMENT AND WAR

Information about these large corporations and their role in global violence is not easily found in the mainstream media messages. Mainstream media sources are often biased, reflecting the views and opinions of the corporations that own the stations, newspapers, and magazines. Six corporations control the major U.S. media: Rupert Murdoch's News Corporation, Time Warner, Disney, Viacom, Bertelsmann, and General Electric. General

Electric owns NBC, CNBC, MSNBC, Telemundo, Bravo, Universal Pictures, and 28 TV stations.[55] The news cannot be considered unbiased when these corporations control the major media sources and the news that is ultimately presented to the public.

The peace movement depends on accurate, honest, and current information from reliable, independent sources to effectively change the corrupt system of corporate control over government policy. One significant effort of the peace movement is to educate the general population on corporate influence on government decisions to engage in violent conflicts. Not-for-profit organizations like CorpWatch and Corporate Accountability report on the corporate role in global violence and mobilize campaign efforts to stop such corporations.

Founded in 1996, CorpWatch is a not-for-profit organization that performs investigative research and journalism to inform, educate, and mobilize the public. CorpWatch "investigates and exposes corporate violations of human rights, environmental crimes, fraud and corruption around the world, [and] work[s] to foster global justice, independent media activism, and democratic control over corporations."[56] Through the CorpWatch.org Web site, the organization provides critical information that exposes corporate abuse and advocates for corporate accountability and transparency in an attempt to "foster global justice, independent media activism, and democratic control over corporations."[57] CorpWatch has mobilized people to participate in numerous campaigns targeting corporations participating in human rights violations and practices that are destroying the environment.

In 1997, the organization began campaigning against Nike's working conditions at their facilities in Vietnam, leading to greater oversight of their factories and changes in their corporate practices. CorpWatch spearheaded a series of other campaigns to expose human rights abuses and dangerous corporate practices from a series of entities, including the United Nations. In 2002 and 2003, CorpWatch began to track companies like Bechtel, DynCorp, and Halliburton, who are profiting greatly from the "war on terrorism." CorpWatch led two investigative journalist teams to Iraq to investigate the outsourced reconstruction efforts after the U.S. invasion. The organization has released a number of reports and films uncovering the truth behind corporate involvement in war and global violence.[58]

For over 30 years Corporate Accountability has successfully campaigned against multinational corporations engaging in irresponsible and dangerous practices that threaten the health and survival of people and the planet. Corporate Accountability was established in 1977 as the Infant Formula Action Coalition (INFACT) in response to Nestlé's marketing of infant formula in developing countries. Nestlé falsely advertised their infant formula to be healthier than breast milk and convinced thousands of women in developing countries to convert to using the formula. The formula, however, was not healthier than breast milk and was too expensive for women to purchase. After finishing the formula samples provided by Nestlé, new mothers were unable to produce breast milk and were forced to continue to purchase the expensive formula. As a result, the formula was often mixed with water to make the supplies last, providing even less nutrition to newborn babies. The World Health Organization reported that 1 million babies a year died of malnutrition and disease related to the introduction of infant formula in developing nations. INFACT began an international campaign against Nestlé and eventually forced the company to stop their exploitive marketing practices.[59]

In 1984, after a successful six-year campaign against Nestlé, INFACT turned their attention to stopping the production of nuclear weapons, specifically targeting General Electric. While General Electric boasted the "We Bring Good Things to Life" motto, INFACT publicly exposed their role as a military contractor, organized protests at GE facilities and corporate meetings, and influenced an international boycott of GE products. By 1985, INFACT organized over 10,000 protests at 12 major nuclear weapons manufacturing corporations. At this time, General Electric had $3.53 billion in nuclear weapons revenues.

By 1986, INFACT's campaign had expanded to all 50 states in America, and over 2 million Americans were boycotting GE's products, causing GE's total revenue to decrease by 16 percent. Through direct engagement with the company and major hospitals and retail stores participating in the boycott, INFACT negotiated with GE to stop producing the nuclear bomb trigger in 1990. Through enormous public pressure and substantial loss in revenue, GE pulled out of the nuclear weapons business in 1993.[60]

CorpWatch and Corporate Accountability also provided critical information that strengthened the efforts that inevitably forced Bechtel out of Bolivia. The successful campaigns against General Electric's production of nuclear weapons and Bechtel's privatization of water in underdeveloped countries demonstrate the effectiveness of organizing. These campaigns illustrate the power of thousands of people working together for a single purpose. It is possible to change the practices of huge multinational corporations.

This chapter illustrates the intricate relationship between corporations and the governments that promote war. In an effort to obtain a peaceful world, people must join together to stop the corporations that fund, support, and profit from war and violent conflicts. Putting an end to the corporations that promote, develop, and manufacture military weapons and equipment would be one effective way to stop the violence. Waging war would be impossible without weapon production.

What happens behind closed doors often dictates what will or will not happen in the occurrence of war and the destruction of the planet. Groups such as CorpWatch and Corporate Accountability help to identify for us the players and their stakes. Advocates for peace urge people not to turn their eyes away from the victims; we need also to look directly at the responsible institutions and hold them accountable.

NOTES

1. Butler, 2003.
2. OpenSecrets.org, "General Electric."
3. INFACT, "Chicago INFACT Newsletter," 1986.
4. Ibid.
5. Ibid.
6. Ibid.
7. Military Industrial Complex, "Contractor/Contract Detail."
8. The Center for Public Integrity, "Windfalls of War."
9. Cray, "General Electric."
10. Ibid.; CleanUpGE.org, "GE Misdeed."
11. INFACT, "INFACT Newsletter: Nuclear Weaponmakers Campaign Update," Fall 1989.
12. Ibid., INFACT, "INFACT Newsletter: Nuclear Weaponmakers Campaign Update." 1990.
13. INFACT, "INFACT Newsletter: Nuclear Weaponmakers Campaign Update," 1991; Chasnoff, 1991.
14. INFACT, "INFACT Newsletter: Nuclear Weaponmakers Campaign Update," 1989; 1990; CleanUpGE.org, n.d.
15. Washington State Department of Health, n.d.; Reaching Critical Will, "The Environment and the Nuclear Age."
16. INFACT, "INFACT Newsletter: Nuclear Weaponmakers Campaign Update," Fall 1989.
17. Ibid.
18. Ibid.
19. US Environmental Protection Agency, "Hudson River PCBs"; The Center for Public Integrity, "Windfalls of War."
20. US Environmental Protection Agency, "Superfund Sites Where you Live."
21. US PIRG, n.d.; The Center for Public Integrity, "Windfalls of War."
22. The Center for Public Integrity, "Windfalls of War."
23. Ibid.
24. Chatterjee, 2003; Pilisuk, 2008.
25. The Center for Public Integrity, "Windfalls of War."
26. Reaching Critical Will, "Bechtel Corporation."
27. Ibid.
28. Werner, 2007.
29. Reaching Critical Will, "Bechtel Corporation."
30. The Center for Public Integrity, "Windfalls of War."

31. Ibid.; Chatterjee, "Bechtel Wins Iraq War Contracts."

32. Food and Water Watch, "Bechtel;" Source Watch Online, "Bechtel Group, Inc."

33. Source Watch Online, "Bechtel Group, Inc."

34. Military Industrial Complex, "Contractor/Contract Detail,"

35. Alternatives Action and Communication Network for International Development, "Untold Suffering in the Congo; Reaching Critical Will, "Bechtel Corporation;" Montague, 2003.

36. Bechtel, "Sustainability and Environment."

37. Chatterjee, "Bechtel's Water Wars."

38. Food and Water Watch, "Bechtel." Pilisuk, 2008.

39. Ibid.

40. INFACT, "Chicago INFACT Newsletter." 1986.

41. Ibid.

42. INFACT, "Twin Cities INFACT Campaign Center Newsletter," 1986.

43. The Center for Public Integrity, "Windfalls of War."

44. Ibid.

45. Reaching Critical Will, "Bechtel Corporation."

46. The Center for Public Integrity, "Windfalls of War."

47. Ibid.

48. Chatterjee, "Bechtel Wins Iraq War Contracts."

49. Ibid.

50. Ibid.; The Center for Public Integrity, "Windfalls of War."

51. The Center for Public Integrity, "Windfalls of War."

52. Ibid.; Chatterjee, "Bechtel Wins Iraq War Contracts."

53. The Center for Public Integrity, "Windfalls of War."

54. Chatterjee, "Bechtel Wins Iraq War Contracts;" OpenSecrets.org, "Bechtel Group."

55. Goodman and Goodman, 2005.

56. CorpWatch.org, "About CorpWatch."

57. Ibid.

58. Ibid.

59. International Baby Food Action Network, "Information to Consumers;" Corporate Accountability International, "Infant Formula Campaign."

60. INFACT, "INFACT Newsletter," 1986, 1990, 1991; Corporate Accountability International, "Our Victories."

CHAPTER 6

Socially Responsible Investing, Peace, and Social Justice

Tessie Petion and Steven D. Lydenberg

Peace and social justice have been among the core values promoted by socially responsible investing (SRI) over the past 40 years as it has transcended its roots as a faith-based activity and has become an integral part of the mainstream investment community. SRI—which goes by many names including socially responsible investing, ethical investing, sustainable investing, triple-bottom-line investing, green investing, best-of-class investing, or simply responsible investing—at its core seeks to maximize a variety of social goods while achieving competitive financial returns.

In its modern form, SRI evolved in the United States in the early 1970s as a response to the Vietnam War, the civil rights movement, and growing environmental concerns. SRI attracted investors who shunned corporate profits that were coming at the price of human suffering and environmental degradation. In addition, investors realized that they could raise their voice on these issues as a way to influence companies. During that era the primary tools of the current SRI movement evolved: screening and advocacy.

Screening involves the setting of certain social and environmental standards to determine the investment eligibility of publicly traded companies. The most common standards applied by socially responsible mutual funds are those related to alcohol, tobacco, gambling, defense/weapons, environmental issues, human rights, labor issues, and community relations.

Through shareholder advocacy or engagement, socially responsible investors exercise their right as owners to influence a corporation's actions. The filing of proxy resolutions on social and environmental issues is the most prominent form of shareholder advocacy—they give socially responsible investors a seat at the table.

In addition to screening and advocacy, SRI has increased the demand for corporate transparency on issues like human rights, defense contracting, and environmental justice. This increasingly detailed Corporate Social Responsibility (CSR) reporting has provided benchmarks for nongovernmental organizations (NGOs) and governments to evaluate corporations' records in these areas, and to act on these evaluations.

Since the 1970s, SRI has grown from a curiosity in the world of finance to a worldwide phenomenon accepted by many of the largest institutional investors. While there are many ways in which SRI can influence human rights, the environment, and economic development, this chapter highlights SRI's ability to promote peace and social justice.

ORIGINS

SRI dates back to the 17th century. Religious institutions such as the Society of Friends (Quakers), Mennonites, and the Methodists believed that investing was not a neutral activity, but implied values. These groups shunned "sin" stocks, which were those of companies involved in alcohol, tobacco, gambling, and in certain cases, weapons.[1]

In the late 1960s and early 1970s, a number of the church investment funds started to explore ways of avoiding investments in companies operating in South Africa or involved in the Vietnam War. At that time, Ralph Nader and Saul Alinsky, two U.S. consumer and community activists, started to make use of the shareholder right to appear at corporate annual meetings and to file shareholder resolutions to raise social and environmental issues directly with corporate management. Nader's General Motors campaign led to the submission of two socially based resolutions on the annual meeting proxy ballot in 1970.[2] These tactics were soon adopted by the SRI movement and became an important tool for the responsible investor.

Historically, many religious investors have drawn connections between war and the companies who profit from war. The first ethical mutual fund, the Pax World Fund, was established in the United States in 1971 by founders who had worked on peace, housing, and employment issues for the Methodist Church and wanted to make it possible for investors to align their investments with their values. Pax challenged corporations to establish and live up to specific standards of social and environmental responsibility.[3] As its name implies, Pax only invested in non–war-related industries.

In 1972 the Corporate Information Center (CIC), a precursor to the Interfaith Center on Corporate Responsibility (ICCR), released a study revealing that several Protestant denominations and the National Council of Churches held sizeable investments in companies supplying materials for the Vietnam War, although they were on record opposing the war as immoral and profoundly sinful. In this case, the groups did not sell their defense stocks, choosing instead to exercise their shareholders' right to speak to management, raising concerns about corporate profiteering from the war. In doing so, they established a modus operandi that came to characterize that of ICCR's members on issues of peace and social justice over the coming decades.[4]

In the early 1980s, SRI started to take root in Europe. In the United Kingdom, the Friends Provident Stewardship Unit Trust was launched in 1984. The Stewardship Unit Trust aimed to invest in companies that made a positive contribution to society and excluded companies providing products or services it viewed as unethical, such as arms, gambling, and tobacco.[5] By the 1990s, SRI became strongly established throughout the Continent, with a strong emphasis on sustainability and the environment. For example, a number of "eco-banks" such as Triodos Bank in the Netherlands were founded during that time.[6]

SRI, which originally developed in a political climate of social protest, has now been transformed from a faith-based activity into an activity promoting a public awareness of the "social responsibility" of corporations and of investing.[7] As it has gained acceptance in the mainstream, it has in part left behind its activist image and become a more broadly accepted investment endeavor. Some of the largest national pension funds in the world, including, for example, those of Norway and Denmark, refuse to invest in manufacturers of landmines or nuclear weapons.

SRI TODAY

SRI is a worldwide movement with assets under management that totaled more than $6 trillion at the end of 2007.

In the United States, SRI assets under management were $2.71 trillion in 2007, representing 11 percent of the $25.1 trillion in total assets under management.[8] In Europe between 2002 and 2007, the number of SRI funds increased by 150 percent to 447 in 2007.[9] According to the European Social Investment Forum, SRI accounts for 17.6 percent of total European funds under management.[10]

Pension funds, as a group, are the largest single owners of corporate stock. Their increasing participation in the SRI movement means that corporate managers must take their responsibilities to society and the environment seriously. In the United States, for example, more than 80 percent of all assets socially screened for institutional clients are managed for public retirement systems or other state and local investment pools.[11] Large institutional investors such as these have access to corporate management and their willingness to raise social and environmental issues with management has furthered the movement.

The United Nations–sponsored Principles for Responsible Investment (PRI) coalition currently demonstrates how SRI has become a worldwide phenomenon and is no longer a niche market among a handful of institutional investors. Signatories to the PRI, who have agreed to incorporate environment, social, and corporate governance issues into their investment analysis and decision making, represented more than $18 trillion in assets by the end of 2008.[12] In addition, in several European countries, legislation and regulations now require pension funds to publicly state the degree (if any) to which they take into account social, environmental, and governance considerations in their investment decisions.[13]

SRI AND MILITARY SCREENS

Weapons screening is today among the most frequently used screen in the SRI world and plays a major role this investment practice.[14] Recently a number of Europe's largest pension funds have adopted screening techniques tied to international norms and standards, entering the screening space by screening out companies involved in the manufacture of landmines and antipersonnel or nuclear weapons.

For example, Norway's sovereign wealth fund will not make investments that may contribute to violations of fundamental humanitarian principles, serious violations of human rights, gross corruption, or severe environmental damages. In March 2009, it divested $36 million in Textron shares because of their production of cluster bombs.[15]

While many social investors around the world have military screens of one sort of another, few investors exclude all companies that sell anything to the military. In most cases, military screens eliminate companies that only sell weapons or weapons systems.[16]

For example, Domini Social Investments, a manager of a family of socially screened mutual funds in the United States, believes that nuclear terrorism and war are grave threats to humanity, that military spending by major powers raises threats to international peace, and that the

international trade in conventional arms fuels internal and regional conflicts around the world. Military spending also diverts funds from much-
needed investments on the range of domestic public goods and international
aid that are essential for the creation of prosperous, stable nations. Therefore Domini does not invest in companies deriving significant revenues
from the manufacture of military weapons. Nor does the company invest in
companies that are significant owners or operators of nuclear power plants,
the spread of which is difficult to divorce from the proliferation of nuclear
weapons.

By contrast, other SRI funds argue that there are legitimate national security threats and needs that require the production of weapons and their
use in certain circumstances. For example, Calvert Investment's weapons
policy avoids investing in companies that manufacture, design, or sell weapons or the critical components of weapons that violate international humanitarian law and companies that manufacture, design, or sell inherently
offensive weapons.[17]

ENGAGEMENT AND MILITARY ISSUES

In addition to using screening to express their concerns, SRI investors
have actively engaged corporate management on issues of peace and social
justice. They have filed shareholder resolutions and joined in coalitions to
enter into public dialogue on issues as diverse as plans for peace conversion,
censorship in China, lobbying and political contributions, support for repressive regimes, access to capital, and environmental justice. ICCR is one
of the longest, strongest centers for such engagement initiatives.

ICCR, established in 1971, is a coalition of faith-based institutional investors, including national denominations, religious communities, pension funds,
foundations, hospital corporations, economic development funds, asset management companies, colleges, and unions. ICCR draws on common religious
values and its goals are social and economic justice.

Through its efforts over the years, ICCR has sponsored or co-sponsored
hundreds of proxy resolutions (more than 100 each year). Individual shareholders in the United States have the right to place issues on corporate
proxy statements for votes by all shareholders at company annual meetings.
These resolutions don't always pass—in fact, they rarely do—but that is
not the most important point. The point is that they allow the expression of
dissent and diversity within a corporation and introduce new issues in new
ways to corporate managers. In response to the filing of these resolutions,
company management frequently sits down with dissident investors to discuss the issues raised and what changes might be required for the

Table 6.1.　Top Ten Targeted Companies, 1972–2009

Company	Number of Shareholder Proposals
General Electric	37
General Dynamics	28
Boeing	23
Raytheon	23
Textron	23
Lockheed	21
McDonnell Douglas	21
Rockwell	19
United Technologies	19
Honeywell	16

Source: ICCR

shareholders to withdraw their resolution.[18] Studies show that 40 to 45 percent of proposals sponsored by religious investors or socially responsible mutual funds are withdrawn each year, often indicating some type of favorable corporate response.[19]

From its earliest days, anti-militarism has been one of the issues that ICCR members have regularly focused on. Through proxy resolutions they have raised issues such as corporate involvement in foreign military sales, weapons in space, nuclear weapons, landmines, and peace conversion. They have targeted the largest military contractors, such as General Electric and Boeing, on a broad range of issues over the years (see Table 6.1 for a list of the 10 companies that have received the most military-related resolutions from ICCR members over the years).

HUMAN RIGHTS AND SOCIAL JUSTICE

In addition to their concerns about corporations' involvement in the military, SRI investors around the world have often pressured governments abusing human rights by publicly refusing to invest in the stocks of companies doing business with them. This practice received wide attention in the 1970s and 1980s in the South Africa divestment campaign and continues today in Sudan and Burma. In addition, they have asked companies to address human rights and labor standards issues directly in their own operations or those of their vendors.

South Africa

The issue of South Africa played a crucial role in the development of the SRI movement during the 1970s and 1980s. The history of the involvement of investors in this issue illustrates its ability to play a supporting role in addressing many of the most important issues of our time.

Post–World War II, South Africa's government officially established the system of racial segregation known as apartheid. The apartheid system classified inhabitants into racial groups and stripped blacks of their citizenship. The government segregated education, medical care, and other public services. The policies drew scrutiny and were denounced, but those outside the country at first did little to foster change.

International opposition to apartheid strengthened after the 1960 Sharpeville massacre when South African police shot a crowd of black protesters. In 1971, the Episcopal Church filed the first church-sponsored shareholder resolution on South Africa. The resolution called on General Motors to withdraw from South Africa. Though the resolution didn't pass, it launched ICCR's divestment campaign.[20]

At the same time, Reverend Leon Sullivan (a General Motors board member) drafted a code of conduct for practicing business in South Africa that became known as the Sullivan Principles (see Table 6.2). The Sullivan Principles gained wide use in the United States. The Principles laid out a series of graded positions that permitted several levels of screening, from very strict to very mild, for pension funds to participate in the divestment process.[21] The framework provided by the Sullivan Principles allowed SRI to establish credibility and made corporations accountable for their records on human rights.

Table 6.2.   The Sullivan Principles for Corporations in South Africa

1. Non-segregation of the races in all eating, comfort, and work facilities.

2. Equal and fair employment practices for all employees.

3. Equal pay for all employees doing equal or comparable work for the same period of time.

4. Initiation of and development of training programs that will prepare, in substantial numbers, blacks and other nonwhites for supervisory, administrative, clerical, and technical jobs.

5. Increasing the number of blacks and other nonwhites in management and supervisory positions.

6. Improving the quality of employees' lives outside the work environment in such areas as housing, transportation, schooling, recreation, and health facilities.

Using these principles as guidelines, cities, states, colleges, faith-based groups, and pension funds throughout the United States began divesting from companies operating in South Africa. Before the end of South Africa's apartheid era, the principles were formally adopted by more than 125 U.S. corporations that had operations in South Africa. Of those companies that formally adopted the principles, at least 100 ultimately completely withdrew their existing operations from South Africa.[22] The subsequent negative flow of investment dollars eventually forced a group of businesses, representing 75 percent of South African employers, to draft a charter calling for an end to apartheid. Although the SRI efforts alone didn't bring an end to the apartheid system, it focused persuasive international pressure on the South African business community.

Sudan

The Sudan divestment movement of today has parallels with that of South Africa from the 1970s and 1980s. The conflict in Darfur, Sudan, started in 2003 when rebel groups began attacking government targets. The government of Sudan responded to the military challenges in Darfur by arming, training, and deploying Arab ethnic militias. The militias and Sudanese armed forces launched a campaign of ethnic cleansing and forced displacement by bombing and burning villages, killing civilians, and raping women. The conflict is believed to have resulted in the death of at least 200,000 people in Darfur and has displaced over 2 million people.[23]

In 2004, a number of institutional investors identified divestment as a possible tool to exert pressure on the Sudanese government. In particular, divestment policies have focused on companies supporting Sudan's oil industry, in part because 80 percent of the government's export revenue is from oil. (Sudan lacks the internal expertise or capital to extract resources itself and is therefore completely dependent on foreign companies to exploit its oil reserves.) Firms such as China National Petroleum Corporation, Oil and Natural Gas Company of India, and Petronas of Malaysia can therefore be regarded as providing an economic lifeline for the regime. Though these firms are aware of the conflict, they are reluctant to disrupt the pipeline of natural resources.

The model for the divestment campaign promoted by the Conflict Risk Network (formerly the Sudan Divestment Task Force) encourages shareholders to exert pressure only on companies that provide significant support to Khartoum and fail to benefit Sudan's marginalized populations. Rather than asking companies to leave Sudan completely, this divestment model asserts that companies can remain in Sudan and use their leverage to contribute to positive change. Shareholder divestment is only used if the company is not responsive to engagement.

A number of companies have responded to this divestment campaign. Rolls Royce, CHC Helicopter, ICSA of India, and others have left Sudan, citing the humanitarian crises in the country. Schlumberger and La Mancha Resources continue their operations, having adopted and implemented responsible business plans in Sudan.[24]

Thus far the Sudan divestment movement has been centered in the United States. U.S. pension funds, like the $210 billion California Public Employees' Retirement System (CalPERS), have banned investments in companies that do business in Sudan. However, investors from abroad are also beginning to address Sudan-linked companies. In 2008, PGGM, one of the largest pension funds in the Netherlands, decided to disinvest from PetroChina because of its involvement in human rights violations in Darfur.[25] Divestment has helped alter company behavior toward Sudan, which in turn has placed pressure on the Sudanese government. Though divestment has raised consciousness of the seriousness of the human rights issues in Sudan among many Western companies, many of the publicly traded companies doing business in Sudan are Chinese companies that have not been so susceptible to this influence.

Though shareholder activism and divestment have not starved the Sudanese government of funds, they have helped to continue to focus international attention on the conflict in the region.

Burma

Burma is another region where social investors hope to bring international pressure to bear on a government on human rights issues. Burma's military dictatorship has been accused of serious and ongoing human rights violations. Though the divestment movement is not as formalized as it is for Sudan, many socially responsible investors believe that corporations should not do business in Myanmar (Burma). The country's economy is almost entirely government controlled—corporations operating there provide direct financial support to the regime.

In particular, Chevron has received pressure from investors to speak against human rights abuses in the country. Chevron, through its acquisition of Unocal in 2005, has become partnered with the Burmese government in a pipeline project that hired the Burmese military to provide security services. In doing so, the military allegedly committed numerous human rights violations, including the use of forced labor. Chevron has been subject to lawsuits alleging human rights abuses filed in U.S. courts.[26] Although Chevron points to the community projects they have in place in the country, many

SRI investors feel that these programs pale in comparison to the hundreds of millions of dollars of revenue the pipeline provides the military regime.

ICCR members have been a major player in the campaign against Burma. They scored two major victories during the 1997 proxy season. After a shareholder resolution was filed calling for withdrawal from Burma, PepsiCo announced that it was leaving the country. Shortly thereafter Texaco divested its holdings in Burma's natural gas industry.

LABOR STANDARDS

Social investors have also asked companies to directly address issues of environmental justice and labor rights in their operations. For example, Freeport-McMoran's operations in the Indonesian territory of Papua have been the subject of substantial shareholder activism within the SRI world. It is alleged that between 1998 and 2004, this U.S. mining company gave military and police officials in Papua approximately $20 million to shield it from environmental regulations. Freeport employs a natural river system to dispose of close to 230,000 tons of tailings each day and releases large quantities of sediments and toxic heavy metals into the water, including copper, cadmium, mercury, and arsenic. In 2006, Indonesia's Minister of the Environment charged that the company was operating in violation of the government's water quality regulations. In May 2006, the Indonesian Friends of the Earth issued a report that alleged that Freeport committed violations of Indonesian environmental laws and regulations.

Faith-based investors were among the first to raise the issue of the company's impact on the environment and indigenous peoples in the region. A number of institutional investors have committed to long-term engagement with Freeport over its operations there. In June 2006, the Norwegian Ministry of Finance ordered the divestment of Freeport McMoran stock from the Norwegian national pension fund citing serious damage to the river system and parts of the rainforest as well as considerable negative consequences for the indigenous people in the area. The government also found that the environmental damage caused by Freeport's mining operations was extensive, long-term, and irreversible.[27]

Over the years socially responsible investors have also encouraged corporations to take responsibility for conditions in the factories where they source their products and to ensure that workers are covered by basic standards concerning safety, working hours, and pay. Gap Inc. released its first Social Responsibility Report after two years of dialogue with a coalition of socially responsible investors. Gap had initially resisted the idea of quantifying its performance in this area and a shareholder resolution served as an important negotiating tool. As a result of this dialogue, Gap became the first clothing retailer to publicly rate the way its contractors treat their workers, and set a new standard for transparency in its industry. This report and subsequent Gap reports tackled the difficult challenges the company faced in enforcing global labor standards, including obstacles imposed by its own business model and purchasing practices. Gap's initial report has also contributed to an informal standardization of reporting with Nike and Hewlett Packard using a similar format of a key chart in their reports.[28]

THE LARGER CONTEXT OF SRI

This chapter has focused on the role of peace and social justice issues within the SRI world, but these are only two of a broad range of social and environmental issues of concern to socially responsible investors. While other issues are as varied as climate change, affordable health care, excessive chief executive officer compensation, and corporate involvement in the marketing of tobacco, alcohol, and gambling, underlying them all is a basic concern for the creation of a safe and equitable society.

In this chapter we have stressed particularly the involvement of religious organizations in the United States because they had been by far the most active over the years in filing resolutions—and among resolution filers, the most active in raising issues about militarism in our society. But they have also raised, and continue to raise, the full spectrum of SRI concerns. And, as SRI has grown over the years, numerous other organizations have joined these religious groups in taking up the tools of screening and engagement to raise these issues. Today they include socially responsible mutual funds, pension funds, unions, and human rights and environmental activist organizations.

SRI has from its earliest days placed a strong emphasis on, and made a constant demand for, increased corporate *disclosure* on an extensive range of social and environmental issues crucial to society. In filing resolutions on many issues, shareholders' first demand is often for a company report to the public on the topic. Through their support for such organizations as the Global Reporting Initiative (GRI) and their frequent surveys on CSR initiatives undertaken by corporations, SRI investors have demonstrated the demand for and catalyzed the evolution of improved CSR disclosure. (The GRI has developed a comprehensive framework and guidance for CSR reporting through a thorough stakeholder consultation process.)

Indeed, one of SRI's most tangible accomplishments has been to turn CSR reporting from an exceptional company practice in the 1980s to something that in certain regions of the world is rapidly becoming the rule. In France, for example, large publicly traded companies have been required to report on some 40 key social and environmental indicators since 2003 and Sweden will require all companies with state ownership to report in accordance with the GRI starting in 2009.[29] The number of CSR reports issued around the world as of 2009 approached the 4,000 mark, up from less than 100 as recently as the early 1990s.[30] These reports form the foundation on which various dialogues between corporations and those concerned with the creation of a better world are often built.

Throughout its development, critics of SRI have raised two broad objections to this practice. The first asserts that limiting one's investment universe by screening out certain companies or whole industries on nonfinancial grounds will hurt financial performance and is therefore a violation of fiduciary duty—the obligation of money managers to act in the best interest of their clients. Literally hundreds of academic studies have been conducted since the 1970s on the effects, or lack thereof, of screening on performance and of CSR on profits. Although results have varied widely, the preponderance of these studies shows either a positive relationship between screening and financial performance and CSR and profits, or a neutral one—it doesn't help and it doesn't hurt.[31] The Web site, sristudies.com, maintains an extensive bibliography with annotations of the most important of these studies.

The second major criticism of SRI is that it is ineffective—no more than a form of window dressing that may make investors feel good, but accomplishes little in reality. It is a criticism that was often heard 20 years ago about divestment of companies involved in South Africa and is heard today about similar policies for involvement in Sudan. These critics assert, for example, that "A fundamental assumption underpinning the decision to divest from a company is that investors are able to affect the financial fate of the targeted firms and therefore induce a change in corporate policy and/or behavior."[32] To back up this assertion, economists point out that that boycotting a stock is unlikely to have any impact on its price.

Socially responsible investors, however, measure success in terms of economic, ecological, and social gains, and their effectiveness in terms of the promotion of public debate about the role of corporations and society. Although numerous specific accomplishments can be cited resulting from direct dialogue between corporations and various players in the SRI world, the long-term strength of SRI lies not primarily in its ability to change the world one company at a time. Rather it lies in SRI's ability to influence the *vocabulary* that is used to discuss and evaluate the relationship of corporations to society and the environment.

SRI has played a strong role in legitimizing the demands of society that corporations disclose their policies and practices on a tremendous range of issues vital to society—and in doing so, has begun to alter the whole framework, the whole range of expectations, within which corporations exercise their license from society to continue their daily operations.

Because they hold an ownership stake in the companies in which they invest, members of the SRI world are uniquely positioned to promote this new vocabulary and demand that dialogue take place on these new concerns. At the core of these concerns and this dialogue is the question of how a more peaceful and sustainable world can be created and how all elements of society, including corporations, can cooperate to achieve that goal.

NOTES

1. Kinder, Lydenberg, and Domini, 1993.
2. Massie, 1997.
3. Pax World Investments, 2009.
4. Kinder, Lydenberg, and Domini, 1993.
5. Ibid.
6. Louche and Lydenberg, 2009.
7. Sparkes, 2001.
8. US SIF, 2008.
9. Lipper, FERI, 2008.
10. Eurosif, 2008.
11. SIF, 2008.
12. Grene, 2009.
13. Lydenberg and Louche, 2009.
14. Eurosif, 2008.
15. O'Dwyer, 2009.
16. Kinder, Lydenberg, and Domini, 1993.
17. Calvert Investments.
18. Makower, 1994.
19. Tkac, 2006.
20. Massie, 1997.
21. Ibid.
22. Ibid.
23. Soederberg, 2009.
24. Wisor, 2007.
25. Eurosif, 2008.
26. Lifsher, 2005.
27. ICCR, 2007.
28. Kanzer, 2009.
29. Baue, 2002.
30. Kropp, 2009.
31. Orlitzky, Schmidth, and Rynes, 2003; Statman, 2006.
32. Soederberg, 2009.

PART II

RESISTING VIOLENCE

Wars, unlike hurricanes and earthquakes, do not "just happen." They come as a result of human decisions and human-created institutions. But wars *do* happen and when they do some people recoil at the horror inflicted and resist. Resisting violence has a long history including illegal efforts to free slaves, soldier revolts, standing between gunmen and civilians, dismantling weapons or drenching them with blood, blocking shipments of weapons, and withholding taxes. Some reach out to help the victims, some to record the casualties and make them known, and others to prevent some of the killings from happening. A special group are the soldiers who come to resistance from their personal experiences with the disparity between what they were led to believe and the consequences they actually see. Some return as veterans opposed to war and join groups reaffirming continuing efforts to end agencies that are designed to recruit and to create warriors and hitmen. Some sign petitions, some march in protest, some dedicate their personal lives to be free from violence, some pray for peace, and many do nothing.

Kathy Kelly has been the coordinator of Voices in the Wilderness, a Chicago-based group that organized over 70 citizen delegations to Iraq to report how sanctions were affecting people in that country during the 1990s. In addition, Kelly twice led delegations that literally camped out in the way of the U.S. invasions of Iraq in 1991 and 2003. Her contribution speaks to one of the most basic truths about war and aggressive policies: that they continue because we lose sight of the human victims of all ages. It also speaks of the heroic courage that can save lives in the face of efforts that destroy them. Christine Schweitzer writes of the work of a nonviolent peace force. The concept is that a coordinated group of trained, unarmed civilians can enter the area of hostilities with a specific mission of working directly with people on the ground—averting violent activities, mediating where possible, interposing where necessary, and bearing public witness. The group takes on major tasks of protecting peacemakers as well as other civilians; negotiating with authorities, with community leaders, and with nongovernmental organizations (NGOs); and building the transitional structures that will aid reconciliation, reconstruction, and healing. Some illustrations in Sri Lanka and in the Balkans point out both the problems and the promise of this activity. The nonviolent force is particularly promising because it illustrates that people are not powerless in the face of hostilities. It shows also a potential for escalation of peacemaking activities. This is the opposite of the escalations of violence that commonly follow hostilities and can stimulate further hostilities and produce the horror of war. Here is a way to break the cycle.

The way that military and foreign intelligence operations of the United States are spread into almost every sector of American society leaves many different professions and businesses actively collaborating with the planning and execution of wars. Jill Latonick-Flores and Daniel J. Adamski describe the involvement of the psychology profession in the program of torture of prisoners, the attempt of the American Psychological Association (APA) to refrain from calling this unethical, and the movement among psychologists to protest this stance of their own professional organization and to demand accountability from the APA.

Over the years of colonial domination, major powers have linked themselves to governments in other countries that were capable of curbing resistance to domination by wealthy corporate elites. These elites are part of the colonial legacy and provide the partners for neo-colonialism. Such wealthy families ruled in much of the global south with the support of police and military forces. Their alliance with Western governments ensured weapons and training sufficient for control of mostly peasant populations, and of the social workers, labor organizers, priests, or guerrilla groups that sought to speak for the poor. To provide the most effective military response, both to protect the oligarchs and to overthrow populist leaders, the United States opened a School of the Americas (SOA) to train Latin American military officers. Because of its reputation for violence—it was popularly called the School of Assassins—it was renamed the Western Hemisphere Institute of Security Cooperation (WHINSEC). Many of its graduates have been implicated in efforts to steal elections and intimidate opponents and even in brutal assassinations conducted with impunity. Father Roy Bourgeois was a founder of School of the Americas Watch, which has been working since 1983 to expose the activities of the SOA and its graduates and to close it down. He and Jill Latonick-Flores write to describe the activity of this group. (In the following part, Hector Aristizábal, a victim of torture by Colombian military provides a first hand account.)

As the Vietnam War was ending, we became aware of the psychological legacy soldiers bring home. Many are deeply scarred. Some return with an internal demon interfering with every aspect of their lives and the lives of their families, and many are homeless, frightened, and confused substance abusers to this day. Among those who return, some find solace in reaffirming the patriotic myths justifying the price they and their comrades paid. Others seek therapy, and for a substantial number their healing has involved participation in soldiers' anti-war movements. The remaining chapters in this part deal with resistance among soldiers. To understand this phenomenom more fully we look into recruitment and training as described by former Marine Sergeant Martin Smith. Inigo Gilmore and Teresa Smith describe the critical element of dehumanizing that will enable soldiers to kill and how the ability to see others as people is important for living with one's conscience. Justin Cliburn writes of the efforts that soldiers make to come to an understanding of the horror they see and even their own part in the violence. The writers have identified with efforts of veterans to speak out for peace. Historian Howard Zinn, himself a veteran of World War II, concludes this section with a review of the history and meaning of soldier resistance and its central importance for the peace movement.

Taken as a whole, this part demonstrates that overt violence can be resisted. For many of us, veterans or not, these documented accounts should provide some inspiration.

—Marc Pilisuk and Michael N. Nagler

CHAPTER 7

A Hand for Peace in a Zone of War

Kathy Kelly

On August 2, 1990, Iraq invaded Kuwait. Four days later, the United Nations began to enforce against Iraq the most comprehensive economic sanctions ever imposed in modern history. But Saddam Hussein did not withdraw from Kuwait, and the United States began a massive military buildup for an eventual war against Iraq.

It seemed unlikely that the United States was preparing to invade Iraq because the U.S. government refused to tolerate either a brutal dictator or an illegal invasion. The United States had recently invaded Panama and before that, Grenada, and the United States had helped install and prop up several dictatorships in Latin America. I believed that the war was being prepared to dominate and control the resources of another country. But nothing could prepare me for the realities encountered in Iraq or in the United States, as an increasingly imperial attitude developed the illusion that the United States was so powerful, militarily and economically, that it could create its own reality, regardless of the consequences borne by people whose lands were attacked by our military and economic policies.

In the fall of 1990, some months before the 1991 Gulf War began, I applied to join the Gulf Peace Team, a nonviolent, nonaligned encampment that would position itself on the Iraq side of the Iraq–Saudi border, between the warring parties. The organizers placed me on a waiting list. In early January 1991, word arrived that I could join a U.S. contingent leaving on a plane that would be the last to land in Baghdad before the bombing began.

Probably the most courageous thing I did during that year was to ride the bus to my family home on Chicago's southwest side and tell my mother what I was about to do. She was vehemently opposed. Leaving my family home, I caught a blast of frigid air in my face and my mother's thick Irish brogue at my back. "What about the incubators?" she cried out. "Kathy, what about the incubators?!"

She was referring to testimony from Nayireh, a young Kuwaiti girl, who told the U.S. Congress that she had witnessed invading Iraqi soldiers barge into a Kuwaiti hospital and steal incubators. With luminous eyes and a compelling presence, Nayireh told of her horror as she watched the menacing soldiers dump babies out of incubators. Months later, when the war was a distant memory, U.S. reporters learned that Nayireh was actually the daughter of a Kuwaiti emir; that doctors in Kuwait could not corroborate her testimony; that in fact the supposedly stolen incubators had been placed carefully in storage during the invasion; and that the Hill and Knowlton Public Relations firm had rehearsed with the young woman how to give *apparently* false testimony effectively.

Was Nayireh's testimony false? We can't be absolutely sure. Did Iraqi soldiers steal or damage valuable medical equipment? I'm not sure of that either. Here are some things of which, unfortunately, we all can be sure.

The Desert Storm bombardment destroyed Iraq's electrical grid. Refrigeration units, sewage and sanitation facilities, and all sorts of valuable equipment were ruined. Life-saving devices found in a modern hospital were rendered useless. As the allied bombing went on and on, my mother's question became more and more relevant, yet went largely unasked. "What about the incubators?"

Years later, when peace teams visited Iraq during 13 years of deliberate siege, we saw incubators, broken and irreparable, stacked up against the walls of hospital obstetrics wards. Sanctions prevented Iraqis from importing new incubators and from getting needed spare parts to repair old ones. And this was only one vitally needed item that sanctions prohibited.

I was in Iraq during the first 16 days of the Gulf War, one of 73 volunteers from 18 countries who formed the Gulf Peace Team. We intended to sit in the middle of a likely battlefield and call for an end to hostilities. I still feel a glimmer of pride recalling that we succeeded in setting up an encampment in the desert almost exactly on the border between Iraq and Saudi Arabia and near a U.S. military camp.

Author Daniel Berrigan, a Jesuit and human rights activist, once said that one of the reasons we don't have peace is because pacifists aren't willing to pay the price of peace. Soldiers are expected to sacrifice their lives in the name of war, but peacemakers often decline to take similar risks. The

Gulf Peace Team was a diverse group, but I think almost every person there was motivated by just the willingness that Berrigan spoke of, a readiness to pay the price of peace to bear witness against the war.[1]

Our U.S. contingent did indeed land in Baghdad on the last plane allowed into the country prior to the war. We had linked with European and Asian contingents in Amman, Jordan, and then traveled together, by bus, beyond Baghdad. To reach the desert camp, our bus passed through Kerbala, in southern Iraq. Our team was mesmerized by the city's beauty. Students, gowned and graceful, sauntered along palm-tree–lined university streets. Mosques shimmered in the sunlight. All of us voiced a hope that we could one day return to Kerbala.

The Gulf Peace Team camp was already humming by the time I got there. Latrines had been dug, tents were set up, food preparation and clean-up tasks were assigned, and in spite of language and cultural differences people were learning about each other. We also began learning to live quite simply. We had to ration our food, eventually reducing our meals to one per day. Water and electricity were very scarce. The camp was an abandoned way station once used by pilgrims on their way to and from Mecca. We slept in huge tents with corrugated tin roofs. The nights were bitter cold, but daytime brought an intense sun. Communicating with each other took great patience because we came from so many different countries and walks of life. It took weeks for us to form ourselves into affinity groups that allowed for at least some democratic process in decision making.

The night the war broke out, our team members took turns clustering around a tiny short-wave radio, anxious to know whether there would be a last-minute resolution to prevent the war. Military experts had predicted that the bombing would begin on a moonless night. That night, there was no moon. At about 2:00 A.M., on January 16, the United States began bombing. We crawled out of our tents and huddled together, watching planes fly overhead.[2]

I remember feeling the deepest dismay I'd ever known. Every dog in the region began barking when the U.S. and allied war planes appeared overhead. Those dogs barked themselves hoarse. I felt that was the most appropriate response to the war. Each night, bombers flew above us, sometimes at five-minute intervals. And each one carried a devastating payload of bombs. I imagined there would be nothing left of Iraq.

On January 27, 1991, as the ground war loomed, the Iraqi government decided to evacuate us. It seems that they believed we actually would be in the way of invading forces if the U.S. military were to attempt a pincer movement designed to block retreating Iraqi soldiers.

An Iraqi government representative instructed us to break down our camp and pack for an early morning departure the next day. Buses would take us to

Baghdad. We were divided about whether to stay or to go. A hard argument ensued. Finally we agreed that 12 of our number would form a circle, holding signs that said, in Arabic and in English, "We Choose to Stay."

The next morning, buses were lined up, awaiting us. The unenviable task of coordinating our removal fell to Tariq, a civilian with the Ministry of Culture who had visited our camp several times before. He seemed genuinely fond of us and was eager to understand why we had placed ourselves in such peril.

When he saw the dozen people seated, holding their placards, Tariq was baffled. I doubt that he had ever read much of Gandhi or the Rev. Dr. Martin Luther King. Maybe he'd never heard of nonviolence. He asked me, "What am I to do?"

"Tariq," I answered, "Nobody here wants to harm you or disrespect you. They're just unable to board the buses voluntarily—it's a matter of conscience." He nodded, and then walked away. Moments later I saw him walk up to Jeremy Hartigan, a gentle British barrister, seated cross-legged on the ground, holding his sign as others softly sang. Jeremy was a Buddhist. At intervals, he chanted, "Omm."

Tariq bent over, kissed Jeremy on the forehead and pointed northward, saying, "Baghdad!" Then he and several aides gently placed their hands under Hartigan—it reminded me of levitation games we played as children—and carried him aboard the bus. With solemn faces, they continued one by one with the others, carefully placing them on the buses.

By late afternoon, we were aboard buses traveling a road that was under constant bombardment. The buses swerved around huge bomb craters and we saw the charred, smoking remains of oil tankers, an ambulance, a passenger bus, and several civilian cars. Later I learned that the station chief for CBS News had been attacked from the air while driving a tiny Toyota.

In Baghdad, we stayed for four days at the plush Al-Rashid hotel, which could offer no running water and was pitch dark because all electrical power had been knocked out.[3]

However, in the women's restroom there was a light. I went there to write and read, from time to time, and there I met mothers and children. The mothers were very friendly to me, and the children, after initial shyness, were glad to play. Sometimes I'd see them again, in the hotel's basement bomb shelter, late at night, when the bombing was more intense. Fathers held children in their arms and reassured them. But the men's faces showed unmistakable anxiety and fear.

We found an old typewriter, abandoned by journalists. It lacked a typewriter ribbon, but I had learned, in Nicaragua and in prison, that if you place a sheet of carbon paper in front of a clean sheet of paper, it will function like a typewriter ribbon. We melted a candle onto the typewriter and soon I was able to produce our team's statement about why we were in Baghdad.

An Iraqi official spotted me managing to type something and soon returned with a document he needed typed in English. We were reluctant, at first—was it right for a team claiming neutrality to assist an Iraqi government official? We asked to read the letter. It was a letter to then Secretary General of the United Nations, Javier Perez de Cuellar, asking him to seek an end to bombardment of the Iraqi highway between Baghdad and the Jordanian border.

This road was the only way out for refugees and the only way in for humanitarian relief supplies. Our team had traveled on this road for some distance, en route to Baghdad, and had seen charred and smoking vehicles. Our bus drivers would swerve to miss craters in the road. It was a very dangerous route.

We agreed to type the letter, knowing that according to Geneva conventions warring parties must provide a way out for refugees to exit and a way in for humanitarian relief. The official returned with crumpled stationery, signed by a cabinet-level official, Adnan Dawoud Al Salwan, and red carbon paper that had been used five times over. Imagine cabinet-level correspondence being typed on wrinkled stationery by an extranational from the country that is bombing you, who is using an abandoned typewriter and working by candlelight. This was the situation of Iraq's government. Then imagine the support available to the Pentagon.

On January 31, in Baghdad, a bomb hit the servant's quarters of the hotel where we were housed. Iraqi authorities, once again concerned about our safety, hurried the whole Gulf Peace Team onto buses and moved us to Amman, Jordan. But they first issued visas to 33 of us who had asked to stay with families in Baghdad, assuring us that we could return at a later date.

In Amman, a large press conference had been arranged for us. I was to speak for U.S. Gulf Peace Team participants, but I felt at a loss for words. "How can I begin?" I asked George Rumens, a British journalist and a member of our team. "Tell them," he said, "that when the war fever and hysteria subside, we believe the lasting and more appropriate responses to this war will be felt throughout the world, deepest remorse and regret for the suffering we've caused."[4] Desert Storm continued. We called it Desert Slaughter.

Many of the Gulf Peace Team members returned to their home countries to campaign for an end to the relentless bombing and destruction. Those of us who had visas for a return trip to Iraq organized, as best we could, medical relief convoys to bring desperately needed medicines into Iraq.

We hoped that we might safeguard the road between the Jordan–Iraq border and Baghdad, thinking that if authorities from the United States and the United Kingdom knew that ordinary citizens from their own countries were traveling along that road, delivering medical relief, they might be less inclined to consider every moving vehicle a military target. Announcing the convoy project would give us a chance to remind the U.S. war planners about the Geneva conventions.

In Amman, a few of us began calling Jordanian pharmacists and charity organizations to learn more about procuring medicines for delivery to Iraq. A Jordanian businessman, Mr. Nidal Sukhtian, heard of our project and decided to donate a semi-truck full of powdered milk. He also volunteered to pay for petrol, hire a driver, and help us out with an interpreter.

Suddenly our project became much more manageable. I took responsibility to contact the media. A NBC TV correspondent decided to cover our departure. I don't remember her name, but I do remember a steady exchange of phone calls setting up the time and date for the convoy to film us loading up trucks with food and medicine and then driving back into the war zone.

The day before our planned departure, someone from the United Nations finally managed to get through to us that our convoy wasn't going to enter Iraq unless we were prepared to ram our way through a UN checkpoint. Sanctions prohibited delivery of almost all goods to Iraq, save for a short list of medical supplies and medicines.

Realizing that our powdered milk shipment could never pass the checkpoint, we divvied up a long list of tasks: offload the semi-truck and return it to the owner, find two small trucks to carry whatever we could find that was on the list, call pharmacies, find a new source for fuel and new drivers, change the press release, and change the departure time. In the frenzy of activity, I completely forgot to call the NBC correspondent. She was out in the field waiting to film us, with a full camera crew, and it was raining.

I saw her that night, at the Red Crescent office, where we both had turned up to get documents that would allow us to enter Iraq. She was livid. "I will assure that you and your team never again get coverage from NBC," she said. I murmured how sorry I was. She turned, walked away, and then paused, looking over her shoulder, to add, "I shouldn't even tell you this, but offloading the truck WAS the story." My heart sank.

Had NBC covered Janet Cameron, the Scottish doctor on our team, tearful as she hauled cartons of powdered milk off of the semi-truck, had this image been beamed into living rooms across the United States, it might have "jump-started" awareness about the most comprehensive sanctions ever imposed in modern history.

I still feel ashamed, even now, recalling that story. I feel shame and sorrow because throughout all the years of the long war against Iraq, offloading the truck never stopped being the story.

By 2007, a combination of sanctions, war, and occupation had brought to Iraq the world's worst deterioration in child mortality rate. Writing for *The Independent*, Andrew Buncombe cited a Save the Children Report, released in 2007, which stated that "in the years since 1990, Iraq has seen its child mortality rate soar by 125 percent, the highest increase of any country in the world. Its rate of deaths of children under five now matches that of Mauritania. . . . Figures collated by the charity show that in 1990 Iraq's mortality rate for under-fives was 50 per 1,000 live births. In 2005 it was 125."[5]

Massive convoys should have been going into Iraq, bearing all manner of humanitarian relief. They should have been, but they weren't, and in December 2006 donor nations cut in half the money they would commit to the United Nations High Commission for Refugees.

Eventually, in late March of 1991, our team did return to Kerbala, the city that had so impressed us when we first traveled into Iraq. We stared in awe as we drove along streets devoid of palm trees, lined by wreckage and smoking ruins.

We entered the main hospital and our feet stuck to the floor because the blood was so thick. Beds were smashed; equipment was torn out of the walls. We saw clusters of badly frightened doctors. Henry Selz, who had lived in Lebanon during the civil war there, spotted bullet holes near the rooftops of buildings as we walked along a side street. One elderly woman pulled us aside and began whispering about mass graves. What had happened?

I learned in fits and starts, fitting together pieces of the horror story that still isn't completed.

Margaret Thatcher remarked once on television that after the ceasefire had been declared, Saddam Hussein's generals asked if they could keep their helicopters and the U.S. generals said, "Yes." Then they asked if they could keep their attack helicopters—again the answer was "Yes." Those attack helicopters swiftly took off in pursuit of insurgents who were rebelling in cities all through southern Iraq: Amarah, Qut, Najaf, Nassiriyeh, Basra, and Kerbala.

Saudi Arabia and Kuwait, U.S. allies in the 1991 war against Iraq who were helping fund the war, had told President George Bush Sr. to keep Saddam Hussein in power because otherwise uprisings of Shi'ite people in the south could give rise to a dominant Shi'a governance in Iraq that would be sympathetic to coreligionists "next door" in Iran.

Hence the long regime of economic sanctions that kept Saddam crippled externally but strengthened internally—punitive sanctions that were always evaluated only on the basis of whether or not they prevented Saddam from acquiring weapons of mass destruction and never with regard to how the sanctions affected innocent and vulnerable Iraqis, particularly children.[6]

After the war, Iraq agreed to let us enter the country with study teams to document the combined effects of the war and economic sanctions. I stayed in the region for the next six months helping to organize medical relief and study teams. In March of 1991, I was with a small team that visited the neighborhood of Ameriyah, Iraq, where, on February 13, 1991, U.S. smart bombs were so smart that they were able to enter the ventilation shafts of a building that sheltered hundreds of Iraqi women and children. The exit doors were sealed shut and the temperature inside rose to 500 degrees centigrade. All save 17 survivors were melted.

I had begun to cry, staring at the scene, when I felt a tiny arm encircling my waist. An Iraqi child was smiling up at me. "Wel-kom," she said. Crossing the street were two women, draped in black. As they approached, I felt sure they were coming to withdraw the children who now surrounded us. I had learned just a few words of Arabic. "Ana Amerikia, wa asif," I stammered. "I'm American, and I'm sorry."

"La, la, la," said the young Iraqi mother. She was saying "No, no . . . ," and then motioned to her son to bring us the glasses of tea that he carried on a small platter.

Perhaps it was for the best that without electricity these women and children couldn't know what was being said, just then, in the United States. It wasn't until I returned that I heard those popular lines, "Rock Iraq! Slam Saddam!," shouted by college students as they hoisted another beer mug to cheer the war on. "Say hello to Allah!" sung out by U.S. soldiers when they blasted Iraqi targets. And the unforgettable words of General Colin Powell, when asked about the number of Iraqis who died in the war: "Frankly, that number doesn't interest me."

Senate and congressional investigating committees should have heard testimony from Iraqi eyewitnesses who survived the Desert Storm war, much as they had heard from Nayirah, the Kuwaiti teenager whose testimony helped market the war. Instead, the U.S. leadership told legislators and the general public very little about the consequences of the war. Very few people understood that when you destroy a nation's infrastructure and then cripple it further with punishing sanctions, as the United States insisted must happen for the next 13 years, the victims are always the society's most vulnerable people—the poor, the elderly, the sick, and most of all the children.

I recall driving out of Iraq, in mid-March 1991, as a passenger next to a brave Palestinian driver, Taha, who had courageously driven along dangerous desert treks to make repeated deliveries of humanitarian relief shipments to Iraq. Taha drove our small team back to Jordan. Along the road, we passed an isolated village. Suddenly, a group of youngsters ran down an embankment toward our speeding vehicle. They stretched out their arms, touched their lips, and then made the motion of forming chapattis, the bread of the poor. They were desperately hungry.

"We cannot stop," Taha said, blinking back tears. "Anyway we have nothing to give." The road had turned into a gauntlet, flanked with wave after wave of child beggars. Taha shook with frustration, then finally heaved with sobs as we drove on through the desert.

In the course of the 1991 Desert Storm bombing, U.S. aircraft alone dropped 88,500 tons of explosives on Iraq, the equivalent of nearly five Hiroshima nuclear blasts. Seventy percent of the so-called smart bombs missed their intended targets, falling sometimes on civilian dwellings, schools, churches, mosques, or empty fields. The 30 percent that blasted on target wiped out Iraq's electrical generating plants and sewage treatment networks. Iraq's infrastructure—bridges, roads, highways, canals, and communication centers—was systematically destroyed.[7]

Just before leaving the United States, a reporter asked me if there were any alternatives to the impending Gulf War. "Yes," I said. "The United States could allow continued usage of UN economic sanctions to coerce Saddam's withdrawal from Kuwait." Who could have known, then, how poorly informed I was? I had no idea how swiftly and violently the economic sanctions would punish innocent Iraqis who had no control over their government. Neither did most U.S. people.

However, crucial information was available to U.S. policy makers. Even though successive U.S. administrations claimed that the sanctions were intended only to contain Iraq and deter Saddam Hussein's regime from acquiring weapons of mass destruction, a 1991 report written by the United States Defense Intelligence Agency (DIA) showed that the United States understood that just six more months of economic sanctions could be expected to thoroughly degrade Iraq's water treatment systems. The report, "Iraq Water Treatment Vulnerabilities," noted that "although Iraq has made a considerable effort to supply pure water to its population, the water treatment system was unreliable even before the United Nations sanctions."[8]

Commenting on the anticipated effect of the economic sanctions, the DIA analysis speculated that, "With no domestic sources of both water treatment, replacement parts, and some essential chemicals, Iraq will continue attempts to circumvent United Nations sanctions to import these vital commodities. Failing to secure supplies will result in a shortage of pure drinking water for much of the population. This could lead to increased incidences, if not epidemics, of disease."[9]

The report also noted that Iraq's rivers "contain biological materials, pollutants, and are laden with bacteria. Unless the water is purified with chlorine, epidemics of such diseases as cholera, hepatitis, and typhoid could occur."[10] By 1991, with importation of chlorine embargoed by sanctions, the chlorine supply in Iraq was, according to the DIA, "critically low." The report concluded that "full degradation of the water treatment system probably will take at least another 6 months."[11]

The sanctions continued for 13 years.

I was a "late arrival" in coming to grips with the question of how to nonviolently resist U.S. addiction to war making. But, with regard to U.S. invasion of Iraq, my involvement was relatively early, as part of the 72-person Gulf Peace Team on the Iraq–Saudi border. Several years later, an even smaller group formed Voices in the Wilderness, aiming to defy the UN/U.S. economic sanctions against Iraq by exercising civil disobedience. We broke those sanctions as often as we could, bringing medicines to Iraqi children and families. We knew, then, what we were doing and why. We felt confident that we could return to the United States with explanations of what we had seen and heard, and we hoped that our testimony could build awareness in the United States about the awful consequences as a silent, economic warfare brutally and lethally punished hundreds of thousands of innocent people, over half of them children under age five.

In the summer of 2000, we spent nine weeks living in the most impoverished area of Iraq's poorest city, Basra. We wanted to show that siege warfare caused intense suffering among people who meant us no harm. During Operation Shock and Awe, the Iraq Peace Team lived alongside Iraqi people, throughout a coming war we hoped we could prevent. We couldn't allow war to sever the bonds that had developed between ourselves and the people who had offered us unstinting hospitality. We remained in Iraq throughout the U.S. bombing and initial months of occupation. In each of these circumstances, we knew what we were doing and why.

But, since the 2003 U.S. invasion and occupation of Iraq, I've been floundering in efforts to nonviolently challenge terrible crimes committed against people bearing the worst consequences of U.S. warfare in Iraq, in Afghanistan, and now, increasingly, in Pakistan. Younger friends of mine, individuals deeply committed to peacemaking in Iraq, maintain a blog titled "War, Endless War."[12] Skillful commentators describe the tsunami of misery caused by the war. The photos of mournful mothers cradling sickened infants poisoned by contaminated water still fill the pages of UN booklets. Asked to speak about conditions we encounter among people who've fled from Iraq, I and several friends deliver heartbreaking stories of bereavement, torture, and displacement endured by people whose entire lives have been marked by "war, endless war." I feel staggered by the bludgeoning force of the U.S. war machine. The war has caused spiraling levels of chaos and revenge. And yet, I generally write or speak from a safe, secure distance.

People sometimes ask me how I find hope or happiness in life, in spite of being intensely aware of so much suffering. Truthfully, the best way to pursue that question is to visit Iraqis who've directly borne the war's consequences. How do they find hope and happiness? They don't receive invitations to speak about their travails, much less find themselves nominated for awards. Since 1991, consistently, in the simplest of homes, I've felt overwhelmed by genuine and generous welcomes from Iraqi friends. The hospitality extended to me and dozens of people who traveled with Voices delegations doesn't obscure impoverishment, loss, pain, and anger. But the friendships and forgiveness extended to us anchors my faith and hope.

In Amman, Jordan, in January 2007, while visiting an Iraqi family living in a wretched home and coping with poverty, disease, and trauma, I felt amazed that in spite of their harsh circumstances, the family extended a warm welcome to me and my friends. Over the course of several visits, I learned that they'd lost their home and all of their material resources in Iraq, because kidnappers holding their 16-year-old son demanded a huge ransom. They sold everything they owned, secured the son's release after he had been tortured for four days, and immediately fled Iraq. Later that year, the family suffered another blow when the father, crushed by the burden of being unable to provide for his family and deranged with anger when he learned that his cousin had been tortured and killed, suddenly disappeared. The 10-year-old son seemed overcome by a numbing depression that wouldn't lift. Each time I visited, he turned away from the family, apparently absorbed in "Tom and Jerry" cartoons on TV. Even when his older brother, the ransomed son, was recognized with medals and applause while playing soccer as an Iraqi representative on an international team, the youngster refused to join in the family's joy. I knew his mother wanted desperately to help her young son emerge from the fog of despair. Certainly his suffering required time for healing. But his knowing mother watched him carefully, and one summer day, when an art teacher and I turned up with a bag of notebooks, art supplies, and small bouncing balls, the boy's mother flashed me an impish smile and began juggling the balls. Her son's eyes widened as he watched his mother playfully juggling, and, slowly, a smile spread across his face. Soon he was shyly giggling in his mother's arms.

The boy's mother did what she could to find happiness and future hope for her family. Here is a story about other mothers, in a U.S. prison, who did what they could to bear a share of the war's burdens. In 2004, I was imprisoned at the Pekin Federal Prison Camp in Pekin, Illinois. I had trespassed at Fort Benning as part of the School of the Americas Watch campaign, and was sentenced to three months in prison. On Saturday, May 1, 2004, several prisoners hurried into the prison library, wanting me to come and see news releases on CNN. "Girl, you gotta' see this," they said. "It's just terrible, what's happening." Together, we watched the photos that are now nearly iconic: "The hooded man," "the man on a leash," "the pyramid," "the man and the dog." The women I knew at Pekin prison would have had good reason to identify with the shame, fear, and anxiety of other prisoners anywhere. But the emotions behind their tearful questions came, I think, from genuine concern for their country. "What's happening to our country?" they asked. "What can we do?"

It was hard to imagine a less relevant spot from which to take action, locked up in a U.S. prison. But, later that day, several of the women approached the warden, seeking permission to gather, twice a day, on the oval track outside the prison, simply to pray. The warden said yes. Initially, a small group of women gathered, holding hands, at sunup and again at sundown, to voice their prayers. Days later, the group enlarged as several dozen women joined the circle. By the time I left the prison, as many as 80 women came together to pray. The women prayed for their children, for children in Iraq, for the children of U.S. military people in Iraq, and for the guards in the prison and their families. They prayed for an end to war. Prayers for forgiveness, prayers for compassion, prayers for peace—these were among the greatest signs of hope I've ever experienced as women held hands, gathered on the oval track at the Pekin prison.

Hand holding hand, we can yet proclaim our nonviolent resistance to what the Rev. Dr. Martin Luther King called "the demonic suction cup" of U.S. militarism. We do that best when we can stand among those who bear the brunt of war and injustice, and therein seek essential compassion and justice.

I think of those who taught me to imagine one hand gently beckoning people into heightened awareness of wrongdoing while the other hand helps offer balance, encouraging people to gain control over their fears. Such hands have been extended to me, throughout my life, but most extraordinarily in prisons, war zones, and impoverished neighborhoods.

When overwhelmed by struggles and fears, when shamed by floundering through preventable calamities wrought by human hands, we can still revere the hands that reach out to us.

NOTES

1. Kelly, 1997, 4.
2. Ibid., 5.
3. Ibid., 5.
4. Ibid., 5.
5. Buncombe, 2007.
6. Balkwill, 2007.

7. Kelly, 1997, 6.
8. U.S. Defense Intelligence Agency, 1991.
9. Ibid.
10. Ibid.
11. Ibid.
12. Electronic Iraq.

CHAPTER 8

HUMAN SECURITY: PROVIDING PROTECTION WITHOUT STICKS AND CARROTS

Christine Schweitzer

This chapter focuses on one sector of the broad field of nonviolent intervention that can be called "nonviolent peacekeeping." Peacekeeping aims to prevent or at least lower the level of violence. While military peacekeeping is dissociative, that is, it aims to keep warring armies apart, unarmed missions try to protect parties within a community: they deal mostly with targeted assassination of individuals, for example, human rights defenders or social activists, or the protection of communities or groups such as refugees returning home. Nonviolent peacekeeping can be used to support those struggling to change their society (nonviolent struggle) or for maintaining their own way of life (nonviolent or social defence), by protecting them and by opening or maintaining open some social space. Sometimes *protective accompaniment* is used as a generic term to describe these activities.

The literature on nonviolent intervention is mainly descriptive. When it does discuss nonviolent peacekeeping, little has been done to put this into a theoretical framework. The important exception is the work on protective

This chapter originally appeared in Howard Clark, ed., *People Power: Unarmed Resistance and Global Solidarity* (London: Pluto Press, 2009).

accompaniment of Mahony and Eguren, especially their book on Peace Brigades International (PBI).[1] They develop a theory of nonviolent deterrence to explain how protective accompaniment works or does not work depending on certain variables.

This chapter, drawing on experiences other than PBI, argues deterrence is not the only mechanism operating in nonviolent peacekeeping and suggests integrating different approaches into a framework of an escalation of conflict without arms.

THE THEORY OF NONVIOLENT DETERRENCE

The deterrent power of international accompaniment is that it raises the costs of attacking an accompanied activist.[2] The aim is to affect the chain of command, from decision makers down, but accompaniment can also give pause to individuals:

> We should not assume that the thugs who pull the trigger are unaffected by international presence. No one wants an unexpected witness around when they are carrying out a crime. The volunteer's presence may have a moral influence on individual perpetrators. It also introduces an uncertainty factor—the attacker does not know what the consequences of this witness will be, so unless he has explicit orders that take the accompaniment into account, he is likely to restrain himself rather than risk getting in trouble with his superior.[3]

Mahony and Eguren go into detail about assessing the impact of accompaniment on political space, and in their subsequent work have further developed procedures on risk assessment for local activists.[4] The key protagonists in their work remain the local activists—those who are primarily exposed to violence, those who invite accompaniment and who at times jointly plan its strategic use.

Two main criticisms have been made of the nonviolent deterrent theory:

1. In many situations, the external governments most likely to apply pressure are North American or European. This could therefore mean, it is argued, that the tactic uses existing power imbalances, neo-colonial dependencies, and patterns of privilege, even to some extent reproducing them.[5]
2. The kind of pressure exerted is usually out of the hands of the nonviolent projects, and might sometimes include military threats. In the case of the OSCE's Kosovo Verification Mission, 1998 to 1999, a large unarmed mission was in effect part of a military escalation: it was introduced by threatening military intervention and its

denunciation of Serbian atrocities in Kosovo prepared the way for
NATO's 1999 military intervention.

Most nonviolent accompaniment organizations are aware of these problems and take steps to mitigate them. This chapter suggests that there is
much to be gained from viewing "protective accompaniment" not just from
the perspective of "deterrence" but also from other perspectives and especially
that of human security.

UNARMED APPROACHES TO HUMAN SECURITY

Human security is distinct from state security. It refers to "freedom for
individuals from basic insecurities caused by gross human rights violations."[6] It widens the notion of threat to include "protection of citizens from
environmental pollution, transnational terrorism, massive population movements, such infectious diseases as HIV/AIDS, and long-term conditions of
oppression and deprivation."[7]

Looking at how NGOs (nongovernmental organizations) provide human
security, Slim and Eguren distinguish five main modes of action:

1. *Denunciation:* publicly pressuring authorities into meeting their obligations and protecting those individuals or groups exposed to abuse.
2. *Persuasion:* further private dialogue to convince authorities to fulfil
   their obligations and protect those exposed to violations.
3. *Mobilization:* discreetly sharing information with selected people,
   bodies, or states with the capacity to influence the authorities to fulfil
   their obligations.
4. *Substitution:* directly providing services or material assistance to the
   victims of violations.
5. *Support to structures and services:* empowering existing national and/or
   local structures by helping projects that enable them to carry out
   their functions to protect individuals and groups.[8]

Methods used include humanitarian assistance, presence, and accompaniment; monitoring and human rights reporting; and humanitarian advocacy.
Apart from substitution, the other modes of action directly refer to the goal
of opening space and protecting civil society in resistance. As well as *deterrence*, two other mechanisms are at work: *persuasion* defined as making
authorities act of their own accord, and *substitution* defined as the NGO acting in place of the authorities.

The Nonviolent Peaceforce Feasibility study—after studying many examples of peace teams, civil peace services, larger-scale unarmed monitoring

missions as well as military peacekeeping—identified the following sources of protection in addition to deterrence.[9]

- *Identity.* Factors here might be age, gender, country of origin, religion, and others.
- *Role* (peacekeeper) and *who you represent* (for example, the UN). This has become important in international missions when members of those missions would probably not have been respected because of their identity alone.
- *Law and tradition.* (For example, social norms against harming unarmed opponents or of hospitality).
- *Communication*: making oneself known and trusted by creating personal relationships, using rational argument and moral appeal, or setting examples, by acting in ways that differ from usual, expected patterns (such as working in teams whose members come from nations known as enemies of each other).[10]

NONVIOLENT PEACEFORCE IN SRI LANKA

Nonviolent Peaceforce (NP) shows some of these nondeterrent factors at work in Sri Lanka. NP is a young international NGO founded with the goal of developing an alternative to military peacekeeping through deploying large numbers of nonviolent field staff. It launched its first project in Sri Lanka in late 2003 at the invitation of and in partnership with local groups. NP in Sri Lanka (NPSL) consists of a headquarters in Colombo and five teams of approximately 20 to 25 internationally recruited field team members (most of them from countries from the Global South), applying unarmed peacekeeping methods such as protective accompaniment, mediation, observing, and reporting in volatile areas in the North and East of Sri Lanka. Their objectives are to reduce the level of tension and prevent violence; support and improve the safety, confidence, and ability of Sri Lankan peacemakers and other civilians to address conflict in nonviolent ways; and work with Sri Lankans to provide human security and deter resumption of violent conflict in partnership with Sri Lankans.

Primary partners and beneficiaries of NPSL's work are Community-Based Organizations (CBOs) working to prevent violence and protect human rights on the ground. In addition NP has entered into agreements with national NGOs to assist with election monitoring, accompaniment, and the creation of a Shanti Sena (Peace Army). NPSL is also partnering and cooperating with international NGOs and a UN agency. It has played key roles in resolving disputes among ethnic and other groups, securing the release of child soldiers, providing protective presence in camps for displaced people and at temple festivals, monitoring the delivery of aid to Tsunami-affected areas, and accompanying local aid workers who are under threat in certain areas.

The first field team members were trained in the approach of George Lakey of Training for Change—emphasizing four elements of nonviolent peacekeeping: accompaniment, presence, monitoring, and interpositioning. They were to apply the first three. However, on arriving in Sri Lanka, it quickly became clear that these elements did not constitute the full repertoire of activity for NPSL.

Ellen Furnari summarizing the early internal reports, noted that specific methods and activities included:[11]

- connecting people to resources
- linking CBOs with national NGOs and International Organizations (IOs)
- facilitating people to connect with local leaders/authorities
- networking CBOs in different places with each other, making them known to other people
- accompanying activists or other threatened people
- providing transportation when appropriate for peace work, crisis management, or protection
- presence at events or places at risk
- facilitation within or between communities including mediation and/or building bridges over communication and community barriers
- documentation of threats to human rights and/or violence
- support of local groups and individuals including accompanying local NGO workers as requested
- documentation, monitoring, and fact-finding that contributes to rumor control or supports nonviolent problem solving
- visiting and listening
- consulting with local activists and people in general on options of what to do in crisis
- supporting the development of the Rapid Deployment Peace Brigade of Sarvodaya
- providing safe places to meet
- introducing International Non-Governmental Organization (INGO) and IOs to areas that are difficult, remote, or familiar to NP
- helping build nonviolent alternatives
- supporting early warning efforts
- supporting new, emerging leaders working for nonviolent solutions to individual and community problems
- training in nonviolence and nonviolent methods and sharing inspiration and experiences of peace and human rights work from different parts of the world or different regions of Sri Lanka

- supporting free and fair elections through work with People's Action for Free and Fair Elections (PAFFREL)
- being a trusted partner to think about and plan difficult issues, especially in a crisis.

This list—together with the detailed team reports not publicly available—indicate that additional elements are necessary to accompaniment, presence, and monitoring.[12] Two major sets of activities link people to authorities or agencies and support meetings and dialogue at the community level, while training is a further addition. Clearly, none of these would fit into the classic "dissociative" definition of peacekeeping. However, they are part of a strategy to provide human security since most have the goal of increasing people's well-being by helping them to get access to aid, solving conflicts that otherwise would probably lead to communal violence and killings, and helping civil society groups to come together to develop their own activities against violence and human rights violations. Moreover, this list matches rather well with the five modes of action of Slim and Eguren—only "substitution" is missing.

NP has neither the means of enforcement available to "robust" (military) peacekeepers, nor does it have "carrots" in forms of humanitarian aid. This has often required explanation and at first some disappointed expectations by local people who associate INGOs with aid. NP found that it needed a lot of time to explain its particular approach of nonviolent peacekeeping, and finding and building trust.

Until recently, if asked what NP's source for security of its own staff was, the answer would have been: "to be known and trusted by the local community." So the impact has depended on personal relations: "our relationships deepen as trust builds over time and as our own understanding of situations matures, we are able to have more impact."

Although NP started to build up an international Emergency Response Network following the example of PBI, this network is much less effective. During the first two years in Sri Lanka it was never used, and when it was used—twice in early 2006—the response rate was disappointing. Therefore NP falls short of having the kind of international clout needed in the eyes of PBI to achieve protection for those they accompany and for their own staff. Nevertheless, NP has been a protection in many cases. Countless times teams have accompanied local activists and aid workers, mediated in community conflicts, and coordinated and maintained a presence at events where forced recruitment (abduction of children) was feared.

In May 2006, however, NP and some other INGOs came under direct attack by unknown perpetrators. A grenade exploded in front of their office, wounding one of its international staff. Although not knowing for sure, the assumption is that NP's nonpartisan approach, which has involved contacts and accompaniment to all sides in the multiple-sided conflicts in that area of Sri Lanka, has become a threat to one or the other of these sides. The trust that NP had built in the community had not been sufficient to protect it from the attack (though of course the perpetrators themselves may have come from outside the community). From this point NP began to engage more forcefully than before in the strategy of nonviolent deterrence, using its contacts to officials, international agencies, and embassies to develop international clout.

BALKAN PEACE TEAM

The Balkan Peace Team (BPT) was an international volunteer project working in Croatia and the Federal Republic of Yugoslavia between 1994 and 2001.[13] It had a broader mandate than PBI or NP, although it shared the goal of opening space for local actors rather than being one of the countless NGOs in the area following their own agendas and doing their own externally-planned projects. Its main focuses were protection and support of dialogue, with protection being more important in Croatia, while support of dialogue at the civil society level had priority in Serbia and Kosovo.[14] Many BPT activities in Croatia had to do with human security. The teams accompanied local human rights activists in trying to prevent the illegal eviction of Serbs from their homes and monitoring the situation in the areas militarily reintegrated into Croatia in 1995 to deter harassment or worse of the remaining Serbs.

BPT was an experiment in combining several roles that other projects tended to keep apart. Unlike many peace building projects, it focused on human security/protection (civil peacekeeping) without rigidly limiting its role to this one aspect. And it allowed itself to get involved in a range of peace building activities without feeling that doing so would lose its character or endanger its nonpartisanship.

The ways in which BPT made a difference included:

- Serving a *preventive* function in regard to potential human rights violations.
- Fulfilling a *mediating* role between local NGOs and international organizations or NGOs. In Croatia, BPT was often called on because, as an international NGO, it had easier access to other international organizations than local activists. Bigger international bodies sometimes paid lip-service to local involvement but rarely took local groups seriously.

- Serving as a *bridge* between local NGOs or private citizens and local authorities in the same way as NP does in Sri Lanka.
- Facilitating *contact* between NGOs from "different sides." As internationals, BPT had more freedom of movement between the conflict areas than local NGOs.
- This placed the organization in the position to *support civil society dialogue.* Meetings mediated by BPT between activists and students from Serbia proper and Kosovo did not take place abroad (as with most dialogue projects), but with people accompanied by BPT to visit each other in their towns, so giving participants more sense of ownership over the meeting than in an international workshop.
- Carrying out an active *advocacy role.* BPT alerted other international organizations about, for example, the policy of Croatia regarding refugees or occasions when the practices of international bodies were not very helpful.

BPT was able to play these different functions because it was an international project. And in many instances its effectiveness probably can be explained by the deterrence theory. But there is one important modification: The former Yugoslavia was an arena with a multitude of international interveners, many—and the most conspicuous—of them being backed by military force. BPT made a point of distancing itself from high-profile international interventions, both on the symbolic level (not using the fancy four-wheel-drive white cars favored by the UN and EU) and on the practical level by seeking dialogue rather than invoking the threat of international power. So while it certainly profited from this power, its approach was different from PBI's, and the sources of its influence consisted rather in their being different from the rest of the international community.

ADDITIONAL EXAMPLES AND DISCUSSIONS

- Peacekeeping is not confined to "internationals." There are more local or national initiatives than tend to be recognized in international literature. The probably best-known examples are the Pakistani and Indian peace armies as developed by Abdul Ghaffar Khan and Gandhi, and a number of local peace teams or peace monitoring missions that can be found in such varied countries as Croatia, Indonesia, Philippines, Sri Lanka, and, of course, India today.[15] Their effectiveness is probably mainly derived from respect in the community, being centered inward, not outward to the international world. The focus of the Indian Shanti Sena is and was on convincing those ready to apply violence and to strengthen the communities to resist that violence, using methods of dialogue, counteracting rumors, physical interpositioning, and aid and reconstruction.[16]

- A relationship of a two-layered protection scheme has been sketched in NP's work to develop a project in Mindanao, Philippines. In brief, this system is that the local communities look after the international field team members, making sure that they do not fall victim to kidnapping or violence, while the internationals would carry with them the "international eye," being witnesses from the outside.

- The Nonviolent Peaceforce Feasibility Study found that larger-scale unarmed peacekeeping missions, mostly governmental, relied on local people for security, albeit to differing degrees. "Relying on the Bougainville people to ensure the safety of peace monitors reinforces the realization that peace on Bougainville is the responsibility of the Bougainville people. They are only too aware that, should the safety of the PMG [Peace Monitoring Mission] be placed at risk, there is a very real danger that the peace process will falter. This was emphasized on a number of occasions when Bougainvillians assisted patrols in difficult circumstances."[17]

- Research on the concept of a nonviolence without deterrence or force by a group of German researchers led by Martin Arnold suggests that there is indeed some almost universal mechanism of principled nonviolence taking effect by making an opponent change his or her behavior through what they call "guetekraft," which they see as an equivalent to "force of love."[18]

LOOKING FORWARD: THE ESCALATION OF NONVIOLENT INTERVENTION

The examples above demonstrate that there are mechanisms other than deterrence to provide human security. In regard to keeping opponents apart, there are obviously different approaches to achieve that. One of the major ones identified is building on trust and protection by the local community, so that attackers would refrain from action not because of fear of sanctions or repercussions from the international wider community, but from within their own community. This seems to be a mechanism working both for international and for local unarmed peacekeepers. But this way of achieving effect seems not always to work as the example of NP showed when in spite of seemingly good relations in the community an attack was carried out against the team. Therefore the idea suggests itself that there is some kind of escalation model of nonviolent intervention. This is the question that will be pursued in the last paragraphs of this chapter.

NONVIOLENT ESCALATION

The activities of international nonviolent intervention discussed here have all been based on an invitation from local activists and have at least to some degree been strategized with local activists. Any escalation model therefore needs to be based on the strategy of local groups and developed as a transnational strategic element. Furthermore, to the extent that the focus of escalation is nonviolent peacekeeping, human security, or protection, it has to be viewed in the context of the range of activities—by locals as well as internationals—under that heading.

Theodor Ebert, building on Gene Sharp's work, has defined three stages of escalation in nonviolent action; each stage having both subversive/opposition and constructive elements.[19] This escalation is presented in the context of the growing extent to which those ruled withdraw their consent and refuse to obey. However, while transnational nonviolent intervention works in alliance with local movements, it does not really include this dimension of struggle. For instance, a powerful weapon of nonviolent movements, such as withdrawal of cooperation, is not available to international nonviolent peacekeepers on the ground, even if ultimately sanctions and boycotts might be tools used by transnational movements of solidarity. Sharp himself has commented on transnational intervention that:

> World opinion on the side of the nonviolent group will by itself rarely produce a change in the opponent's policies. Frequently a determined opponent can ignore hostile opinion until and unless it is accompanied by, or leads to, shifts in power relationships, or threatens to do so.[20]

This finds support from John Paul Lederach who argues that, for conflict transformation to take place, a counter power has to be developed to challenge the unequal distribution of political power, to clarify the issues in conflict, and to bring about a new relationship between the parties in conflict.[21] It may be helpful to lay out some of the functions of intervention according to a scale of nonviolence.

1. Protection through persuasion of those who would otherwise threaten protected parties.
2. Protection through sources of power internal to the society in which the conflict takes place. Here the interveners may be either locals (Shanti Sena) or internationals who have gained respect and trust through their previous work.
3. Protection through mobilization (discreet sharing of information with those who can influence those responsible).

4. Protection through shaming (public denunciation) that often goes together with the threat of undefined or vague sanctions ('the international eye')—the PBI deterrence approach.

At this point the escalation ladder becomes increasingly coercive and the mechanisms are more likely to be carried out by governments than by nonviolent groups.

5. Protection through the threat of concrete sanctions. As the UN has applied other sanctions when military peacekeeping is failing, it should be possible that a nonviolent peacekeeping mission could also be backed up in this way.
6. Protection through international sanctions.

By now, the escalation ladder is in transition from coercive to military action.

7. Protection through the threat with direct enforcement—an example would be the (unarmed) Kosovo Verification Mission of the OSCE in Kosovo from 1998 to 1999, that made the threat with a NATO intervention as backup.
8. Direct military action.

This chapter needs to end with two warnings. The first is that all this is highly speculative and based more on intuitive insights and on assumptions held by local partners or the interveners themselves than on hard-core facts. The second is that this escalation ladder does not necessarily reflect growing effectiveness. It would need much further and comparative research into projects and missions of this type of unarmed or nonviolent intervention to be able to draw conclusions on that question.

NOTES

1. Mahony and Eguren, 1997. See also Nagler, 2004, 28–35.
2. As proposed by Mahony and Eguren, 1997; also Mahony, 2004, 2006.
3. Mahony, 2004, 8.
4. Mahony and Eguren, 1997.
5. Kinane, 2000; Boothe and Smithey, 2007.
6. A Human Security Doctrine for Europe, 2004.
7. Human Security Now, 2003, 6.
8. Derived from Slim and Eguren, 2004.
9. Schweitzer et al, 2001.
10. Ibid., Chapter 2, Summary
11. Furnari, 2006, 260–268.
12. Nonviolent Peaceforce, 2006.

13. The Balkan Peace Team was founded and run by a group of mainly European-based peace organizations from Austria, France, Germany, the Netherlands, Switzerland and the United Kingdom. They included Austrian Peace Service, International Fellowship of Reconciliation, Peace Brigades International, War Resisters' International, Federation for Social Defense (Germany), Brethren Service (U.S.), and MAN (Mouvement pour une alternative nonviolente [France]). Its tightly-run coordinating office was based in Germany.

14. Müller, 2004; Schweitzer and Clark, 2002; Schweitzer 2005.

15. Further examples include Shanti Sena, Sri Lanka; peace teams set up in eastern Croatia; the Philippine NGO, Bantay Ceasefire monitoring in Mindanao.

16. Weber, 1996, 116–117.

17. Foster, 1999.

18. See www.guetekraft.de (only in German) and Arnold, 2011.

19. Ebert, 1981.

20. Sharp, 1973, 662.

21. Lederach, 1997.

CHAPTER 9

Psyched up to Save Psychology: A Tale of Activists' Efforts to Resist Complicity in U.S. Human Rights Violations Post–9/11

Jill Latonick-Flores and Daniel J. Adamski

Individuals form social activist groups based, in part, on shared values and on aspects of their own identity that support these values. As professionals ethically committed to "do no harm," psychologists began organizing among themselves when, in late 2004, the *New York Times* reported that detainees at the U.S. detention center at Guantanamo Bay, Cuba, were being treated in strange and seemingly abusive ways.[1]

The International Committee of the Red Cross (ICRC), a decidedly independent source for the monitoring of international human rights compliance, reported that a group of "psychologists and psychological workers" had played an uncertain role in the mistreatment of persons held in detention centers worldwide, including the center at Guantanamo Bay, Cuba.[2] One aspect of this mistreatment was described as mental torture and was conceptualized as distinct from physical torture. So-called Behavior Science Consultation Teams had advised military interrogators in a manner that raised suspicions about their role in potential human rights violations. Alarmingly, the ICRC declared that due to the conditions of their confinement, the treatment of detainees in some instances was "tantamount to torture."[3] The article highlighted core issues about the role of psychologists in these circumstances, including the ethical considerations of psychological workers as related to secret national security situations, and it specified the obscure characteristics of abuses, noting ". . . one regular procedure was making uncooperative prisoners strip to their underwear, having them sit in a chair while shackled hand and foot to a bolt in the floor, and forcing them to endure strobe lights and loud rock and rap music played through two close loudspeakers, while the air-conditioning was turned up to maximum levels."[4]

After 9/11 Vice President Dick Cheney told the American public that it was time to remove constraints on human rights protections and to work the "dark side" of intelligence gathering.[5] And according to Cofer Black, onetime director of the Central Intelligence Agency's (CIA) counterterrorism unit: "After 9/11, the gloves came off."[6] *Newsweek* reporters Michael Isikoff and Stuart Taylor Jr., said the term "the legal equivalent of outer space," which was widely used to describe the detention center at Guantanamo Bay, Cuba, was first used by a Bush administration working group in the immediate aftermath of 9/11 as the group looked for ways to circumvent U.S. obligations to international human rights laws.[7] Without Geneva protections, detainees were afforded less legal protection than were iguanas on the island.[8] These events and others like them drew anger from citizens and social activists alike. The Convention Against Torture, which the United States signed in 1988, states no public emergency or state of war can be used as a reason to disengage from human rights commitments.[9]

When the *Times* report was released, institutional policies and domestic adherence to international law was in disarray. In some situations, certain high-ranking public officials, such as attorneys John Yoo and David Addington, were wittingly complicit in the remaking of American's commitments to international human rights treaties and obligations. In other situations, the purpose and implications of Bush administration legal changes led to confusion and unwitting participation in the abuses.[10]

According to White House legal advisor Alberto Gonzales, the Geneva Conventions were rendered "quaint" in the aftermath of 9/11.[11] Secretary of Defense Donald Rumsfeld proclaimed the detainees at Guantanamo Bay were the "worst of the worst" of terrorists and they likely held information that could be used to prevent further attacks.[12] Discussions as to whether the practice of water boarding constituted torture dominated political conversations. At a White House press conference, President Bush questioned the meaning of human rights protections: "And that Common Article 3 says that, you know, there will be no outrages upon human dignity. It's like – it's very vague. What does that mean, outrages upon human dignity? That's a statement that is wide open to interpretation."[13]

While the administration overtly professed to a commitment to human rights, it worked to redefine torture and abuse. Domestic law now permitted tactics long known to be violations of human rights and granted impunity to purveyors of the new tactics. Nevertheless, like other professionals, psychologists have the privilege and duty to uphold the highest standards of morality within the ethical and legal realms of their science. To these ends, two principles are foundational to the ethical practice of psychology: to improve human welfare and to "do no harm." If professional ethics conflict with laws, then these basic principles must supersede the law. Post–9/11 concerns brought into question whether national security was a sufficient reason to re-define professional psychology ethics in such a way that the moral dictum to "do no harm" was relegated from a mandate to an elective.

A few persons within the top echelon of the American Psychological Association (APA), the largest group of psychologists in the United States, made efforts to redefine the practice of psychology in a way they believed would best meet national security goals. One example of their efforts is this message from Dr. Gerald Koocher, APA president in 2006:

> In many of the circumstances we will discuss . . . [how] the psychologist's role may bear on people who are not "clients" in the traditional sense. Example, the psychologist employed by the CIA, Secret Service, FBI, etc., who helps formulate profiles for risk prevention, negotiation strategy, destabilization, etc., or the psychologist asked to assist interrogators in eliciting data or detecting dissimulation with the intent of preventing harm to many other people. In this case the client is the agency, government, and ultimately the people of the nation (at risk). The goal of such psychologists' work will ultimately be the protection of others (i.e., innocents) by contributing to the incarceration, debilitation, or even death of the potential perpetrator, who will often remain unaware of the psychologists' involvement.[14]

The early challenges of the psychologists' anti-torture advocacy were twofold. First, the profession needed greater understanding of the processes of legal exceptionalism that permitted widespread abuses. Second, they needed greater understanding of how they had obscured these changes in public conversation and of how they were replicated within the APA. For many activists-psychologists, nothing less than the "soul of psychology" was at stake.[15]

Psychologists began to mobilize by targeting myths about the effectiveness of torture and psychology in interrogation and resolved to uphold their "do no harm" commitments. Psychologists-turned-activists urged the APA to adhere to international law standards and appealed to its constituents' ethical integrity as a means of maintaining a core professional identity.

Using broad strokes, this chapter outlines the key developments in the psychologist–human rights activists' efforts to restore integrity to the APA.

HISTORICAL MISUSE OF PSYCHOLOGY

After 9/11, many human rights organizations were well aware that for over 50 years, from Vietnam to Honduras to Guatemala, psychologists had been involved in the development and dissemination of torture and abuse in general and the development of mental torture in particular.[16] The public, including many people engaged in the profession of psychology, seemed less aware of the misuse and abuse of psychological knowledge. Central to this condition was the government's effort to cover up the misuse of psychological knowledge through use of a sanitized language.

In 1963, after years of research into Soviet mind control experiments, the KUBARK manual (a CIA code name for itself) was published. The manual outlined ways that the military could make use of psychological knowledge to further its goals. Specifically, it outlined the nature of the use of psychological knowledge and the militarization of scientific findings:

> It is true that American psychologists have devoted somewhat more attention to Communist interrogation techniques, particularly "brainwashing," than to U.S. practices. Yet they have conducted scientific inquiries into many subjects that are closely related to interrogation: the effects of debility and isolation, the polygraph, reactions to pain and fear, hypnosis and heightened suggestibility, narcosis, etc. This work is of sufficient importance and relevance that it is no longer possible to discuss interrogation significantly without reference to the psychological research conducted in the past decade. For this reason a major purpose of this study is to focus relevant scientific findings upon CI [counterintelligence] interrogation. Every effort has been made to report and interpret these findings in our own language, in place of the terminology employed by the psychologists.[17]

This tradition continued post–9/11 in the APA's use of Orwellian language.[18] In a letter to the American Psychological Association, the American Civil Liberties Union (ACLU) urged the organization to stand firm on its ethical commitment, declaring: "The history of torture is inexorably linked to the misuse of scientific and medical knowledge. As we move fully into the 21st century, it is no longer enough to denounce or to speak out against torture; rather, we must sever the connection between healers and tormentors once and for all. As guardians of the mind, psychologists are duty bound to promote the humane treatment of all people."[19]

THE DARK SIDE

On September 16, 2001, Vice President Dick Cheney met with Tim Russert on the television show, *Meet the Press.* Cheney detailed the administration's response to the recent terrorist attacks. In doing so, he outlined procedures he thought were essential to American success in the fight against terrorists. Cheney encouraged the necessity of "working the dark side" of the intelligence world.[20] In time, his short description would prove central to anti-torture advocates' illumination of the immorality of Bush administration tactics:

MR. RUSSERT: When Osama bin Laden took responsibility for blowing up the embassies in Kenya and Tanzania, U.S. embassies, several hundred died, the United States launched 60 Tomahawk missiles into his training sites in Afghanistan. It only emboldened him. It only inspired him and seemed even to increase his recruitment. Is it safe to say that that kind of response is not something we're considering, in that kind of minute magnitude?

VICE PRES. CHENEY: I'm going to be careful here, Tim, because I— clearly it would be inappropriate for me to talk about operational matters, specific options or the kinds of activities we might undertake going forward. We do, indeed, though, have, obviously, the world's finest military. They've got a broad range of capabilities. And they may well be given missions in connection with this overall task and strategy.

We also have to work, though, sort of the dark side, if you will. We've got to spend time in the shadows in the intelligence world. A lot of what needs to be done here will have to be done quietly, without any discussion, using sources and methods that are available to our intelligence agencies, if we're going to be successful. That's the world these folks operate in, and so it's going to be vital for us to use any means at our disposal, basically, to achieve our objective.

MR. RUSSERT: There have been restrictions placed on the United States intelligence gathering, reluctance to use unsavory characters, those who violated human rights, to assist in intelligence gathering. Will we lift some of those restrictions?

VICE PRES. CHENEY: Oh, I think so. I think the—one of the byproducts, if you will, of this tragic set of circumstances is that we'll see a very thorough sort of reassessment of how we operate and the kinds of people we deal with. There's—if you're going to deal only with sort of officially approved, certified good guys, you're not going to find out what the bad guys are doing. You need to be able to penetrate these organizations. You need to have on the payroll some very unsavory characters if, in fact, you're going to be able to learn all that needs to be learned in order to forestall these kinds of activities. It is a mean, nasty, dangerous dirty business out there, and we have to operate in that arena. I'm convinced we can do it; we can do it successfully. But we need to make certain that we have not tied the hands, if you will, of our intelligence communities in terms of accomplishing their mission.

MR. RUSSERT: These terrorists play by a whole set of different rules. It's going to force us, in your words, to get mean, dirty, and nasty in order to take them on, right? And they should realize there will be more than simply a pinprick bombing.

VICE PRES. CHENEY: Yeah, the—I think it's—the thing that I sense— and, of course, that's only been a few days, but I have never seen such determination on the part of—well, my colleagues in government, on the part of the American people, on the part of our friends and allies overseas, and even on the part of some who are not ordinarily deemed friends of the United States, determined in this particular instance to shift and not be tolerant any longer of these kinds of actions or activities.

In an ironic twist of fate, and perhaps unknown to Cheney himself, his framing of the "dark side" term facilitated greater understanding of the secret activities by allowing people to generalize meaning of the term across multiple domains of experiences: that is, to connect the dots between overt support of human rights and covert violation of U.S. treaties and obligations.

During the interview, Cheney specifically described a reassessment of U.S. operations around wartime tactics and in forming alliances with those persons who violate human rights. In short, "No discussions" meant don't ask questions of your government. "Operating in the shadows" meant secrecy without accountability. "Having on the payroll some very unsavory characters," meant colluding with those who violate international standards for human rights. "Certified good guys" implied that adhering to international human rights laws was restrictive. "We have to operate . . . in the mean, nasty, dangerous dirty business" to be "successful" was a warning that further harm could come to the American people if the "dark side" was not accommodated. Further, Cheney implied that there was no other choice in the matter.

Over the ensuing years, according to popular opinion polls, Cheney's advocacy of "dark side" strategies seemed in line with many of those people surveyed. A January 2005 Associated Press poll found that 53 percent of Americans would agree to torture, with 37 percent opposed. In late 2005, similar results were obtained with 61 percent of Americans surveyed believing torture is justified and only 36 percent saying it could never be justified.

By 2008, a Pew Survey found that 48 percent of those surveyed believed that torture is acceptable. Eighty-two percent of FOX News Channel viewers said that torture is acceptable in "a wide range" of situations.[21]

SAYING "YES" TO TORTURE BY DEHUMANIZING OTHERS

> Torture is a war crime; a crime against humanity. And, assuming the polls have it right, also part of the "accumulation" is the fact that a majority of our fellow citizens have been frightened into believing that it is permissible to dehumanize others to the point of torture.[22]
>
> —Ray McGovern, Ex-CIA Analyst and Antiwar Activist

Popular culture characterized torture as an effective means of gaining information for national security purposes. In the United States and the United Kingdom, public understanding of torture was influenced by portrayals on television of its circumstances and forms. Jack Bauer, the anti-hero policeman played by Keifer Sutherland in the series 24, is credited with making great strides for the good using torture tactics. Military interrogators in Guantanamo Bay and Abu Ghraib reported soldiers imitated the tactics portrayed on the television series.[23]

In a series of articles titled "Torture Hits Home," *Mother Jones* magazine discussed the FOX News Channel series *Voluntary Confinement*. The reality show subjected people to "days of isolation . . . just a few hours of sleep and minimal food. [And] . . . to the amplified screams of infants and hours stuffed into a small box that kept getting hotter." One contestant saw "little gray rabbits staring up at him." The producers of the show felt as if their tactics were safe and ethical because the process was vetted by psychologists and physicians who monitored the participants' destabilization.[24]

Mother Jones magazine reporter Michael Mechanic asked psychologist Philip Zimbardo, a professor emeritus at Stanford University well known for his 1971 Stanford Prison Experiment, whether he thought the television show had any redeeming characteristics. "My sense," Zimbardo replied, "is it's a debasement of human nature, and it doesn't matter if the process is a competition, a game show, or a war."

Psychologists, like other human rights organizers, recognized that this sort of entertainment desensitizes audiences to the suffering of others. In the process everyone involved is dehumanized. Public figures engaged in the same practice, repeatedly depicting the detainees at Guantanamo Bay as the "worst of the worst."[25]

When coupled with the myth that torture was an effective means of dehumanization, these descriptions seemed likely to foster the acceptance of torture and abuse. Psychologists for Social Responsibility, an organization of psychologists working to build cultures of peace with social justice, collaborated with military interrogators to deconstruct the myth that torture was an effective means of gaining information for national security purposes.[26] The findings from this collaboration were distributed to human rights organizations in the United States and around the globe.

Survivors of torture taught human rights advocates about abuses and the processes that enfold them after the events of 9/11. Among untold dozens of others, the stories of Moazzam Begg, an Islamic bookstore owner of British descent who was captured by U.S. forces in Afghanistan and psychologically and physically abused at Bagram, Afghanistan, and Guantanamo Bay, Cuba, helped human rights advocates weave together the insidious processes of legal exceptionalism and psychological torture.[27] Mahar Arar, a Canadian citizen born in Syria, was abducted by U.S. officials as he traveled through New York. He was taken to Syria and tortured. On his release, he made efforts to communicate to the public how innocents could be kidnapped and abused during the United States's practice of "extraordinary rendition."[28] Anti-torture advocates communicated stories of the tortured and disappeared when they could not speak for themselves. Physicians for Human Rights, an organization of health professionals who work to investigate the health consequences of human rights violations and stop them, was instrumental in informing concerned persons about the insidious nature of psychological torture. This effort culminated in the subsequent release of an in-depth report titled "Leave No Marks." In addition to specifying differences between physical torture and psychological torture, the report sheds light on ways that psychological torture could be concealed from human rights observers and how to obscure the ways that it harmed prisoners. Torture Abolition and Survivors Support Coalition, the only organization founded by and for survivors of torture, gave their accounts of the effects of mental torture in a video presentation called *Breaking the Silence.*[29]

ORGANIZING FOR A MORAL PSYCHOLOGY: THE EFFORT TO BE HUMAN

After the ICRC report was leaked, several professional associations in the United States began issuing resolutions clearly stating their expectations for ethical conduct within the confines of their professional ethics. The APA and the American Medical Association set clear standards by stating their members should not participate in interrogations. The APA responded to member dissent by setting up a task force called Psychological Ethics and National Security (PENS).[30] Eventually, in opposition to the APA efforts to include psychologists in potentially unethical positions during military interrogations, two members of the task force, psychologists David Wessels and Jean Maria Arrigo, called on the APA to set aside the report and its conclusions. Wessels resigned from the task force and Arrigo went on to develop guidelines for ethical interrogation practices. Arrigo was also instrumental in developing support networks for whistleblowers who came forward during the Abu Ghraib scandal. Amy Goodman, host of *Democracy Now!*, spoke with Wessels and Arrigo in the first of many interviews on APA complicity with Bush administration torture and abuse tactics.[31]

Many psychologists continued to work within the auspices of the APA to create needed change (the APA has many subdivisions in which psychologists address specific areas of the science). Other concerned psychologists sought to effect change by forming alliances with human rights organizations, lawyers, and other anti-torture activists. The most outspoken psychologists submitted suggestions to the APA leadership council and encouraged the highest attainable ethical positions.[32]

The Coalition for an Ethical Psychology is a small group consisting of research psychologists, psychoanalysts, an attorney, and at least one psychologist specializing in military ethics. This group was highly successful in capturing media attention, which helped explain the political affairs within the APA and its tendencies to undermine "do no harm" principles. *Newsweek*, the *Boston Globe*, and the *New York Times* covered their efforts.[33]

Frustrated with APA leadership between 2007 and 2008, the group successfully orchestrated the bid of one of its members, Steven J. Reisner, for the APA presidency. Reisner obtained an overwhelming majority of support in preliminary rounds of membership polls but lost in the final vote. Nevertheless, his human rights—based platform was publicized throughout APA candidacy forums, and in the process large numbers of APA members obtained necessary background information about the wrongs of the APA engagement policy. Significantly, Reisner's candidacy statement contained a plea for humanizing values in face of life's tragedies:

> I come from a family of Jewish refugees. My mother is from a small town in Poland. She is the only member of her immediate family who survived the Auschwitz concentration camp. My father is from Warsaw. When the war began, and the Soviet Union and Germany conquered and divided Poland, my father fled into Soviet Russia. He was picked up by the secret police and interrogated with the classic Soviet methods (which now have become American methods).

My mother told me a story about the first roundup of Jews in her small town when she was 14. The Nazis pushed all the Jews into a small circle and beat those on the outside of the circle with clubs. My mother observed that some of the Jews tried to protect the weak, the elderly, and the very young, while others pushed the weaker ones to the outside to protect themselves. "I knew from that moment that to be human would not always come naturally," she told me. "I knew that I would have to make an effort to be human."[34]

RESOLUTIONS

Between 2005 and 2008, the APA leadership was presented with a series of resolutions stating that the association should adhere to the highest possible ethical standards. Each submission was met with increasingly stronger statements that the APA was "unequivocally opposed" to torture, yet the APA's complicity in human rights violations remained. All resolutions contained contradictions and large loopholes that permitted violations of international human rights obligations and subjected psychologists to unethical situations, even if unwittingly.[35] Furthermore, the principles expressed could not be practically applied to the problems described by APA critics and human rights advocates, nor could they be overseen by the APA.

During the summer of 2007, when the APA held its annual convention in San Francisco, 85 percent of the APA council refused to endorse an independent amendment to its resolutions on psychological ethics that stated ". . . the roles of psychologists in settings in which detainees are deprived of adequate protection of their human rights should be limited as health personnel to the provision of psychological treatment."[36]

This refusal led many psychologists to believe the APA leadership endorsed the use of psychological knowledge for harm under the guise of national security operations.[37] A town hall meeting was held to discuss the status of the changes in ethics and the efforts the APA was making to address the participation of psychologists in detention centers and interrogations. During this meeting, the APA leadership informed Amy Goodman of *Democracy Now!* that the media were permitted just 10 minutes to cover the discussions. Goodman took to the microphone and told meeting participants of the APA's attempts to censure large portions of the public discussion. Tellingly, participants voted that the media should continue to cover the event and they did.[38] The membership wanted transparency in its workings, even if the leadership did not.

In later months, Goodman continued to inform the public about APA/ Bush administration collaborations by claiming many other psychologists were "in denial" about these relations.[39]

Those within the APA who advocated psychologist engagement in military interrogations did so, in part, because they felt psychologists could help ensure interrogations were "safe, legal and effective."[40] In acting as "safety officers" psychologists could ensure that the treatment of prisoners during interrogations did not slide into the realm of torture. Critics, however, claimed psychologists were being used as experts that could provide legitimacy to the Bush administration's legalization and legitimization of torture and abuse.[41]

To protest the APA's participation in interrogations under the guise of acting as safety officers, bestselling author Mary Pipher returned her Presidential Citation award from the APA. In a letter to the association's president, she wrote, ". . . I do not want an award from an organization that sanctions its members' participation in the enhanced interrogations at CIA 'black sites' and at Guantanamo."[42] In August 2008, the Raging Grannies, a peace and advocacy group, many of whom were dressed in brightly colored aprons, protested the claim of the APA's "safety officers" outside the Boston convention by "sounding off" on this uneasy relationship:

I don't know but I've been told
Psychologists are way too bold

They're in bed with Rice and Bush
Ethics gone with a great big whoosh!

They're "guardians" "saving lives"
We don't buy one-uh their lies

Waterboarding, it's a game
Career advancement, with no shame

Dealers of death—torture and pain
They do it for financial gain

They're not Doctor, Mister, Miz
Let's call them what they really is

Murderers with PhDs
Torturing with impunity

We demand that APA
Stop all torture, right away.

Sound Off, Sound Off
Sound Off, Sound Off
Sound Off, 1-2-3-4
NO MORE!

Many more psychologists began to distance themselves from the APA. With the intention of pressuring the APA to increase its commitment to international human rights law, psychologist Ghislane Boulanger founded the "Withhold Apa Dues" activist group. Her effort resulted in several hundred APA members withholding their yearly dues from the APA. Group members were encouraged to write a letter of protest to the Chief Executive Officer of the APA stating their demands for change and offering to resume membership dues once changes were implemented. Members advertised their cause by sporting blue ribbons during APA conventions. After withholding dues for a period of two years, some members chose to leave the APA. Individual letters of resignation were publicized to highlight the outrage of well-known APA members.[43]

Michael Jackson, Associate Professor of Psychology at Earlham University, made a resolution requesting changes in APA policy.[44] Focusing on the conflicts between international human rights laws and changes in domestic laws and APA policies, the resolution called for the adoption of ethical congruency between these areas. Jackson submitted his resolution to his department and then to the APA. His efforts were publicized in *The Chronicle of Higher Education*. Over the next year, 10 universities adopted similar resolutions and sent them to the APA.[45]

The APA continued to create the appearance of complicity in human rights violations as late as 2008 by contributing to the misuse of psychological principles and practices (acts of commission) and failing to respond to well-documented abuses of psychology (acts of omission). With the slogan, "There is no right way to do a wrong thing!" Psychologists for Social Responsibility's End Torture Action Committee outlined ways the APA side-stepped ethical principles and urged the following corrections:

Acts of Commission

- Militarization of psychological knowledge and practice. The APA still lauds its Psychological Ethics and National Security (PENS) report, developed by a task force dominated by military-intelligence officials and consultants, several with direct involvement in chains of command implicated in torture.[46] Given the conditions under which the PENS report was produced, the APA needs to heed the call of the two independent members and set aside the report and its conclusions.
- Dual roles. After Bush administration policies redefined torture from "pain and suffering" to "prolonged pain and suffering," psychologists and others became complicit in calibrating cruelty, under the guise of acting as "safety" officers. This dual role imposes an intractable burden upon psychologists and stands in opposition to established UN human rights procedures and medical ethics.
- Escape clauses. Ethics code 1.02 states that psychologists can choose to follow the ethics code or U.S. law when faced with a conflict between the two. Because U.S. law has been altered to circumvent Geneva

principles, this standard would permit persons to discard Geneva principles and remain compliant with APA ethics. The APA needs to provide clear direction and mandates for international human rights laws
and increase the involvement of the entire membership when making
these decisions.

Acts of Omission

- "Black sites." The APA must advocate to stop torture and to refrain
  from allowing psychologists' participation in secret detention centers.
  Psychologists implicitly lend credibility to structural cruelties when
  operating in settings where persons are held outside of or in violation
  of international law.
- Extraordinary renditions/disappearances. It is unethical for psychologists to actively participate in situations where enforced disappearances and incommunicado detention occur without charge or trial.
  Current APA policy does not address these practices.
- Inadequate safeguards against charges of torture place psychologists
  in jeopardy of charges of war crimes. Of the 19 techniques prohibited
  by the APA in 2007, many techniques—such as isolation and sensory
  deprivation—are used to gather intelligence for national security
  purposes *and* they are often routine conditions of confinement.
  Isolation for up to 30 days was Standard Operating Procedure (SOP)
  at Guantanamo in 2004.[47] In darkened cells or in cells that are
  constantly flooded with light, isolation can contribute to the increased
  dependency of a person on other human beings and to problems
  with concentration, memory, and orientation. Isolation can result in
  hallucinations. Psychologists served as Behavioral Science Consultants
  aiding interrogations during the time this SOP was developed and
  implemented. The APA needs to make clear that these techniques and
  similar ones are unethical, whether used in interrogation or as part
  of the conditions of confinement. Further, it needs to investigate
  potential involvement of psychologists in the implementation of
  isolation and other abuses.
- Unanswered ethics complaints. In 2005, Major John Leso was documented to have been present during portions of the interrogation of
  Mohamed al Qahtani. Despite ethics charges having been filed against
  Major Leso in 2006, two years later, the APA has made no statement
  about these serious charges.[48]

Anti-torture activists asserted psychologists held inadequate authority in
military chain of command situations and were no better equipped to end abuses
than were other professionals. The Red Cross is the official organization whose
duty it is to monitor adherence to international human rights, not the APA.

PSYCHOLOGISTS REJECT THE DARK SIDE[49]

Gradually, the "dark side" metaphor became an easily recognized term that described how the Bush administration veered from its international human rights obligations and encouraged public acquiescence for their new torture paradigm.

Activists, investigators, and human rights organizations made use of the dark side metaphor to expose the underbelly of abuses and related human rights violations along with the processes of legal exceptionalism that accompanied them. Jane Mayer detailed the military's use of psychologists Mitchell and Jenson in her book, *The Dark Side*.[50] Her investigations illuminated the connections between psychological knowledge and psychological practitioners who were said to "reverse engineer" military survival teachings (also known as SERE training) by transforming them into torture tactics that could be used against detainees. Likewise, the documentary *Taxi to the Dark Side* described the kidnapping, torture, and death of an innocent taxi driver presumed to be a terrorist in Afghanistan. An editorial in *The Washington Post* revealed, "Cheney's Dark Side Is Showing."[51]

In late 2007, APA members Dan Aalbers, Ruth Fallenbaum, and Brad Olson took the issues into their own hands after learning of an APA bylaw that allowed the entire membership of the organization to develop policy through voting on referendum proposals. The bylaw requires that 1,000 members support a proposal, which can then be sent to the entire association for a vote. A petition Web site was used to track progress toward obtaining 1,000 signatures and to explain the referendum.[52]

Members produced the following:

Whereas torture is an abhorrent practice in every way contrary to the APA's stated mission of advancing psychology as a science, as a profession, and as a means of promoting human welfare;

Whereas the United Nations Special Rapporteur on Mental Health and the UN Special Rapporteur on Torture have determined that treatment equivalent to torture has been taking place at the United States Naval Base at Guantánamo Bay, Cuba;[53]

Whereas this torture took place in the context of interrogations under the direction and supervision of Behavioral Science Consultation Teams (BSCTs) that included psychologists;[54]

Whereas the Council of Europe has determined that persons held in CIA black sites are subject to interrogation techniques that are also equivalent to torture,[55] and because psychologists helped develop abusive interrogation techniques used at these sites;[56]

Whereas the International Committee of the Red Cross determined in 2003 that the conditions in the U.S. detention facility in Guantánamo

Bay are themselves tantamount to torture,[57] and therefore by their presence psychologists are playing a role in maintaining these conditions;

Be it resolved that psychologists may not work in settings where persons are held outside of, or in violation of, either International Law (e.g., the UN Convention Against Torture and the Geneva Conventions) or the U.S. Constitution (where appropriate), unless they are working directly for the persons being detained or for an independent third party working to protect human rights.[58]

In a video taped presentation that highlighted the urgency of voting for the referendum, Psychologists for Social Responsibility members explained the referendum's goals, sent the tape to pertinent divisions within the APA, and posted it on their Web site and on YouTube. The referendum was also endorsed by a multitude of anti-torture advocates including the School of Americas Watch, Torture Abolition and Survivor Support Coalition, and Physicians for Human Rights.

By 2008, members of the APA held a clearer understanding of the marriage of institutional and government torture tactics. They knew that like the Bush administration, top officials of the APA had taken the wrong side of the struggle. The referendum passed by a majority of votes, 8,792 to 6,157.[59] In an article about the passing of the referendum, psychologists Stephen Soldz and Brad Olson declared "Psychologists Reject the Dark Side."[60]

According to Withhold APA Dues, the passage of the APA membership-wide referendum banning psychologists' work within the U.S. military chain of command in detention facilities that operate outside of or in violation of U.S. law, international human rights statutes, and/or the Geneva Conventions was historic in several respects. It represented the first member-sponsored referendum brought under Article IV, section 5, of the APA bylaws in the APA's history. Second, it was passed with one of the largest voter responses in APA history for any vote, including presidential elections. Third, it represented a resounding repudiation on the part of the full population of American psychologists of the APA's policy of supporting psychologists' consultation in detainee interrogations in such settings.[61]

As of this writing, the APA is failing to implement the changes expressed in the referendum by claiming that previous resolutions accomplished the same goals.

ACKNOWLEDGMENT

This chapter is gratefully dedicated to those survivors of torture who have made grueling sacrifices to bring their horror to light and, in doing so, have made the greatest contributions to anti-torture advocacy. And to those who did not survive or whose horrors remain hidden, you are not forgotten.

NOTES

1. Lewis, 2004.
2. Report of the International Committee of the Red Cross (IRCR), 2004.
3. Ibid.
4. Lewis, 2004.
5. "The Vice President Appears on Meet the Press with Tim Russert," 2001.
6. Gaston, 2007.
7. Isikoff and Taylor, 2006.
8. Guantanamo Voices, 2009.
9. United Nations, 1997.
10. Mayer, 2008; Sands, 2008.
11. "Geneva Accords Quaint and Obsolete," 2006.
12. Fisher, 2009.
13. "Geneva Accords Quaint and Obsolete," 2006.
14. Kaye, 2009.
15. Soldz and Olson, 2008.
16. McCoy, 2006.
17. KUBARK, 1963.
18. "Guantanamo Bay Use of Psychologists for Interrogations 2006–2008."
19. Goodman, 2008.
20. "The Vice President Appears on Meet the Press with Tim Russert," 2001
21. McGovern, 2005.
22. Ibid.
23. Lagouranis and Mikaelian, 2007.
24. Mechanic, 2008.
25. Fisher, 2009.
26. Arrigo and Wagner, 2007.
27. Begg, 2006.
28. Mayer, 2005.
29. Pilger, 2003; Torture Abolition and Survivors Support Coalition, n.d.
30. "American Psychological Association Presidential Task Force on Psychological Ethics and National Security," 2005.
31. Goodman, 2007.
32. Soldz and Olson, 2008.
33. Ephron, 2008; Soldz and Olson, 2008; Carey, 2008.
34. "Candidates for APA President: Dr. Steven J. Reisner," 2008.
35. Soldz and Olson, 2008.
36. Ibid.
37. "WithholdAPADues," n.d.
38. Goodman, "APA Members Hold Fiery Town," 2007.
39. Goodman, "Psychologists in Denial," 2007b.
40. "American Psychological Association Presidential Task Force on Psychological Ethics and National Security," 2005.
41. Soldz and Olson, 2008.
42. Goodman, "Renowned Psychology Author," 2007.
43. "WithholdAPADues," n.d.

44. "Resolution Regarding Participation by Psychologists in Interrogations in Military Detention Centers," 2007.

45. "Resolutions Urge Psychology Assn. to Take Tougher Stand on Interrogating Prisoners," 2007.

46. "American Psychological Association Presidential Task Force on Psychological Ethics and National Security," 2005.

47. "Changes in Guantanamo Bay SOP Manual," 2007.

48. Bond, 2007.

49. Soldz and Olson, 2008.

50. Mayer, 2008.

51. Froomkin, 2005.

52. "Petition to APA," n.d.

53. United Nations Commission on Human Rights, 2006.

54. Miles, 2007.

55. Council of Europe Committee on Legal Affairs and Human Rights, 2007.

56. United Nations Commission on Human Rights, 2007.

57. Information Clearing House, n.d.

58. It is understood that military clinical psychologists would still be available to provide treatment for military personnel.

59. Interrogations and Ethics, 2008.

60. Soldz and Olson, 2008.

61. "WithholdAPADues," n.d.

CHAPTER 10

SHUT IT DOWN! A BRIEF HISTORY OF EFFORTS TO CLOSE LA ESCUELA DE ASESINOS (THE SCHOOL OF ASSASSINS)

Jill Latonick-Flores with Father Roy Bourgeois

The School of the Americas Watch (SOA Watch) is a grassroots peace movement based on principles of nonviolent direct action as exemplified by Dr. Martin Luther King Jr. and Mahatma Gandhi. Founded in 1983 by Maryknoll Missionary Father Roy Bourgeois, the movement has mobilized many thousands of people toward a distinct goal: to close a military training institute located at Fort Benning, Georgia, once called the School of the Americas (SOA) but renamed in 1998 the Western Hemisphere Institute of Security Cooperation (WHINSEC). The school is known widely throughout Latin America as La Escuela de Asesinos, or the School of Assassins.

As a symbol of U.S. foreign policy, the SOA Watch/WHINSEC site is used by SOA Watch activists to educate Americans of the effects of unjust policies and the human costs of a militarized global economy. Racial discrimination, economic deprivation, human rights violations, and environmental injustice are but some of the trajectories of militarized economic policies.

The SOA Watch affirms through word and deed that these systems can be converted to more just and peaceful systems, ones that are rooted in cooperation and the affirmation of human connections to the earth and to each other. Once a person's eyes are opened to the structures that perpetrate injustice, it becomes harder to accept conditions that contribute to the suffering of so many for the benefit of so few. It then becomes easier to say "Nuncas más!" (No more!) and to undertake the task of enacting a new way of being in the world. We can learn to say "A better world is possible!" and "Si se puede!" (Yes, we can!).

The SOA Watch movement aims to increase public awareness of a multitude of issues that create conditions of injustice, inequality, and repression. The SOA Watch's vision for a better future and its willingness to celebrate and affirm life in the midst of struggle provide the inspiration and hope that have energized the movement for close to two decades. The effectiveness of the SOA Watch lies in its ability to communicate a common purpose, to mobilize multiple avenues of activity toward that purpose, and to work both within and outside of conventional systems to meet its goals. The movement has adapted its strategies across time and circumstance to accommodate shifting political and social realities. Through the perspective of Father Roy Bourgeois, the following account examines a brief history of the SOA Watch movement and explores its origins, its structures, and some of its strategies.[1]

ORIGINS

How do you teach democracy behind the barrel of a gun?
—Father Roy Bourgeois, SOA Watch founder

During the 1980s, the populations of Bolivia, Guatemala, Honduras, Peru, Chile, El Salvador, and Nicaragua lived under the constant threat of death squads, torture, and forced disappearance (the kidnapping, abuse, and frequent murder of citizens). The financial elite in these countries relied on military force to carry out certain economic policies that benefited the powerful few and exploited the resources and cheap labor of the poor.

Terror tactics such as demonstration violence—kidnapped and tortured bodies left in public places—were prevalent. In the village of El Mozote, El Salvador, over 900 innocent people were massacred in two days.[2] Under such repressive conditions, to speak out against the powerful was to dig your own grave. Untold thousands who were killed, "disappeared," or tortured into silence were left with no prospects, no "voice" for social or political change. Indeed, help did not come from the North. The U.S. government contributed to the repression in these countries by backing certain military dictators and providing training to soldiers in commando tactics, torture, and various counter-insurgency methods at the U.S. Army's School of the Americas. Although the United States claimed that it was operating to support democratic regimes, all too often it propped up military dictators and contributed to the overthrow of democratically elected leaders.

Despite rhetoric to the contrary from the SOA/WHINSEC military training school in Fort Benning, Georgia, soldiers typically returned to their countries and waged war against their own people. The insurgents in these instances were poor peasants, religious leaders, human rights leaders, and intellectuals—primarily student and university leaders. Labor leaders and union organizers were also among the prime targets of SOA violence because they worked to change economic conditions.

In El Salvador, Archbishop Oscar Romero began pleading to the military to stop the killing. For his efforts he was assassinated on March 24, 1980. But before he was killed, Archbishop Romero avowed that the struggle for justice would continue if he were to die. "I do not believe in death without resurrection. If I die, I will be resurrected in the voice of the Salvadorian people," he said. He urged those with a voice to speak for those who are voiceless.[3]

Today a sea change is occurring throughout Latin America. The people are no longer voiceless. They are not powerless. The people of Latin America are louder and stronger than ever. Yet still, too many children in the region live in abject poverty and will die before reaching adolescence. And the militaries are still very much feared and powerful.

There is, therefore, still much work to be done to bring an end to U.S. foreign policies wherein the powerful elite throughout the Americas is enriched and the poor continue to suffer.

TORTURE AND MURDER

After serving as a navel officer during the Vietnam War, Roy Bourgeois became a priest with the Maryknoll Missionary Order and began working in Bolivia among poor peasants. The poor became his teachers. They taught him how the quality of their lives was harmed by U.S. foreign policy. At that time Bolivia was under the military dictatorship of General Hugo Banzer Suarez, a SOA graduate who is prominently featured at SOA/WHINSEC's "Hall of Fame" and a brutal dictator responsible for the torture and killings of innocents.[4] As a religious person aiding the poor, Father Roy was viewed by the political elite in Bolivia as subversive. He worked in that country for five years before being tortured, imprisoned, and banished from the country.

On returning to the United States, Father Roy heard similar stories of torture and oppression mostly from religious persons who had served in South and Central America. On December 2, 1980, four churchwomen from the United States, Maryknoll Sisters Maura Clarke and Ita Ford, Ursuline Sister Dorothy Kazel, and Cleveland Lay Mission Team member Jean

Donovan, were arrested, raped, and murdered by members of the National Guard of El Salvador. Consequently, these killings brought increased international attention to the gross human rights violations in the region. Two of these women were Father Roy's close friends. Salvadorian activists, nuns, and priests began to investigate the likelihood of U.S. complicity in these horrors. They discovered that the U.S. army was training Salvadorian soldiers at an army base located in Fort Benning, Georgia.

THE SOA WATCH'S FIRST NONVIOLENT DIRECT ACTION

"Have You Been to Jail for Justice?"

—song by Anne Feeney

In 1946, the School of the Americas was opened in Panama. It was forced to close in 1984 under the conditions of the Panama Canal Treaty. Thus, in 1983, the School of the Americas was still officially located in Panama. Unofficially, it was training Salvadorian soldiers at Fort Benning. With the skills they received at the training school, Salvadorian soldiers returned home and waged war against their own people.

To draw attention to this development, in August 1983, Father Roy and two Salvadorian activists donned military garb and sneaked onto the base after dark. They had a flashlight, some rope, a portable stereo cassette player, and a recording of the speech Archbishop Oscar Romero delivered the night before he was assassinated, his last homily. The base housed 525 Salvadorian soldiers. While the soldiers were sleeping, the trio scaled a large pine tree and blasted Archbishop Romero's message from the cassette player:

> I would like to appeal in a special way to the men of the Army, and in particular to the troops of the National Guard, the Police, and the garrisons. Brothers, you belong to our own people. You kill your own brother peasants; and in the face of an order to kill that is given by a man, the law of God should prevail that says: "Do not kill!" No soldier is obliged to obey an order counter to the law of God. No one has to comply with an immoral law. It is time now that you recover your conscience and obey its dictates rather than the command of sin.
>
>   The Church, the defender of the rights of God, of the law of God, of the dignity of the human person, cannot remain silent before so much abomination. We want the government to seriously consider that reforms mean nothing when they come bathed in so much blood. Therefore, in the name of God, and in the name of this long-suffering people, whose laments rise to heaven every day more tumultuous, I beseech you, I beg you, I command you in the name of God: "Cease the repression![5]

As Romero's voice rang through the military base, lights from the dormitories flickered on. Soldiers poured out into the night. The trio, Linda Ventimiglia, Father Larry Rosebaugh, and Father Roy Bourgeois, were apprehended and arrested. All three activists spent over a year in federal prison. This trio would be the first of several thousand to trespass on the base or "cross the line" by enacting nonviolent direct actions, a hallmark of the SOA Watch movement, to close the school.

THE FIRST SOA WATCH VIGIL: NOVEMBER 16, 1990

On the night of November 16, 1989, a Salvadorian Army patrol entered the University of Central America in San Salvador and massacred six Jesuit priests, their housekeeper, and her daughter. Nineteen of the military officers cited for this atrocity had received training at the U.S. Army School of the Americas.

On November 16, 1990, the first anniversary of this carnage, Father Roy and 10 activists camped outside of the gates of Fort Benning. For the next 35 days, they participated in a hunger strike during which they only drank water. The hunger strike was successful in generating publicity about the SOA and the atrocities perpetrated by its graduates. This first vigil was made up of religious people. Most of them were nuns and priests who had witnessed first-hand the atrocities in the region. As an extension of their missionary service, their faith was foundational to their effort. But as the movement began to grow, many people who joined were not Catholic and many were not particularly religious. Father Roy aimed to be sensitive to these differences so that the gatherings could be as inclusive as possible: "What brings us together is a desire for peace and our love for others. We are people of goodwill."

Since 1989, an annual vigil with direct action (the pinnacle of which is a solemn funeral procession on Sunday morning) is held every third weekend in November.

THE SOA CLOSES AND RE-OPENS AS WHINSEC

"New Name, Same Shame!"

—SOA Watch Slogan

Beginning in 1990 and spearheaded by Joseph Kennedy II (D-Mass.), several congressional members began researching connections between the SOA and reports of human rights abuses from Latin America. A real boost to the effort came on March 15, 1993, when the United Nations Truth Commission Report was released. It cited the names of specific officers charged with committing atrocities in El Salvador.[6] Vicky Imerman of the SOA Watch matched the names cited in the UN Report with names in a U.S. government document. The Freedom of Information Act (FOIA) permitted Vicky and other SOA Watch researchers to seek the truth about the crimes and those responsible for ordering and carrying them out.

In the meantime, SOA Watch activists spent 40 days on the steps of the U.S. Capitol engaging in a juice-only fast to draw congressional attention to the documents that validated what they had been saying for years. These actions coincided with the 103rd and 104th Congresses in which legislation was introduced to investigate the school and cease its funding. Two separate congressional votes came increasingly close to shutting down the school.[7] Then, in 1995, the SOA Watch released the documentary, *The School of Assassins*, narrated by actress Susan Sarandon. The video sold 20,000 copies and was later nominated for an Oscar award.[8] The documentary detailed the struggle to educate Congress about the misuse of military funds and the shame the institution had brought on the United States.

On August 16, 1996, more than 300 religious leaders organized by Leaders Conference of Women Religious held a prayer vigil outside of the military base at Fort Benning. "We believe our action is critical in breaking through the wall of ignorance concerning the true nature of the SOA," said Sister O'Brien, a Sister of St. Joseph from New York. "The veil of silence about U.S. financing and training of Latin American militaries that abuse and violate human rights must be lifted," she added.[9]

In 1996, a Pentagon report revealed that between the years 1982 and 1991, the United States instructed South and Central American military officers in extortion, torture, beatings, coercions, and various forms of disappearance and demonstration violence.[10] Thousands of military officers from 11 countries in South and Central America including Guatemala, Honduras, and El Salvador were issued the manuals, which were printed in Spanish. This "veil of silence" was raised when on September 24, 1996, a news story by Dana Priest, "U.S. Instructed Latins on Executions, Torture," appeared in the *Washington Post*.[11] The article detailed portions of the content of the torture manuals used at the SOA between 1982 and 1991 and gave the names of some of the SOA graduates and the human rights violations attributed to their command. The graduates included Roberto D'Aubuisson, "the leader of El Salvador's right-wing death squads; 19 Salvadorian soldiers linked to the 1989 assassination of six Jesuit priests; Gen. Manuel Antonio Noriega, the deposed Panamanian strongman; six Peruvian officers linked to killings of students and a professor; and Col. Julio Roberto Alpirez, a Guatemalan officer implicated in the death of an American innkeeper living in Guatemala and to the death of a leftist guerrilla married to an American lawyer."[12] The *Washington Post* article generated a number of related newspaper articles and editorials. Public indignation swelled. The following spring, between April 19 and April 29, approximately 200 people demonstrated every day on the steps of the U.S. Capitol. They held signs and large banners protesting the School of Assassins. They handed passersby lists documenting human rights abuses in Latin America and distributed the lists to their congressional representatives. Several of the activists fasted during the 10 days. Others held a mock trial of human rights abusers in a street theatre production that told of the injustices, the plight of those who suffered, and the role of the SOA behind the veil of secrecy and denial.[13]

Also in 1997, 17 people were arrested for digging a mass grave on the grounds of the Pentagon in Washington, D.C.[14] Street theatre was used to draw attention to atrocities in Latin America and the grave was made to bury the massacred. That same year, news reports told the story of Medal of Honor recipient Charles Liteky who together with six other SOA Watch activists "painted anti-SOA messages on the Fort Benning main gate and threw a blood-like substance on the brick wall that marks the entrance to the Army base."[15]

During the 106th Congress, a bipartisan amendment to close the school and conduct a congressional investigation came within 10 votes of passing.[16] In December 2000, a Department of Defense Proposal included in the Defense Authorization Bill for fiscal year 2001 closed the SOA.[17] It reopened, however, on January 17, 2001, with a new name: the Western Hemisphere Institute for Security Cooperation (WHINSEC). According to Father Roy, this change was the result of a slick public relations campaign designed to clean up the school's image.[18]

After the events of September 11, 2001, the Freedom of Information Act was restricted in the sense that researchers have found it increasingly difficult to track human rights abuses because the names SOA and WHINSEC are blacked out on the documents released to the public. In spite of SOA/WHINSEC's claim that they have nothing to hide, they have become increasingly secretive in this manner.[19]

In October 2009, the U.S. House of Representatives approved the McGovern (SD)—Sestak-Bishop (GA)—Lewis (GA) amendment to the National Defense Authorization Act for fiscal year 2010 with a 224 to 190 vote. The amendment forced the public release of names, country of origin, rank, courses taken, and dates of attendance of SOA/WHINSEC's graduates and instructors to the public.[20]

STRUCTURES

> Trying to explain how so many pulled together in the Oaxaca struggle, Kiado, a young Zapoteca leader, said "in our language, there is no word for 'I'. We only exist in relation to one another."[21]
>
> —Lisa Sullivan, SOA Watch Latin American Coordinator

The organizational structure of the SOA Watch is egalitarian and nonhierarchical. Although Father Roy is the founder and figurehead of the movement, he is not the sole person in charge of the SOA Watch. This organization's structure is marked by cooperation, equality, nonviolence, nonracism, and nondiscrimination. The organization aims for transparency and accountability in all of its endeavors and decision making, as well as in its communications with the general public. Interested activists are included in all major decisions. Like many social change movements, SOA Watch has a Web site, a Facebook page, and can be found on Twitter. The SOA Watch newsletter, *Presente!* is published three times a year. Communications are in both Spanish and English. Sign language is provided at the annual vigil.

In Washington, D.C., five SOA Watch staff share a strip of small rooms adjacent to Catholic University of America, the national university of the Roman Catholic Church. The Maryknoll Missionary order owns the building. The Latin American coordinator and the Latin American Communications coordinator are located in Venezuela. Father Roy's efficiency apartment, located on Fort Benning Drive, is home to the SOA Watch movement in Georgia.

The council meets face to face at least twice a year to coordinate major decisions for the movement. Representatives are elected at regional levels or self-nominated, depending on the number of activists from the region. In between meetings, teleconferencing and e-mail are important ways of communicating. The national council consists of representatives from 12 regions of the United States and Latin America. Leaders from Veterans for Peace and Torture Survivors and Support Coalition International have seats on the council as do persons from the SOA offices in Washington, D.C., and Georgia.

The national council coordinates suggestions from the working groups and makes decisions that affect the entire movement. Conflict management strategies are built into a consensus model of decision making. Each decision is shaped by the input of every person or group on the national council. Decisions are not final until an agreement that is acceptable to all members has been reached. Every person has the power to refuse the group decision. Depending on the issue, decision making can last days or months. One major decision, the possibility of moving the annual vigil to Washington, D.C., has been discussed for years.

SOA Watch working groups allow individuals to affirm issues that are most important to them, to highlight their issue's relevance to the movement's goals, and to carry out particular actions. Working groups consist of like-minded persons that come together with a particular focus: Spanish-language media, research, legislative action, anti-discrimination, media, translation and interpretation, women's issues, and direct action are among a number of working groups. There are working groups to bring together the sound equipment for the vigil and there are working groups to raise money.

SOLIDARITY

Closing the SOA/WHINSEC is more than simply putting an end to the physical structures of the facilities at Fort Benning. The SOA/WHINSEC represents the militarized arm of oppressive economic, political, and social injustices. Military might is used to enact the unjust policies that benefit multinationals and elite populations at the expense of the poor. These social and economic injustices are rooted in various types of discrimination that include, but are not limited to, race, gender, class, physical ability, and sexism.

At meetings and at the annual vigil, people who have suffered the most from the gross human rights violations in Central and South America inform people in the movement of accounts of injustice. Torture survivors speak for themselves, as do peace activists, labor organizers, and students. Indigenous farmers share their knowledge and experience. The SOA Watch learns from the speakers and seeks to collaborate with them in providing information and logistical support for peace and social justice efforts in their regions. Speakers' stories guide and inspire others in the movement and offer sustenance for activists as they continue the struggle on return to their communities. However, SOA Watch activists acknowledge that speaking out is difficult or impossible for some persons who have been traumatized by past horrors or the possibility of current death threats, as in Colombia. There are those, too, who cannot afford to travel inside the United States to come to the vigil or do not have the appropriate papers and are fearful of speaking out in this country.

Workshops, teach-ins, and creative presentations by SOA Watch activists address these types of discriminations and the struggles to change them. In this way and others, the movement strives to examine itself for hidden and obvious sources of white supremacy and discrimination-based activity. SOA Watch organizers scrutinize power dynamics involved between alliances when a privileged population, such as SOA Watch activists in the United

States, seeks to support a less privileged and oppressed population such as human rights organizers in Latin America.

Individual and collective efforts to end inequalities in power relations are ongoing. The newsletter *Presente!* outlines the connectedness between social and economic injustices, racism, and militarism.

Challenging racism in the world may cause activists to more quickly recognize discrimination on personal, interpersonal, and community levels. Person-to-person discrimination can be just as difficult as challenging global injustices.

But, rather than just talking about anti-oppression goals, activists attempt to enact more egalitarian ways of being in community with others. Most recently, Father Roy has run into difficulties with the Vatican by giving his support to women who desire to enter the priesthood. Despite being threatened with excommunication, he continues to support the effort to make real the equal standing of women in the church. "Justice is not something you can be selective about" he says.[22]

STRATEGIES

In February of each year, a strategy meeting takes place in one of 12 regions. Activists review recent events that have affected the movement's goals. Lobbying tactics and talking points are developed. People generate new ideas, practice effective ways of communicating important points, and develop plans for direct action and legislative efforts. These meetings oftentimes coincide with the SOA Watch's "Lobby Days," when activists instruct members of Congress and foreign policy staffers about SOA/WHINSEC.

The movement's strategies are as diverse as its constituents. Creative nonviolence that includes fasting, street theatre, and sit-ins is used in conjunction with more traditional methods of achieving social change, such as letter writing campaigns, petitioning, and lobbying members of Congress. People then can decide for themselves what type of action they can contribute toward the movement's goals.

THE SOLEMN FUNERAL PROCESSION: *NO MÁS! NO MORE!*

The ritual of the annual vigil doesn't name God but appeals to a universal spirituality that connects us all. No one would call the SOAW movement a Christian movement and no one would call it a secular movement. Our movement's power comes from a diversity of people that view the task of closing the SOA as a moral issue.[23]

—Eric Le Compte, SOA Watch Organizer

Musty incense rises into the towering pines that line the road leading to the gates of the U.S. military post at Fort Benning, Georgia. This weekend, like every third weekend in November for almost two decades, the mile-long road is blocked to traffic. A large stage is positioned at one end of the street before the entrance to the base. A 10-foot chain-link fence topped with barbed wire restricts civilians from access to the base. A "No Trespassing" sign is posted on the fence. On the stage speakers from countries across the Americas tell of their experiences of life and struggle. A group of musicians has traveled from Colombia and is sending out the light and gentle thump of Andean music.

The street is full of art and action. Near the opposite end of the busy street, puppetistas, enormous puppets held in the air by two men each, symbolize the processes of death and rebirth. Black and gray-faced puppets symbolizing death mix with equally large sunshiny yellow, green, and orange smiling faces affirming life. Street artists dramatize the plight of indigenous farmers. Flower-draped men, women, and children walk on stilts. Farm workers, black-masked teens, and allages and nationalists tread slowly alongside somber-faced nuns, brown-cloaked monks, and families carting young children. The Coalition of Immokalee Workers, Women Religious, Torture Abolition and Survivors Support Coalition International, Colombia Support Network, Grandmothers for Peace, Veterans for Peace, Witness for Peace, the AFL-CIO, and Christian Peacemaker Teams are but a sample of the many groups gathered here. A cluster of orange-shrouded Buddhist monks has walked for miles to gather with the crowd. But not all those at the vigil are SOA Watch supporters: uniformed Military Police observe the crowd lazily but assuredly. They gaze up on the regularity of its movement with a strange mix of fascination and boredom.

The crowd becomes silent. Shortly thereafter, in unison, a commitment to nonviolence is affirmed by all of the participants. Willowing through the breeze, a song affirms the solidarity of the people who have suffered so from the brutalities: *Nuncas más! Never again! No más, no more! shout the hills of Salvador. Compañeros, compañeras, we cry out, "No más, no more!"* Within minutes, a Gregorian-tuned voice rings through the crowd announcing the first of several hundred names of the dead: "Archbishop Oscar Romero." The crowd affirms the presence of the memory and spirit of Romero by sounding, slowly, in unison: "Pre-sen-te!"

Hundreds of people in the crowd raise religious symbols over their heads. Countless white crosses have the names of the dead written on them. Then the mass of demonstrators takes a small step closer to the fence that divides those gathered today from the military base at Fort Benning. Thus begins the solemn funeral procession of the annual vigil of the School of the Americas Watch.

LEGISLATIVE ACTION

Since 1993, legislative action has been at the forefront of strategies used by SOA Watch activists to close the school. In addition to shutting down the school completely, shutting off funding for the school has been a method to advance the movement's goals. SOA Watch's legislative action committee provides training for activists to research congressional representatives and to learn how to set up meetings with them. Postcards outlining details of proposed amendments are provided by the movement to local organizers and the interested public, for a small fee.

Non-violent direct action
You can Jail the Resisters but you can't Jail the Resistance!
—SOA Watch T-Shirt

Since its inception, SOA Watch activists have used nonviolent direct action to draw attention to their purpose. Nonviolence is decisive noncooperation with injustice. It is not passivity; it is not revenge oriented. Nonviolence requires self-discipline, goodwill, sacrifice, persistence, and guts. Nonviolence requires love.

In the years since 1983, over 275 people have carefully planned and carried out nonviolent direct action in an effort to increase public attention to the effort to close the school. Referred to as Prisoners of Conscience (POCs), each person has spent about six months in federal prison, typically for trespassing on government property by walking onto the base or "crossing the line." The charge is a misdemeanor punishable by a fine of up to $1,000 and six months in federal prison. Although it is rare in this country to be sentenced to federal prison for a misdemeanor charge such as trespassing, most activists who have crossed the line expect to receive this punishment and a fine.[24] Many activists choose to waive the fine and instead, they spend increased time in jail. Most of the 275 protesters had never been arrested before engaging in this nonviolent direct action.[25]

Activists can choose to receive training in nonviolence at the SOA Watch workshops scheduled to occur prior to the annual vigil. Legal advisors inform activists about what to expect on their arrest. The purpose of crossing the line is to educate the general public about the SOA/WHINSEC through media attention of the direct action, through prison witness, and through books, articles, and public speaking engagements.

During the 1998 vigil, 2,319 activists risked arrest by crossing onto the base. In 1999, that number almost doubled, reaching 4,408.[26] In 2000, up to 3,500 people "crossed the line." During those years demonstrators walked onto the base en masse and were not always arrested and taken to jail. Instead, they were taken by bus to a local park and released. In the form of a "ban and bar" letter, those arrested and processed were warned not to return to the base for five years.[27]

After the attacks of September 11, 2001, the SOA/WHINSEC officials formally requested that the SOA Watch withhold its protests. The army claimed that the political conditions post–9/11 indicated a demonstration could be unsafe. Eventually, a court order ruled in favor of the SOA Watch. In discussing his decision, Federal Magistrate G. Mallon Faircloth said, "It was a question of First Amendment rights, and you can't play with that. I am sworn to uphold the U.S. Constitution. I think I did that today." SOA Watch Council member Ken Hayes reported rumors that Judge Faircloth said that if the army at Fort Benning needed this kind of protection against the SOA Watch, with its lengthy history of nonviolence, then "we are all in a lot of trouble."[28]

Later in 2001, the *New York Times* reported on two siblings, both of whom were nuns who had been barred from the base for previous acts of trespass.[29] Sister Dorothy Marie Hennessey, aged 88, and Sister Gwen L. Hennessey, aged 68, spent six months in federal prison for their dedication to protesting human rights abuses. The *Times* story gave a history of the SOA/WHINSEC and recounted human rights abuses committed by graduates of the school. Of course, this was the goal of the women's actions.

Octogenarian Ed Lewinson, a Professor Emeritus of History at Seton Hall University, further exemplifies the persistence and dedication of SOA Watch activism. Lewinson crossed the line during the vigils in 2003, 2004, 2005, and 2007, but the state initially refused to prosecute him for his first three acts of civil disobedience because he is blind. It would appear that the judge did not want to draw the media's attention by sentencing an elderly blind man to jail for advocating the SOA Watch cause. Eventually, in 2007, he was ordered to pay a $500 fine and sentenced to 90 days in federal prison.[30]

Of the hundreds of activists who have chosen arrest, thousands of others have supported them through letter writing, financial gifts, and legal aid. Singing protest songs outside of the Columbus jail is one of the ways that SOA Watch activists who do not choose arrest support the cause of the people who do. As in all cases of creative nonviolence, the action should bring increased attention to the cause and make clear the hidden benefits of SOA Watch creative nonviolence to energize other activists in the movement and further the overall goal. Not all activists can risk the sacrifices that going to jail for six months entail, yet witnessing the sacrifice of others can be an inspiration to continue to work hard to address the movement's goals.

FUNDING THE MOVEMENT

Funding and material resources come from donations and grants. The movement is funded by its members through direct mail campaigns or through voluntary donations during the annual November vigil. Those in attendance are encouraged to give a minimum of one dollar. Grant monies, typically between $1,000 and $5,000, come from various religious groups. Women's Religious and the Maryknoll order are but two of the contributors. Father Roy receives donations from speaking events that generate close to half the SOA Watch's income.[31] In addition, activists support one another by funding travel expenses and sharing transportation to the vigil. A "ride" board is posted on the organization's Web site. It designates travel routes to the November vigil and connects riders and drivers from all regions of the country. An annual "Journey for Justice" in which Salvadorian torture survivor Carlos Mauricio and others travel from San Francisco to Fort Benning to inform others about the SOA/WHINSEC is funded by small donations along the way. Food is also generously donated during the days-long gathering in November. Typically, it is provided by charitable organizations, from various religious orders, and from "Food Not Bombs" for those who cannot afford to purchase food during the November weekend.

CITIZEN DIPLOMACY

Prior to 2006, SOA Watch activists took delegations to regions in Latin America to learn from fellow activists and to see how U.S. foreign policies such as Plan Colombia and NAFTA/CAFTA affected the people there. They saw how military force served to undermine populations struggling for dignity and survival. Christian Peacemaker Teams and Witness for Peace delegations collaborated with locals and informed U.S. activists of ongoing human rights violations. They detailed activities needed for change.

In 2006, at the annual strategy meeting in Washington, D.C., a suggestion was made to form a working group in Latin America, composed of Latinos and Latinas to coordinate efforts with the SOA Watch in the United States. A working group, Partnership America Latina (PAL), was founded in Venezuela and has been successfully organizing citizen diplomacy meetings in eight countries. At these meetings, SOA Watch delegations meet directly with heads of state and military defense officials to urge them to cease sending soldiers to the SOA/WHINSEC.[32]

SOA Watch activists wanted to see more of these sorts of collaborations on the ground in the countries where the SOA/WHINSEC trains soldiers. The goal of the Latin American Project was to ask the leaders from different countries to stop sending soldiers to the school. This effort was a slight twist on the usual strategies for closing the school: If there are no soldiers at the school there can be no school.

At the national strategy meeting in early 2006, organizers voted to begin a Latin American Project in which people-to-people grassroots efforts would be coordinated by Latinos in their own countries. Lisa Sullivan-Rodriquez, a Maryknoll lay leader who had lived and worked for peace throughout Latin America for 29 years, was chosen to bring together this effort. Asking high-level government leaders to stop sending soldiers to the SOA/WHINSEC is but one of the aims of the Latin American Project. They also increase the issue of the SOA in public debate and further engage local human rights activists in insisting on their country's withdrawal from this institution.

Since 2005, the Latin American Project has met with human rights organizers, indigenous leaders, military defense leaders, vice-presidents, and presidents throughout Central and South America. SOA Watch delegations have met with high-level government officials from 14 countries. In 2005, President Hugo Chavez of Venezuela was the first President to withdraw soldiers. Since then three more countries have made a commitment to stop sending soldiers—Argentina (2005), Uruguay (2005), and in 2007, Costa Rica. (Costa Rica has no army but was sending members of its police force.)[33]

Although formal channels for requesting contact with government and military officials exist in most countries, this novel approach to international diplomacy (or citizen diplomacy) was made possible by the efforts of partners in the struggle in many countries. During trips by certain delegations, such as that to Colombia, local organizers risked their lives to speak out about the human rights violations during meetings between military personnel and SOA Watch organizers. Men with machine guns listened attentively as displaced people struggling to survive talked of the injustice.[34]

When SOA Watch delegates spoke to leaders about the SOA/WHINSEC, its graduates, and its atrocities, the officials were woefully aware of the painful legacy of its operations. Many high-level government officials that the SOA Watch delegates met with are themselves torture survivors and were at one time political prisoners. In Bolivia, SOA Watch delegates met with President Evo Morales, the first indigenous leader to be elected to that office. In Argentina, alongside the renowned mothers of the disappeared (Madres de la Plaza de Mayo) and thousands of others who had gathered to mourn and remember, the group marked the 30th anniversary of the dictatorship. They shared hugs with Argentines who thanked them for coming and for speaking out to close the school. In Panama, delegates met with Jorge Illueca, who was the President of Panama when the SOA was kicked out of that country in 1984. It is he who first referred to the School of Americas as "the School of Assassins."[35] The leaders would consistently give SOA Watch delegates considerably more information than they had obtained to date. Human rights violators and dictators trained at the SOA are household names in many countries the delegations visit.

As of this writing, the United States continues to train soldiers, such as those that implemented the coup that illegally ousted democratically elected President Zelaya of Honduras in June 2009. General Romeo Vasquez Velasquez, widely credited with spearheading the military coup, appears to have been trained at the SOA when torture manuals were used.[36]

The struggle continues.

Howard Zinn, 1922–2010, died leaving both a lifetime of dedicated work for peace and justice but also the narratives that may make peace possible. He added the voices of ordinary people, dissenting soldiers, slaves, civil rights workers to the telling of history. Their voices now stand along side the generals and the corporate scientists as makers of history and as prophets for an era of peace and justice. We are honored by his granting us permission to include his work.

NOTES

1. Bourgeois, 2009.
2. Danner, 1994.
3. Wright, 2008.
4. School of the Americas Watch, 2007.
5. Wright, 2008.
6. Report of the UN Truth Commission on El Salvador, 1993.
7. Legislative Action Index, n.d.
8. Richter, 1994.
9. The School of the Americas Watch, "Three Hundred Religious Leaders Hold Prayer Vigil."
10. Ibid.
11. Priest, 1996.
12. Ibid.
13. The School of the Americas Watch, "Action History."
14. The School of the Americas Watch, "Grave Diggers."
15. Le Compte, 2009.
16. Legislative Action Index.
17. Ibid.
18. Fr. Roy Bourgeois, telephone conversation with Jill Latonick-Flores, September 12, 2009.
19. Ibid.
20. Legislative Action Index, n.d.

21. The School of the Americas Watch, "SOA Watch Delegation to Mexico and Costa Rica."

22. Bourgeois, 2009.

23. Kjos, 2004.

24. Bourgeois, 2009.

25. Ibid.

26. School of the Americas Watch, n.d.

27. Bourgeois, 2000.

28. Hayes, 2009.

29. Goodstein, 2001.

30. School of the Americas Watch, 2007.

31. Hayes, 2009.

32. The School of the Americas Watch, "The SOA Watch Latin American Project."

33. Ibid.

34. Ibid.

35. Ibid.

36. Institute for Southern Studies, 2009.

CHAPTER 11

STRUCTURED CRUELTY: LEARNING TO BE A LEAN, MEAN KILLING MACHINE

Martin Smith

I will never forget standing in formation after the end of our final "hump," Marine-speak for a forced march, at the end of the Crucible in March 1997. The Crucible is the final challenge during Marine Corps boot camp and is a two-and-a-half-day, physically exhausting exercise in which sleep deprivation, scarce food, and a series of obstacles test teamwork and toughness. The formidable nine-mile stretch ended with our ascent up the "Grim Reaper," a small mountain in the hilly terrain of Camp Pendleton, California.

As we stood at attention, the commanding officer made his way though our lines, inspecting his troops and giving each of us an eagle, globe, and anchor pin, the mark of our final transition from recruit to Marine. But what I recall most was not the pain and exhaustion that filled every ounce of my trembling body, but the sounds that surrounded me as I stood at attention with eyes forward.

Mixed within the repetitive refrains of Lee Greenwood's "God Bless the USA," belting from a massive sound system, were the soft and gentle sobs emanating from numerous newborn Marines. Their cries stood in stark contrast to the so-called "warrior spirit" we had earned and now came to

Originally published on 2-20-07 by CounterPunch, http://www.counterpunch.org/smith02202007 .html.

epitomize. While some may claim that these unmanly responses resulted from a patriotic emotional fit or even out of a sense of pride in being called "Marine" for the very first time, I know that for many the moisture streaming down our cheeks represented something much more anguished and heartrending.

What I learned about Marines is that despite the stereotype of the chivalrous knight, wearing dress blues with sword drawn, or the green killing machine that is always "ready to rumble," the young men and women I encountered instead comprised a cross-section of working-class America. There were neither knights nor machines among us.

During my five years in active-duty service, I befriended a recovering meth addict who was still "using," a young male who had prostituted himself to pay his rent before he signed up, an El Salvadorian immigrant serving in order to receive a green card, a single mother who could not afford her child's health care needs as a civilian, a gay teenager who entertained our platoon by singing Madonna karaoke in the barracks to the delight of us all, and many of the country's poor and poorly educated.

I came to understand very well what those cries on top of the Grim Reaper expressed. Those teardrops represented hope in the promise of a change in our lives from a world that, for many of us as civilians, seemed utterly hopeless.

U.S. Marine Corps (USMC) boot camp is a 13-week training regimen unlike any other. According to the USMC's recruiting Web site, "Marine Recruits learn to use their intelligence . . . and to live as upstanding moral beings with real purpose." Yet if teaching intelligence and morals are the stated purpose of its training, the Corps has peculiar way of implementing its pedagogy.

In reality, its educational method is based on a planned and structured form of cruelty. I remember my first visit to the "chow-hall" in which three drill instructors (DIs), wearing their signature "smoky bear" covers, pounced on me for having looked at them, screaming that I was a "nasty piece of civilian shit." From then on, I learned that you could only look at a DI when instructed to by the command of "Eyeballs!" In addition, recruits could only speak in the third person, thus ridding our vocabulary of the term "I" and divorcing ourselves from our previous civilian identities.

Our emerging group mentality was built on and reinforced by tearing down and degrading us through a series of regimented and ritualistic exercises in the first phase of boot camp. Despite having an African American DI and a Latino DI, recruits in my platoon were ridiculed with derogatory language that included racial epithets. But recruits of color were not the only victims, we were all "fags," "pussies," and "shitbags." We survived through a twisted sort of leveling based on what military historian Christian G. Appy calls a "solidarity of the despised."

We relearned how to execute every activity, including the most personal aspects of our hygiene. While eating, we could only use our right hand while our left had to stay directly on our knee, and our eyes had to stare directly at our food trays. Our bathroom breaks were so brief that three recruits would share a urinal at a time so that the entire platoon of sixty-three recruits could relieve themselves in our minute-and-a-half time limit. On several occasions, recruits soiled their uniforms during training.

Every evening, DIs inspected our boots for proper polish and our belt buckles for satisfactory shine while we stood at attention in our underwear. Then, we would "mount our racks" (bunk beds), lie at attention, and scream all three verses of the Marine Corps hymn at the top of our lungs.

While the DIs would proclaim that these inspections were to ensure that our bodies had not been injured during training, I suspect that there were ulterior motives as well. These examinations were attempts to indoctrinate us with an emerging military masculinity that is based on male sexuality linked to respect for the uniform and a fetishization of combat.

After the playing of "Taps," lights went out. At which time, a DI would circle around the room and begin moralizing. "One of these days, you're going to figure out what's really tough in the world," he would exclaim. "You think you've got it so bad. But in recruit training, you get three meals a day while we tell you when to shit and blink," he continued. The DI would then lower his voice, "But when you're out on your own, you're gonna see what's hard. You'll see what tough is when you knock up your old woman. You'll realize what's cruel when you get married and find yourself stuck with a fat bitch who just squats out ungrateful kids. You'll learn what the real world's about when you're overseas and your wife back in the states robs you blind and sleeps with your best friend."

The DI's nightly homiletic speeches, full of an unabashed hatred of women, were part of the second phase of boot camp, the process of rebuilding recruits into Marines.

The process of reconstructing recruits and molding them into future troops is based on building a team that sees itself in opposition to those who are outside of it.

After the initial shock of the first phase of training, DIs indoctrinate recruits to dehumanize the enemy to train them how to overcome any fear or prejudice against killing. In fact, according to longtime counter-recruitment activist Tod Ensign, the military has deliberately researched how to best design training for how to teach recruits how to kill. Such research was needed because humans are instinctively reluctant to kill.

Dr. Dave Grossman disclosed in his work, *On Killing*,[1] that fewer than 20 percent of U.S. troops fired their weapons in World War II during combat.

As a result, the military reformed training standards so that more soldiers would pull their trigger against the enemy. Grossman credits these training modifications for the transformation of the Armed Forces in the Vietnam War in which 90 to 95 percent of soldiers fired their weapons. These reforms in training were based on teaching recruits how to dehumanize the enemy.

The process of dehumanization is central to military training. During Vietnam, the enemy in Vietnam was simply a "gook," "dink," or "slope." Today, "rag head" and "sand nigger" are the current racist epithets lodged against Arabs and Muslims. After every command, we would scream, "Kill!" But our call for blood took on particular importance during our physical training, when we learned how to fight with pugil sticks, wooden sticks with padded ends, how to run an obstacle course with fixed bayonets, or how to box and engage in hand-to-hand combat. We were told to imagine the "enemy" in all of our combat training, and it was always implied that the "enemy" was of Middle Eastern descent. "When some rag head comes lurking up from behind, you're gonna give 'em ONE," barked the training DI. We all howled in unison, "Kill!" Likewise, when we charged toward the dummy on an obstacle course with our fixed bayonets, it was clear to all that the lifeless form was Arab.

Even in 1997, we were being brainwashed to accept the coming Iraq War. Abruptly interrupting a class (one of numerous courses we attended on military history, first aid, and survival skills), a Series Chief DI excitedly announced that all training was coming to a halt. We were to be shipped immediately to the Gulf, because Saddam had just fired missiles into Israel. Given that we lived with no knowledge of the outside world, with neither TV nor newspapers, and that we experienced constant high levels of stress and a discombobulating environment, the DI's false assertion seemed all too believable. After a half-hour panic, we were led out of the auditorium to face the rebuke and scorn of our platoon DIs. It turned out that the interruption was a skit planned to scare us into the realization that we could face war at any moment.

The trick certainly had the planned effect on me, as I pondered what the hell I had gotten myself into. I also now realize that we were being indoctrinated with schemes for war in the Middle East. Our hatred of the Arab "other" was crafted from the very beginning of our training through fear and hate.

Almost 10 years since I stood on the yellow footprints that greet new recruits at the Marine Corps Recruit Depot in San Diego, I express gratitude for my luck during my enlistment. I was fortunate to have never witnessed a day of combat and was honorably discharged months after 9/11. However, joining the military is like playing Russian Roulette. With wars raging in Iraq and Afghanistan, and the likelihood of military action against Iran, troops in the Corps today are playing with grimmer odds.

In these "dirty wars," troops cannot tell friend from foe, leading to war crimes against a civilian population. Our government is cynically promoting a campaign of lies and deception to justify its illegal actions (with the complicity of both parties in Washington), and our troops are fighting to support regimes that lack popular support and legitimacy.

With over 3,100 U.S. troops now dead and thousands more maimed and crippled, I look back to the other young men I heard sobbing on that sunny wintry morning on top of the Reaper. The reasons we enlisted were as varied as our personal histories. Yet, it is the starkest irony that the hope we collectively expressed for a better life may have indeed cost us our very lives. When one pulls the trigger called "enlistment," he or she faces the gambling chance of experiencing war, conflicts that inevitably lead to the degradation of the human spirit.

The war crimes committed by U.S. troops in Iraq, such as the brutality exhibited at Mahmoudiya, in which soldiers allegedly gang-raped a teen-aged Iraqi girl and burned her body to destroy the evidence, are, in fact, part and parcel of all imperialist wars. The USMC's claim that recruits learn "to live as upstanding moral beings with real purpose" is a sickening ploy aimed to disguise its true objectives. Given the fact that Marines are molded to kill the enemy "other" from TD One (the first training day), combined with the bestial nature of colonial war, it should come as no surprise that rather than turning "degenerates" into paragons of virtue, the Corps is more likely capable of transforming men into monsters.

And yet as much as these war crimes reveal about the conditions of war, the circumstances facing an occupying force, and the peculiar brand of Marine training, they also reflect a bitter truth about the civilian world in which we live. It speaks volumes that in order for young working-class men and women to gain self-confidence or self-worth, they seek to join an institution that trains them how to destroy, maim, and kill. The desire to become a Marine, as a journey to one's manhood or as a path to self-improvement, is a stinging indictment of the pathology of our class-ridden world.

NOTE

1. Grossman, 1996.

CHAPTER 12

If You Start Looking at Them as Humans, Then How Are You Gonna Kill Them?

Inigo Gilmore and Teresa Smith

At a press conference in a cavernous Alabama warehouse, banners and posters are rolled out: "Abandon Iraq, not the Gulf coast!" A tall, white soldier steps forward in desert fatigues. "I was in Iraq when Katrina happened and I watched U.S. citizens being washed ashore in New Orleans," he says. "War is oppression: we could be setting up hospitals right here. America is war-addicted. America is neglecting its poor."

A black reporter from a Fox TV news affiliate, visibly stunned, whispers: "Wow! That guy's pretty opinionated." Clearly such talk, even three years after the Iraq invasion, is still rare. This, after all, is the Deep South and this soldier less than a year ago was proudly serving his nation in Iraq.

The soldier was engaged in no ordinary protest. Earlier this month, for more than five days, around 200 veterans, military families, and survivors of Hurricane Katrina walked 130 miles from Mobile, Alabama, to New Orleans to mark the third anniversary of the Iraq war. At its vanguard was Iraq Veterans Against the War (IVAW), a group formed less than two years ago, whose very name has aroused intense hostility at the highest levels of the U.S. military.

Originally published March 29, 2006 by Guardian Unlimited Available at http://www.guardian.co.uk/Iraq/Story/0,,1741942,00.html.

Mobile is a grand old southern naval town, clinging to the Gulf Coast. The stars and stripes flutter from almost every balcony as the soldiers parade through the town, surprising onlookers. As they begin their soon-to-be-familiar chants—"Bush lied, many died!"—some shout "traitor," or hurl less polite terms of abuse. Elsewhere, a black man salutes as a blonde, middle-aged woman, emerging from a supermarket car park, cries out, "Take it all the way to the White House!" and offers the peace sign.

Michael Blake is at the front of the march. The 22-year-old from New York state is not quite sure how he ended up in the military; the child of "a feminist mom and hippy dad," he says he signed up thinking that he would have an adventure, never imagining that he would find himself in Iraq. He served from April 2003 to March 2004, some of that time as a Humvee driver. Deeply disturbed by his experience in Iraq, he filed for conscientious objector status and has been campaigning against the war ever since.

He claims that U.S. soldiers such as him were told little about Iraq, Iraqis, or Islam before serving there; other than a book of Arabic phrases, "the message was always: 'Islam is evil' and 'They hate us.' Most of the guys I was with believed it."

Blake says that the turning point for him came one day when his unit spent eight hours guarding a group of Iraqi women and children whose men were being questioned. He recalls: "The men were taken away and the women were screaming and crying, and I just remember thinking: this was exactly what Saddam used to do—and now we're doing it."

Becoming a peace activist, he says, has been a "cleansing" experience. "I'll never be normal again. I'll always have a sense of guilt." He tells us that he witnessed civilian Iraqis being killed indiscriminately. It would not be the most startling admission by the soldiers on the march.

"When IEDs [improvised explosive devices] would go off by the side of the road, the instructions were—or the practice was—to basically shoot up the landscape, anything that moved. And that kind of thing would happen a lot." So innocent people were killed? "It happened, yes." (He says he did not carry out any such killings himself.)

Blake, an activist with IVAW for the past 12 months, is angry that American people seem so untouched by the war, by the grim abuses committed by American soldiers. "The American media doesn't cover it and they don't care. The American people aren't seeing the real war—what's really happening there."

We are in a Mexican diner in Mississippi when Alan Shackleton, a quiet 24-year-old from Iowa, stuns the table into silence with a story of his own. He details how he and his comrades in Iraq suffered multiple casualties, including a close friend who died of his injuries. Then he pauses for a moment, swallows hard, and says: "And I ran over a little kid and killed him . . . and that's about it." He has been suffering from severe insomnia, but later he tells us that he has only been able to see a counselor once every six weeks and has been prescribed sleeping pills.

"We are very, very sorry for what we did to the Iraqi people," he says the next day, holding a handwritten poster declaring: "Thou shall not kill."

As we get closer to New Orleans, the coastline becomes increasingly ravaged. Joe Hatcher, always sporting a keffiyeh and punk chains, reflects on his own time in the military and the hostility he has met from pro-war activists at home in Colorado Springs, Colorado, a town with five army bases where he campaigns against the war at town hall forums. He says: "There's this old guy, George, an ex-colonel. He shows up and talks shit on everybody for being anti-war because 'it's ruining the morale of the soldier and encouraging the enemy.'"

"I scraped dead bodies off the pavements with a shovel and threw them in trash bags and left them there on the side of the road. And I really don't think the anti-war movement is what is infuriating people."

When we reach Biloxi, Mississippi, the police say that there is no permit for the march and everyone will have to walk on the pavement. This is tricky because Katrina has left this coastal road looking like a bomb site.

Jody Casey left the army five days ago and came straight to join the vets. The 29-year-old is no pacifist; he still firmly backs the military but says that he is speaking out in the hope of correcting many of the mistakes being made. He served as a scout sniper for a year until February 2006, based, like Blake, in the Sunni triangle.

He clearly feels a little ill at ease with some of the protesters' rhetoric, but eventually agrees to talk to us. He says that the turning point for him came after he returned from Iraq and watched videos that he and other soldiers in his unit shot while out on raids, including hour after hour of Iraqi soldiers beating up Iraqi civilians. While reviewing them back home he decided "it was not right."

What upset him the most about Iraq? "The total disregard for human life," he says, matter-of-factly. "I mean, you do what you do at the time because you feel like you need to. But then to watch it get kind of covered up, shoved under a rug. . . . 'Oh, that did not happen.'"

What kind of abuse did he witness? "Well, I mean, I have seen innocent people being killed. IEDs go off and [you] just zap any farmer that is close to you. You know, those people were out there trying to make a living, but on the other hand, you get hit by four or five of those IEDs and you get pretty tired of that, too."

Casey told us how, from the top down, there was little regard for the Iraqis, who were routinely called "hajjis," the Iraq equivalent of "gook."

"They basically jam into your head: 'This is hajji! This is hajji!' You totally take the human being out of it and make them into a video game."

It was a way of dehumanizing the Iraqis? "I mean, yeah—if you start looking at them as humans, and stuff like that, then how are you going to kill them?"

He says that soldiers who served in his area before his unit's arrival recommended them to keep spades on their vehicles so that if they killed innocent Iraqis, they could throw a spade off them to give the appearance that the dead Iraqi was digging a hole for a roadside bomb.

Casey says he didn't participate in any such killings himself, but claims the pervasive atmosphere was that "you could basically kill whoever you wanted—it was that easy. You did not even have to get off and dig a hole or anything. All you had to do was have some kind of picture. You're driving down the road at three in the morning. There's a guy on the side of the road, you shoot him . . . you throw a shovel off."

The IVAW, says Hatcher, "is becoming our religion, our fight—as in any religion we've confessed our wrongs, and now it's time to atone."

Just outside New Orleans, the sudden appearance of a reporter from the Washington office of al-Jazeera electrifies the former soldiers. It is a chance for the vets to turn confessional and the reporter is deluged with young former soldiers keen to be interviewed. "We want the Iraqi people to know that we stand with them," says Blake, "and that we're sorry, so sorry. That's why it was so important for us to appear on al-Jazeera."

A number of Vietnam veterans also on the march are a welcome presence. For all the attempts to deny a link between the two conflicts, for both sets of veterans the parallels are persuasive. Thomas Brinson survived the Tet offensive in Vietnam in 1968. "Iraq is just Arabic for Vietnam, like the poster says—the same horror, the same tears," he says.

Sitting on a riverbed outside New Orleans, Blake turns reflective. "I met an Iraqi at one of the public meetings I was talking at recently. He came up to me and told me he was originally from the town where I had been stationed. And I just went up to this complete stranger and hugged him and I said, 'I'm sorry. I'm so sorry.' And you know what? He told me it was OK. And it was beautiful. . . ." He starts to cry. "That was redemption."

CHAPTER 13

WHERE IS THE RAGE?

Justin C. Cliburn

Where is the rage? I had drill this weekend. Drill has been a forever-evolving presence in my life for the past six years. I went from looking forward to drill to hating it to missing it while I was in Iraq and back to looking forward to it when I returned. I used to hate drill, but found myself liking the weekends where I was reunited with those with whom I spent a year in Iraq.

Over the past few months, that [thought of returning] has turned into dread, and I am questioning whether or not I can remain an effective member of the military. Over the course of our many bull sessions at drill, the topic of Iraq inevitably came up. We exchanged stories and shared laughs as the new guys who didn't deploy looked on with wonder. Stories about clandestine drunken nights, the anger that comes with being kicked out of the chow hall for being sweaty, and getting to the point where you ignore gunfire took up most of the time; however, not all of the stories were so innocent. The same set of soldiers that in 2005 said they couldn't wait to kill "ragheads" were now bragging about times they scared Iraqis, bent the rules of engagement, and generally enjoyed playing bully for a year. I like these guys a lot, but I don't know why I was surprised. I had thought that maybe being there for a year would eventually change them and open their eyes to how their actions were inhumane, but I was wrong.

Adapted from a Sept. 7, 2007, blog post at http://www.progressiveu.org/224930-where-is-the-rage.

Someone who had not deployed before asked if we would go again. "In a heartbeat!" one soldier replied. Others assured him that they would have no problem going back. Now, the eyes were on me.

"No, I am not going back to participate in that war." The look of shock and awe on their faces quickly gave way to a flurry of questions about how I would get out, what I would do, how could I do that to my comrades, why did I feel the way, what did I think I was proving, and why did I think I could make a difference. The question that got me on a roll, however, was none of the above.

"What are you going to do . . . become a conscientious objector?" one soldier and friend said with a smirk and a chuckle.

"In fact, I just may do that. That's what I am, essentially, isn't it?" You could have heard a pin drop as the smirks fell from their faces; this appeared to be the worst thing I could have said. It amazes me how they had just gotten done talking about taking pleasure in bullying Iraqis and I was somehow demonized for stating that I had a moral objection to the occupation and subjugation of a Third World nation. I have a conscience, and that upset them more than anything else I could have said for some reason. I then spent about 20 minutes explaining why I had a moral objection to scaring Iraqis for the fun of it, occupying a country that didn't attack us, risking my life and the lives of my comrades for a war that does nothing but make the world more dangerous and less stable, and giving complicit approval to policy that has failed on every front. What stuck out to my comrade, however, wasn't about killing or risking my life. "Why do you keep talking about how unstable the Middle East has become as a result of the war? I mean, you almost seem to take it personally. Why do you care if wars break out there?" I was exasperated, but I kept trying to make him get it. I care because where there is war, there are innocent people dying. It doesn't matter if they're Iraqi, Syrian, Lebanese, Israeli, Palestinian, Iranian, or Turkish; I do not want them to experience the horrors of the war. On a more selfish front, the more unstable the region is, the more chance there is that we'll have to eventually intervene. The region has gotten worse and worse since our invasion to "stabilize the region," and constitutes a gross failure of the Iraq War. "Yeah, but why take it so seriously? I mean, you've got to defend your country either way. You've got to have the balls to go even if you don't agree with it."

No, it takes balls not to go when you don't agree. The courage to resist is oftentimes more honorable than the courage to enter a foxhole. These same friends of mine told me that they concede that the situation did nothing but get worse in our year in Iraq and that they didn't see how we could really "win." One went so far as to say he didn't believe in the war, but could never "abandon" his country. One said he agreed with everything I said . . . he just lacked the political will to do anything about it. Another stated his agreement with me, but said he was just going to hope that his contract runs out before they ever call us up again. Out of all those sitting there, only one fully supported the war, but all were willing to go back either for some misguided belief in honor or because they were too lazy or scared to do anything about it. I thought I could do this; I thought I could oppose the war and remain in the military. Change from within, I thought. I realized this weekend that that was a pipe dream, for me at least. I spend half my time in that uniform cringing at exaggerated stories; expressed pleasure in other peoples' pain; and empty, misguided proclamations of honor, integrity, and selfless service. I am done with the military.

I don't know how exactly I will leave the service just yet, but I know that I will. I entered the army in an honorable fashion and I will leave it that way, but leave it I will. I participated in the September 15, 2007, protests in Washington, D.C., with tens of thousands of other concerned Americans, including representatives of Iraq Veterans Against the War, Military Families Speak Out, Gold Star Families, and the ANSWER Coalition. I am taking more and more responsibility within IVAW to end this war, take care of our veterans, and provide reparations for the Iraqi people and it feels right. I accepted the position of Regional Coordinator-Gulf Coast Region and look forward to working with other IVAW Regional Coordinators in the future.

In the meantime, I simply ask, "Where is the rage?!"

CHAPTER 14

SOLDIERS IN REVOLT

Howard Zinn

As the situation in Iraq worsens with increasing attacks on U.S. troops, increasing numbers of roadside bombs, and increasing casualties, there are growing signs of resistance from the ranks of U.S. servicemen and service-women who do not want to fight the war.

The United States has a long history of resistance from within the military. Probably the most astonishing examples came from Vietnam with the appearance of what came to be called "fragging," the use of grenades and other explosive devices by disgruntled soldiers against their commanders. By the time U.S. soldiers were withdrawn from Vietnam in March 1973, there had been 86 deaths due to fragging.

In Vietnam, African American soldiers and sailors were more prone to rebellion than others, and GIs who came from the working class were less enthusiastic about the war than those from more privileged backgrounds. In short, racial resentment and class anger fueled much of the disaffection from the war in Vietnam.

Historically, rebellion in the ranks long predates Vietnam—from the Revolutionary War, the War with Mexico, the Civil War, the War with the Philippines and onward—although the antiwar activities of the Vietnam era were certainly the most massive, and the most successful in the nation's history.

Originally published in Howard Zinn, *A Power Governments Cannot Suppress* (San Francisco: City Lights Publishers, 2007), 173–77.

In his book *Soldiers in Revolt*,[1] David Cortright documents the rebellion of U.S. soldiers during the Vietnam years in stunning detail. Cortright's work is especially important to recall today because the war makers in the White House have been so anxious to put to rest what they call "the Vietnam syndrome." The word "syndrome" refers to a disease, in this case the disease against popular opposition to a war of aggression fought against a small country half the world away.

The word "disease" has shown up again, as more Americans declare their opposition to the war in Iraq. Surely, one of the factors in this national disapproval is the resemblance of the Iraq war to the war in Vietnam. The bombing and invasion of Iraq, the public has begun to realize, is not to defend the United States, but to control an oil-rich country already crushed by two wars and more than 10 years of economic sanctions.

It is undoubtedly the nature of this war, so steeped in deceptions perpetrated on the American public—the false claims that Iraq possessed "weapons of mass destruction" and was connected to 9/11—that has provoked opposition to the war among the military. Further, the revelations of torture, the killing of Iraqi civilians, and the devastation of the country from bombardment, foreign occupation, and sectarian violence, to which many of the dissenting soldiers have been witness, contribute to their alienation.

A CBS News dispatch on December 6, 2004, reported on American GIs who have deserted the military and fled north across the border to live in Canada. Theirs were among the first 5,000 desertions that have occurred over the opening years of the war in Iraq. One soldier told the CBS journalist: "I didn't want 'Died deluded in Iraq' on my gravestone."

Jeremy Hinzman, of Rapid City, South Dakota, went to Canada after being denied conscientious objector status by the army. He told CBS: "I was told in basic training that, if I'm given an illegal or immoral order, it is my duty to disobey it, and I feel that invading and occupying Iraq is an illegal and immoral thing to do." His contract with the government, Hinzman said, was "to defend the Constitution of the United States, not take part in offensive, preemptive wars."

According to the *Toronto Globe and Mail* report on December 8, 2004: "Jimmy Massey, a former marine staff sergeant, told an immigration and refugee board hearing in Toronto that he and his fellow marines shot and killed more than 30 unarmed men, women, and children, and even shot a young Iraqi who got out of his car with his arms in the air."

A *New York Times* story of March 18, 2005, told of an increasing number of soldiers seeking to escape in Iraq. One soldier from Hinesville, Georgia, was reported to have asked a relative to shoot him in the leg so he would not have to return to war. The deserters in Canada, according to this story, came from various parts of the country but reported the same kinds of motivations for wanting out of the military. "Some described grisly scenes from their first deployment to Iraq. One soldier said that he saw a wounded, weeping Iraqi child whom no one would help. . . . Others said they had simply realized that they did not believe in war, or at least not in this war."

Not all the dissension in the military has been due to an analysis of the moral nature of the war. As in other wars, very often, the soldiers simply feel maltreated by their officers, sent into dangerous situations without proper defenses, their lives considered cheap by higher-ups. On October 18, 2004, the *New York Times* reported that a platoon of 18 men and women refused to deliver a shipment of fuel from one air base to another because they said their trucks were unsafe and lacked proper armed escort.

In November 2004, the *New York Times* reported that the army was having trouble calling into duty members of the Individual Ready Reserve. These were former soldiers being ordered back into the military. And of 4,000 given notice to return to active duty, more than 1,800 of them requested exemptions. Furthermore, reports were multiplying, in the spring of 2005, of the difficulties army recruiters were finding in getting young people to enlist.

In early 2005, Naval Petty Officer Third Class Pablo Paredes refused to obey orders to board an assault ship in San Diego that was bound for the Persian Gulf. He told a U.S. Navy judge: "I believe as a member of the armed forces, beyond having a duty to my chain of command and my President, I have a higher duty to my conscience and to the supreme law of the land. Both of these higher duties dictate that I must not participate in any way, hands-on or indirect, in the current aggression that has been unleashed on Iraq."

For this, Paredes faced a year in the brig, but the navy judge, citing testimony about the illegality of the Iraq War, declined to give him jail time, instead gave him three months of hard labor, and reduced him in rank.

Especially disturbing are the stories of female soldiers who desert to escape sexual harassment by their male superiors. On June 26, 2006, *National Public Radio* reported the story of 21-year-old army specialist Suzanne Swift, who "deserted because of sexual harassment she suffered during a year-long appointment to Iraq." Police arrested Swift at her home in Oregon and transferred her to Fort Lewis, Washington. Since her story has been publicized in national media, Suzanne Swift's family has been contacted by scores of other female soldiers who have also been sexually harassed by fellow soldiers, but had not reported it.

In a reminder of the creation of the Vietnam Veterans Against the War, a number of men and women returning from Iraq formed Iraq Veterans Against the War. One of its founders, Kelly Dougherty, asked an audience at Harvard University in February 2005 to follow the precedent of Vietnam protests. In Iraq, she felt: "I'm not defending freedom, I'm protecting a corporate interest."

The level of GI protest in the current Iraq war is still far from what it came to be during the war in Vietnam, but as the war in Iraq continues, a point may be reached where men and women in uniform can no longer tolerate the injustices they witness and experience. It is encouraging to be reminded of the basic desire of human beings to live at peace with one another, once they have seen through the official lies and have developed the courage to resist the call to war.

NOTE

1. Cortright, 2005.

PART III

HEALING THE WOUNDS

When considering whether the cost of any new war is worth taking on, we rarely take into account the many costs that are unseen. After experiencing violence, major loss, and situations of deep fear, individuals carry lasting wounds. Trauma often appears to heal on the surface but remains to affect the quality of people's lives—and their propensity for violence in the future. Our ability to ameliorate the suffering caused by such human tragedy has much to do with whether we can break the cycle of violence at any point. In the previous section we noted the trauma experienced by soldiers. Here we focus on the circumstances of others who used the experience of trauma to reduce the enduring psychological pain and anger in order that such violence might not be repeated. Hector Aristizábal, a Colombian-born psychologist, actor, and torture survivor, recounts, with Diane Lefer, the mental state that made it possible for him to survive his torture and to share the perspectives of victims and perpetrators to audiences as a path toward healing.

In recent years there has been attention directed to the process of forgiveness. Azim Khamisa, whose son was the victim of random violence, went on to forgive his son's murderer, *and* to teach forgiveness and prevent future occurrences of violence through a foundation that he set up for these purposes. As forgiveness becomes a larger part of human cultures, we lay the foundations for a justice system based not on retribution or revenge but on restoration. In *restorative justice*, as this system is now called, the perpetrator of the violent crime takes responsibility, shows remorse, and takes on the tasks of compensating for the harm and sometimes working to build a society in which such violence is eliminated.

After the Rwandan genocide, people returned to live in the same areas as family members of people they had killed. The Gacaca court, a community justice system, was brought into play to help alleviate an overwhelmed judicial system and to assist a population needing closure for psychic wounds. These courts focus on confession, indications of remorse, and opportunities for forgiveness. In one instance a woman faced the man who killed her children and her husband and told him that she could never forget but she accepted his apology and he was welcome to find shelter in her home where she would treat him as a son. Ervin Staub and Angel Ryono report a study of a major reconciliation effort in Rwanda working with groups of people, with leaders, and with media to create a shared narrative, incorporating the historical context of the problem and establishing a shared history as a basis for peace.

Some of the healing after violence depends on a settlement between warring parties. The conflict between Israel and Palestine has been present since the inception of the state of Israel. A modern, highly militarized democratic state is pitted against territories holding the world's largest number of refugees, and in the case of Gaza, led by groups that carry out violent attacks on Israelis. Israeli military acts are defended in the name of security and attacks on Israelis are defended as retaliation for repression and killing of Palestinians. A political resolution of the conflict is made difficult by the unquestioning support of the Israeli military by the United States as well as by hardened extremist positions, which feed on the repetition of violence. In this climate one essential component of healing is the ability to keep people of goodwill, on both sides of the issue, in a dialogue outside of the posturing and blaming of the official political process. A specific project aimed at such healing is described by Laura Bernstein in Volume 3, and a basis for humanizing the Muslim "other" by understanding Muslim beliefs is described by Mohammed Abu-Nimer and Jamal Badawi in Volume 1. Herbert Kelman describes a long-term process bringing people positioned to be influential in policy into quiet dialogue out of the spotlight but highly important for preserving a necessary voice for peace.

In war, children are often kidnapped or lured into the role of child soldiers. They are easily forced or persuaded to accept the absolutely subservient roles to soldiers on whom they depend and to accept killing as normal. Some grow to be warriors in numerous civil clashes often extending beyond national boundaries. Michael Wessells deals with the circumstance of child soldiers and the culturally sensitive efforts, sometimes successful, in bringing them into a role as advocates for peace.

Without declared war, 27 million people are currently enslaved in every continent. Their daily traumatic abuse reflects the even grander displacement of people in the global economy and the willingness of most people not to notice. Melissa Anderson-Hinn describes the issues raised by slavery for the movement for peace and against violence. These issues are public information, rescue, rehabilitation, and prevention of this ultimately inhuman practice.

In Volume 1 the case was made that humans are not naturally inclined to kill others of their species (Nagler and Ryono, Pilisuk and Hall), that but must be programmed to do so by experience or psychological intervention. Even with such programmed efforts the trauma of knowingly killing another human being is often profound. Rachel MacNair presents the evidence for a special form of posttraumatic stress disorder (PTSD), that is, perpetration-induced traumatic stress (PITS), that is highly prevalent among those who have killed. As militaries in the course of war have created ways to make soldiers more likely to pull the trigger, they have simultaneously created a larger pool of people afflicted by this syndrome whose need for treatment becomes critically important not only for their own well-being but to forestall future violence. Their treatment is thus a necessary component of the search for peace. More than this, the recognition that we have badly underestimated human nature by overlooking this powerful innate empathy in every one of us provides an irresistible demand that we get on with that task.

—Marc Pilisuk and Michael N. Nagler

CHAPTER 15

OUT OF THE INNER WILDERNESS: TORTURE AND HEALING

Diane Lefer and Hector Aristizábal

This is a story of helplessness. It's also a story of agency and of healing.

THE NARRATIVE OF HELPLESSNESS

It was 4:00 A.M. at a low-income housing project on the outskirts of Medellín, Colombia. The whole neighborhood shook as military trucks rumbled into the barrio on the hunt for subversives. It was 1982 and I was 22 years old. We were living under the Estatuto de Seguridad, a repressive law that looked on almost any opposition to the government as communist-inspired. It was dangerous to talk politics. Sometimes it was even more danger-ous to create art. Friends of mine from the university had been seized and they disappeared only to reappear as cadavers found in a ditch, bodies covered with cuts and burns, toes and fingers broken, tongues missing, eyes gouged out.

It could happen to me. With my theater company, I performed plays that encouraged dissent by poking merciless fun at the military and the rich, at presidents and priests. I'd participated in protests and human rights demon-strations and had organized cultural events that included free and open discussion.

It could happen to my younger brother. It might already have happened. Juan Fernando had left the house two days earlier to go camping with three other kids. Then my family got word he had been arrested. My father and I went searching for him and were told he'd been turned over to the army, but we hadn't been able to learn his whereabouts or anything about his case. Did that mean he had been "disappeared"? I'd spent a restless night, my sleep troubled by fear for my brother.

Now I was instantly alert. I pulled on a T-shirt and warm-up pants and ran to look out through the blinds. A truck was stopped in front of our house directly beneath my window. Should I try to escape? A cold mist made everything indistinct, but by the light of the streetlamp I could see Juan surrounded by soldiers in the open back of the truck. So at least he was alive. But there was no running for it now. I couldn't try to save myself if the army had my brother.

"Open the door! This is a raid!" shouted a soldier, as a platoon of 10 soldiers and a sergeant burst in, pointing their weapons at my terrified parents. My father grabbed our little dog, his beloved Chihuahua, trying to keep her still. "All of you! Sit there!" ordered the sergeant. There was my teenage sister Estela, scared and embarrassed to be seen in the old nightclothes she slept in. And there were my brothers, Hernán Darío, who was fighting demons of his own that had nothing to do with politics, and Ignacio, the steady, reliable one who worked as a delivery boy to help support the family.

"You! What's up there?" said one of the soldiers as he pointed his rifle at me.

"It's where the boys sleep. Me and my brothers," I answered.

I led them up the stairs. They overturned furniture, threw clothes and papers everywhere, and tossed my mattress as they ransacked my room. As I watched them search, I started to calm down. I figured they weren't after me for anything I'd done. They expected to find something and I knew they wouldn't. I always cleaned the house when a government crackdown was expected. Pamphlets that criticized the president, leaflets demanding social justice, anything that mentioned trade unions or socialism—including books assigned at school—I'd gotten rid of everything. That's what I thought, and I was wrong.

When I was 14 years old, I'd written a letter to Radio Havana Cuba asking for books and magazines about the revolution. I was so proud of that letter that I'd kept a copy for myself. I had forgotten all about it. Now it was in the hands of the soldiers. And worse. Among my school papers, they found a booklet from the ELN, the Ejército de Liberación Nacional, the second largest guerrilla group in the country. This little pamphlet could mean a death sentence. It had to be Juan Fernando's. No one else in the family had any interest in the ELN. Was he hiding it? Or had he left it for me to find, a follow-up to our recent disagreement? Then they picked up the photos. As a psychology student, I had been documenting the degrading treatment of mental patients at the charity hospital. According to the sergeant, these wretched looking human beings were hostages held by the guerrillas.

My mother cried and begged the soldiers to let me go, but I was handcuffed and pushed out to the street. It was August, winter in Colombia, and a cold gray dawn was breaking. All the world's colors seemed washed out, gone. And it was quiet, abnormally quiet. No shouts, no street vendors, no radios. But hundreds of neighbors had come out of their houses to see what was happening. They watched in silence and I remember thinking, *witnesses*, hoping that it would make a difference, hoping that the Army would not be able to just disappear us when so many people had seen us detained.

I was put in the back of the truck with my brother.

"Juan," I cried. Soldiers kicked us and struck us with their rifle butts and told us to shut up but I had to talk to him. If we couldn't explain away that ELN booklet, one or both of us might die. "I'm going to say you've been in the mental hospital, okay?" I said. We could admit he might have picked up some guerrilla propaganda, but I would explain that he wasn't capable of understanding what it meant. My brother said nothing, but his eyes were full of pain.

We were driven to an army post in another part of town. Followed by three more trucks, we entered the compound. Each truck carried one of the boys who'd gone camping. Soldiers ordered us out and stood us facing a wall. I remember the sun breaking through at last, throwing shadows against the whitewashed adobe, and the brief touches of warmth, now on my shoulders, now my back.

"Comunistas!" "Subversivos!" they shouted. Soldiers ran by in formation, hollering insults: "Hijueputas!" The firing squad stopped and aimed their rifles. Someone shouted: "The one with the red shirt!" Bang! "The one with the long hair!" My heart exploded in my throat. "Long hair" meant me. Bullets slammed into the wall again and again just above my head, but they didn't hit me.

What were they going to do to us? We stood under guard for hours at that wall. The day went on and on and I shivered in the cold, waiting.

"Don't look!" they ordered, but I looked and saw a short fat man lead my brother's friends away one by one. They were so young, just kids. What would happen to them? At last the soldiers brought them back. "Don't look!" But I saw the boys were soaking wet and trembling. "Shut up! Don't talk!" But there were whispers. We were tortured. They were tortured.

A man took Juan Fernando. Minutes went by. Then hours. He didn't bring my brother back. Images roared through my mind: mutilated bodies, my brother's face. Torture. When the man came back, he was alone.

The man came for me.

He led me up a hill to a cell at the end of a long one-story building. He blindfolded me. He barked out questions: "Name?" "Nickname?" "What organization do you belong to?"

"Sir, I don't belong to any organization."

The blow knocked the wind out of me. The fists slammed into my stomach again. I doubled over and he kicked me.

"What actions have you planned? Where do you cache your weapons?" he demanded.

I had no answers for him, and so he beat me. Except for when he knocked me to the ground, I was not permitted to lie down or sit but had to remain standing day and night. When he left, the torture became psychological as I waited for his return with no hope of rescue. The door creaked open. No food. No water. No sleep. But still more questions for which I had no answers.

A second interrogator came to see me. From his way of speaking, this one seemed to be an educated, well-mannered man. He pretended to be my friend. "If you don't give me names," he said in a kind voice, "that man is going to come back. Your brother is already in very bad shape, and if that man comes back, I can't guarantee you will survive." But I had no names to give him.

The torturer called for soldiers to help him.

They hold my head under water, and they bring me to the verge of drowning again and again. They strip me and attach electrodes to my testicles and send jolts of electricity tearing through my nerves. I scream, but only they can hear me. Then, el potro—an ingenious technique that can leave permanent damage but no scars. Soldiers I cannot see cover my hands and my lower arms with what feels like a wet sweater. Something is pulled tight, then my arms are jerked behind me and somehow I'm hanging painfully in space over an abyss, arms wrenched from sockets, my body extended so that the pain is everywhere.

I'm utterly abandoned. The pain disseminates itself to every cell. It extends to the brain and blows out all conscious thought, all sense of self. Was there always a void in the center of me? It's there now. I disintegrate and fall into it.

Days later, soldiers drove me around in a small Jeep. One pushed the barrel of his rifle into my mouth. "You're going to die now," he said. "Just like your brother."

Instead, they forced me into an underground passage where I found Juan and his friends alive, all of us hidden from view—as we later learned—while a human rights delegation searched for us somewhere aboveground. The ceiling of our dungeon was so low we had to crawl. The air was hot and thick, and the stench unbearable from human waste and from the festering wounds of a black man from Chocó we found chained and shackled there, bleeding to death in the dark. He told us he had no idea why he'd been arrested and tortured. "Worse than a street animal," he said. There was nothing we could do to help him or ease his pain till it turned out another prisoner had bribed a guard for marijuana which he offered to the dying man. "Here, brother," he said. The man dying in shackles filled his lungs and began to laugh and the smoke filled the dark and filthy crawlspace. We all filled our lungs and laughed and I believe I'll hear our laughter echoing in that cave and in my nightmares for the rest of my life.

It must have been the witnesses and the human rights delegation that saved us. We could have been executed in secret. Instead, we were brought before a judge. Our mental hospital story worked. The ELN booklet was deemed harmless, but my brother went to prison for carrying a subversive weapon—a machete. He went in an idealistic young man: He came out a committed revolutionary, convinced there was no alternative to the armed struggle.

As for me, 10 days after my arrest, the Army let me go, but the ordeal marked me. It marks me still.

My torturer. I could never forget what he looked like: short curly hair, thick eyebrows, a small moustache, stocky body, broad shoulders, a small but noticeable belly, and penetrating greenish eyes. If I ever found him, I would have my revenge.

My torturer. That's a pronoun I need to lose, and one I hear from so many other survivors—*my* perpetrator, *my* rapist—because while the state-sponsored violation of a person's body is a very specific assault, it has much in common with other atrocities. When you're in that room, that isolated place where no help can reach you, where you can no longer count on family or friends or human decency, there is one person there with you. He was entirely focused on controlling me, watching me, listening to my breath, keeping me alive, yet all the while holding over me the power of life and death. And I had never in my life paid such close attention to anyone. I was alert to him and to his every response, trying to predict his every move with all my senses until pain overwhelmed everything and I lost my very identity. In that moment of utter surrender, when everyone else had abandoned me, when my own body and mind betrayed me, only he was there.

For a long time the man who tortured me was a primary figure in my mental life.

I now understand that one of the long-lasting effects of such trauma is to confuse that enforced and claustrophobic connection with intimacy. I need to break that connection and recreate the loving connections in my life.

I need to think of that man as *a* torturer, not *my* torturer, and to understand that he belonged to the army, to the system of repression, and not to me.

THE NARRATIVE OF AGENCY

What I've told you so far is true, but it's not the whole truth.

There's a slightly different narrative I tell myself, a form of recycling. I look at a dirty experience, one I instinctively wish to get rid of, and instead try to find in it something of value. I will not allow myself to remain obsessed with my weakness. I tell myself: *I survived.* I revisit my wound to remember what made me strong.

So here's the other, equally true, version of my story—a narrative not of my helplessness, but of my resistance.

A man blindfolded me. Someone pushed me into a room. About 20 minutes later, I heard the lock turn, the door creak open, and I recognized the same smell of tobacco and sweat. Though the man who came to torture me tried to disguise his voice, I realized I was dealing with the same fat man in civilian clothes who had led me up the hill. At that moment, I lost all respect for him. He thought he could hide his identity. He thought I was completely vulnerable and at his mercy but at that moment, I felt superior. I could identify him. That meant I was holding a card he didn't know I had and that gave me a feeling of power.

It is true the pain was often unbearable. It is also true that I often exaggerated it. As I'd done so much physical training as an actor, I could make myself fly back through the room when he hit me. I'd land back against the wall and get some idea of the dimensions of this terrible space. When they submerged my head, I put on such a great act of drowning that I scared them. I pretended to be more exhausted than I was, falling against the torturer. And when he instinctively reached out to catch me, I sighed and pretended to fall asleep in his arms. He didn't like that one bit! Though I could not resist the things they did to me, I refused to be passive. Would my ploys be of any use? I had no idea, but each time I believed I'd outwitted my tormentors, I felt stronger.

"Your brother has told us everything," he said. "We know you're an urban guerrilla commander. You're the one who's training those kids."

The son-of-a-bitch had to be lying. Juan Fernando would never have said such a thing. Again, I assured myself I knew more than he did.

"He's crazy," I said. "My brother has been hospitalized." The worst pain was imagining what they might do to him. "Please don't hurt him," I pleaded.

I tried to learn as much about my situation as I could even when I had no idea how the information might serve me. A loose paving stone in the passageway echoed with a clunk every time the torturer or a guard came within

9 or 10 steps of the cell. At first, the sound made me panic. It meant I was going to be hurt. But then I realized it gave me warning. I knew when the torturer was coming back. More important, the sound let me know when I was alone and when I was being watched. I counted out the time it took for the guard to make his transit up and down the passage, so then I knew how long I had before I'd be seen. There was something else I could use to my advantage: my hands had been bound behind my back when I was arrested, but after the mug shot, the soldier had handcuffed me in front. That meant I could raise my wrists and push back the blindfold . . . if I dared.

Clunk. With my heart pounding, I waited. Then I slowly raised my wrists but I didn't have the guts to go further. I counted the minutes. I waited. Clunk. I tried again. Were they watching? I let myself touch the blindfold. I scratched my forehead, waiting to see if anything would happen. I waited. No one hit me. I counted out the time. Clunk. I had to remove the blindfold but—*Next time*, I kept telling myself. *I'll do it next time. But they'll catch me*, I thought and then again promised myself *next time*. It took me what felt like forever but then I did it. I pushed the blindfold back.

There through the bars I could see down the hill. There was the wall, and there was Juan Fernando, alive, looking scared. Even at a distance I could sense his tension, but he was alive. He was okay. They had lied to me.

In the story I tell myself now, I saved my brother and he saved me. Every time the torturer entered, all I could talk about was Juan Fernando. *Where is my brother? What are you doing to him? He's fragile. If anything happens to him, our mother will die.* I named people I knew at the mental hospital and claimed they had treated him. By holding onto my love and concern for my brother, I never entirely lost my connection to humanity outside that room. My emotional ties were not completely broken.

Once I finally pushed the blindfold back and got away with it, I did it again and again; however, each time the torturer returned, I was standing obediently in exactly the same place in the room. Each time I *looked*, my first act was to reassure myself that my brother was still all right. Then I went further. To my surprise, I saw my cell had a toilet. Though I had kept complaining of hunger and exhaustion and thirst, now, when unobserved, I was able to drink from the tank. The interrogators had left a pile of evidence in the middle of the room. There was the ELN pamphlet. There was a photo of one of the mental patients from the hospital in a barred cell—the so-called guerrilla hostage. And there, at the bottom of the pile, was the only evidence with my name and with my handwriting—the copy of the letter to Radio Havana Cuba. I tore it up and flushed it down the toilet. The noise was a risk, but not taking that risk seemed the greater danger.

At the end of 10 days, I was released for lack of evidence.

HEALING

Besides revising the narrative I tell, I have tried to see the time of my torture as an initiatory ordeal. The initiate is separated from his accustomed world. He doesn't know where he has been taken. Naked and unprotected, he will face severe trials. He won't know what comes next. He must accept the unknown outcome. Afterward, he returns to his society and is recognized in celebration.

I am not saying the torture *was* an initiation, but that for my own sake, to move past the victim position and claim my own power, I have tried to *resignify* it as such. I had gone through an ordeal—not at the hands of the elders, but at the hands of perpetrators. The elders would have taught me to love life and to value my culture. Instead, the torturers made me lose faith in life. They made me wish I could die just to end the pain. They left in me a desire for revenge, fueled by a violent and deadly rage. I had survived but unlike the traditional initiate, I wasn't brought back to the community and celebrated. The perpetrators left me in the wilderness and it was up to me, through my own resources, to find the way home.

But merely returning home is not enough. Like the shaman—though I would not presume to claim that title—the torture survivor has experienced a break with the reality on which most of us rely. His identity has disintegrated. He has descended to hell but he has also returned and that means he knows the path. He can go and come back, descend and return. From the terrible depths the shaman brings back medicine and knowledge.

For me, this means that to return in the fullest sense, I must take a story back to the world, I must speak out against torture, I must provide healing to those who've been to hell and are finding it hard to rediscover the path back to life.

Today, approximately half-a-million torture survivors live in the United States. Many survivors speak reluctantly, if they are able to speak at all. Besides sometimes permanent or chronic physical damage, the psychic disintegration that accompanies torture leaves the survivor on unstable ground. Survivors cope with the symptoms of post-traumatic stress, with impaired memory, anxiety, depression, and difficulties in forming or maintaining relationships. You may know a survivor without being aware of it. You may have a neighbor, friend, partner, teacher, student, patient, client, or colleague who copes silently with torture's long-term effects.

We Latin Americans who survived the horrific repression of the 1970s and 1980s (often sponsored by the U.S. government and carried out by military officers trained by the U.S. Army at the School of the Americas) have had decades to process our emotions and to learn that breaking silence is part of healing. The trauma robs you of your community, your language, and your relations. All of these connections are broken. If we don't reconnect, we replicate the isolation of the torture chamber over and over. We have to find the door and the key to unlock it.

I had spoken out against torture for years, but when photographs surfaced of the hell of Abu Ghraib, old feelings of helplessness and rage threatened to overwhelm me. In collaboration with my friend Diane and my friend Enzo Fina, a musician, I created "Nightwind," an autobiographical solo performance about my arrest and torture; I've toured performing the program over thousands of miles and through several countries to mobilize public opinion.

After a performance, someone always asks how it affects me to relive the trauma. The truth is, I'm not sure, though I have many answers. Turning the experience into art, into an aesthetic object, gives me a sense of control and, I hope, creates beauty where once there was only pain. And that very pain empowers me as an activist as I seek allies in the struggle against such horrendous practices. Performing has become for me a way to unlock that chamber door. I used to think I needed to unlock it to get out; however, now it occurs to me an open door also serves to invite people in. Torture occurs in isolation, in secret. When I bring an audience into the experience with me, I am supported by their active participation as witnesses, and the space can no longer be a torture chamber. The space itself is transformed.

To help others heal, I joined the board of the Program for Torture Victims (PTV), the first program in the United States dedicated to treating survivors suffering the physical and psychological consequences of state-sponsored violence. PTV got its start in 1980, after two Latin American exiles met in Los Angeles. Dr. José Quiroga, a cardiologist, had been Chilean president Salvador Allende's personal physician before the military coup that cost Allende his life. Ana Deutsch, a psychologist, survived the dirty war in Argentina, escaping to the United States along with her family after the military government threatened to arrest them for their opposition activities. Ana and José knew there were survivors in Los Angeles who weren't getting the care they needed due to poverty, fear, or a powerful reluctance to speak of what they had endured. The two simply began offering their services, often in their own living rooms, free of charge.

In 1994, PTV gained nonprofit status and the founders were finally able to seek outside funding, rent offices at Mercado La Paloma, and expand a staff of therapists, social workers, and administrators, as well as build a roster of cooperating doctors and immigration asylum attorneys.

Initially, most clients came from Latin America. Today, PTV serves people from more than 65 countries around the world, from Afghanistan to

Zimbabwe. As a board member, I often speak on behalf of PTV while also reaching out to my fellow survivors through the Healing Club. We get together to dance and play theatre games and soccer. We have fun, but also serve a serious purpose. When a severely traumatized person cannot make eye contact or speak, how will this person be able to go to an asylum hearing and face the immigration judge and answer questions about torture and rape? The games we play are a way to prepare them. I don't do anything threatening. I don't bring up the big issues, at least not at first. And there is nothing at stake. We just play, and in this way we come back into our bodies and reclaim our voices.

I recently worked—or played—with a survivor from Cameroon who arrived in the United States rendered mute. Months later, he was able to make a statement to a group of college students. Admittedly, his presentation was brief and he spoke in general terms, offering no personal account. More privately, he told me he loves the United States because in this country, everyone gets a fair trial and only terrible criminals go to prison. He asked: "Why doesn't the United States care about Cameroon? President Bush invades Iraq to get rid of a dictator. Why won't he invade my country?" This man had suffered horribly for speaking out against his government in his homeland. Now, as much as I quietly disagreed with his opinions, what mattered to me most was that he could express them.

Then there's Meluleki. He's a tall, handsome young man, always clean cut and, like many Africans I've met in Los Angeles, he's rather formal. For his first two years in the United States, my friend Meluleki sat in an apartment, doing nothing, utterly depressed as he waited for the government to decide whether to grant his application for asylum.

"Go out," I suggested once. "Get a job, even if it's a crummy job. It would be something to do."

"No," he said. "They told me since I asked for asylum I'm not allowed to work. If they catch me working, I don't get it."

So Meluleki waited. No money. Nothing to do. All he had were memories of the life he used to lead and the political violence and torture that made him leave that life behind.

I imagine he was like me in that chamber, tormented not just with the pain, not just with the interrogator's questions, but the bigger questions that never leave you: *Where is everybody? Where are my family, my friends, the country, and the values of this society? Why can this happen apparently with such ease? How can people treat other human beings like this? Why doesn't anyone care? Where are the people?*

In Zimbabwe, Meluleki was an actor, which is why his therapist, Ken Louria, wanted us to meet. Now he speaks so softly, the words come out and are swallowed back almost before I can hear what he's said. Someone who doesn't know the consequences of torture might find it hard to believe this man once projected his strong voice in street theatre performances, out in the open air.

I take him to buy a drum—a djembe drum, a healing drum. We find drums painted in the colors of Africa, and another in a multi-mask design, adorned with brightly patterned swirls. But the drum Meluleki chooses isn't painted. Instead, it's the grain of the wood and the simplicity of the braided cord around the drumhead that give it beauty. The sales clerk comes over to offer help, but for the first time since I've known Meluleki, it is clear he needs no help from anyone. As soon as his hand touches the goat-skin, my friend is fully alive.

Over lunch, I ask Meluleki about the initiation rites of his tribe. "The older men of the village initiate you," he explains. "Your uncles, not your father. If something is bothering me or I am in some trouble, I tell my uncle. He may then talk to my father or instruct me, but in our custom, I never go directly to my father."

"Who would be the equivalent of your uncle in Los Angeles?" I ask.

He names his therapist. He names the whole PTV program. "And you," he says, "because you went with me to get this drum."

"When you get your asylum, we should celebrate," I say. "Your uncles should offer you a welcoming ceremony."

He smiles, saying, "That will be good, and I will tell you how."

And so one day in May, we all sit in a circle in the meeting room downstairs at Mercado La Paloma. The conference table is gone and the walls are decorated with African fabrics. We are survivors and staff and children and friends. We come from the United States and Sri Lanka, Congo, Guatemala, Eritrea, France, Italy, Palestine, El Salvador, and more. We speak English, Spanish, Shona, Russian, Armenian, Georgian, Tigrinya, Singhalese, Arabic, Italian, Amharic, and more African languages than I can name.

"I am Hector," I say, moving my arms in a flourish. Everyone repeats, "I am Hector," and the whole circle copies me, waving their arms. "I am Melu," says Meluleki. One by one, we introduce ourselves with a name and gesture, to be imitated and celebrated by all. At last, we're back to Meluleki. Now it is his chance to say more than his name, to tell us all exactly how he wants to be known.

He begins to drum. He speaks in remembrance of those who have died in Zimbabwe and then he says:

My name is Meluleki. My umbilical cord was buried in the red soils of kwaGodlwayo omnyama. . . . [Instantly the Zimbabwean women in the room begin to ululate, galvanizing us all. They join in Meluleki's praise of his people:] . . . umahlaba ayithwale owadeluku biya ngamahlahla wabiya ngamakhand' amadoda. This is how I praise my chief and identify with the sons and daughters of the soil, the people of my origin, the Ndebele tribe. I remember growing up in the presence of the Fifth Brigade, commonly known as the "gukurahundi," one of the most ruthless armies that have ever existed on this planet. They massacred more than 30,000 of my beloved brothers and sisters on the instructions of the so-called angel of death, Robert Gabriel Mugabe, who has successfully destroyed my motherland for the past 27 years. I tried with my fellow comrades to voice our concerns through staging theatre shows in the schools, crèches, youth centers, and streets of Bulawayo, but the message was too clear to go unheard by the little dogs that he has planted all over. These people visited me without an invitation and, believe me, it was not a pleasant visit. This is what they did to me.

He doesn't speak now, but his hands fly as he drums, hard and fast, and then faster.

"Today I have a scar on my forehead. When I look at the mirror I see a defeated warrior, but it's only for the moment," he tells us.

Will Mugabe fall at last? Will Meluleki someday return home?

He taps his drum. His fellow countrymen join him as they sing the national anthem: *Mayihlom' ihlasele, nkosi sikelel' izwe lase Zimbabwe.*

We welcome him to the PTV family, first with words. He receives a welcome from his therapist, Ken Louria. A man from Cameroon talks of the support people must give each other: "No matter where you are or how bold, you need someone in front carrying the torch." We welcome him then with our drums. I've got mine. Enzo is playing, too, and so is case manager Saba Kidane who's brought a drum of her own and can't stop smiling as she joins in.

We teach each other songs in our different languages and when we start to dance, I see the African woman—the one who has sat silent and stiff with tears on her expressionless face—suddenly rise. She's out in front now, leading the dance, swaying and clapping.

"Look, look," says her friend. "This is the first time I see her happy since she arrives in the United States."

Now we have welcomed Meluleki and this woman, too, into the PTV community. It remains to be seen whether they will be welcomed by Los Angeles and into the wider community of the United States of America.

Where is everybody? We are here.

CHAPTER 16

FROM GRIEF TO GRATITUDE: THE TARIQ KHAMISA FOUNDATION

Azim N. Khamisa

If we are to have real peace in the world, we shall have to begin with the children.

—Mahatma Gandhi

The Tariq Khamisa Foundation (TKF) is dedicated to empowering kids to say "no" to gangs, guns, and violence, to saving lives, and to teaching peace. I founded it as my life's mission in response to a tragedy. On January 21, 1995, my 20-year-old son Tariq Khamisa, a San Diego State University student, was delivering pizzas when he was shot and killed by a stranger, a 14-year-old named Tony Hicks, who fired the fatal bullet on orders from an 18-year-old gang leader. While I will mourn Tariq's tragic death for the rest of my life, I have channeled my grief into a powerful commitment to stop kids from killing kids through the violence-prevention educational programs of TKF, established in October 1995 in loving memory of my son.

TKF was inspired in a beautiful instant when I was embraced with love in the arms of God. In the midst of that peace and safety, I understood that there were victims at both ends of the gun. My son was a victim of the

This chapter is an adaptation from Azim Khamisa, *From Forgiveness to Fulfillment* (ANK Publishing, 2007).

shooter, Tony Hicks. And Tony himself was a victim of early childhood abuse and neglect. Although living with his loving grandfather, Tony was still angry because of many early problems. When the gang leader told him to shoot a pizza deliveryman for two pizzas, he did. Holding the gun, he was an angry 14-year-old who had come from an extended family of violent gang members. In that murderous moment, he didn't value any life, including his own. Then Tony realized this was the worst thing he'd ever done and that it could not be reversed.

Who is responsible for causing, and for stopping, youth violence in our society? Every day 75 kids, aged 12 to 18, get shot, and 13 of them die. Another 237 youth are arrested daily for violent crimes involving a weapon. About 760,000 kids are in 24,000 youth gangs. Homicide is the leading cause of death in California for youth aged 15 to 19. Fifty percent of kids do not feel safe at school. Statistics reveal the tragic likelihood that if a kid joins a gang, he or she will either be in prison or dead by the age of 25. No less than the combined hearts of every one of us needs to be caring for all of our children faced with such daunting challenges.

Before Tariq's death, I rarely considered the overall welfare of society's children. I took care of my own children and thought, as many people do, that other children were the responsibility of their own parents. Little did I know how many parents and guardians are violent role models for their kids. How then are these children supposed to live differently when violence is promoted as a way of life?

When I became aware of the violent youth statistics in our country, I began to ask, "Why do our kids join gangs?" The answers I found horrified me. Joining gangs is macho. Kids join to get a sense of respect. Or they join for protection because they live in an area where if they don't join *this* gang, then *that* gang will target them. Kids also join gangs for a sense of belonging. The fact that kids join gangs indicates a gross lack in what our families and communities offer children. Otherwise, no youth would need to join a gang to gain respect, to feel safe, or to have a sense of belonging.

After learning the truth about gangs and youth violence, I knew in my heart that I had to do something to save children from becoming victims like Tariq and Tony. I also knew that I couldn't do it alone. As these thoughts were arising, my spiritual teachers reminded me that there is a time to grieve and a time to stop grieving. After our 40-day ritual, it was time to let Tariq's soul fly to freedom. My teachers affirmed that by doing good deeds I could accumulate spiritual currency to help my son's soul on its way.

TKF was born of this dual inspiration: to do good deeds to advance Tariq's journey and to give my life's attention to helping children learn to make nonviolent and peaceful choices. If I could save one child, I would feel that

I had made a difference. My desire to stop kids from killing kids took root. Today it has blossomed into a fully staffed, nonprofit organization that successfully implements several youth and parent programs.

Since 1995, the work of the foundation to end the epidemic of violence has touched millions of children through in-school assemblies, video presentations, and broadcasts into the classroom. We have touched at least as many adults through extensive national and international print and electronic media coverage, as well as television and radio exposure. These students, teachers, and parents—as well as many others I reach through forgiveness workshops and speaking at conferences and other venues—are coming to the self-empowering realization that they always have choice. They learn that even though they've been exposed to violence, they do not have to pattern their lives after it. Violence begets violence. It is never a good choice.

Through violence-prevention education, TKF inspires students away from a destiny of violence. Through community and educational partnerships, we're cultivating new attitudes and behaviors by role modeling integrity, kindness, empathy, understanding, peace, forgiveness, compassion, and respect. TKF empowers future leaders by inspiring young people to choose nonviolence. Through our programs, we are nurturing a generation of peacemakers who will create a world free from youth violence. We provide antidotes to negative influences, whether from violent family members and peers or from the media where extreme violence and aggression are sensationalized.

Since gang members begin pressuring kids at the fifth-grade level to join gangs, our prevention strategy focuses on youths in the fourth to eighth grades. Our messages of nonviolence and forgiveness instill in the kids the desire to be peacemakers, not gang members. And the strength of our belief that TKF's programs make a difference is backed up by measurable results.

MISSION AND CORE VALUES

TKF's mission is stopping kids from killing kids and breaking the cycle of violence by inspiring nonviolent choices and planting seeds of hope for our children's future. Three core values guide the implementation of the mission. They are integrity, compassionate confrontation, and forgiveness.

Integrity means being honest and genuine in our dealings with others and holding fast to our commitments rather than our desires. We make many commitments to TKF, to ourselves, and to our community. At times these commitments may be in conflict. To remain steadfast to our deepest commitments, we bring these conflicts to light and work together to resolve them.

Confrontation involves openly and honestly facing our differences, conflicts, and contradictions. Compassion means caring about the suffering and well-being of others. At TKF, we embrace compassionate confrontation to achieve a higher understanding with mutually beneficial results. This practice requires compassionate listening and is a healthy ingredient to human interactions. It creates opportunities for change. We confront one another with a loving and compassionate intent.

Forgiveness means letting go of resentment. It starts with acknowledging that harm has been done. Through feeling this pain, we tap into the power of forgiveness, the release of resentment. Ultimately, we reach out with love and compassion to the offender. We forgive others when they have wronged us or someone else. We ask for forgiveness when we have wronged others. We acknowledge that at times we will fail to forgive. We help each other to forgive, to accept forgiveness, and to accept each other through the process. We strive to forgive.

The core values are important to our foundation because they ensure that we are doing everything possible to walk our talk. When we go into the schools to teach peace, nonviolence, and forgiveness to the students, they know whether or not we are speaking the truth. Kids are very much in tune with "vibes," and if they sense that we are not speaking from a place of integrity, they'll stop listening.

BREAKING THE CYCLE OF VIOLENCE

In breaking the cycle of violence, prevention is clearly the ultimate solution. We must keep our vulnerable youth from joining gangs and engaging in other risky behaviors that can destroy their own futures and cause serious harm to others.

How do we approach breaking the dreadful cycle of violence, so often promoted in our society? We raise awareness in children, especially those predisposed to vengeful and aggressive behaviors, of the consequences of their actions, consequences beyond just doing some time in juvenile hall. We show how one mindless, violent decision, such as the one Tony made, can affect many lives for generations to come. We instill awareness that other decisions can be made. We want them to discover the power of a peaceful decision and a forgiving heart. We show that Tony had a choice that night to pull the trigger on that gun or not to pull it.

TKF executive director Lisa Grogan said, "When Tony made that one violent choice in that one moment, not only did Tariq's and Tony's lives change, but also so did other lives of infinite proportions. Maybe Tony, who wanted to become a doctor, would have saved people's lives and in turn would have affected so many other people. Perhaps Tariq and his fiancée would have had children, who then would have had more children, who all would have done wonderful things. The world will never know. That is the power of one poor, thoughtless, violent choice."

THE POWER OF CHOICE AND THE SIX KEY MESSAGES

TKF's mission is to teach kids they have choices and to lead them toward lives of peace and nonviolence. To this end, we have developed several programs within the framework of our comprehensive strategy. Two of these programs are the Violence Impact Forum Assembly (VIF) and Ending the Cycle of Violence. Both are held during school hours and are facilitated by TKF and/or school staff. All of our programs are designed to inspire the kids to learn and essentially live by TKF's six key messages:

1. Violence is real and hurts everyone.
2. Actions have consequences.
3. Youth can make good and nonviolent choices.
4. Youth can work toward forgiveness as opposed to seeking revenge.
5. Everyone deserves to be loved and treated well.
6. From conflict, love and unity are possible.

Our programs deliver these messages and are designed to transform kids by offering them education beyond the basics of reading, writing, and mathematics. Many of the principals, teachers, and counselors at the schools where we speak tell us that our messages are important, because no matter what other future life choices these kids make, most of them are going to become parents one day. As parents, the skills that they will most certainly need are those that we teach: nonviolence, compassion, and forgiveness.

The kids in our programs learn to cope with loss and trauma and with emotional highs and lows. They discover they are not alone in experiencing these sorts of things. They learn to give a direction to their lives to be of benefit to others, not just themselves. They learn how to release anger without causing harm, and they look at alternative, win-win ways to resolve conflicts nonviolently. We do our best to instill the values and practices of empathy, compassion, and forgiveness through our teaching and example.

VIOLENCE IMPACT FORUM ASSEMBLY (VIF)

Our first program, the Violence Impact Forum Assembly (VIF), is an interactive, in-school assembly that shares the real-life TKF story of Tariq and Tony. It demonstrates to students the devastation and consequences of violence. A video presentation reenacts the shooting and its aftermath and shows the truth about gangs and prison life. The goal is to empower youth for resiliency and positive choices. Through our focus on forgiveness and choices, students come to understand the lifelong consequences of Tony's one deadly choice and the critical importance of choosing nonviolence.

As mentioned, we take the VIF into elementary and middle schools, beginning with the fourth grade. If we can get to the kids first and impress on them that they have the personal power and free will to make nonviolent and peaceful choices, then we may save them from the lives of violence that they may otherwise have chosen. Some teachers say our assembly is more needed than almost any other curriculum. Not every child is going to join a gang or be pressured to join. However, violence comes in many forms: bullying, starting a rumor, name calling, segregation. Every child has experienced some violence, so we teach what violence looks like in varied forms.

Before the day of the VIF, an information sheet is sent out to the students' parents, along with an opt-out letter in case a parent does not want his or her child to attend. Many of these kids come from families where gang activity is the norm. The opt-out letter is rarely returned.

We also provide a teacher's guide for the VIF. Each school that participates agrees to do a follow-up session with their students. Our teacher's guide facilitates that follow-up with the TKF vision statement, an abbreviated version of the TKF story, a description of the VIF, objectives, the teacher's role, and a student debriefing agenda. "Tariq's Philosophy of Life" essay and Tony's sentencing speech are also included.

The VIF is a transformative experience for the kids. As the video plays, the kids are immediately drawn in by the rap music. Those who are still talking to their friends quiet down as the dramatic scene unfolds before them of street-smart youths hanging out in the shadows while the pizza delivery man becomes more and more frustrated by his inability to find the right address.

When "Tony" points the gun at "Tariq," any remaining noise from the students' normal energetic distractions dissolves, and the school auditorium is perfectly still. The hush is palpable, the students' breaths drawn in. And then, with the sound of the shot, it's as if the students exhale in one united breath. What they have just witnessed is something they may never have witnessed before. Or, if some of them have, the dramatic video likely may have triggered memories of events from their own lives.

With the video over and the lights becoming brighter, Sal Giacalone, Tariq's boss from the Italian restaurant where he was working the night of the shooting, comes on stage and welcomes the students. He thanks them for having TKF come to their school, for their respect, and for paying close attention to the video and to the speakers who will be coming on stage.

He tells the kids that members of TKF have come to talk to them about making choices, and he instills in them the idea that each of them has the power to make different choices than Tony did. He impresses on them the notion that they can make positive choices to stop the cycle of violence.

"Today you are going to be meeting people who have been deeply affected by violence and how it hurts," he tells them. "Each of you is important. We care deeply about each and every one of you, and we don't want to lose any of you to violence."

Sal then talks about his relationship with Tariq and how they were more than boss and employee, about how they had grown to be good friends. "I was at home on my day off the night I got the call saying Tariq had been shot. I thought it must be a mistake and told my employee to find out what happened and call me back. The next call was from my store manager. He said it was true. Tariq was lying in the street . . . dead."

As Sal continues with his personal story of the events of that tragic night, some of the students are antsy. Some of them are captivated. All of them are listening. He describes how he went to the restaurant and told the police officers every detail he could remember about Tariq's last day at work. Not yet knowing who had shot him, the officers were trying to accumulate as much information as possible.

"The restaurant phone rang," Sal says. "It was Jennifer, Tariq's fiancée, wondering where he was. I told her I didn't know and that she should call back in a little bit. A little while later, the phone rang again, and one of the police officers grabbed me by the shirt and said, 'Don't answer that. We have people trained to make those phone calls.' The phone kept ringing and ringing and ringing, but I didn't answer it."

"Still to this day," Sal tells the kids, "when I hear a phone with that tone, it brings me right back to that night that my friend was murdered. And I don't care where I am. I don't care if I'm at a show, at a store, at work, in somebody's office, I relive his death every time."

By the time Sal finishes his story and introduces me and Tony's grandfather, Ples Felix, the kids are curious. "What exactly does all of this have to do with me?" some of them might be wondering. "I'm not in a gang. I'm not robbing pizza delivery men."

Ples and I walk out on stage and take two seats next to each other. Sal walks behind us and lifts his hand over Ples's shoulder and then mine saying, "This man's grandson murdered this man's son." He repeats it. "This man's grandson . . . murdered this man's son. And today they sit in front of you in the spirit of compassion and forgiveness."

Sal introduces me, and I stand up to speak. The kids are intent on finding out more about this story about Tariq and Tony, me and Ples. I share with them the pain I felt when I heard my son had been shot and killed. I talk about how he was my only son and had been shot for no good reason.

"Violence is extremely painful," I say. "It hurts very deep. It scars the soul, and sometimes it scars it forever." I talk to them about how we see a lot of violence in our culture through movies, television, and video games. "But you don't see the pain that violence causes," I tell them. "I really believe that if we knew this excruciating pain that violence causes, as human beings we would never, ever be violent."

The kids listen as I speak to them about the different forms violence takes, whether it's bullying someone, spreading rumors, starting fights, or harassing others in some other way. Some of the kids shuffle in their seats. Maybe they've been the bully. Maybe they've been on the receiving end. They all know what I'm talking about.

Then I ask the hard question, the one that will really open some of their hearts to our assembly. Without their knowing it, they've been prepared for the question by watching the video reenactment and by listening to the stories Sal and I shared about our pain and our loss. Because of the groundwork we so carefully laid, they are willing to answer my question.

"How many of you have lost family members as a result of violence?" I ask. Often, two-thirds of the students raise their hands. Two-thirds! On many occasions TKF staff are approached post-assembly by teachers, counselors, or vice principals with shock and sadness on their faces. "We didn't know," they'll say. "We had no idea so many of our children had been exposed firsthand to this kind of violence."

I tell the students who've raised their hands (and I know that I'm also speaking to some of those who didn't), "I understand the pain of losing someone you love. When Tariq died I felt like a nuclear bomb went off in my heart. How many of you have brothers and sisters?" Many hands go up.

"Tariq had an older sister, Tasreen. Maybe you lost a brother or a sister, a mother or a father, an aunt, an uncle, or a cousin. Perhaps this violence has happened in your family. If not, imagine that your brother or sister was killed in an act of violence. How many of you would seek revenge? Raise your hand if you would seek revenge." Almost all of the hands in the auditorium fly up in unison.

"I completely understand that you would feel like you wanted to have revenge," I tell them. "But what would revenge do? Would it bring Tariq back? Would it stop the pain in my heart?" The kids shake their heads no. "What would it do?" I ask them.

"Make it worse," they say. "Cause more violence." They understand in their hearts that violence doesn't make things better. Deep inside of them, they know that revenge and violence are never the answer.

"I understand that it can be difficult," I say. "In some of your homes you are encouraged not to be violent and at the same time you're told to get revenge if anyone is bullying you or harassing you. These mixed messages can be difficult to understand. But I'm here to tell you," I say emphatically, "never to choose revenge. I'm here to tell you that violence is never a solution. The consequences of violence are always going to be negative. When Tariq was killed, instead of revenge I chose forgiveness, and I reached out to Tony's grandfather, who is now like a brother to me and is one of my best friends." I point to Ples sitting in his chair on stage. He is looking at me. "I would do anything for Ples, and he would do anything for me," I say. "How many of you would like a friend like that?" All the hands go up. "Would we have this kind of friendship if I was seeking revenge?" They shake their heads back and forth in unison. "No," says the chorus of voices in the auditorium. I take a moment and then say, "This kind of friendship comes from forgiveness. And you find forgiveness in your heart."

The kids look at me standing in front of them wearing my pain on my sleeve and at Ples still sitting in his chair. They know that his grandson shot and killed my son. And they know that I have forgiven both Tony and his family for the tragedy. But they still don't know why.

I tell the kids that I know forgiveness is hard to do and that it is absolutely okay to be angry and to want revenge. I let them know it's okay to have the feelings, but that they don't need to act on them. I acknowledge the feelings they might have, and I offer an alternative to transform the negative emotions into something positive. "Forgiveness is letting go of your anger toward a person who has done something wrong to you. Every morning I wake up and I forgive Tony. Because I practice every day, my forgiveness muscle is very strong. It takes courage to let go of your anger, but I am healing from my pain because I forgive Tony every day."

My Brother Ples

When I introduce Tony's grandfather, Ples, and the kids see us hugging like loving brothers, they are very curious about nonviolence and forgiveness. Not all the pieces completely fit for them yet, but once Ples starts talking, it all begins to come together and make sense.

Ples is savvy and street smart and knows how to reach the kids at their "I wanna be tough" level. He tells it like it is and makes no secret of the fact that his grandson adversely affected many lives—including his own—by his one act of violence. Ples gets down to the nitty-gritty and talks to the students about Tony and the bad choices he made—those bad choices that put him into the prison system. He talks about how he, too, lost a son, since Tony was as close to a son as he'd ever had.

He doesn't hold back any punches when he tells the kids that Tony's been serving a 25-years-to-life sentence in an adult prison since the age of 16.

> Tony's entire life has changed because of one bad choice he made after a day of hanging with his friends, drinking alcohol, and smoking pot. Tony woke up angry that day. And though he didn't know it when he woke up, this was going to be the last day of his life as he'd known it. Everything was about to change . . . for Tony and for all of us.

He tells the students that when we're angry, we're not thinking people. We're only reacting people. "And when we're reacting people," he says, "we're not aware people. We're not aware of what's going on around us. We're not aware of what's going on inside us. We're not aware of how on the edge we are to doing something that will put our lives off track. Because we're angry and reacting," he says, "we are not aware."

He tells them how Tony woke up angry that morning and decided to run away from home. He ran away because he was angry and didn't like the discipline at home where his grandfather required him to study, do well in school, and choose friends wisely so that he could have a successful life. Ples talks to the kids about what makes a good friend.

> You might think someone's your friend, but if they bully you or tell you to do something that you don't really want to do, they're not a friend, so don't think they are. Tony thought these people were his friends. They weren't. One of them put a loaded gun in his hands. And after Tony pulled the trigger that night, these so-called friends told him to run, run, run and not drop the gun. They weren't concerned. They didn't care about Tony.

Ples tells the kids how Tony made his first bad choice when he decided to be angry that morning and that all day long he continued to make bad choices that finally resulted in his shooting and killing Tariq. "Azim and his family lost Tariq. I lost my grandson to the prison system. And as a result of one bad decision, Tony has lost his freedom. Even after he gets out, he will always have to report to the state of California. He will be living with the consequences of this one bad choice for the rest of his life."

Ples then asks the students how many of them have dreams. All the hands go up. He tells them:

> It's important that you keep your dreams close to you. Don't let anybody tell you that you can't live your dreams. People will tell you that.

They'll tell you that you can't have your dreams. But you have to be strong enough to understand, this is *your* dream. It doesn't have anything to do with those folks. This is *your* dream. Accomplish your dreams. But you don't want to set obstacles up to prevent you from realizing your dreams by committing yourself to choices that are violent, that are not peaceful, that create consequences for you, your family, and the community.

Before Ples closes, he makes sure the kids understand who's responsible for the death of my son. He says, "Let me hear it loud and clear. Who's responsible for the death of Tariq Khamisa?"

"Tony," the kids shout back.

Ples says,

Tony is responsible. You have to be able to take responsibility for your choices. Nobody makes you do something. When you do a violent act, you do it because you choose to do it. And you're responsible for it. So when you're out there making choices, understand that the choices you make are going to have consequences or benefits to you. So make the right choice. Be peacemakers.

Panelists

After Ples speaks, our panelists come on stage to talk to the kids. These speakers have been there, exactly where the students are now. They've been exposed to violence on the streets and in their homes. And they've been tempted to join the gang family for a sense of belonging and safety. They tell the kids that when they were their ages, they made the wrong choice. Our panelists, both male and female, engage the kids' attention because they speak from the heart about their choices, painful consequences, and how they turned their lives around to choose the ways of peace and nonviolence.

The TKF Peacemaker Pledge

At the closing of the assembly, we ask all the kids to stand and join us in a pledge of nonviolence:

I pledge on my honor to be a peacemaker;
In my home
In my school
And in my community.
I am a peacemaker.
I AM A PEACEMAKER

Garden of Life

Being able to express grief is a first step in healing, and so following the VIF elementary school assemblies we hold a special "Garden of Life" ceremony on campus. A tree is planted in memory of Tariq and any family members the students have lost, and the kids also plant flowers in memory of their loved ones. This garden becomes a place they can visit every day, a place they can go for healing or remembrance.

Ples expresses a beautiful perspective about the programs and especially about the Garden of Life.

I see and experience the programs as an opportunity to help children see the potential of divinity within themselves. I always project that when we finish one of the VIFs, I see these students walking around with this great, glowing light coming from their hearts. The light itself is symbolic of the inspiration having been turned on to make decisions that will change them for the rest of their lives. That's the kind of vision I walk away with from every VIF.

But the Garden of Life accentuates that even more for me, because it ritualizes for the students and everyone else in attendance an opportunity through the planting of a flowering plant for the expression of grief. And for the expression of caring for someone lost. And it's done in such a loving, reverential, nonreligious kind of way that whenever that's done, I visualize those lights coming from these students being one thousand times brighter.

Each of these students touched a living plant, dug a hole in God's earth, and planted this flower with loving intention for its growth, blossoming, and beauty as a means of expression to memorialize or to say goodbye or to honor someone they've lost. Some of these children are so reverent with respect to the application of the Garden of Life, even after they plant the flowers, they step back and just close their eyes briefly in silence. Then when the kids have completed that process, you can see that they have been unburdened. They have not only been unburdened, but they have also been freed to make choices that will prevent them from engaging in violence in a way that will really help their lives.

HOPES

I wish that Tariq were still with me. And I sometimes wish that TKF programs had existed before Tony decided to join a gang. I think that maybe if he had participated in a VIF or had gone through the Ending the Cycle of Violence curriculum, he would have been transformed from a life of violence to a life of peace. But these wishes are only impulses of the heart and have no substance in reality.

I know only too well that it is because of the death of my son at the hand of Tony Hicks that TKF came into existence. This is what makes this story both a tragedy and a blessing. "He always wanted to leave this world a better place . . . and he has," Tasreen says about her brother. Yes, he has. Without the ultimate sacrifice of his death, TKF would not exist. And without the programs of TKF, many more children would remain lost in lives of violence, living without hope, living in the darkness of despair, revenge, and hatred.

I have great hopes for TKF. I believe that as we continue to accumulate data and results, more and more school districts will hear of our work and choose to make TKF a part of the mainline curriculum in all of their schools, bringing our message of hope and nonviolence to more and more kids. Just like going to a math, reading, history, or science class, kids will go into a TKF class and learn the core values we teach through our six key messages.

It is my dream that once we have achieved this goal in the U.S. school system, we'll go to places like Iraq, Israel, Palestine, and North Korea, where there is such dire conflict. I would like to see TKF go all over the world, because when we have been able to touch all the kids of the world and they have learned how to create brotherhood, sisterhood, love, and unity from conflict, then we will manifest a world at peace.

I've always maintained that no child is born violent. It follows that since violence is a learned behavior, nonviolence can also be learned. But who in our society teaches nonviolence? TKF does and does it successfully. In fact, San Diego State University has been so impressed with the results of our programs over the past 12 years, they have proposed creating a TKF-endowed professorship on peace and nonviolence.

Since San Diego State is the highest teacher-producing university in the country, with the professorship in place, every graduating teacher will have been trained in our curriculum. The university also has 20 international centers, so through our partnership we will be able to take our programs into these other countries. Being involved with an institute that can support the research and development of our programs is a dream come true. Ples and I have committed the rest of our lives to the principles of peacemaking and teaching nonviolence, and when the TKF meets its mandate, we will see the beginning of a peaceful society.

CHAPTER 17

Steps toward Reconciliation: Understanding and Healing in Post-Genocide Rwanda and Beyond

Ervin Staub and Angel Ryono

During the era of its colonial rule, the policies of Belgium greatly influenced the identity and shaped the relationship between the major groups in Rwanda, Tutsis and Hutus. The Belgians favored the Tutsis and had them rule in their behalf. Under their oversight the already existing differences between the two groups increased and political and social divisions intensified. The oppression of the Hutus and the hostility that developed between the groups established a foundation for violent conflict.[1] The period just preceding and the decades following the formal pronouncement of Rwandan independence were marked by violence against, and at times mass killings of, Tutsis. In 1994 there was a horrific genocide—a 100-day massacre of over 700,000 Tutsis, and about 50,000 Hutus because they were seen as politically moderate or enemies for other reasons.[2]

For decades since Rwanda's independence, Tutsis have left Rwanda to escape the violence against them and sought refuge in neighboring countries. In 1990, a rebel group consisting mainly of descendants of Tutsi refugees, calling themselves the Rwandan Patriotic Front (RPF), entered the homeland from Uganda. A civil war followed. There was a cease fire and an opportunity for political conciliation was presented by the Arusha Accords in 1993. However, animosity toward the Tutsis continued and Hutu extremists planned a genocide. The plane of the President of Rwanda was shot down, and immediately the genocide began, on April 7, 1994. Fighting between the RPF and the government army resumed, and with the international community remaining passive bystanders, the RPF brought the genocide to a halt. The RPF assumed leadership over a new government. Following the genocide, there was continued armed conflict between the RPA (the Rwandan Patriotic Army, the new name of the government army) and Hutu perpetrators of the genocide who escaped into Zaire, now the Congo, and killed Tutsis in the course of incursions into Rwanda. The violence spread into the Congo, resulting in over five million deaths by 2009, due to killings, violence, and disease.[3]

Since 1994, national and international efforts have included a focus on reconciliation and reconstruction. These efforts include but are not limited to the following: government-supported memorial sites and media programs; government-sponsored education and re-education camps espousing unity; United Nations (UN)-funded International Criminal Tribunal for Rwanda (ICTR); and grassroots and community-based platforms for truth telling and justice (Gacaca).[4]

However, overcoming the rift between groups after mass violence is an enormous task. In the aftermath of a genocide perpetrated by residents of the same nation and locality, as in Rwanda, how can formerly opposing groups continue to live together and build a non-violent future? How can they resolve the traumatic past and establish harmonious relations? Among the many steps toward reconciliation, there is a critical role for processes that address the psychology of individuals and groups.

Of great importance is understanding the roots of violence. What are the external conditions, and what are their psychological effects that lead to violence? Understanding these factors that lead to violence can help people resist the influence of these external conditions and enable them to take action to prevent violence. It can also help them act out their psychological effects in constructive ways. What is the impact of past violence, the psychological woundedness it creates? How can healing or psychological recovery, and other aspects of reconciliation be promoted? To promote reconciliation and thereby both prevent new violence and contribute to harmonious societies requires a comprehensive approach, including changes in how the community attends to problems in human relationships, particularly to conflict and the imbalance of power and injustice. Otherwise, violence is likely to recur.[5]

The intent of this chapter is to describe and to illustrate an approach to post-conflict healing and reconciliation that uniquely draws upon the principles of psychology. Understanding the influences leading to violence and healing from psychological trauma and emotional scarring are stressed as important steps to reconciliation and preventing future violence.

This understanding and healing approach builds on previous theoretical work and research done by the lead author and his associates, in particular, Laurie Anne Pearlman, a trauma specialist. The approach was used in seminars, workshops, and trainings with community workers, journalists, national leaders, and then in collaboration with George Weiss and the Dutch NGO he directs, LaBenevolencija, applied to educational radio programs. This project was supported by multiple philanthropic foundations, including the John Templeton Foundation, and by the U.S. Institute of Peace (USIP), the U.S. Agency for International Development (USAID), University of Massachusetts at Amherst, Netherlands, Belgium, the European Union, and individual donors.

The approach to understanding, healing, and reconciliation in Rwanda showed indications of success. An evaluative study is described showing the effects of implementing this approach in reconciliation-related activities in Rwanda.[6] We believe that adaptations of the same model can find useful application in other post-conflict settings.

GENOCIDE IN RWANDA—A BRIEF HISTORY

There were differences between Hutus and Tutsis before colonial rule; European colonialists exploited and enhanced the differences, increasing the divisions between the two groups socially, politically, and economically, in service of control of the country.[7] The Belgians institutionalized the divisions by requiring Hutus and Tutsis to carry identification cards. Tutsis were regarded and treated as superior to Hutus. These colonial policies and visibly unjust practices cemented the Hutus' bitterness towards Tutsis. In 1959 Hutus revolted against the oppression, killing Tutsis, (thousands of them according to earlier reports, hundreds according to later reports) with many thousands seeking refuge in neighboring countries as Hutus assumed power.[8]

The massive transfer of power to the Hutus led to discrimination against Tutsis and periodic violent attacks, some on the scale of mass killing. In 1990, the RPA entered from Uganda, initiating a civil war with Hutu forces. In 1993, after a cease-fire, the Arusha Accords were signed, intending to establish a shared government. However, on April 6, 1994, Hutu President Habyarimana was killed when his plane was shot down. An intense public campaign of hostility towards Tutsis had led to the planning of genocide, which began after Habyarimana's plane was shot down. Over a 100-day period beginning on April 7, 1994, about 800,000 Rwandans, mostly Tutsis, were killed. The perpetrators in this government-organized violence included members of the military, young men organized into paramilitary groups, and ordinary people including neighbors and even family members in mixed families.[9] The community of nations watched in horror, but remained passive, while about 10,000 Tutsis a day were slaughtered. The genocide ended only when the RPA defeated the government army and took over leadership.

In recent years, the RPF-led government has taken active steps towards reconciliation and is espousing national unity. However, the government has been increasingly intolerant of "divisionism," even accusing those who are potential opponents, non-compliant, or dissenters as propagators of genocidal ideology. Little open public discussion and political opposition interfere with reconciliation. Eugenia Zorbas considers this a "papering over of cleavages" and a systematic denial of the still deep wounds left by the complex history of violence.[10]

DEFINITION AND GENERAL PRINCIPLES OF RECONCILIATION

Reconciliation is a result of a change in attitudes and behaviors of an individual or group toward the other. Reconciliation means that groups in conflict do not see past relationship as defining the present. It means that they come to see and accept the humanity in one another, welcome forgiveness, and have a vision of the possibility of a future, constructive relationship. Political and social processes, structures, and institutions are part of the context of conflict and also play a role in reconciliation.[11] They solidify or maintain the progress of psychological transformations that result from reconciliation. This psychological definition of reconciliation is consistent with Louis Kriesberg's, which focuses on the relationship between parties.[12] The definition is also compatible with Broneus' definition stating that changes in attitude and behavior between parties are important in bringing about mutual acknowledgment of past suffering.[13]

Following great violence, such as genocide and mass killing, reconciliation is achieved through a difficult and long-term process.[14] Theory, research, and practice in this area are in their early phases. Demands and challenges exist for developing effective and expeditious interventions that promote reconciliation because, in many post-conflict settings, perpetrators and victims continue to live next to each other.

THE IMPACT OF MASS VIOLENCE ON SURVIVORS, PERPETRATORS, AND PASSIVE BYSTANDERS

Genocide and mass killing deeply affect survivors, their perception of themselves and of the world. Victims of such violence see the world as dangerous and feel diminished and vulnerable.[15] Victimization has a negative effect on survivors' identity, interpersonal relationships, and their view of the world.[16] Because individual identity is rooted in group identity, members of the victim group who were not directly involved in the conflict are also traumatized by the destruction of their group or group identity.[17]

In Rwanda, "returnees" are children of Tutsi refugees from earlier violence who repatriated from neighboring countries after the 1994 genocide. Returnees come back to devastated families and communities. With the Tutsis' return to govern Rwanda, the impact of genocide on Tutsis' psychology and the early experiences of the returnees can have significant political consequences.

The psychological effects of victimization include heightened sensitivity to new threats.[18] If new conflict arises, then this sensitivity makes it challenging for survivors to balance their needs against the needs and concerns of others. Corrective experiences, an important element of which can be community healing with neighbors helping each other to promote psychological recovery, can promote social healing. Without such experience, survivors of mass violence will not easily be open to reconciling damaged relationships. They may believe that they need to defend themselves forcefully or aggressively against new threats—even when aggression is unnecessary or inappropriate. They may strike out in response to new threats or conflict, hence becoming perpetrators.[19] An aggressive response continues the cycle of violence.

Perpetrators also suffer psychological wounds. Past experiences of political persecution, being forced into servitude, or past violence against them can be a source of trauma and lead to unhealed wounds.[20] As they engage in violent actions, perpetrators psychologically distance themselves from their victims to avoid feeling empathy or acknowledge the victims' humanity. This psychological distance from and devaluation of the targeted, or victim, group is likely to generalize to other groups and situations of conflict.[21] But it does not provide perpetrators with sufficient psychological protection. Recent research shows that people who engage in varied forms of violence against others are psychologically wounded by their own actions[22] (See also Rachel MacNair, chapter 21 in this volume).

Passive bystanders are defined as members of the perpetrator group who did not enact violence but were in a position to know about it (in a "position to know" because bystanders often close their eyes and try to avoid knowing) and in a position to take action. Passive bystanders witness the evolution from hostile social conditions, to indirect violence, to direct violence. They may have joined their group in discriminatory behaviors and passively accepted harmful actions that preceded the genocide or mass killing. Their passivity in the face of harm to others is likely to wound passive bystanders as well. They progressively distance themselves from victims in order to maintain connection to their own group, which is perpetuating this violence. They do this by increasingly devaluing the victims, seeing them in increasingly negative light, and as deserving their fate.[23]

The extent and nature of psychological woundedness of the three groups are different. Its moral meaning is also different: survivors of violence are wounded because they, their relatives, their group has been harmed, perpetrators because they have inflicted great harm. However, to achieve reconciliation it is important to address the woundedness of all groups. For the purpose of this discussion, woundedness is defined as enduring psychological distress accompanied by feelings of vulnerability.

When violence ends, perpetrators and passive bystanders tend to assume a defensive stance. The tend to continue to devalue and blame the victims and tend to be unwilling to assume responsibility for their own or their groups' actions.[24] To address perpetrators' woundedness and trauma helps diminish their defensiveness and increase their capacity for reconciliation. Helping perpetrators become aware of their usually unacknowledged guilt and shame, and engaging with their historic losses and distress due to their actions, in a safe environment, can open them to the humanity of their victims. This can lead them to feel and express empathy, regret, and sorrow, which in turn lead to positive responses from survivors.

Together with other aspects of reconciliation, this process can lead, in turn, to such positive responses from survivors as understanding the context of the perpetrators' behavior, wishing for reconciliation and considering a measure of forgiveness.[25] In summary, healing that is inclusive and obtained at the community level appears an important requirement for reconciliation.[26]

AN OVERVIEW OF CONCEPTS AND PRACTICES THAT CONTRIBUTE TO RECONCILIATION

Truth and justice are important concepts in a comprehensive approach to promote reconciliation.[27] In working with survivors of genocide, one comes to understand their yearning for the truth about what was done to them and for their suffering to be acknowledged.[28] For example, the Armenian people continue to suffer when Turkey refuses to claim responsibility for the genocide in the early 1900s. All groups, including survivors of the Holocaust, respond with pain and anger at those who deny mass violence perpetrated against them.

When the global community recognizes and condemns victimization of a group of people, the message helps survivors feel that moral order is reinstated and increases their sense of security. Truth and the acknowledgment of suffering may repair diminished identity. Acknowledgment from perpetrators, through expressions of regret and empathy, is of special importance to victims' psychological recovery. Unfortunately, perpetrators typically continue to justify their actions and to devalue and blame their victims. Empathy with perpetrators, difficult as it may be given the nature of their actions, can help them heal, reduce their defensiveness, and enable them to act in a way that helps to heal the victims and contribute to a reconciliation process.

The history of group conflict in Rwanda adds complexity to post-conflict dialogue and reconciliation. While the genocide in 1994 targeted Tutsis, as the woman who was the justice minister during the genocide told Ervin Staub when he interviewed her in prison, Hutus focus on their servitude (she called it "slavery") before 1959.[29] Hutus also refer to RPF violence against Hutu civilians during the civil war and violence against Hutu refugees in Zaire, now the Congo.[30] Unacknowledged and unexamined violence in the past cause conflicting groups to focus on their own suffering and attribute blame to the other. Reconciliation is advanced as in the course of coming to understand the roots of violence and engagement with each other. A healing process is promoted when each side is able to acknowledge the suffering of the other. However difficult this may be, the acknowledgment of pain on both sides, the mutual search for truth, and groups in conflict moving toward a shared history, advance reconciliation.

The importance of justice in promoting reconciliation has also received substantial attention.[31] Survivors of genocide need justice, as it is another form of acknowledgment and it re-establishes a moral order. Truth is a prerequisite for justice. One form of justice is punishment, it is important for survivors and may deter future perpetrators to some extent. However, excessive punishment risks rekindling antagonisms. Procedural justice is especially important in reconstruction and developing the capacity for a lawful society. Justice can also be compensatory or restorative, engaging the parties with each other and with perpetrators, contributing to the rebuilding of society. Restorative justice is likely to contribute to the healing process.[32]

Empirical evidence about the role of truth in reconciliation is limited.[33] However, it is clear that the absence of truth and justice inhibits or stalls reconciliation. As mentioned earlier, the Armenian community struggles to heal and move beyond the genocide of early 1915–1916 because Turkey has persistently denied responsibility and has used its political influence to stop others from acknowledging the genocide. It has attempted to influence scholars and exerted pressure on countries, including the United States.[34] When overt acknowledgment and justice are not forthcoming, a community will need to find internal healing processes.[35]

An important aspect of justice is economic. This includes labor by perpetrators or members of their group that helps rebuild survivors' lives. It also includes establishing equitable relations between groups within a society. In Northern Ireland, the possibility of resolving the conflict between Catholics and Protestants was greatly increased by improving economic and educational access and opportunities for the Catholic minority.[36]

Contact also contributes to reconciliation, especially if it includes deep engagement of people belonging to hostile groups. Social psychological theories and a meta-analysis of a large body of research on contact affirms its positive effects.[37] People from different groups working together for shared goals can overcome devaluation and prejudice. In the face of incidents that were incitements to violence, Hindus and Muslims from some cities responded differently from their counterparts in other cities. In three Indian cities where Hindus and Muslims belonged, and were committed to the same organizations, members from both groups worked together, responding to the incitement in ways that prevented the outbreak of physical violence. In three other cities where such inter-group contacts did not exist, similar incitements did result in violence.[38] Some Indian cities are beneficiaries of the Shanti Sena, an organization begun by both Hindu and Muslim followers of Gandhi. Shanti Sena are peace-keepers, mediators, diplomats, and crisis counselors whose voluntary intervention as a third party has been useful in preventing violence from occurring or from spreading, even when customary interactions between groups may be less strong than desired.[39]

Forgiveness is also an important aspect of reconciliation.[40] Both theory and research suggest that forgiveness eases the anguish of victims as they learn to let go of hostility and desire for revenge and develop a more positive attitude toward the perpetrators.[41] An important difference between forgiveness and reconciliation is that the former is one-sided and the latter requires mutual participation and mutual change. Anecdotal information gathered in

Rwanda points to instances in which forgiveness by a survivor may draw out expressions of regret and apology from the perpetrators. However, it is more typical that regret and apology expressed by perpetrators facilitate forgiveness.

Many practical interventions that can promote reconciliation have been developed.[42] Dialogue between members of conflicting groups is a centerpiece in conflict resolution. Sometimes influential members of groups, at other times ordinary members of the communities, are participants. Dialogue between leaders is important. Dialogue groups can set goals that are both material and psychological, helping to resolve both practical and emotional challenges to coexistence. Dialogue is an important form of contact, and can create deep engagement between participants. For dialogue groups to be able to resolve practical issues of living together, there have to be psychological changes.[43] Participants need to move from negative attitudes to experiencing some degree of empathy with each other and developing the capacity to accept responsibility for their own group's actions.

THE COMBINED ROLE OF PSYCHOLOGY AND THE SOCIAL STRUCTURE

Psychological elements that advance reconciliation are essential. However, social structure plays an important role in supporting the reconciliation process. Psychological elements are defined as perceptions, interpretations, evaluations, attitudes, memory, and emotional responses associated with an individual's or a group's past history and future expectations. Social structure is defined as policies, social practices, and institutional rules and procedures. The equality or equity of policies and their perceived fairness can contribute to the success and sustainability of reconciliation goals. When institutions provide just social and legal structures, and when they promote and create access to resources and opportunities for contact, they help make reconciliation possible.

It is hoped that psychological change, over time, can have a progressively expanding influence. This influence can be achieved through a combination of efforts, some directed to the training of people for direct work with the local community, others directed toward community and national leaders and to the national media. In the work of Ervin Staub and his associates, bringing about change involved training community workers, members of the media and national leaders, and public broadcast of educational radio programs that directly reach a majority of the population. Engaging the population and promoting psychological change in the public, can in turn shape policies and institutions.

UNDERSTANDING AND PSYCHOLOGICAL HEALING: THEIR PLACE IN RECONCILIATION

The theories and scholarly work of the lead author about the origins and prevention of genocide and reconciliation, drawing also on the work of others, informed this project on promoting reconciliation in Rwanda.[44] Research and experiential work related to trauma and healing by the lead author's associate in this work in Rwanda, Laurie Anne Pearlman, also drawing on others' work, provided another basis for the psychological approach to reconciliation.[45]

The first focus for the approach to understanding and healing was the use of psychological concepts to promote understanding of the roots of mass violence. A second and related focus was to help people understand the human impact of violence. A third focus was psychological recovery and healing. One ultimate aim of the approach was to prevent new violence by effectively contributing to reconciliation. The specific goals in the Rwanda project included mitigating trauma, strengthening diminished identity, educating about psychological woundedness, establishing in each group a degree of openness to the other group, developing understanding of mass violence and genocide, encouraging critical dialogue, and promoting awareness of social justice to provide for basic human needs. Through all this the intent was to empower people to be active bystanders, to help each other heal and promote coexistence and peace.

These goals were incorporated into education and communication programs and activities that reach the majority of Rwandans. They included trainings and workshops at the community level, and with journalists and national leaders who can influence the community, and educational radio programs that reached the whole population. Participants in trainings and listeners to the radio programs are encouraged to engage with each other, share experiences, and support each other. This helps to heal and strengthen all members of the community, thereby making important contributions towards reconciliation.[46]

PROMOTING UNDERSTANDING AND HEALING AT ALL LEVELS OF RWANDAN SOCIETY

In early 1999, during a visit by the lead author and his associate, Laurie Pearlman, to Rwanda, the tremendous psychological impact of the genocide was visible in the many faces on the streets, seemingly frozen in pain, people immediately talking about their horrible experiences to strangers in a country known for such conversations before only with family. The need for healing and reconciliation was evident. Rwanda, a country of eight million people, has a culture that is rooted in communal experiences; both because of this, and because both victimization and perpetration happened in groups, healing in groups was likely to be most effective.[47]

The project began training thirty-five Rwandans, both Hutus and Tutsis, employed at various local organizations working with the community. The training composed of psycho-educational lectures, extensive group discussions, and experiential components that included sharing experiences and developing ways to use the lessons gained from the seminar in future community work. The training introduced the following main ideas:

- Origins of genocide and mass killing—Introduce a broader context so that participants learn about the origins of other genocides, the specific influences that have led to violence in other communities. Understanding influences that shape the thinking and actions of perpetrators can mitigate the tendency for victims to blame themselves and to see perpetrators as purely evil.
- Trauma and victimization—Information and awareness about widespread behavioral, physiological, cognitive, emotional, interpersonal, and spiritual impact of violence.
- Avenues to psychological healing recovery. One example is to create settings in which people can safely talk about their painful experiences.[48] Talking about the trauma has contributed to psychological recovery.[49]
- Basic psychological needs—Basic human needs play a role in both the origins of genocide and in post-conflict reconstruction and reconciliation. Thus, understanding basic psychological needs—security, positive identity, feelings of effectiveness, trust, positive relationships, a world view that makes reality comprehensible—can help people meet them more effectively, and constructively, and combat scapegoating and destructive ideologies that occur after violence.[50]
- Positive engagement with the others—Encourage empathic responses to others' experiences with listening skills and emotional support— and thus person-to-person healing.
- Integration of methods—Combine psychological healing with existing or traditional approaches in community building activities.

CHANGES CREATED BY THE UNDERSTANDING–HEALING APPROACH

Some participants in training expressed the realization that their tragedy is part of a larger, albeit horrific, human history and experience—that the genocide in Rwanda was not divine punishment that targeted their group.

There was a shift toward "rehumanizing" the opposing group. Participants reported that they understood the influences that lead to genocide, and believe that it is possible to prevent future violence. Participants gained experiential understanding of the roots of mass violence by connecting the facts and framework of violence from other genocides with the Rwandan genocide and their own experience.

A field study was conducted to assess how members of the community who received training in newly set up community groups, facilitated by the members of local organizations trained in the approach had changed.[51] Working with Rwandan research associates, trauma symptoms, attitudes toward members of the other ethnic group, and about "conditional forgiveness" were assessed. The results showed that the understanding—healing approach helped to move Rwandans closer to reconciliation.

Information was obtained from a time before the training, immediately after it, and again two months later. Findings from participants in the program were compared to members of groups led by facilitators who were not trained in the approach and to members of other groups that received no training. Trauma symptoms decreased in the groups that were facilitated by participants in the workshops/seminars, and positive orientation by Tutsis and Hutus towards one another also increased. Positive orientation included the following components: (1) seeing the genocide as having complex origins; (2) willingness to work with the other group for important goals; (3) indicating awareness or belief that some Hutus resisted the genocide and some saved lives; and (4) willingness to forgive provided that there was acknowledgment of suffering and sincere apology. Evidence of such positive orientation may indicate that each group is ready to reconcile with the other. The changes were significantly greater in groups led by the facilitators who received the training, prior to the onset of sessions and two months later, and in comparison to change in the other groups.

WORKING WITH NATIONAL LEADERS

In 2001, two seminars were conducted with national leaders as participants. There were about 32 national leaders: government ministers, members of the Supreme Court, heads of national commissions and of the national prison system and the main Kigali prison, an advisor to the president, and members of the National Unity and Reconciliation Commission. In 2003, a one-day seminar, similar to the first, was conducted with 69 participants including the addition of members of Parliament and political parties. After exposure and discussion of information about the origins and impact of violence and avenues to prevention and reconciliation, the participants considered, in small groups, whether particular government policies and practices would make violence more likely, or would help prevent violence and promote positive relations. Would they contribute to devaluation by one group of another or humanize the "other," intensify or appropriately moderate respect for authority, and so on? The leaders discussed what they could do to shape policies and practices to reduce the likelihood of future violence and address the need for psychological recovery.

There was active discussion with national leaders about the creation of a shared history. Collective memories have been recognized in prevention and promoting reconciliation; stressing the importance of working for the creation of shared histories.[52] Some participants argued that history is objective. But the majority of the participants recognized that history could be told from different perspectives. Hence, national leaders came to a consensus that it is important to create a shared view of history. A small group discussion from the 2001 seminars resulted in a variety of proposals for creating a shared history. One proposal suggested asking each group to take the role of the other in describing Rwanda's history. Another proposal emphasized the peaceful coexistence between Hutus and Tutsis in Rwanda's early history. In the end, many participants expressed doubt that it would be possible to achieve a shared history so soon after the genocide.

During the second national leaders' seminar, a participant referred to an earlier "genocide." In 1959, the Hutu revolt against Tutsi rule led to the killing of Tutsis (earlier believed to be in large numbers but more recent investigation suggests hundreds rather than thousands were killed at that time). There is a general understanding that colonial rule intensified and institutionalized prior divisions between Hutus and Tutsis, elevating Tutsis further. The persistent injustice during colonial rule fueled the revolution, which led to some killings, but not to genocide. The discrimination and violence against Tutsis under subsequent Hutu rule could be understood as the outcome of the psychological woundedness, fear, and anger felt by the Hutus, and their intense devaluation of Tutsis.

Policies and practices of Hutu leadership after 1959 created new injustices. The past became a "chosen trauma" for Hutus.[53] They were further wounded by their own dehumanizing actions towards the Tutsis. The "understanding approach" of the seminar worked to inspire a mutual and balanced awareness of the past.

Lectures about the origins of genocide were used to help participants understand how mass violence usually comes about.[54] Social conditions, characteristics of cultures, and their psychological effects that breed violence were identified: severe economic problems, political instability, persistent conflict, intense devaluation of the other, scapegoating and destructive

ideologies, and the evolution of increasing violence. These and other concepts were then applied in the analysis of other examples of genocide. Participants in every workshop were then asked to apply the concepts to
Rwanda.[55] This activity is a part of helping the group to develop a sustainable understanding about their experiences. Creating a story and constructing meaning out of tragic experiences have been identified as important
contributors to healing from trauma.[56] But understanding also has positive
psychological effects and creates the possibility of constructive actions. The
lectures and subsequent discussion also considered avenues to prevention
and healing that were suggested by understanding the origins.

WORKING WITH JOURNALISTS, THE MEDIA, AND COMMUNITY LEADERS

A number of seminars were conducted with the media and community
leaders similar to the national leaders' seminars. Participants concluded that
the media have the power to humanize people or to devalue them; hence they
have the potential to add to or dissuade violence. Media influence was intense
during the months leading up to the Rwandan genocide. Radio and other
media communicated hate against Tutsis; they were the vehicles that propa-
gated destructive ideologies. But media can also have positive effects. Following inter-ethnic violence in the case of Macedonia, journalists belonging to
different ethnic groups joined together to write collaborative newspaper
articles about the lives of families from various ethnic groups. In this instance,
media portrayed the humanity of members of each group in the service of harmonious relations.[57] Individuals who are in leadership roles within their communities possess similar capacities to influence inter-group acceptance.

The Gacaca trials were a special issue brought to discussion. The Gacaca
court, a community justice system, was created both to serve justice and
help to alleviate an overwhelmed jail system that detained about 120,000
accused genocide perpetrators. About 250,000 Rwandans were elected to
act as judges in the Gacaca trials and serve as administrative personnel,
with about 10,000 Gacaca courts created. Later the number of judges was
reduced. The Gacaca, which ended in 2009, was conducted in every community once a week. Members of the local community were to attend and participate. Their goal included establishing the truth of what was done,
bringing about justice and promoting reconciliation.

Participants and the leaders' workshops/seminars talked about potential
psychological consequences of these courts, such as testimonies about
the genocide retraumatizing survivors and generating renewed anger in
both groups. Children attending the trials would be newly traumatized.

Participants discussed what could be done to mitigate possible trauma. Ideas were put forth stressing community support, positive presence, and empathic listening. They thought that promoting the understanding of the societal, cultural, and psychological roots of violence presented in the seminars/workshops to a larger community would be useful. As people engage with, listen to and respond to the testimonies at the Gacaca court, the psychological changes in thinking and feeling that can result from people adopting an understanding orientation can limit the severity of re-traumatization and make the Gacaca a more effective tool of reconciliation.

After the first leaders' workshop, discussions with the then general secretary of the RPF—later to be appointed foreign minister—and the justice minister at the time, led to an agreement to initiate educational radio programs for this purpose.

EDUCATIONAL RADIO PROJECTS

Radio is the primary form of media that Rwandans use to access information and current events. While not every person owns a radio, village members will often listen to radio together. In 2001, the lead author and his collaborator, Laurie Pearlman, began to work with George Weiss of LaBenevolencija, a Dutch non-government organization (NGO), to produce two types of radio programs, aimed at the same goals of reconciliation, healing, and violence prevention as Staub and Pearlman's previous work in Rwanda.

A radio drama titled "Musekeweya," or "New Dawn," deals with two neighboring villages in conflict. The understanding and healing approach was embedded in the story to provide information about the roots of violence, possibilities of healing and prevention, and traumatic impact of violence on individuals and groups. "Musekeweya" also reflected complexities of human society with subplots about love between a young woman and man from the two villages, friendships, and family relations. Rwandan writers authored weekly episodes based on the objectives of understanding the roots of violence and its prevention, psychological healing, and reconciliation. Starting in 2004, and continuing since then, the radio drama broadcasts twice a week in the national language, Kinyarwanda.

A survey of general radio listening in 2005 reported that 90 percent of the population listens to radio, and 89 percent women and 92 percent men among them listened to this program, reflecting the program's popularity among a nationwide audience. A large study has evaluated the impact of the program on knowledge, and on behavioral and cognitive changes that resulted from listening to the radio drama.[58] The results indicate changes in both attitudes and behavior after a year of airing the program.

Participants who as part of an experimental study listened to the radio drama when compared to those who listened to a different program were found to:

- Have greater empathy for victims, perpetrators, leaders;
- Understand more the importance of talking as a means of healing trauma;
- Express greater willingness to speak out when they disagree;
- Engage more in discussions about when there are issues to resolve;
- Act more independently of authority.[59]

Some of these findings suggest that the radio drama can help society move to more critical thinking and greater pluralism, in contrast to an authority-oriented culture.

An informational/journalistic radio program was launched in September 2004 and aired monthly. Elements of the understanding–healing approach were integrated into discussions that involved local commentators, experts, and citizens with relevant experience.

In January 2005, the radio drama began airing in Burundi, which has the same Kinyarwanda language, and where there was also a great deal of violence between Hutus and Tutsis, with new programs starting in 2006. The Rwandan's civil war and genocide have led to intense violence in the Eastern Congo. Between 1996, two years after the Rwandan genocide, and 2010, about five million Congolese people have died due to violence that spilled over from the Tutsi-Hutu conflict, but also partly resulted from the instability and corruption under Mobutu's leadership before 1996, and the intense disease and hunger brought on by long-term violence. In 2006, both types of radio programs were also created for and began to broadcast in the Eastern Congo. The radio programs were adapted to fit the nature of violence and conditions in the Congo—a society with more ethnic groups vying for influence, power, and security.

CONCLUDING THOUGHTS

Understanding the influences that lead to violence and its enduring impact and the ways of healing at the individual, local community, and national level promote a positive orientation of one group toward another. In Rwanda, this approach opens an important door to reconciliation and helps the society move towards creating a shared history. A psychological approach that promotes "experiential understanding"—understanding that connects with people's own experience, which furthers healing—can be essential to create the motivation to work together to rebuild society in the wake of violence. In a post-conflict setting, restoring the community's sense of safety, facilitating healing activities, promoting group contact, and supporting dialogue are among ways to re-build a community. Understanding, healing, and individuals becoming active bystanders in building a better society can be advanced by education and mass communication programs.

The success of the project must be viewed in the context of continuing socioeconomic and political problems. Large numbers of people have been displaced and lost family members been impoverished and have engaged in violence. The conflict between Hutus and Tutsis has carried over to the Eastern Congo, when the RPF brought the genocide to an end and both perpetrators and over a million other Hutus escaped into Zaire, later renamed the Congo. The RPA moved into the Congo to fight the genocide perpetrators.[60] Conflicts and violence have been aggravated by exploitation of the Congo's natural resources. Incursions by and fighting between foreign armies, starting in 1998, and the creation and emergence of many militias including the Tutsi-led National Congress for the Defense of the People (CNDP) and Hutu-led Democratic Forces for the Liberation of Rwanda (FDLR), have exacerbated existing conditions of violence and instability. Both the armies and militias have committed grave offenses against the residents of the Congo. Reconciliation in Rwanda will not only increase long term security for the Rwandan people, but it may shape the Rwandan governmental policies in ways that help promote reconciliation and peace in the Eastern Congo as well.[61]

Research, theory and practices that promote reconciliation are in nascent stages of development. However, these efforts are important as they have implications for the prevention of future violence. The project's apparent success in Rwanda, even though tested by challenge of the intense impact of violence on all parties, the political conditions and restrictions on public discussions, encourages further application of the approach and practices of Staub, Pearlman, and LaBenevolencija in promoting reconciliation in real world settings. This approach is unusual in that it is based on past research and theory in psychology, points to the importance of using research and theory in psychology, and points to the importance of using research scholarship in developing methods to prevent violence, promote reconciliation, and build harmonious societies.[62]

NOTES

1. Mamdani 2002.
2. des Forges, 1999.
3. United States Committee for Refugees and Immigrants, 2002.
4. Zorbas, 2004.

5. Lederach, 1997; De la Rey, 2001.

6. Staub et al., 2005; Staub and Pearlman, 2001; Staub and Pearlman, 2006.

7. Lederach, 2001.

8. Powell, 2008.

9. des Forges, 1999.

10. Zorbas, 41.

11. Staub and Pearlman, 2001.

12. Kriesberg, 1998.

13. Broneus, 2003.

14. Staub and Bar-Tal, 2003.

15. Staub, 1998.

16. McCann and Pearlman, 1995; Pearlman and Saakvitne, 1995.

17. Tajfel, 1982; Staub, 1998.

18. Herman, 1992; Staub, 1998.

19. Mamdani, 2002.

20. Staub, 1998; Volkan, 1997.

21. Staub, 1989.

22. MacNair, 2002; Rhodes et al., 2002.

23. Staub, 1989.

24. Staub and Pearlman, 2001; Staub and Pearlman, 2006.

25. Staub, 2005a.

26. Montville, 1993.

27. Gibson, 2004; Proceedings of Stockholm International Forum on Truth, Justice and Reconciliation, 2002.

28. Hovannisian, 2003.

29. Staub, 2006.

30. des Forges, 1999.

31. Gibson, 2004.

32. Tyler and Smith, 1998.

33. Gibson, 2004.

34. Hovannisian, 2003.

35. Staub, 2003a.

36. Cairns and Darby, 1998.

37. Pettigrew and Tropp, 2006.

38. Varshney, 2002.

39. Helmick and Petersen, 2002; Staub and Bar-Tal, 2003.

40. "Report of the American Psychological Association Presidential Task Force on Psychological Ethics and National Security," 2005.

41. Kelman and Fisher, 2003.

42. Kelman and Fisher, 2003; Kriesberg, 1998; Staub, 2011; Volkan, 1998.

43. Cairns and Darby, 1998.

44. Staub, 1989; 1996; 1998; 1999; 2003b; Chorbajian and Shirinian, 1999; Totten et al, 1997; Staub and Bar-Tal, 2003.

45. McCann and Pearlman, 1990; Pearlman and Saakvitne, 1995; Saakvitne et al, 2000; Staub, 1998; Allen, 2001; Herman, 1992; Staub, 1998; Esterling et al, 1999; Nadler, 2003; Nadler, Malloy, and Fisher, 2008.

46. "Report of the American Psychological Association Presidential Task Force on Psychological Ethics and National Security," 2005.

47. Staub and Pearlman, 2006; Herman, 1992; Wessells and Monteiro, 2001.

48. Foa et al, 2000.

49. Pennebaker, 2000.

50. Staub, 1989; 2003a, 2011; Pearlman and Saakvitne, 1995; Saakvitne et al., 2000.

51. Staub et al., 2005b; Staub, 2011.

52. Bar-Tal, 2002; Cairns and Roe, 2002; PRI 2004; Staub and Bar-Tal, 2003; Staub, 2011; Willis, 1965.

53. "Chosen trauma" was proposed by Vamik Volkan (1997) to describe the focus of a group on a historical trauma and its psychological and behavioral consequences.

54. Staub, 1989, 2003c, 2011.

55. Staub and Pearlman, 2006; Staub, 2011.

56. Herman, 1992; Pennebaker, 2000.

57. Information Clearing House, n.d.

58. Paluck, 2009; Staub and Pearlman, 2009; see also Staub, 2011 for a detailed discussion of both the workshop-trainings and radio programs and their results.

59. Interrogations and Ethics, 2008.

60. Prunier, 2009; Staub, 2011.

61. A detailed description of the work promoting healing, reconciliation and the prevention of new violence in Rwanda (and the Congo) can be found in Staub, 2011.

62. A detailed description of the work promoting healing, reconciliation, and the prevention of new violence in Rwanda (and the Congo) can be found in Staub, 2011.

CHAPTER 18

INTERACTIVE PROBLEM SOLVING: INFORMAL MEDIATION BY THE SCHOLAR-PRACTITIONER

Herbert C. Kelman

For nearly 40 years now, my colleagues and I have developed and applied an unofficial, academically based, third-party approach to the resolution of international and intercommunal conflicts known as "interactive problem solving." The approach is derived from the pioneering work of John Burton[1] and is anchored in social-psychological principles. It is a form of unofficial—or what is now often called "track two"—diplomacy. It has also been described as "informal mediation by the scholar-practitioner"[2] to emphasize the unofficial and facilitative form of the intervention and the academic base of the third party. My own special emphasis has been on the Israeli-Palestinian conflict.

Interactive problem solving is quintessentially social-psychological in its orientation in that its goal is to promote change in individuals—through face-to-face interaction in small groups—as a vehicle for change in larger social systems: in national policies, in political culture, in the conflict system at large. The core of interactive problem solving is a particular *microprocess*,

This chapter is a revised version of an article that appeared in *Zeitschrift für Konfliktmanagement* (Verlag Dr. Otto Schmidt, Cologne), 2009, Volume 12(3): 74–79. It is based on remarks presented at the Thirteenth Mediations-Kongress, April 2, 2009, in Berlin, on the occasion of receiving the Sokrates Prize for Mediation from the Centrale für Mediation, Cologne.

best exemplified by problem-solving workshops, which is intended to produce changes in the *macroprocess* of official negotiations—in the peace process.[3]

The microprocess relates to the macroprocess in two ways. Most important, it provides *inputs* into the macroprocess. Furthermore, it can serve as a metaphor for what needs to happen in the macroprocess of conflict resolution.[4] The three components of the term *interactive problem solving* suggest what is required at the macrolevel of conflict resolution: (1) the process has to address the *problem*, which is in essence a shared problem in the relationship between the parties—a relationship that has become entirely competitive to the point of mutual destruction; (2) the process has to search for a *solution* that addresses the underlying causes of the problem—that can be located in the parties' unfulfilled or threatened needs—and that leads to a transformation of the destructive relationship; and (3) solution of the problem is best achieved through an *interactive* process, in which the parties share their differing perspectives and learn how to influence each other through mutual responsiveness. A solution arrived at through the direct interaction between the parties is more conducive to a stable, durable peace and a new, cooperative relationship than an imposed solution, because it is more likely to address the parties' fundamental needs and to elicit their commitment to the agreement and sense of ownership of it. Moreover, the interactive process of arriving at the solution in itself initiates the new relationship that the solution is designed to foster.

This view of the macroprocess of conflict resolution suggests some key components of the process that must take place somewhere in the system if the process is to fulfill itself and ultimately lead to a peace agreement (see Table 18.1):

1. *Identification and analysis of the problem*—requires mutual exploration of each other's basic needs and fears, from the perspective of the other, as well as of the escalatory dynamics of the conflict.
2. *Joint shaping of ideas for a solution*—involves identification of options, reframing of issues to make them more amenable to negotiation, and generating creative approaches to a win-win solution, all of which are necessary ingredients of a process of "pre-negotiation."

Table 18.1.   Components of the Conflict Resolution Process

1.   Identification and analysis of the problem
2.   Joint shaping of ideas for resolution
3.   Influencing the other side
4.   Creating a supportive political environment

3. *Influencing the other side*—calls for a shift from the heavy reliance on force and the threat of force to the use of positive incentives, including mutual reassurance that it is safe to enter into negotiations and mutual enticement through the promise of attractive gains; to this end, the parties must learn (as I have already suggested) how to influence the other by being responsive to the other's needs and fears.

4. *Creating a supportive political environment for negotiations*—calls for an environment marked by a sense of mutual reassurance fostered by sensitivity to each other's concerns and the development of working trust, by a sense of possibility that a mutually satisfactory solution can be found, and by a shift in the dominant political discourse from power politics to mutual accommodation.

These components of the conflict resolution process, as I have suggested, must occur somewhere in the larger system if conflict resolution is to become possible. Problem-solving workshops and related activities in the spirit of interactive problem solving seek to provide special opportunities for these processes to occur. Let me turn, then, to a brief description of the microprocess of problem-solving workshops, which bring together members of the political elites of the conflicting societies for direct, face-to-face interaction, facilitated by a third party knowledgeable about international conflict, group process, and the conflict region.

The precise format of problem-solving workshops may vary as a function of the phase of the conflict, the nature of the participants, the particular occasion and setting, and the specific purpose. Whatever their format, these workshops represent a microprocess that is specifically designed to insert—in a modest, but systematic way—the components of conflict resolution that I have outlined into the macroprocess. One can think of problem-solving workshops in the literal sense of the term, like a carpenter's or an artisan's workshop: a specifically constructed space, in which the parties can engage in a process of exploration, observation, and analysis, and in which they can create new products for export, as it were. The products in this case take the form of new ideas and insights that can be fed into the political debate and the decision-making process within the two societies and thus penetrate their political cultures.

Workshops are not negotiating sessions. They are not intended to substitute for negotiations or to bypass them in any way. Negotiations can be carried out only by officials who are authorized to conclude binding agreements, and workshops, by definition, are unofficial and nonbinding. But it is precisely their nonbinding character that represents their unique strength and special contribution to the larger process. They provide an opportunity for the kind of exploratory interaction that is very difficult to achieve in the context of official negotiations. The nonbinding character of workshops allows the participants to interact in an open, exploratory way; to speak and listen to each other as a means of acquiring new information and sharing their differing perspectives; and to gain insight into the other's—and indeed their own—needs, fears, concerns, priorities, and constraints and into the dynamics of the conflict relationship that leads to exacerbation, escalation, and perpetuation of the conflict.

Even though workshops are not negotiations and not meant to be negotiations, they are directly linked to the negotiations and complementary to them. I view them as an integral part of the larger negotiation process, potentially relevant at all of its stages (see Table 18.2). At the *pre-negotiation stage*, they can contribute to creating an environment that is conducive to moving the parties toward the negotiating table. Alongside of negotiations, at the *para-negotiation stage*, they may be particularly useful in helping the parties deal with the setbacks, stalemates, and loss of momentum that often mark the negotiations of intense, protracted conflicts—as we have observed in the Israeli-Palestinian conflict and many other cases. Thus, they may contribute to creating momentum and reviving the sense of possibility. They can also deal with issues that are not yet on the table, providing an opportunity for the parties to identify new options and reframe the issues in ways that make them more amenable to successful negotiation by the time they get to the table. In periods marked by a *breakdown of negotiations*, such as the current stage in the Israeli-Palestinian case, workshops can contribute to rebuilding trust in the availability of a negotiating partner and a sense of possibility and hope, and thus help the parties find a way back to the negotiating table. Finally, at the *post-negotiation stage*, workshops can contribute to resolving the problems of implementation of the negotiated agreements, as well as to the post-conflict process of peace building, reconciliation, and transforming the relationship between the former enemies.

Until 1991, our Israeli-Palestinian workshops were all obviously in the pre-negotiation phase. Moreover, until 1990, all of our workshops were one-time, self-contained events, usually consisting of separate pre-workshop

Table 18.2.   Relationship of Interactive Problem Solving to Negotiations

Pre-negotiation stage: creating an environment conducive to moving to the table

Para-negotiation stage: helping to create momentum, identify options, reframe issues

Breakdown of negotiations: rebuilding trust in the negotiating partner and sense of possibility and hope

Post-negotiation stage: contributing to implementation, peace-building, and reconciliation sessions (of 4 to 5 hours) for each party and two-and-a-half days (often over a week end) of joint meetings. Some of the individual participants in these workshops took part in more than one such event, but the group as a whole met only for this one occasion. In 1990, we organized our first continuing workshop with a group of influential Israelis and Palestinians who participated in a series of meetings over a three-year period. We have since had a Joint Working Group on Israeli-Palestinian Relations, which met between 1994 and 1999 and—for the first time in our work—was explicitly dedicated to producing joint concept papers on issues in the final-status negotiations. We now have another joint Israeli-Palestinian working group that began in 2001, after the failure of the Camp David summit and the onset of the second intifada, with a special focus on rebuilding trust in the availability of a negotiating partner, and which has met periodically since then.

To give some indication of what happens at workshops and the principles that govern them, I shall describe a typical one-time workshop between Israelis and Palestinians. There are, understandably, important differences between one-time and continuing workshops. There is also considerable variation among one-time workshops, with respect to the nature and number of participants, the size of the third party, the occasion for convening the workshop, the setting, and other considerations. But despite such variations, there is a set of key principles that apply throughout and can be gleaned from the description of an ideal-type one-time workshop.

The typical workshop participants are politically involved and, in many cases, politically influential members of their communities. However, with occasional exceptions, they have not been current officials. They have included parliamentarians; leading figures in political parties or movements; former ministers, military officers, diplomats, or government officials; journalists or editors specializing in the Middle East; and academics, many of whom are important analysts of the conflict in the public media and some of whom have served in advisory, official, or diplomatic positions and are likely to do so again in the future. We look for participants who are part of the mainstream of their societies and close to the center of the political spectrum. But they have to be interested in exploring the possibilities of a negotiated solution and willing to sit with members of the other society as equals. With some exceptions, our workshops have generally included three to six members of each party, as well as a third party of two to four members.

The academic setting is an important feature of our approach. It has the advantage of providing an unofficial, private, nonbinding context, with its own set of norms to support a type of interaction that departs from the norms that generally govern interactions between conflicting parties. Conflict norms require the parties to be militant, unyielding, and dismissive of the other's claims, interests, fears, and rights. To engage in a different kind of interaction, which enables each party to enter into the other's perspective and to work with the other in the search for mutual benefits, requires a countervailing set of norms. The academic setting is one setting (a religious setting is another) that can provide such norms that both permit and require participants to interact in a different way.

The third party in our model performs a strictly facilitative role. We do not generally propose solutions or participate in the substantive discussions. Our task is to create the conditions that allow ideas for resolving the conflict to emerge from the interaction between the parties themselves. The role of the third party is important. We select and brief the participants, set and enforce the ground rules, and propose the main lines of the agenda. We moderate the discussion and make a variety of interventions: content observations, which often take the form of summarizing, highlighting, asking for clarification, or pointing to similarities and differences between the parties; process observations, which suggest how interactions within the group may reflect the dynamics of the conflict between the two societies; and occasional theoretical observations, which offer concepts that might be useful in clarifying the issues under discussion. Finally, we serve as a repository of trust for the parties who, by definition do not trust each other: They feel safe to come to the workshop because they trust the third party and rely on it to make sure that confidentiality is maintained and that their interests are protected.

The ground rules governing the workshop, which are presented to participants several times—at the point of recruitment, in the pre-workshop sessions, and at the beginning of the workshop itself—are listed in Table 18.3. The first ground rule, privacy and confidentiality, is at the heart of the workshop process. It stipulates that whatever is said in the course of a workshop cannot be cited for attribution outside of the workshop setting by any participant, including the third party. To support this ground rule, the typical workshop has no audience, no publicity, and no record. To ensure privacy, we have no observers in our workshops; the only way our students are able to observe the process is by being integrated into the third party and accepting the discipline of the third party. To ensure confidentiality, we do not tape workshop sessions.

Confidentiality and nonattribution are essential for protecting the interests of the participants. In the earlier years of our work, meetings between Israelis and Palestinians were controversial in the two communities. The very fact that they were taking part in such a meeting at times entailed political, legal, or even physical risks for participants. Now that Israeli-Palestinian meetings have become almost routine, most (though not all) people are not concerned if their participation becomes known. Privacy and confidentiality—particularly the

Table 18.3. Workshop Ground Rules

1. Privacy and confidentiality

2. Focus on each other (not constituencies, audience, third parties)

3. Analytic (non-polemical) discussion

4. Problem-solving (non-adversarial) mode

5. No expectation of agreement

6. Equality in setting

7. Facilitative role of third party

principle of nonattribution—remain essential, however, for protection of the process. This ground rule makes it possible for the participants to engage in the kind of interaction that problem-solving workshops require. Confidentiality gives them the freedom and safety to think, listen, talk, and play with ideas, without having to worry that they will be held accountable outside for what they say in the workshop.

Ground rules 2 through 4 spell out the nature of the interaction that the workshop process is designed to encourage and that the principle of privacy and confidentiality is designed to protect. We ask participants to focus on each other in the course of the workshop: to listen to each other, with the aim of understanding the other's perspective, and to address each other, with the aim of making their own perspective understood. Workshops are radically different, in this respect, from debates.

Focusing on each other enables and encourages the parties to engage in an analytic discussion. The purpose of the exchange is not to engage in the usual polemics that characterize conflict interactions. Rather, it is to gain an understanding of each other's needs, fears, concerns, priorities, and constraints. A second purpose is to develop insight into the dynamics of the conflict, particularly into the ways in which the conflict-driven interactions between the parties tend to exacerbate, escalate, and perpetuate their conflict.

Analytic discussion helps the parties move to a problem-solving mode of interaction, in contrast to the adversarial mode that usually characterizes conflict interactions. In line with a "no-fault" principle, the participants are asked to treat the conflict as a shared problem, requiring joint efforts to find a mutually satisfactory solution, rather than try to determine who is right and who is wrong on the basis of historical or legal argumentation. We are not asking participants to abandon their ideas about the justice of their cause, nor are we suggesting that both sides are equally right or equally wrong. We are merely proposing that a problem-solving approach is more likely to be productive than an attempt to allocate blame.

The fifth ground rule states that in a workshop—unlike a negotiating session—there is no expectation to reach an agreement. Like any conflict resolution effort, we are interested in finding common ground, but the amount of agreement achieved in the discussion is not a measure of the success of the enterprise. If the participants come away with a better understanding of the other side's perspective, of their own priorities, and of the dynamics of the conflict, the workshop will have fulfilled its purpose, even if it does not produce an outline of a peace treaty.

The sixth ground rule states that, within the workshop setting, the two parties are equals. Clearly, there are important asymmetries between them in the real world—asymmetries in power, in moral position, in reputation. These play important roles in conflict and, clearly, must be taken into account in the workshop discussions. But the two parties are equals in the workshop setting in the sense that each party has the same right to serious consideration of its needs, fears, and concerns in the search for a mutually satisfactory solution.

The final ground rule concerns the facilitative role of the third party, which I have already discussed. In keeping with this rule, the third party does not take positions on the issues, give advice, or offer its own proposals, nor does it take sides, evaluate the ideas presented, or arbitrate between different interpretations of historical facts and international law. Within its facilitative role, however, it sets the ground rules and monitors adherence to them; it helps to keep discussion moving in constructive directions, tries to stimulate movement, and intervenes as relevant with questions, observations, and even challenges.

One of the tasks of the third party is to set the agenda for the discussion. In the typical one-time workshop, the agenda is relatively open and unstructured, as far as the substantive issues under discussion are concerned. The way in which these issues are approached, however, and the order of discussion are structured so as to facilitate the kind of discourse that the ground rules seek to encourage. The workshop begins with personal introductions around the table; a review of the purposes, procedures, and ground rules of the gathering; and an opportunity for the participants to ask questions about these. We then typically proceed with a five-part agenda, as outlined in Table 18.4.

The first discussion session is devoted to an exchange of information between the two sides, which serves primarily to break the ice and to set the tone for the kind of discourse we hope to generate. Each party is asked to talk about the situation on the ground and the current mood in its own community, about the issues in the conflict as seen in that community, about the spectrum of views on the conflict and its resolution, and about their own position within that spectrum. This exchange provides a shared base of information and sets a precedent for the two sides to deal with each other as mutual resources, rather than solely as combatants.

Table 18.4. Workshop Agenda

1. Information exchange
2. Needs analysis
3. Joint thinking regarding solutions
4. Discussion of constraints
5. Joint thinking regarding overcoming constraints

The core agenda of the workshop begins with a needs analysis, in which each side is asked to talk about its fundamental needs and fears—those needs that would have to be satisfied and those fears that would have to be allayed if a solution is to be acceptable in its society. Participants are asked to listen attentively and not to debate or argue about what the other side says, although they are invited to ask for elaboration and clarification. The purpose of this phase of the proceedings is to help each side understand the basic concerns of the other side from the other's perspective. We check the level of understanding by asking each side to summarize the other's needs, as they have heard them. Each side then has the opportunity to correct or amplify the summary that has been presented by the other side. Once the two sides have come to grasp each other's perspective and understand each other's needs as well as seems possible at that point, we move on to the next phase of the agenda: joint thinking about solutions to the conflict.

There is a clear logic to the order of the phases of this agenda. We discourage the participants from proposing solutions until they have identified the problem, which stems from the parties' unfulfilled and threatened needs. We want the participants to come up with ideas for solution that are anchored in the problem—that address the parties' felt needs. What we ask the parties to do in phase 3 of the agenda is to generate—through a process of joint thinking (or interactive problem solving)—ideas for the overall shape of a solution to the conflict, or to particular issues within the conflict, that are responsive to the fundamental needs and fears of both parties, as presented in the preceding phase of the workshop. The participants are given the difficult assignment of thinking of solutions that respond, not only to their own side's needs and fears (as they would in a bargaining situation), but simultaneously to the needs and fears of *both* sides. It goes against the grain for parties engaged in a deep-rooted conflict to think of ways in which the adversary too can "win"—but that is precisely what joint thinking requires.

Once the parties have achieved some common ground in generating ideas for solutions that would address the fundamental needs and fears of both sides, we turn to a discussion of the political and psychological constraints within their societies that stand in the way of such solutions. Discussion of constraints is an extremely important part of the learning that takes place in workshops, because parties involved in an intense conflict find it difficult to understand the constraints of the other, or even to recognize that the other—like themselves—has constraints. However, we try to discourage discussion of constraints until the parties have gone through the phase of joint thinking, because a premature focus on constraints is likely to inhibit the creative process of generating new ideas. We try to see whether the particular individuals around the table can come up with new ideas for resolving the conflict. Once they have generated such ideas, we explore the constraints that make it difficult for these new ideas to gain acceptance in their societies.

Finally, to the extent that time permits, we ask the participants to engage in another round of joint thinking, this time about ways of overcoming the constraints against integrative, win-win solutions to the conflict. In this phase of the workshop, participants try to generate ideas for steps that they personally, their organizations, or their governments can take—separately or jointly—to overcome the constraints that have been identified. Such ideas may focus, in particular, on steps of mutual reassurance—in the form of acknowledgments, symbolic gestures, or confidence-building measures— that would make the parties more willing and able to take the risks required for innovative solutions to the conflict.

The ground rules and agenda that I have described are designed to help achieve the dual purpose of workshops (see Table 18.5), to which I alluded earlier. The first purpose is to produce change in the particular individuals who are sitting around the workshop table—to enable them to gain new insight into the conflict and acquire new ideas for resolving the conflict and overcoming the barriers to a negotiated solution. However, these changes at the level of individual participants are not ends in themselves, but vehicles for promoting change at the policy level. To this end, the second purpose of workshops is to maximize the likelihood that the new insights and ideas developed by workshop participants will be fed back into the political debate and decision-making procedures in their respective societies.

What is interesting, both theoretically and practically, is that these two purposes may be and often are contradictory to each other. The requirements for maximizing change in the workshop itself may be contrary to the requirements for maximizing the transfer of that change into the political process. The best example of these dialectics is the selection of participants. To maximize transfer into the political process, we would look for participants who are officials as close as possible to the decision-making process and thus in a position to apply immediately what they have learned. But to maximize change, we would look for participants who are removed from

Table 18.5.   The Dual Purpose of Interactive Problem Solving

Change in individual workshop participants: development of new insights, new ideas for conflict resolution

Transfer of these changes into the political debate and the decision-making processes in their societies

the decision-making process and therefore less constrained in their interactions and freer to play with ideas and explore hypothetical possibilities. To balance these contradictory requirements, we look for participants who are not officials but politically influential. They are thus freer to engage in the process, but at the same time, their positions within their societies are such that any new ideas that they develop can have an impact on the thinking of decision makers and the society at large.

Another example of the dialectics of workshops is the degree of cohesiveness that we try to engender in the group of participants. An adequate level of group cohesiveness is important to the effective interaction among the participants. But if the workshop group becomes too cohesive—if the Israeli and Palestinian participants form too close a coalition across the conflict lines—they may lose credibility and political effectiveness in their own communities.[5] To balance these two contradictory requirements, we recognize that the coalition formed by the two groups of participants must remain an uneasy coalition. By the same token, we aim for the development of *working trust*—of trust in the participants on the other side based not so much on interpersonal closeness, but on the conviction that they are sincerely committed, out of their own interests, to the search for a peaceful solution.

Let me conclude with a brief summary of our Israeli-Palestinian work over the past four decades. Our earliest work, in the 1970s and 1980s, clearly corresponds to the pre-negotiation phase of the conflict. Our workshops and related activities during those years contributed to the development of a sense of possibility, of new ideas for resolving the conflict, and of relationships among members of the political elites across the conflict lines.

By 1989, in the wake of the resolution of the 1988 Palestine National Council that in effect endorsed a two-state solution, the atmosphere for negotiations had greatly improved. The time seemed ripe in 1990 for Nadim Rouhana and me to convene, for the first time, a continuing workshop with a group of high-level, politically influential Israelis and Palestinians.[6] A year later, in 1991, official negotiations began with the Madrid conference. As it happened, four of the six Palestinian members of the continuing workshop were appointed to the official negotiating team. A year later, a Labor Party government took over in Israel and several of the Israeli members of the continuing workshop were appointed to high positions in the new administration. The political relevance of the continuing workshop was enhanced by these developments, but they also created some ambiguities and role conflicts. Several members left the group in light of their official appointments and were replaced by new members. At our meeting in the summer of 1993, some of the discussion focused on the role of a group like ours at a time when official negotiations were in progress. Within days of that meeting, the Oslo agreement was announced and, in close consultation with the members of the group, we decided to close the continuing workshop and to initiate a new project in keeping with the new political requirements.

Our work up to that point, along with many other track-two efforts, played a modest but not insignificant role, directly or indirectly, in laying the groundwork for the Oslo agreement. In my own assessment, three kinds of contributions can be identified:[7]

1. Workshops helped to develop *cadres* experienced in communicating with the other side and prepared to carry out productive negotiations.
2. Workshops helped to produce *substantive inputs* into the political thinking and debate in the two societies. Through the communications of workshop members—and to some degree of members of the third party—ideas on which productive negotiations could be based were injected into the two political cultures and became the building stones of the Oslo agreement. These ideas, as summarized in Table 18.6, focused in particular on what was both necessary and possible in negotiating a mutually satisfactory agreement.[8]
3. Workshops, along with many other efforts, helped to create a political atmosphere favorable to negotiations and open to a new relationship between the parties.

Table 18.6. Evolving Ideas for Resolving the Israeli-Palestinian Conflict (1967–1993): The Building Stones of the Oslo Agreement

Focus of the Ideas	Target of the Ideas	
	Negotiation Process	Negotiation Outcome
What is necessary	Negotiations between legitimate national representatives	Mutual recognition of national identity and rights
What is possible	Availability of a negotiating partner	The two-state solution

Source: Kelman, 2005, p. 53. Reprinted by permission of the editor, R.J. Fisher, and the publisher, Lexington Books.

The major new project that we initiated after the signing of the Oslo Accords corresponded to the new phase of the conflict, which focused on implementation of a partial, interim agreement and movement to final-status negotiations. The project was the Joint Working Group on Israeli-Palestinian Relations, which was co-chaired with Nadim Rouhana, and which met between 1994 and 1999. The purpose of the group—for the first time in our work—was to produce and disseminate joint concept papers on some of the issues that the Oslo Accords left for final-status negotiations, placed within the context of the desired future relationship between the two societies. We published three joint papers: one on general principles for the final agreement,[9] a second on the Palestinian refugee problem,[10] and a third on the future Israeli-Palestinian relationship.[11] Each was translated into Arabic and Hebrew and widely disseminated in all three versions. A fourth paper, on the settlements issue, was close to completion, but overtaken by events.

This brings us to the current phase of our work, which began with the failure of the Camp David summit in the summer of 2000 and the onset of the second intifada. It corresponds to a phase of the conflict characterized by the breakdown of once-promising negotiations. My major effort during this period—in partnership with Shibley Telhami—has been the formation of a new joint Israeli-Palestinian working group, focusing on the theme of rebuilding trust in the availability of a credible negotiating partner and of a mutually acceptable formula for a two-state solution.

The effort started with two planning meetings in 2001 but, for a number of reasons beyond our control, the group's substantive work did not begin until 2004. Over the course of four productive sessions between 2004 and 2006, the group seemed ready to work on a joint concept paper on how to frame a final peace agreement in a way that would reassure the two publics and elicit their full support. At subsequent meetings, however, the members of the group felt that—in light of the significant changes in the political land-scape due to elections on both sides, the wars of 2006, and the Hamas take-over of Gaza—the time was not ripe for a paper focusing on a final agree-ment. They were very eager, however, to exchange information and ideas, to discuss new obstacles and possibilities, and to explore the growing role of Hamas in the equation. They made it very clear that they wanted to continue the group and that they considered track-two efforts, if anything, more criti-cal than ever at this juncture. The group has continued to meet in this spirit and to engage in productive exchange of information, analysis of events, and joint thinking. At a meeting in 2009, the discussions yielded some concrete suggestions for statements by the leadership on each side that might help overcome the profound distrust of the public on the other side. At their most recent meeting, in June 2010, the participants developed ideas for actions on the part of the U.S. administration that might advance negotiations, and asked the third party to convey these ideas to relevant U.S. officials on behalf of the working group.

As for the larger picture, what is required, in my view, to break through the profound mutual distrust in the ultimate intentions of the other side and energize public support for peace negotiations, is a visionary approach that transcends the balance of power and the calculus of bargaining concessions. Paradoxically, perhaps, this calls for a step toward reconciliation—which is generally viewed as a post-negotiation process—to move negotiations forward. In this spirit, a final agreement would have to be framed as a principled peace, based on a historic compromise that meets the fundamental needs of both peoples, validates their national identities, and declares an end to the conflict and to the occupation consistent with the requirements of fairness and attainable justice. The framework I propose would start with the recognition that both peoples have historic roots in the land and are deeply attached to it, that each people's pursuit of its national aspirations by military means may well lead to mutual destruction, and that the only solution lies in a historic compromise that allows each people to express its right to national self-determination, fulfill its national aspirations, and express its national identity in a state of its own within the shared land, in peaceful coexistence with the neighboring state of the other. The framework would proceed to spell out what the logic of a historic compromise implies for the key final-status issues (including borders, Jerusalem, settlements, and refugees); and offer a positive vision of a common future for the two peoples in the land they have agreed to share—and of the future of the shared land itself. If such a framework is constructed through a joint Israeli-Palestinian process, it can reassure the two publics that the agreement is not jeopardizing their national existence and promises mutual benefits that far outweigh the risks it entails.

The framework I propose requires visionary leadership on both sides. Until such leadership emerges, the primary initiative for constructing and disseminating such a framework rests with civil society in the two communities. A track-two approach like interactive problem solving can contribute to such efforts by providing a joint process of "negotiating identity," in which each side can acknowledge and accommodate the other's identity—at least to the extent of eliminating negation of the other and the claim of exclusivity from its own identity—in a context in which the core of its identity and its associated narrative are affirmed by the other.[12] Ideas that emerge from such an interactive process can then be injected into the political debate and the political culture of each society.

NOTES

1. Burton, 1969, 1979, 1984, 1990.
2. Kelman, 2002.
3. Kelman, 1997: 212–220.
4. Kelman, 1996: 99–123.
5. Kelman, 1993.
6. Rouhana and Kelman, 1994, 157–178.
7. Kelman, 1995, 19–27; Kelman, 2005.
8. Kelman, 2005.
9. Joint Working Group on Israeli-Palestinian Relations, 1999, 170–175.
10. Alpher and Shikaki, 1999, 167–189.
11. Joint Working Group on Israeli-Palestinian Relations, 2000, 90–112.
12. Kelman, 2001.

CHAPTER 19

FROM YOUNG SOLDIERS TO YOUNG PEACE BUILDERS: BUILDING PEACE IN SIERRA LEONE

Michael Wessells

Although the number of armed conflicts under way has declined recently,[1] large numbers of societies—about 25 to 40 in any particular year—are just emerging from wars, many of which have raged for a decade or more.[2] In some of these societies, there are no peace movements as such since the wars had shattered civil societies, militarized large numbers of people, and made "peace" a taboo subject. In addition, many presumably post-conflict societies remain ripe for further violence. Not uncommonly, large numbers of former combatants, including many children, remain under arms and lack the livelihoods and life options needed to transition into civilian life.[3] Also, many armed conflicts leave in their wake deeply divided societies that contain the seeds of future violence.

In such transitional contexts, it is unrealistic to expect a full blown peace movement to emerge, particularly if levels of social cohesion are very low and people are desperate to meet basic survival needs such as those for food, water, shelter, and health care. Nevertheless, it may be possible to organize peace building activities that limit the impulse to fight and lay a foundation on which subsequent peace movements can stand.

Although many post-conflict peace building activities have focused on adults, it is equally important to focus on young people, defined in this chapter as including children (people 0 to 18 years) and also those between 18 and 24 years of age. In many war zones, young people such as teenagers are highly sought after as soldiers since their physical strength, cognitive capacities, and political consciousness, not to mention their limited sense of their own mortality and the ease with which they can be manipulated, make them valuable members of fighting forces and armed groups.[4] Even those under 18 years of age may be regarded not as children but as adults since they may have completed cultural rites of passage or do work regarded as the work of adults. Not only boys but also girls are recruited and used as fighters, porters, spies, or sex slaves.[5] Having been socialized into systems of violence, these young men and women are at risk, even following the signing of a ceasefire, of engaging in crime and banditry, being recruited into local "security forces," or becoming mercenaries in neighboring countries. A highly significant task, then, is to help young people transition out of their soldier roles and identities, enabling them to integrate into civilian life.

This chapter shows how it is possible for youth to transition from life as soldiers to life as civilians and peace builders at community and societal levels. It focuses on Sierra Leone, where the conflict engaged large numbers of young people and where the conflict raged for over a decade, leaving behind a society that was widely regarded as highly prone to further conflict. During the 1990s, there had been considerable pessimism internationally regarding the prospects for the integration of former child and youth soldiers into civilian life in Sierra Leone owing to the nature of the fighting and roles that youth played. These challenges to integration are outlined below together with a description and analysis of the programmatic steps needed to gain community acceptance of former young soldiers and to enable formerly recruited young people to become local peace builders.

CHALLENGES OF REINTEGRATION

The challenges of young people's reintegration were linked closely with the roles of young soldiers. Many young people performed roles such as combatants, porters, cooks, spies, and bodyguards, and these roles were often performed in the same time period. Some individuals, however, had specialized roles such as torturers or sex slaves, with girls serving mostly in the latter. Most young recruits lived lives that were thoroughly militarized and either witnessed or caused deaths.

The Revolutionary United Front (RUF), the opposition group that was the main recruiter of young people, regularly recruited young people via abductions, which began a brutal process of indoctrination. The RUF abducted many children at gunpoint and then forced them to kill members of their villages or families.[6] This horrific practice aimed to terrorize people and destroy the bonds between the young person and the village, thereby decreasing the motivation to escape and return home. Typically, girls were taken as sex slaves whose refusals to provide sex on demand led to brutal beatings or death. Many girls served also as porters, carrying heavy loads long distances with little to eat or drink. They and male porters avoided death by continuing to carry their loads, as anyone who lagged behind or complained was usually killed.

Both girls and boys served as combatants, though the majority of young combatants were boys. To prepare them for combat, commanders often plied them with drugs such as alcohol, marijuana, and amphetamines. As a result, many young people said they entered combat very high and feeling neither fear nor pain. To increase even further their willingness to fight, traditional healers often administered ritual treatments believed to make the young soldiers bulletproof. To promote obedience, commanders controlled young recruits through a mixture of terror tactics and positive incentives for fearless behavior and enthusiasm in combat. The best fighters often got promoted and received privileged access to coveted items such as medicines.

Young people also played a role in some of the worst atrocities. Small Boys Units that consisted entirely of soldiers less than 12 years of age often committed amputations.[7] Also, young soldiers demonstrated considerable machismo, taking names such as "Rambo" or "Cock and Fire" to trumpet their ferocity and combat deeds. Because of the bad things that young soldiers had done, many people regarded them as bloodthirsty predators and animals.

Former girl soldiers faced particularly severe challenges to integration due to the heavy burden of stigma toward formerly recruited girls. Many girls were regarded as "bad" not only because of their unruly behavior but also because they had been sexually violated out of wedlock. Also, many girls were HIV-positive and had babies who carried the double stigma of having been born out of wedlock and being "rebel children." In rural areas of Sierra Leone, rape in the bush brands one as damaged goods and is believed to cause contamination by angry spirits, which can harm a girl's family or community members. These spiritual challenges underscore the importance of local cosmologies and indigenous understandings.[8]

REINTEGRATION AND PEACE BUILDING

Following the conflict, high priorities were to integrate former young soldiers into civilian life and enable them to contribute to peace building at the community level. These priorities were closely linked since reintegration into civilian life would have been impossible without steps to reconcile young returning soldiers with their communities. In addition, the process of reintegration entails a transformation of young people's military identities together with a shift in community perceptions away from the "youth as troublemakers" stereotype toward a view of young people as valued, peaceful members of communities.[9] The two projects described below sought to enable community reconciliation of formerly recruited young males and females, respectively. A distinctive feature of the men's project was that it engaged young people as peace builders who conduct community service projects and work to improve their relations with former adversaries.

Reconciliation, Employment, and Community Service for Male Youths

At the end of the war, the Northern Province was the RUF stronghold and a site of significant tension since former soldiers from different sides were returning to the same village. Many of the male former soldiers identified jobs and income as their greatest needs and stated bluntly that they would not disarm and return to villages without proper clothing or a means of earning an income. To address these needs, Christian Children's Fund (CCF)/Sierra Leone worked in the Northern Province to defuse tensions and improve intergroup relations using a superordinate goals approach[10] wherein previously competing groups of youth cooperated on the achievement of common goals, earning an income as they worked. The common goal was to improve the well-being of children, who comprised half the population, had suffered greatly during the war, and had few supports.

The CCF staff, who were Sierra Leonean and understood the local language, culture, and situation, met first with the paramount chiefs and local chiefs, explaining their purpose and requesting the chiefs' approval, which was enthusiastically granted. To enable inter-village cooperation, CCF staff facilitated community dialogues that involved four or five elected representatives from neighboring villages and focused on children's needs and how to support them. This strategy was designed to reduce inter-village tensions and restore the norms of neighborliness that the war had shattered. CCF worked with a total of 26 communities, thereby reaching a relatively large number of children and helping to rebuild the torn social fabric in the North. The focus on children served to deemphasize political differences and to create a common goal that bound everyone together. The planning discussions considered multiple ideas about community projects to support children and then selected one project as the top priority. Projects included building a health post, rebuilding schools, or repairing bridges that improved access to markets, thereby boosting local incomes. To promote reconciliation, the projects were built by community work teams consisting of formerly recruited youth, including former soldiers who had fought on different sides, and other village youth. CCF played a facilitative role and purchased the local construction materials for the projects.

To enable acceptance of formerly recruited youth, CCF staff conducted community dialogues to build empathy, which is typically among war's first casualties.[11] To break the negative stereotypes of young former soldiers, CCF staff emphasized that all children and young people had suffered and that many young people had been abducted by the RUF and forced to commit horrible acts. As people told how they and their families had suffered, people communalized their suffering, overcame their sense of isolation, and experienced empathy and a sense of unity.

To prepare the youth who formed the work teams, CCF staff organized a two-day workshop on reconciliation, in which they emphasized the need to put the war behind them and to work in unity to build a better future. Village elders and healers promoted reconciliation using traditional proverbs, songs, and dances and also by rekindling collective memories of how the communities had overcome adversity together in the past. The elders and CCF staff set ground rules such as no name calling or use of threatening gestures that might escalate tensions on the work teams. Extensive discussion also focused on the importance of working together as a team to help support vulnerable children.

Next the work teams built the designed projects, with each worker contributing 20 days' labor and earning US$27, which was sufficient to purchase necessities such as food and clothing. During the construction, youth received vocational counseling about which sources of livelihood they might want to pursue. Subsequently, selected youth participated in vocational training and income-generating activities under the guidance of artisans who taught marketable skills to the mentored youth, who used loans to work and then repaid their loans.

Triangulated, semi-structured interviews and focus group discussions with youth, elders, and other community members indicated that the project had supported reconciliation and reintegration. Many formerly recruited youth said that when they left the armed groups they had feared rejection and stigmatization by the community, particularly by the youths they had attacked. Many had doubted their ability to earn a living and find a place in civilian life. However, the formerly recruited youth reported that they had learned how to get along with other youth. The youth who had not been recruited said that they had cast off their images of former youth soldiers as demons and had come to see them as citizens who gave back to their communities. Community members, too, said that they saw and appreciated the former youth soldiers' contributions to the community and no longer feared the former soldiers but accepted them as civilians. This shift in the role of the former soldiers enabled the desired shift in social identity. Indeed, many former soldiers stopped speaking of themselves in military terms and took pride describing themselves as husbands, fathers, and community members. Many reported feeling pride in helping to build peaceful relations at a community level.

A valuable lesson from this project is that former youth soldiers can become peace builders when they are provided with the appropriate space and support for giving back to their communities. The shift from soldier to peace builder is not only an individual process but also a communal process in which communities learn to see former recruits in a different role and manner, thereby enabling the transformation of the former soldiers' social identities. Another lesson is that some of the same skills of communication and mobilization for hard physical labor that had been useful inside the armed group can be harnessed for peaceful means. Too often, reintegration programs have failed to build on the skills of formerly recruited youth.[12] Of course, this project was only a first step in a much longer process of reintegration, which is measured in years. Still, it succeeded in engaging youth as agents of communal reconciliation and peace building, thereby providing a foundation for the longer-term work of reintegration.

Young Women's Reintegration

Although the situation of young men at the end of the Sierra Leone war was very serious, the situation of young women who had been recruited was arguably worse. The official Disarmament, Demobilization, and Reintegration (DDR) process had discriminated against women, as has occurred in other countries as well.[13] Of the estimated 12,000 formerly recruited girls, only 4 percent had received official DDR benefits.[14]

The magnitude of young girls' needs was illuminated by the results of a preliminary assessment conducted in 2002 by CCF/Sierra Leone in the Northern Province Districts of Bombali, Portloko, and Tonkolili. The main finding was that in some villages, nearly every household had at least one girl who had been abducted by the RUF. The girls reported (and health workers confirmed) the wide prevalence of reproductive health problems such as sexually transmitted infections, genital damage, and pelvic inflammatory disease. Having carried heavy loads sometimes for long distances without food or health care, many girls had head and neck pains, stomach pains, other somatic issues, and skin diseases. Over half the former girl soldiers had become mothers as a result of having been violated in the bush.

Among the greatest stresses reported by the girls was their lack of community acceptance.[15] Many girls said they had been stigmatized as "rebel girls" or "kolonkos" (prostitutes) following their return home. Girls also reported being harassed sexually and physically by community members. Few if any former girl soldiers had received health support, and their high disease prevalence made them unacceptable. Some said their "heads were not clear," which in the local idiom meant they were spiritually impure. Saying they could not work because their "minds were not steady," the girls suggested they could be helped by local healers who could conduct traditional cleansing ceremonies to rid them of their spiritual impurity. Lacking a means of earning a living, most girls expressed strong desire for skills training and loans to conduct a small business. Girl mothers particularly sought livelihoods as support since they had no means of providing food or medicines for their babies. Girls reported that out of desperation, some girls had turned to sex work as their only means of survival. A high priority for the girls was education, which was seen as a source of hope.

The girls' concerns resonated with the narratives of their families and communities. Family members said they had initially feared and rejected the girls, who demonstrated little respect for others, were unwilling to help the families, and engaged in highly aggressive, unruly behavior. Community members also feared and rejected the girls, many of whom spent significant time idling, fighting, and engaging in promiscuous behavior. In general, the girls were viewed as undesirable marriage prospects. Those who were married were often rejected by their husbands or had their "rebel" children from the bush rejected by their husbands.

To enable young women's reintegration, CCF/Sierra Leone organized in 2001 to 2005 a community-based program called Sealing the Past, Facing the Future (SEFAFU) to assist 600 sexually abused girl mothers and their families. The joint focus on the girls and their families reflects an ecological view asserting that children's well-being is inextricably interconnected with that of their families[16] and also an understanding of the harm caused in collectivist societies by the use of highly individualized supports.[17] The project objectives were: (1) to increase the girls' access to Western health care and, where appropriate, traditional cleansing, (2) to develop the girls' livelihood skills and income, reducing their risk of sexual exploitation and enabling them to achieve a positive social role, (3) to increase the girls' successful participation in education, and (4) to strengthen community mechanisms for protection and reconciliation.

A key program strategy was to avoid helping only formerly recruited girls—a widely used practice that often produces jealousies—by supporting a mixture of formerly recruited young women and other highly vulnerable girls such as those separated from their families. The vast majority of the girls were former soldiers between 10 and 18 years of age. Of the 600 girls who were directly supported, 57 percent were mothers who had borne children as a result of sexual exploitation inside an armed group. Additional strategic elements were reliance on narrative methods and an empowerment approach; the building on existing community resources such as chiefs, elders, health workers, and women's groups; the activation and support of cultural resources such as traditional healers and appropriate cleansing rituals; a multi-sectoral approach designed to address the holistic nature of the girls' needs; efforts to rebuild civil society, a key condition for peace through steps toward community reconciliation and mobilization; and use of a multi-year approach that recognized the impossibility of resolving in the span of year-long funding allocations problems that had been decades in the making.

Following the pilot phase, the project was taken to scale first in Bombali and Koinadugu Districts in 2003 to 2004 and subsequently in Kaihalun District. Broadly, there were four main foci of the program activities, the first of which was community engagement and mobilization to support the young women. Having met with the Paramount and local chiefs, the CCF staff organized community dialogues to raise awareness about the girls' situation, their suffering during the war, and the need for girls' reconciliation with their families and communities as part of the process of building peace. In addition, the staff mapped community resources such as women's groups, healers, religious leaders, health workers, social workers, and youth groups. These were subsequently mobilized by a community selected by the community and the girls. Mobilization was also catalyzed from within the communities. For example, local women and men in one community organized a Girls' Welfare Committee that limited sexual harassment and violence toward the young women. With the support of the wider community, the Committee established clear rules of appropriate behavior (for example, no name calling, no harassment) and imposed fines for infractions of the rules. This process, which rapidly eliminated the harassment and violence toward the girls, was soon copied by other villages.

Second, the program supported the girls' health by enabling health screening at the local health clinic. Although resource shortages made it impossible to cover the costs of the girls' medical treatment, the program's livelihood elements, described below, enabled some girls to pay their health care costs. The health work built linkages with the Ministry of Health and Sanitation and also with UNICEF, both of which helped to define basic health messages and were part of an emerging network that promoted sustainable health service access.

Third, the program worked with traditional healers, where it was appropriate to do so, to cleanse the girls of spiritual impurities. In many rural areas of Sierra Leone, as in other parts of Africa,[18] people view spiritual harmony with the ancestors as central to well-being. Particularly in Koinadugu District, girls said they needed to see a local healer for cleansing of bad spirits taken in during their stay in the bush. They and their villages saw their pollution as a communal affliction since, left untreated, the girls would bring into the community the evil spirits, which were believed to cause problems such as crop failure, poor health, and even additional fighting. In communities that held these traditional beliefs, CCF worked with healers to provide the necessary materials for a group cleansing. Typical elements of cleansing ceremonies included ritual washing with black ash soap, fumigation with boiled herbs believed to have purgative properties, the sacrifice of goats or chickens, and the subsequent conduct of a feast at which the girls were dressed in white and presented to the community as clean and acceptable.[19] Considerable regional differences existed; in the North, some communities used a mixture of traditional methods and Islamic methods such as writing sacred Koranic verses on a slate which was then wiped clean by the imam. This diversity is a useful reminder that so-called "traditional" methods are, like culture itself, fluid and dynamic.

Fourth, the program organized livelihood supports since the young women identified their lack of income as a significant source of distress and also a barrier to engaging effectively in civilian social roles such as mother or wife. Since the girls lived in predominantly rural areas, they received training in crop production and advice from the Ministry of Agriculture and Marine Resources. To support income generation, the girls also participated in training on skills that a preliminary market analysis had indicated were sustainable. Over several months, paid community artisans trained groups of girls in skills such as sewing, tailoring, soap making, and weaving. CCF provided the necessary materials and sewing machines and organized a workshop in which the girls learned basic business skills.

Following this training, the girls formed solidarity groups consisting of 10 girls each. Each girl received a loan of 150,000 leones (US$50) that could be used to start a business, with the loan repaid over a year together with a 10 percent service fee. When one girl had repaid her loan, the loan rotated to another girl, and this loan rotation continued even following the end of the funded period of the program.

Although a full evaluation was not undertaken by the program, comparisons were made between the program villages in Kaihalun and two similar villages in Kaihalun that had not participated in the project. The two nonprogram villages were inside the same chiefdom targeted by the program. It was decided to bring to these villages the same supports girls had received in the other villages, making the interviews conducted in the two villages a baseline assessment as well as a source of comparison with the project communities. Overall, 200 young women in 10 project communities participated, as did over 100 elders and parents in those communities. The data were triangulated with data from key informant interviews conducted with traditional healers, local chiefs, elders, social workers, and health workers.

The project yielded significant benefits in regard to health, social acceptance, and education. Nearly 80 percent of the former girl soldiers in the project villages received health screening, in contrast with only 10 percent of the former girl soldiers in the comparison villages. Particularly in the Northern Province, both girls and their families reported that their access to health screening and care, including traditional cleansing, had contributed to their physical, spiritual, and social well-being. Reported physical improvements, which included reductions in skin diseases, sexually transmitted infections, and physical ailments such as stomach problems, had marked psychosocial impact since they reflected the girls taking charge of their health situation. Also, the girls felt increased self-esteem and were less likely to be viewed as diseased or somehow untouchable. The girls who had participated in traditional cleansing ceremonies said their minds had become steady, their somatic issues had been reduced, and they felt ready to participate in skills training, business, or education.

The program significantly improved girls' ability to achieve their top priority of gaining acceptance by family and community. Compared to girls in the comparison villages, former girl soldiers in the program villages showed higher rates of marriage and family acceptance, lower rates of stigma and isolation, and increased likelihood of being seen as contributing, self-reliant citizens. Marriage was important because marriage is the norm for older Sierra Leonean girls, who regard being unmarried as a form of social death. Marriage is essential to the girls' role as wife, mother, and member of an extended family. Also, to be married is to be sought after and viewed as a contributing member of one's family and community. Adults in the project communities said that they had seen the young women's behavior change from unruly and aggressive to becoming more prosocial and aligned with local norms. The conduct of the cleansing ceremonies was viewed as having cleansed the girls and made them acceptable for full interaction with families and communities. Speaking the local idiom, adults said that following the conduct of the cleansing ceremonies, the girls were free to "eat off the same plate as us."

In regard to livelihoods, the girls in the program villages reported that before the program, they had had only 2 to 3 cups of rice per day, whereas after the program implementation, they had 5 to 6 cups of rice per day. In the nonprogram villages, girls reported no significant increase in rice availability and said currently they had access to 2 to 3 cups per day. The girls' increased earning ability and income boosted their self-esteem since they were self-reliant, contributed to their families, and had the money needed to go to school. In most cases, the girls reported improved family relations since they shared their loans or small businesses with other family members, making businesses a family operation. Many girls said they were sought after as marriage partners because they had an income and higher status. Similarly, community members often said they saw the girls differently. Whereas previously they had seen the girls as unruly and even as animals, they now saw the girls as productive family members and mothers who contributed as community citizens. Also, key informants reported that the girls' access to income had successfully deterred their involvement in sex work.

The program also had educational benefits. Whereas only 10 percent of formerly recruited girls in the comparison villages attended school, nearly half the former girl soldiers in the program villages attended school regularly. For the latter girls, their income earning ability enabled them to pay the school fees and purchase necessary school materials. Often, they attended school half the day and conducted business the other half. In some communities, their children also attended school and reportedly faced little discrimination.

Given appropriate supports, then, formerly recruited girls, including girl mothers, are reintegrated with their communities and play positive social roles within their families and communities. Although this girls' project did not focus on peace building, it laid a foundation of community acceptance and role-appropriate behavior that could subsequently enable young women to become community peace builders.

YOUNG PEACE BUILDERS AT SOCIETAL LEVELS

Although the work described above focused on the community level, youth in post-conflict environments have also been influential peace builders at wider, societal levels. Two examples concern the role of young people in the Sierra Leone Truth and Reconciliation Commission and in using public media to address the issues situation of formerly recruited young people.

The Truth and Reconciliation Commission

The Sierra Leone Parliament established the Truth and Reconciliation Commission (TRC) in Sierra Leone to give people the opportunity to disclose the truth of what happened, to record a full and impartial history of the war, and to recommend steps that would enable people to recover. Using methods such as public hearings, expert submissions, and research, the TRC collected many children's testimonies in a confidential, ethical manner. In addition, thematic hearings on children were conducted in 2003, enabling representatives of child protection agencies to speak directly to the Commission.

Through drawings and reports, children and youth in Sierra Leone helped to tell accurately the horrors of the war and its impact on children. As a 12-year-old girl said,

> At about 2:00 A.M. the rebels attacked our town. . . . They lined up a number of people, sent for a mortar, and asked each of us to put our hand out and they cut them off. . . . I placed my right hand and it was chopped off.[20]

Similarly, a 12-year-old boy described the attack on his village:

> Everyone was running helter-skelter. It was as if the world was coming to an end. I only heard my parents shouting my name but could not see them and neither could they see me. We went our different ways and that was the last time I ever heard the sweet voices of Mama and Pappa.[21]

These testimonies helped to tell the story of war-affected children and put the atrocities committed by children in a different perspective. Other testimonies captured young people's hopes for peace. As one youth put it,

> Peace Love and Unity
> This is what we want
> in Sierra Leone
> With Love and Unity
> Join hands together
> Let's join our hands
> For Peace today[22]

Although there was much that the TRC did not accomplish,[23] the inclusion of young people gave voice to vulnerable youth and helped to empower them for building peace. After all, peace cannot be built following such a brutal war without enabling children's voices and participation.

Talking Drums Studio

Throughout Africa, large numbers of people listen to radio daily. Using radio as one of its main media, Search for Common Ground (a U.S.-based NGO) has worked with diverse groups in Sierra Leone, including youth, to mobilize various groups to address issues such as the reintegration of young former soldiers, HIV/AIDS, poverty, and corruption. The process facilitated the formation of alliances between groups at different levels, ranging from community groups to national coalitions and government agencies. These alliances become primary actors in deciding which issues to address and how to address them via radio; they formed independent radio stations that actively developed programs and community actions to address the issues.

An example is Talking Drums Studio, which distributed programs to seven national and 18 district-level radio stations throughout Sierra Leone and other West African countries. A soap opera called *Atunda Ayenda* (Lost and Found) addressed issues of concern to youth. Because the shows featured the perspectives of youth, often presented in contrast to the perspectives of adults, the programs engaged young people and stimulated peer discussion. Another program, *Golden Kids News*, enabled young people to serve as producers, reporters, and actors who presented issues of concern to young people and also advocated on behalf of young people. *Unity Boat* is a drama series that addresses issues of nonviolence and reconciliation and that also includes young people's perspectives.

The Talking Drums Studio is listened to by over 85 percent of people living in broadcast areas.[24] In Sierra Leone, the inclusion of youth perspectives and youth actors raised awareness of young people's situation and stimulated empathy with them. In addition, the participation of young people as reporters and advocates presented them as positive role models who can change adult perceptions of young people as trouble makers and who invite positive behavior on the part of other youth. The radio programs have been combined with other activities in ways that have engaged young people as peace builders. In Bo and Makeni, the broadcast of peace festivals stimulated the formation of coalitions of youth groups that subsequently undertook projects such as peace carnivals and the various community projects.[25]

CONCLUSION

Collectively, these results contradict the dire forecasts heard frequently that formerly recruited youth are a "Lost Generation" who will never be able to reintegrate or that they are damaged goods who are traumatized and incapacitated. They give strength to the view that young people are active agents who, given the appropriate support and opportunities, can be effective peace builders at multiple levels. The fact that some formerly recruited young Sierra Leoneans have not transitioned into civilian life should not obscure the reality that most have reintegrated and become peace builders against formidable odds. Their resilience testifies to the fact that war-affected young people are precious societal resources who ought to be supported as citizens who can help their families and societies turn the corner toward peace. Our task is to support them and to learn from their resilience.

NOTES

1. Human Security Report, 2005.
2. Smith, 2003.
3. Brett and Specht, 2004; Wessells, 1997, 2006.
4. Brett and Specht, 2004; Coalition to Stop the Use of Child Soldiers, 2008; Wessells, 2006.
5. McKay and Mazurana, 2004; Stavrou, 2005; Wessells, 2006.
6. Human Rights Watch, 1998.
7. Human Rights Watch, 1998.
8. Honwana, 2006; Wessells, 2006; Wessells and Monteiro, 2004.
9. Wessells, 2006.
10. Deutsch, 2000; Sherif, Harvey, White, Hood, and Sherif, 1961.
11. White, 1984
12. Wessells, 2006; Wessells and Kostelny, 2009.
13. Wessells, 2006.
14. McKay and Mazurana, 2004.
15. Kostelny, 2004.
16. Bronfenbrenner, 1979; Dawes and Donald, 2000.
17. cf. Bracken and Petty, 1998.
18. Honwana, 2006; Wessells, 2006; Wessells and Monteiro, 2004.
19. Kostelny, 2004; Stark, 2005.
20. Truth and Reconciliation Commission of Sierra Leone, 2004, 19.
21. Ibid., 19.
22. Ibid., 21.
23. Shaw, 2005.
24. Everett, Williams, and Myers, 2004.
25. Everett et al, 2004.

CHAPTER 20

Modern-Day Slavery

Melissa Anderson-Hinn

I barely notice the breathtaking views of the sunset over San Francisco as I focus intently on the parlor door. After a week of investigation, still no signs of the girls pictured in the ads and evaluated on social sites. Numerous men, and a few women, enter and exit all day as we watch. We talk with people discreetly so as not to put the girls in greater danger. We know what is going on behind the security cameras, iron gates, and darkened windows. This is our third massage parlor to investigate this month. It seems all we can do is wait and watch and hope for the opportunity of rescue and justice.

The story does not end with massage parlors. In popular restaurants there are fear and submission on expressionless faces as they take orders, cook, serve, and clean. Trafficked thousands of miles from home, they arrive with great expectation for the opportunities of work and education they are promised. Beaten into submission and held in bondage, slaves work constantly for the profit and pleasure of their owners. Picked up before the sun rises and dropped off when the city is already asleep, they rarely see the light of day. They have no control. Even worse, they sign contracts in languages they cannot read, trusting the oppressors who promise them everything.

Throughout the city I observe storefront warehouses that are seemingly abandoned. The doors rarely open and the windows are darkened and painted shut. Inside are sweatshops, operated by hundreds of slaves. On the streets and social sites, baby girls are being pimped around the city. They work for "Daddy" now, beaten severely and addicted to the stench of violent love. A 15-year-old girl sits and waits in a hotel room to turn her next trick while five others wait in neighboring rooms. The next john will be the eighth for today, and it already seemed slow. She is exhausted, malnourished, suffering, and 22 weeks pregnant with no idea what the future holds or whether she has one.

I walk the streets realizing we live in a consumer paradise. We are inundated with bargains, new products, anything and everything that brings short-lived pleasure. I read labels. I imagine all the hands and lives that are involved along the way from the harvest to the mines to open waters and quarries, through manufacturing, production, and retail. It is the story of stuff. We only see the finished product enticing us from the shelf or menu. Look into the products and the stories can be found, the countless stories of abused bodies, invisible identities, oppressed souls, and lost lives.

Cautiously gathered statistics show that in the world today, there are approximately 27 million slaves, more than twice the number involved in the entire 350-year history of the trans-Atlantic slave trade.[1] Modern-day slavery is an industry built on profit and vulnerability. Those who acquire, sell, buy, and control slaves do so to get rich by means of violent domination and exploitation of others. Slavery is the essence of dehumanization. It is more than oppressive working conditions, labor violations, poorly paid workers, or people who face poverty and disease. Other than the fact they are still alive, slaves are stripped of their humanity.

In the history of colonization, slavery consisted of legal ownership, and slaves were not cheap. In the 19th century, a slave in the American South cost an average of $40,000, a substantial amount of money at the time.[2] Slaves were a significant investment that required protection and carrying costs. Slaves were not *usually* considered disposable. Today, the average cost of a slave is only about $90 with few additional carrying costs. Real people have become disposable commodities with a bargain price tag.

Despite being a crime, slavery lives and breathes as a lucrative and growing industry. In fact, the cautious 27 million count may drastically underestimate the number of lives enslaved around the world.[3] Behind the illegal trade of drugs and weapons, slavery is the third largest and most profitable criminal industry. The countless stories of lives already lost and the millions currently held in violent bondage should be enough to bring the world to a state of desperate action; yet, the industry continues to thrive as an ominous threat to the human narrative.

In places like Northern Thailand, the depth of poverty forces children to leave school and pursue work to help their families. Without an education or marketable skills they are easily driven into the commercial sex trade. Walking the streets, in and out of bars in Bangkok or Chiang Mai, little girls are seen approaching and seducing men, offering themselves for sexual favors. In other parts of Southeast Asia, India, and Pakistan, people are sold into slavery deceptively as a measure to make ends meet for the family. Any family member may enter a contract that leads to debt bondage for generations to come. In places like Uganda, Kenya, Nepal, and Peru, locals are abducted, forced, and born into enslavement of all kinds. Their bodies and souls are exploited in a variety of dangerous and demeaning jobs. Children become collateral for loans that are impossible to repay. Some are even forced to kill family members to erase memories of home and the desire to escape and return. Other slaves are trafficked across borders. According to the United Nations Office on Drugs and Crime (UNODC), slaves are found in and from every country in the world.

Individuals at higher risk of slavery often exist in vulnerable and impoverished communities facing scarce resources, growing populations, displacement, political instability, severe health problems, and limited education opportunities. With the effects of globalization, impoverished communities are more cognizant than ever of what they lack, increasing their willingness to take risks to progress. Perpetrators find ways to manipulate and corrupt law enforcement to foster the exploitation of these communities. Local officials can be bribed or threatened for support. They often fear for their own personal, job, and family security as oppressors use power and violence to intimidate. Some local officials may participate in beating victims who try to escape, return them to their holders, incarcerate them without cause, or simply dispose of them for extra profit. As systems of justice and government remain corrupted, impoverished communities become more disempowered and increasingly vulnerable.

Slavery also thrives on the choices of everyday consumers. Slaves are found along the supply chain in just about every industry. Slaves lose their freedom and often their lives so we can have bananas, chocolate, coffee, refined sugar, fruits and vegetables, and manufactured goods. Slaves may be held captive in restaurants, businesses, and homes in our own neighborhoods. Child slaves in Uzbekistan pick the world's largest supply of cotton for our clothes made by slaves elsewhere. The accessories we buy, toys for our children, and the electronic equipment we use every day are often the product of slave labor. Companies aware of their use of slaves may be part of our investment portfolios or mutual fund pensions. The work slaves are forced to do impacts everyone and it is difficult to know precisely when and where without significantly investing in that particular pursuit of awareness.

It is also difficult to precisely define its role in the global economy. Slavery generates an estimated $32 billion in profits; however, due to the nature and complexity of the industry, the total profit margin is difficult to track and could be much larger.[4] One certainty is that the majority of the profits are generated by the global sex industry.[5] The UN, UNICEF, and U.S. Department of Justice have spent significant time working to understand this phenomenon. According to the UN, statistics suggest that more than 2 million women and children enter or are forced into the commercial sex industry every year, though any age and gender can be at risk.[6] The same set of statistics estimates that more than 10 million sex slaves exist in the world at any given time.

Sex slavery is incredibly lucrative, generating high profits with few expenses. A young girl in Thailand, Peru, or India may enter forced prostitution as young as 6 years old. She may be tricked, abducted, or purchased for a one-time fee of less than $150 by a brothel owner and sold up to 10 or 12 times a day for sex, bringing in $10,000 or more per month until she is "worn out."[7] Because virgins generate higher profit, some girls are forced into procedures that "restore their virginity" until their vaginas are destroyed. A slave who becomes a troublemaker or liability (due to sickness, disease, pregnancy, or exhaustive condition) is easily disposable and conveniently replaceable. The worst part is that supply and profit continue to increase because there is increasing demand. It boils down to a simple economic equation.

The two concepts, slavery and human trafficking, are often used synonymously but they are not exactly the same. The United Nations Office on Drugs and Crime defines human trafficking in its Trafficking Protocol as "the recruitment, transportation, transfer, harboring, or receipt of a person by such means as threat or use of force or other forms of coercion, of abduction, of fraud, or deception for the purpose of exploitation."[8] Human trafficking is the major conduit for the slave industry, and it proves that within the context of globalization even human beings are easily bought, sold, and transported in substantial numbers without detection. Most victims of trafficking have not been moved across borders. In Thailand, young girls are commonly forced into prostitution in nearby cities, held captive in basements and dark rooms, disconnected from the world outside sex slavery. Traffickers have a keen sense of where to look for the human property that is most vulnerable, that will generate the highest profit with the lowest expenses, and how to easily acquire and/or move this property. Traffickers are known to work with ruthless efficiency toward a bottom line of profit and invisibility.

WHEN DID IT ALL START?

It is hard to pinpoint an exact time for the origins of modern slavery. As far back as ancient civilizations, slavery was an integral part of society. According to Milton Meltzer, "Slavery is not and has never been a peculiar institution, but one that is deeply rooted in the history and economy of most countries."[9] It persisted through the years and across continents until it was supposedly eradicated almost 200 years ago.

In ancient times, conflicts were usually about land and resources. A stronger group would take over an area and enslave those captured. Groups in power held all the wealth and "delegated" the labor; thus, slaves were necessary to make economies flourish and build labor-intensive monuments. More technologically developed castes attained wealth and status using violence and intimidation as means to exert power and authority, managing massive numbers of slaves. Slaves were a vital part of socioeconomic life.

People still fight over land, resources, status, and power, but wealth and status have become entitlements to many. Slavery is not vital to the global economy, but the aspects of human nature that created the oppressive values that made slavery work throughout history still exist. Understanding modern slavery starts with recognizing the same underlying concepts of old as well as its distinct nuances today. Once considered an economic necessity, slavery is now a social obscenity. Once justified by principles for an orderly and progressive society, slavery is now held in place by the insatiable hunger for power and wealth at the expense of others.

What makes people capable of owning, trafficking, and exploiting others for any purpose? Slavery as an economic reality is replaceable with practical solutions that foster a stronger and better economy. What solutions quench the deep strivings of those who seek to control and exploit the lives of others for personal gain? What solutions can prevent adult men from sexually exploiting 6-year-old girls? What solutions can lessen and even eliminate the risk of slavery among vulnerable communities? These questions require more than economic answers.

MAPPING SLAVERY

The largest number of slaves in the world today is found in India, Pakistan, Bangladesh, and Nepal.[10] This form of captivity is called debt bondage or bonded labor. This means that people are sold into slavery as security against a loan, or they inherit the debt from ancestors. The length and nature of service are never defined and the labor fails to reduce the amount of the loan. In fact, debt tends to increase based on miscellaneous, fraudulent costs. The debt is passed down the generations in a family; thus, justifying the seizure and enslavement of children.

The second largest and fastest growing method of trafficking is contract slavery. It often looks like a legitimate business relationship. Slaveholders have contracts, cover stories, and corroborating witnesses. Often, victims are promised advanced education opportunities, job training, health care benefits, and money for their families. They are given contracts in a foreign language that they anxiously sign. Slaveholders become masters of their disguise. Even in cases where investigations are active, they bribe and intimidate others to receive tips and can quickly dispose of all evidence, flee to set up elsewhere, or just avoid prosecution for lack of evidence and reliable testimony. This type of slavery is rapidly spreading and can be found anywhere. However, it heavily affects parts of Southeast Asia, South America, some Arab nations, and parts of the Indian subcontinent.

The third form of slavery is called "chattel slavery." It comprises the smallest percentage of slaves in the modern world and is found predominantly in parts of Africa and Arab nations. This type most closely resembles the traditional understanding of slavery where the slave is purchased, or acquired, as property.

A growing type, "war slavery," is related to the geography or politics of an area. This often includes slavery sponsored by the government, military, or rebel groups. War produces slaves because it creates political instability and vulnerable refugees. War also requires human resources. A well-known example is found in East Africa where a guerrilla group called the Lord's Resistance Army (LRA) formed in an effort to create a theocratic government in Northern Uganda. Since 1987, tens of thousands of Ugandan children have been abducted by the LRA from their home villages and forced into slavery as child soldiers and objects of abuse. The girls usually become sex slaves and the boys are trained to be killers. Hearing the stories of children who somehow escape or get rescued is powerful and heartbreaking. Their physical freedom is a strange first step on a treacherous journey of recovery, many without families to return to. They must re-story their existence and build sustainable lives.

The U.S. State Department, other humanitarian task forces, and numerous human rights organizations are increasingly pouring resources into mapping all types of slavery. One open source movement, instigated by the organization Not For Sale in San Francisco, is www.slaverymap.org to get more people involved in telling the stories of slavery. Storytelling is powerful tool, one that gives presence and voice to those who have been invisible and voiceless for so long. Mapping slavery is a job accomplished by the process of thorough and sometimes dangerous investigation. Though slavery is well hidden in most places, it is not impossible to discover. It does not matter what the laws are or that a place is well developed. In fact, it is in the backyard of respectable communities and businesses that slavery may be more effectively hidden and more violent.

In 2005, I met a girl[11] from Latin America whose drug-addicted mother began to prostitute her at age 3 along with her two older sisters (ages 5 and

7). After six years of this life, the oldest sister ran away and the other two were abducted by a local pimp and trafficked to foreign cities in the United States. Before leaving their home, they were forced to watch the pimp kill their mother. I met the youngest sister at age 15 shortly after her escape. One evening, she managed to talk a john into sneaking her out of the parlor. Once they exited, he tossed her into an alley and ran away. She managed to crawl into the street, was arrested, and taken to a hospital.

Terrified, with no advocate, and no ability to speak English, she was intimidated by authorities and mistreated by hospital staff. If anyone tried to get close enough to touch her, she nearly had a nervous breakdown. The local police and hospital staff on the scene deemed her "uncooperative" and assumed that she voluntarily chose prostitution. They restrained her with handcuffs and sedated her for examination. She was actively losing blood, dehydrated, with a collapsed lung, and needed surgery to repair broken bones that healed incorrectly. She had bruises on 90 percent of her frail, 5-foot-5-inch, 80-pound body. By the time a translator arrived, the young girl was barely conscious. The translator chose to sit by her bedside comforting her until she regained the strength to speak. Her story finally began to come out.

She was placed in protective custody and shuffled through a variety of social and legal services, including group homes and investigative hearings. Though she described all the men and women who abducted and enslaved her, no one was ever caught. She learned that her oldest sister was never found and her middle sister, after becoming diseased, was found dead nearly 300 miles from the massage parlor in which she "worked." After five years of addiction, voluntary prostitution, intense therapy, and chronic health problems, the 20-year-old fought her way to a GED and plans to attend college to become a nurse who works with survivors of global exploitation.

This young girl's story is not dissimilar from other trafficking survivors. Though slaves face various vulnerabilities to put them at risk and differing slave conditions, all are oppressed against their will, and those who survive face significant challenges to overcome in their reintegration to society. It is crucial for health care providers, legal officials, and even neighbors to become educated to the issue and help in the reintegration process. Working together as a community from within our own community roles allows survivors a chance to heal and successfully reintegrate.

LIBERATING SLAVES

One of the foremost researchers in modern-day slavery, Kevin Bales, suggests that slavery represents an insignificant portion of the global economy. Assuming this is true, Bales suggests that the world's slaves could simply be purchased out of slavery, that the same motivation (money) for holding and trafficking slaves can be used to free them. The problem is what happens when the severance package runs out and the cycle of oppression repeats itself. As long as the global economy accentuates widespread oppressive conditions for much of the world's population, slavery is likely to continue. These oppressive conditions are compounded by deficiencies in resources for rescue and legal action, lack of public awareness, the problem of apathy, and the interconnection with poverty, overpopulation, and war. The complex needs of survivors for healing and reintegration are expansive and complex. Efforts must be made not only to rescue slaves but also to create sustainable solutions for its ultimate eradication.

Deficiency in justice systems is a significant deterrent to sustainable freedom. In June 2007, the UNDP released a report acknowledging that more than 4 billion people live in places where the justice system is corrupt and/or dysfunctional.[12] Deficiencies in law enforcement and political leadership easily reinforce the acts of criminals both directly and indirectly. Gary Haugen, of the International Justice Mission (IJM), has worked since 1997 to address this problem. IJM makes strides to free those who are oppressed by this corruption and offers solutions through supporting local law enforcement, retraining public authorities/officials, prosecuting criminals, providing legal advocacy for survivors of injustice, and offering resources for grassroots efforts to stay involved with aftercare and reintegration. Haugen understands the significance of due process as well as the importance for citizens to feel protected by their own justice system. If survivors of trafficking experience justice as corrupt or inadequate, they are less likely to participate in prosecution and may be labeled as uncooperative, leading to further oppression and even fear for their own lives and families.

Another major deterrent is the lack of public awareness and interest. A responsibility falls on those who are indirectly affected by trafficking, consumers who benefit from the products of slave labor. On Christmas day 2008, tens of thousands of children and families were slaughtered and enslaved in the war in Uganda. On the same day, millions of others were forced to do whatever demeaning job they were enslaved to do. Still others found themselves abducted, abused, and trafficked. Every year, for much of the world, Christmas simply serves as a chilling reminder of what little they are worth. At the same time, Americans spend approximately $450 billion every year for Christmas alone to overindulge in food, gifts, and events.[13] Consumerism is a reality of everyday life. It fluctuates with the seasons of life and the condition of the economy. It is possible to be a socially conscious consumer. One way is to choose not to spend money on goods and services that involve slave labor. Another way is to intentionally spend money on goods and services that foster freedom and sustainable solutions through fair and direct trade methods or purchase from second-hand stores.

To be a socially conscious consumer requires sacrifices, significant effort, and often a willingness to spend more on certified slave-free goods or go without something we want. It is impossible to be perfect, but as more people choose to be aware and responsible, making sacrifices that uphold transformative values and priorities, it will reflect an increased demand for social accountability among corporations, marketing experts, and perpetrators. Being actively engaged in the movement to end slavery is a step we need to take. Imagine the difference we could make by simply spending half of what we spend on Christmas and using the money we save to give toward efforts to rescue and care for survivors of global exploitation.

To listen carefully to the stories of slavery and become engaged with the issue means that some customary practices have to change, expectations have to shift, values have to evolve, and sacrifices have to be made. Reality is that one person's actions may not make a difference in the bigger picture but it affects that person's community and the impact will grow. It is about participating in a global movement, but it starts with personal transformation. We are all part of the same human narrative and it will change only as more of us become socially conscious and actively engaged.

As long as there are demand and profit, traffickers will generate supply, slaveholders will escape accountability, and the slave trade will continue. The world is not running low on vulnerable people so supply is not a problem. Much of the world's population lives on only a few dollars a day, lacking access to clean water, food, health care, education, and housing. Further, over the course of 50 years, the population has more than tripled, reaching more than 6.5 billion people.[14] When a species reproduces faster than the natural resources it depends on, a tremendous strain is placed on everyone, our resources, and the ecosystem in which we exist. A large percentage of the world's poor live in rural settings, dependent on the land for survival; however, in many areas the carrying capacity of the land is exceeded, forcing people into the vulnerable context of migration, engaging in desperate measures for survival. Desperation breeds vulnerability. To achieve a truly sustainable end means it is necessary to address the complex systems of global poverty as well as environmental degradation, war, technology, and other aspects of the global economy. If slaves can be set free, where do they go? With freedom comes the process of reintegration. How would they remain free? Without sustainable solutions to integrate with freedom, a world without slavery seems like an unlikely ideal.

Freedom for slaves also means freedom for oppressors. It is important to focus on prosecution, prevention, and aftercare; however, when slavery comes to an end, what happens to the predators and perpetrators? Can they all be apprehended, redirected, and rehabilitated as part of the effort needed for restorative justice? In the same way that we are all connected to victims of human trafficking, in the reality of our humanity, we are also connected to those who prey on the vulnerable and profit (or find pleasure) from slavery. The same humanity that is capable of goodness and compassion and justice is also capable of violence, intimidation, and evil. Almost as important as liberating slaves is to liberate their oppressors from the bondage that allows them to make others suffer.

Imagine the world as one large system composed of numerous subsystems woven together to give it structural integrity. Slavery is one of those systems within which exist slaves, traffickers, slave owners, consumers, families, and communities. Buying all slaves out of the system, though a great ideal, would still leave the rest of the problematic system intact and integrated. Freedom can only be short-lived in this scenario. Ending slavery means addressing all of the issues at the same time. Efforts to free slaves without sustainable solutions for a post-slavery world could risk making the slave problem worse in the long term. I am not suggesting that we avoid measures to liberate slaves but rather that we acknowledge more is needed.

One particular organization, the Sold Project, began work in Northern Thailand a couple years ago as an effort to inspire and empower individuals to stop sex slavery among children before it begins. In their research, they discovered that the best solution was to generate access to quality, "holistic education" beyond primary school, especially for girls. In that area, all children can access free public education from ages 6 to 11, which takes them through sixth grade. At that point, more than 50 percent are forced to drop out and seek employment.[15] Being under-qualified for any job, they easily fall prey to sex traffickers. *Sold* has a vision to partner with locals to create models for holistic education and raise support for children to receive scholarships and continue being educated beyond what they normally can afford. The purpose is to give them every opportunity to learn the concepts and skills they need to build sustainable lives rather than remain vulnerable to forced labor.

Equally important is holistic intervention with survivors. Slavery is undeniably traumatic. Slaves suffer from severe and potentially irreversible physical, emotional, and spiritual damage. After minimal time in slavery, complex aftercare efforts are necessary not only for treating psychological issues but also meeting basic physical needs, emotional support, and rehabilitative services for addiction or disabilities. Holistic aftercare also includes job training and sustainable community development. Effective aftercare strategies often take years, involving whole communities. Currently, significant gaps exist in the realm of aftercare because of its complexity and the time and energy commitments it requires. Because of this reality, the recidivism rate for survivors to some form of exploitation after release is rather high and often voluntary.

A component of slavery that seldom gets attention and relates directly to recidivism is addiction. Whether it is addiction to substances, power, violence, sex, love, or money, it has powerful influence over behavior. Addiction can make people do unimaginable things and cause people to be incapable of making reasonable decisions. Addictions alter the essence of one's being, making someone more capable of violence and abuse as well as more vulnerable to exploitation. The purpose of mentioning this is not to excuse the behavior of criminals but to become more aware of why and how slavery continues and what we need to address to end it. Addiction not only is a reason that people act with blatant disregard for human life but also a reason slaves become and remain victims.

MODERN-DAY ABOLITIONISTS

As people become more vulnerable, they easily lose their sense of belonging and identity that once gave their lives meaning. In a post-slavery world it is easy to force survivors to assimilate with the wider global culture and hope for the best. As long as life is not sustainable, people will not have the choice to lead lives that they value even in their freedom. The global abolition movement is not only about liberating slaves but also about giving survivors the opportunity to re-story their lives, rediscovering meaning and purpose.

The movement starts with political leadership. On October 28, 2000, U.S. Congress passed the Trafficking Victims Protection Act (TVPA), the first legislation combating modern slavery. The original legislation, renewed and improved every 3 years, is focused on the following: prevention of domestic and global slavery; protection of victims after rescue or escape; and prosecution of traffickers and oppressors under stringent criminal penalties. It is easy to access each version of the TVPA (called the TVPRA in subsequent years).[16] Each version improves on its predecessor by addressing unintended barriers, unforeseen limitations, systems that are affected, and processes/policies that are cumbersome or ineffective. Included in the evolution of this legislation, the United States. created a temporary visa for survivors to avoid deportation before receiving aftercare services. They created an extensive global watch system as an attempt to hold other governments accountable to participation and collaboration in abolition efforts.

Some countries have followed suit, hosting conferences, establishing task forces and/or national action plans to create and implement goals for anti-slavery efforts. The U.S. State Department continues to make efforts to be a leader in the abolition movement worldwide, establishing diplomatic tools and cooperative strategies to use to engage various governments abroad.

The Trafficking Protocol under the jurisdiction of the UNODC, known as the Protocol to Prevent, Suppress, and Punish Trafficking in Persons, is the only international legal means for addressing the issue of human trafficking as a global crime.[17] It is designed as a supplement to the UN Convention Against Transnational Crime and also serves to supplement and encourage other national efforts of preventing the crime, protecting survivors, and prosecuting criminals. The UNODC strives to provide the most accurate and helpful information possible to the public-at-large, easily accessible in its *Global Reports on Trafficking in Persons*.

Another crucial component to the abolition movement is support and leadership from key corporate representatives and social responsibility officers. A number of large corporations across the world are choosing to accept this responsibility and make the changes in policy and regulation as well as demands on licensees that are necessary to end slavery. At the 2009 Global Forum on Human Trafficking, sponsored by the Not For Sale campaign, several corporations were present to discuss the role of corporate leadership and social responsibility, such as Disney; Manpower, Inc.; International Labor Rights Forum; and the Corporate Social Responsibilities Program.

The rising popularity of fair trade organizations like Global Exchange and Trade as One is helping support conscious consumerism. Fair trade and direct trade are organized social movements and market-based approaches to promoting socioeconomic sustainability among vulnerable communities. Consumers can look for the fair trade or direct trade labels on goods and know that stringent social and environmental standards were met throughout the process of production and retail. At this point, only a limited number of goods are available with fair trade labels. The best tool is still consumer responsibility. Consumers need to show their concern by speaking up and increasing demand for mainstream availability of fair and direct trade products.

Emerging over the years is a growing network of individuals and organizations working to end slavery. Every organization has its niche and its own specialized skills, functioning in specific aspects of the abolition movement from raising awareness to training advocates, rescuing victims, providing aftercare, rebuilding communities, hosting political advocacy campaigns, and addressing justice issues. It is global efforts like those led by Kevin Bales at Free the Slaves, David Batstone with the Not For Sale campaign, Justin Dillon with SlaveFree and Call+Response, and Gary Haugen at IJM that generate tremendous energy for abolition. The emerging grassroots efforts such as She Dances in Birmingham, AL, and the SAGE Project in San

Francisco are equally crucial in their respective contexts. The use of social media through such film efforts as *Call+Response*, *Invisible Children*, and *Slumdog Millionaire* is a powerful tool as well as propaganda through the new media technology of Facebook, Twitter, blogging, and other social/ online networking tools.

Journalists and authors like Ben Skinner are making a significant impact on the work of abolition. Publishing *A Crime So Monstrous* in early 2009, Skinner shared his shocking and dangerously inspiring experience of investigating the global slave trade for himself. Skinner was able to infiltrate all sorts of trafficking networks both at the source and destination, to come face-to-face with the horrifying reality of slavery. According to his biography, Skinner became the first person in history to see firsthand the trafficking of human beings on four different continents. He did not do it to satisfy a curiosity or become famous but rather to understand reality and do his part to tell the stories that he discovered, sharing his own personal story of transformation in the process. His work, and his willingness to sacrifice his own safety at times, along with so many other abolitionists, is awe-inspiring.

On April 25, 2009, more than 10,000 individuals in 100 cities around the world gathered for the Rescue, a sociopolitical campaign to walk in solidarity with child soldiers in Uganda and remain "captured" until rescued by a prominent societal figure.[18] This activist movement was sponsored by Invisible Children (IC) and had profound impacts on participating communities. My 9-month-old daughter participated in the event, a story she will hear about for the rest of her life. On July 26, 2009, we dedicated my daughter's first birthday to participating in the San Francisco marathon in an effort to raise more than $1,000 for the work of IC on the ground in Uganda. Everyone has a role to play and the opportunities to participate are endless. It is going to require some people to be more actively engaged, traveling abroad, and taking necessary risks on the ground. However, the groundwork is impossible without supportive fundraising efforts, propaganda campaigns, and the response of the public acknowledging how our choices, actions, and lifestyles can affect the movement.

SUMMARY

Modern-day slavery is a horrifying reality. Though some try to ignore this reality, it is one of the world's most significant issues because it destroys the very essence of humanity for millions of the world's people. Today's slaves are disposable commodities, cheap to buy, cheap to maintain, and convenient to replace. They also generate high profits. Modern-day abolitionists are working hard in the field to liberate slaves, care for them, and help to transform systems and rebuild communities to break the vicious cycle. What is clear is that survivors are deeply wounded physically, psychologically, emotionally, and spiritually when they are held in this type of bondage even for short periods of time. It is hard enough to restore someone's dignity and health but to restore someone's humanity is possibly one of the most complex and challenging tasks. In some aspects it is like bringing dead people back to life. Then, once they are back to life, they have to rebuild an identity, to understand who they are, what they are worth, and how to live in freedom. Even if all of this can happen, the tools for sustainability have to be in place. It is a goal of aftercare and restoration that has no textbook answer or universal strategy. It is truly important for all organizations, governments, individual leaders, and everyday consumers to share information and resources with one another and work as collaboratively as possible to bring an end to slavery. Partially, it is about money. Partially, it is about sustainability. But mostly, it is about compassion and justice and whether the world is ready to say that enough is enough.

NOTES

1. Kevin Bales, 2004, 2007. His statistics are widely used by most new abolitionist organizations around the world and more information can be obtained from www.freetheslaves.net.

2. Ibid. Based on his study of the historic slave trade.

3. Arkless, 2009.

4. As presented in the social media piece *Call+Response*, a rockumentary, released worldwide in 2008 directed by Justin Dillon and produced by Fair Trade Pictures.

5. UNODC on their Web site: http://www.unodc.org/unodc/en/human -trafficking/faqs.html determines that the most widespread statistics show sex slavery as the most common form of human trafficking; however, I agree that this could be the result of statistical bias. Most nonprofit abolitionist organizations and NGOs believe that forced labor is still more common and frequently slaves subjected to forced labor also endure sexual exploitation.

6. UNODC.

7. Bales, 2004. References to conditions of sex slavery also provided in Dillon, 2008.

8. UNODC, "Protocol to Prevent, Suppress, and Punish Trafficking in Persons.".

9. Meltzer, 1993.

10. Most organizations in the new abolitionist movement cite the four main categories for slavery as follows (listed respectively by estimation of largest number to the least number affected): bonded labor, contract slavery, chattel slavery, and all other categories such as war slavery. Sex slavery is most often associated with contract slavery though it can happen on its own without contracts (such as bonded labor) as well as within any and every other category of slavery.

11. Name and identifying information withheld to protect the confidentiality and anonymity of survivor's story and treatment.

12. UNDP Human Development Report, 2007.

13. www.adventconspiracy.com

14. Numbers and statistics as determined by thorough research of reports by United Nations Population Division: http://www.un.org/esa/population/publications/publications.htm.

15. The Sold Project. www.thesoldproject.com statistics provided in their participatory action research reports and local organizations with which they build coalitions.

16. Trafficking Victims Protection Act (TVPA 2000, TVPRA 2003, TVPRA 2005, TVPRA 2009.

17. UNODC, Protocol to Prevent, Suppress, and Punish.

18. www.therescue.invisiblechildren.com—A Web site dedicated to the event held worldwide, sponsored by Invisible Children: www.invisiblechildren.com

CHAPTER 21

PERPETRATION-INDUCED TRAUMATIC STRESS

Rachel M. MacNair

When wars and other forms of violence are over, there is more to do than to send people home and hope they stay there. Although it is obvious that there are therapeutic needs for those who have been unjustly traumatized, there is also evidence that those who caused the traumatic events—or aggressively responded with violence within those events—can also be traumatized. Whether such actions were seen as justified or not is a separate question. Healing needs to occur for those who commit violence, both for their own benefit and to prevent further violence against others.

HISTORICAL INDICATIONS THAT KILLING IS TRAUMATIC

"I am King Kong," screamed the headline of the added material to the DVD of the original 1933 *King Kong* movie. This sentiment was expressed by its director, Merian C. Cooper. The sense of identification becomes all the more interesting when we consider that Cooper put himself in the final scene as the pilot of one of the airplanes that shot King Kong down. He was shooting himself.

His biography showed how this could work psychologically. A bomber pilot in World War I, he had become a post-war Soviet prisoner of war and killed people on his escape. He got himself into dangerous situations frequently after that—he filmed a tiger in the process of trying to pounce on him. In several ways, he was showing signs of the symptoms of posttraumatic stress disorder (PTSD). King Kong represented the beast that was out in the killing jungle. When coming back to civilization and beauty, the beast that was within him had to die. As the last line of the movie said, it was beauty that killed the beast.

Nevertheless, he later volunteered to fight in World War II, reviving the beast. How does it work that being traumatized by killing can lead to more killing? People normally try to avoid that which traumatized them. Perpetration-induced traumatic stress (PITS), that form of PTSD in which committing violence is the stressor that causes the symptoms, does have some distinctive features as compared to PTSD caused by being a victim. That and the associated consequences of the act of killing can help explain this.

It was with combat veterans that the concept of PTSD originated. In the U.S. Civil War, it was called "soldier's heart," and could lead to being executed. In World War I, the term "shell shock" was used to describe the phenomenon, and it was essentially thought to be a physical problem. The Germans regarded it as something that should be discouraged and, to avoid coddling those who got it, sent them immediately back to the front lines—a strategy that may be one of the factors to help explain the rise of Nazism. In World War II, it was called "battle fatigue" or "combat fatigue," and it was finally admitted to be psychological in origin. Though the terms sound euphemistic, the conceptual development was focused on understanding that this was not an insult to the soldier, a disparagement of courage or patriotism, but rather a common reaction to the situation into which these human beings were placed.

Peace activist and innovative social worker Jane Addams interviewed hospitalized soldiers during World War I and thereby became a pioneer in describing PTSD symptoms as the concept was forming. She was also a pioneer in understanding that the symptoms could come from the act of killing. Using the terminology of the time, she talked of insanity among the soldiers in various places, and of their being dazed after participating in attacks. She talked of hearing "from hospital nurses who said that delirious soldiers are again and again possessed by the same hallucination—that they are in the act of pulling their bayonets out of the bodies of men they have killed."[1] This is clearly symptom B(3) from the definition of the American Psychiatric Association, which will be covered below.

Combat veterans throughout history have also noted in their poems this particularly strong symptom of intrusive imagery that cannot be shaken. George Gascoigne participated in war in the 1500s and writes in his *Dulce Bellem Inexpertis*, "The broken sleepes, the dreadfull dreames, the woe, Which wonne with warre and cannot from him goe." M. Grover was British, and after fighting in the Anglo-Boer war, wrote (about 1899): "I killed a man at

Graspan/I killed him fair in fight;/And the Empires' poets and the Empire's priests/Swear blind I acted right/But they can't stop the eyes of the man I killed/From starin' into mine." Yuliya Drunina, a Russian who witnessed World War II, translated from the Russian says: "So many times I've seen hand-to-hand combat/Once for real, and a thousand times in dreams." Shakespeare's Macbeth and Lady Macbeth show signs of PTSD symptoms arising from their assassinations. Signs of this psychological phenomenon can be found across many cultures throughout history.

The U.S. war in Vietnam had a higher percentage of soldiers actually engaged in killing compared to previous wars. Several studies of different wars show that throughout history, only 15 to 25 percent of soldiers have worked against the natural inclination against killing.[2] Vietnam was different because the U.S. military was aware of this problem and solved it by "better" training. For one thing, the military used more realistic human-shaped targets that went down when they were hit. With this and other forms of operant conditioning, the firing rate in soldiers rose dramatically. If the act of killing is not only traumatic, but according to many observations more traumatic than just being a victim of trauma, then it would make sense that the PTSD rate among American veterans of the war in Vietnam would be much higher than in previous wars.

Although the concept of PTSD was originally castigated by such groups as Veterans of Foreign Wars as an anti-war propaganda ploy, the evidence became strong enough that it was defined in the 1980s as a psychiatric disorder. Since then, it has been applied to large numbers of groups in addition to combat veterans, ranging from concentration-camp inhabitants and crime victims to victims of car accidents and hurricanes. Recent evidence also suggests it can also be caused by other forms of killing, such as carrying out executions or police shooting in the line of duty, as well as criminal homicide.[3]

This understanding about how trauma impacts the human mind is exceedingly important and useful for knowing what kinds of therapeutic needs there are after violent conflicts or with refugees or concentration camp survivors. There is additionally such a thing as vicarious trauma, also called second-hand trauma, whereby the people who are helping the people who were traumatized find the exercise of hearing about the traumatic circumstances to be difficult. The South African Truth and Reconciliation Commission, for example, had commissioners showing signs of post-trauma symptoms who had listened to the tales day after day.[4] Because of this, there has been an upsurge of thousands of studies on PTSD and several scholarly associations devoted to the subject.

However, the idea that the act of killing can be inherently traumatic has been scant. Though commented on occasionally, it is primarily a blind spot.

After all, the main people doing therapy for combat veterans are with various countries' governmental veterans administrations. Considering that a task such as carrying out executions might be traumatizing to those assigned to do it will be contentious—any socially approved killing tends by its nature to be controversial. Killing that is not socially approved—criminal homicide—brings with it such a lack of sympathy for the perpetrator that suggestions that they are human enough to have been traumatized by their act are often met with disdain. Therefore, while the information for helping those who everyone understands to have been victims or to have been helping victims is freely discussed, the assertion that killing is traumatic has suffered from a lack of appropriate attention.

The need for attention to this is obvious for those who care about the mental health needs of human beings, and whose commitment to nonviolence is such as to pursue meeting those needs even for (or especially for) those people to whose actions they so strenuously object to. But there is far more to it than helping those individuals. The symptoms of PTSD can themselves be causes of further violence. Therefore, those who want to help establish peace by trying to nip further violence in the bud before it brings about yet more tragedies will want to pay attention to the psychological aftermath of past violence.

VIOLENCE BEGETS VIOLENCE

The National Vietnam Veteran Readjustment Study found that combat veterans with PTSD reported an average of 13.3 acts of violence for the preceding year compared to 3.5 acts for those without PTSD.[5] Several features of the symptoms of PTSD can help account for how it might exacerbate the likelihood of future acts of violence.

There are two official definitions of those PTSD symptoms: one by the American Psychiatric Association[6] and the other from the World Health Organization.[7] First, there must be an actual traumatic event or events; if the events are imaginary, or if they are ones that most people would not think were traumatic, then the condition is something else. For the APA's *Diagnostic and Statistical Manual of Mental Disorders*, that is criterion A. They then group the symptoms into clusters, which are summarized below with their symptom numbers, with additional notes.

Cluster B: Re-experiencing the trauma:
    1. Recurrent, intrusive recollections
    2. Dreams

3. Sudden acting or feeling the event is recurring
4. Intense distress at cues resembling the trauma
5. Physical stress reactions to trauma cues (rapidly beating heart, blood pressure rise, and so on).

This is the cluster that gives the best indication that the symptoms are actually the result of having participated in killing (or other horrific violence, such as torture) rather than merely being from other forms of trauma that might have been happening at around the same time. Unlike the rest of the symptoms, these have content to them. Studies of the U.S. government data on its veterans of the war in Vietnam have shown that this cluster of symptoms is especially strong in those who killed as compared to those in combat who did not kill.[8]

Cluster C: Numbing
1. Avoiding anything associated with the trauma
2. Avoiding things that remind about the trauma
3. Inability to recall something important about the trauma
4. Markedly diminished interest in significant activities
5. Feeling detached or estranged from others.

Note especially that fifth symptom, because feeling estranged from other people can feed into mental strategies that lead to violence: dehumanizing others,[9] blaming the victim, minimizing the damage done to victims, scapegoating, euphemisms, and other mental mechanisms of moral disengagement.[10] It can also facilitate the destructive obedience to authority made famous in the Milgram electric-shock experiments.[11]

Cluster D: Increased arousal
1. Sleep problems
2. Irritability, outbursts of anger
3. Trouble concentrating
4. Hypervigilance
5. Exaggerated startle response

It takes little imagination to ascertain how outbursts of anger can lead to more violence, especially in situations of domestic abuse and street violence. One article classifying violent behavior as a consequence of PTSD symptoms calls it "Mood Lability Associated Violence."[12]

Again, as with intrusive thoughts, the symptom patterns showed that the outbursts of anger were especially strong as a symptom for those who had killed among American veterans of the war in Vietnam.[13] For a literary portrayal of hypervigilance resulting from assassination activities, see Steven Spielberg's movie, *Munich.*

A more detailed discussion of applying psychological theories of violence causation to the exacerbation of violence by PTSD symptoms can be found in the book *Perpetration-Induced Traumatic Stress: The Psychological Consequences of Killing.*[14]

Alcoholism, drug abuse, and workaholism are all methods that have been used to drown out and push away the symptoms—this is called "self-medication." Substance abuse is associated with causing violence in domestic abuse and street crime. Workaholism is the most functional of these, but there have been cases where the intrusive symptoms that have been held at bay for many years come flooding in at retirement.[15] Nor is the workaholism much good for society if the work involves maintaining organizations of structural violence, which on occasion might become more likely with the symptom of detachment and estrangement from others.

There is another even more sinister possibility of the psychological consequences of violence leading to more violence: the concept of addiction to trauma.[16] The physical stress reaction of opioids in the brain is a sensible biological arrangement for those in danger, as it relieves pain at a point when pain can impede the actions needed for survival. Yet the artificial forms of this are cocaine, morphine, and heroin, well known for their addictive nature. This includes a sense of euphoria at the time, but also a problem of withdrawal afterward. This is why the "thrill of the kill" can still be understood as traumatic. The euphoria is not happiness, but a physical reaction that leads to a let down, which then leads to needs for greater and greater "fixes." This helps to account for mercenaries and other people who volunteer in future wars even though they have been traumatized by past wars. In some cases, this may be entirely ideological. Yet in some cases, that need for a "fix" may be a component of their motivation.

CONCLUSION

How to go about healing is still being explored as a matter of psychological research. Techniques such as prolonged exposure, a practice of continually gradually exposing people to reminders of the trauma to desensitize them to it, appear to be a bad idea for this kind of trauma. Group therapy has been rather successful, and so has Eye-Movement Desensitization and Retraining (EMDR), which uses simple eye movements as a physiological way of adjusting the brain while the subject is talking through a problem. Whether pharmacy drugs that help in other cases would help here has not been studied.

Knowing about the universality of this kind of experience can help substantially. Those who have committed violence have often found friends and family, and sometimes even therapists, not wanting to hear the details of what they did, in sharp contrast to the victims. An inability to express these feelings may be one of the reasons symptoms are more severe. When people do not talk about it, and others around them also do not talk about it, they never come to understand that their experience is due to the situation in which they were put and the symptoms are actually a rather normal reaction. This knowledge can help them work through the trauma.

More understanding of PITS may have a role to play in prevention of cycles of violence, because it is one of the mechanisms that continues those cycles. Further research can offer a variety of options for interventions to prevent the cycle or the escalation of violence. If we understand this phenomenon better, we may be able to evaluate various methods of intervention, including therapy, public policy, national reconciliation efforts, and education. Public policy can take PITS into account and not treat those who are expected to carry out killing as unfeeling automata or as people simply doing unpleasant jobs.

Part of the ideology of genocide, torture, or massacres is that those who carry them out benefit from the activity. Efforts at arranging punishment through political means have been used to counter this idea. It may help to add education on how perpetrators do not escape with impunity even if political arrangements are inadequate; there are natural consequences.

Beyond the practical implications that show us one of the many methods to intervene in cycles of violence, it is also important to understand this to counter part of the ideological justifications for violence: it is not inevitable due to human nature. Killing is not merely something that is not in our nature, as the field of psychology has ascertained for some time (although early forays suggested otherwise). Killing as a stressor that can cause PTSD symptoms shows that killing can be understood as being *against* our nature; it tends to make us sick.

NOTES

1. Addams, 1960, 273.
2. Grossman, 1995.
3. MacNair, 2002.
4. Tutu, 1999.
5. Kulka, Schlenger, Fairbank, Hough, Jordan, Marmar, and Weiss, 1990.
6. American Psychiatric Association, 1994.
7. World Health Organization, 1992.
8. MacNair, 2002, chap. 2.

9. Brennan, 1995.
10. Bandura, 1996.
11. Blass, 2000.
12. Silva, Derecho, Leong, Weinstock and Ferrari, 2001.
13. MacNair, 2002, chap. 2.
14. Ibid., 100–106.
15. Sleek, 1998.
16. MacNair, 2002, 140–142.

PART IV

PEACE MOVEMENTS WORLDWIDE

The U.S. Peace Registry is an online database of individuals and organizations in the U.S. who are in one way or another working on peace. In existence only for a few years now, the names still scroll by page after page. The Peace Resource Book of 1986 was 426 pages long. Most of those pages were simple listings, in three columns, of the names and addresses of organizations working one way or another on peace primarily in the United States. Our back-of-the-envelope calculation says that there were more than ten thousand known groups in the United States at time of that writing.

Obviously, the following section is a mere geographical sampling, offering insights by peace practitioners from West Germany, Korea, India, Asia, Iran (with a comparison to a similar group in the U.S.) and the Middle East, with one chapter by Hildegard Goss-Mayr that briefly recounts highpoints from Colombia, Burundi, Southern France, and the Philippines to bring out the unexpected power of nonviolence and individual courage, which we have come to regard as the infrastructure of peace movements, and hence of peace. Other peace movements around the world are of course touched on under different headings elsewhere in these three volumes.

Andreas Buro approaches the post-1945 peace movement in what was then West Germany from the perspective of history and of social movement theory, bringing out the ways that the peace movement can be analyzed and understood as any social movement despite its acute focus on the peace issue. He brings us into the politics of the time and the various ways the German peace movement adjusted its positions to take advantage of them.

He brings out the relationship between immediate goals (questioning missile deployment) and long-term goals (stable peace in Europe), and also points out that the idea of a peace movement may be a misnomer, as one German directory listed about 250 groups in 2004 alone.

The next three studies take us to the East. With Jujin Chung we have another insider's view, and again from a divided country where peace action is relatively new, (much more so in Korea than Germany), and where reunification has been a movement goal. Her chapter furnishes an arresting example of the balance that has to be struck, particularly by would-be interveners from outside a given country, between the eternal principles of peacekeeping (and the next and deeper stages of peacemaking and peace building) that contact human universals and the indigenous strengths and weaknesses of a given culture and region—an awareness that the peace-team movement, for example, has learned well in the last twenty or so years. It was a surprise to us, for example, to learn that the South Korean peace movement has mainly arisen from Christian and not Buddhist centers.

As one would expect, the peace movement (loosely defined) in modern India has, by contrast, roots that are historically and philosophically deep. Ramu Manivannan, a political scientist active with the Nonviolent Peaceforce, gives us masterful insight into the complex traditions that are more often than not unfolding in areas that are indirectly related to anti-militarism and peace—areas like the environment, the expulsion of corporate exploitation in one quarter or another—but which, since Gandhi, many participants would indeed consciously connect with that overriding goal.

In the interests of time, we single out the article of another political scientist, Cynthia Boaz, because it is a comparative study of two roughly parallel women's movements in, respectively, Iran and the United States. Boaz goes a long way (as does Zunes, and of course Abu-Nimer and Badawi in Volume 1, Chapter 12) toward dispelling the current stereotypes that are so damaging to peace. She is particularly well grounded in the principles of nonviolence, which inform her analysis and lend it cogency throughout. And like many other contributors whose focus is a given region—this may emerge as a unifying lesson of this book—she is well aware that it is somewhat imprecise to talk about the Iranian Women's Movement as there is in reality a unity-in-diversity of such movements that are now underway and will no doubt always be. We are particularly pleased that Prof. Boaz was able to interview Nobel Peace Prize laureate Shirin Ebadi for the Iran part of her chapter.

Collectively, these studies raise a fascinating question: when will there be a world peace movement? Not the 'movement toward peace' only, but a concerted (we do not say, hierarchically organized) single effort to put down decisively whatever wave of war-frenzy is happening at the time and put definitively in its place a regime of peace? We came a step closer to that millennium when, in 2002, popular resistance to the impending invasion of Iraq began to take on momentum and climaxed on February 15, 2003 in the largest planetary protest of all time, counting on the order of twelve million active participants in sixty countries. The protest in Rome involved around 3 million people, and is listed in the 2004 Guinness Book of World Records as the largest anti-war rally in history. But that is the limitation: it was an anti-war rally, and not, as several writers in these volumes have pointed out, a rally for peace, not to mention something even more enduring and constructive than a rally. Nonetheless, it was a start: people in sixty countries became aware that they were indeed the collective body of what Jonathan Schell calls "The Unconquerable World." This may just have been the first warning to the war system that indeed it is progressing by its own logic into the dustbin of history.

In the short term, of course, it failed. And few participants had much notion of a longer viability for their efforts. Few realized that Gandhi had chalked out years before a line of escalation between those low-level conflicts in which appeals to reason are still likely to be heard and the more entrenched hostilities in which, as he put it, "things of fundamental importance to the people are not secured by reason alone but have to be purchased with their suffering . . . If you want something really important to be done you must not merely satisfy the reason, you must move the heart also". When then-President Bush dismissed the huge protest as a 'focus group' he was signaling that that line from the efficacy of argument to the need for Satyagraha (nonviolent resistance) had been crossed: but neither he nor most of the protestors were aware of it.

It seems at times as if everything in the world, good or bad, but mostly bad, has been globalized. Espionage, crime, especially the reborn horror of human trafficking (see Anderson-Hinn, Chapter 20 in this volume), of course the most exploitive aspects of the economy (Volume 3, Chapter 27)—in short, everything but peace has been globalized. Note that most of the destructive examples just mentioned are global but not centralized and hierarchical: in other words they are informal arrangements like what the peace movement or any civil society movement would naturally be like. Perhaps it will be only a matter of time before the peace movement goes global and everyone will see that day when, as President Eisenhower said, 'people want peace so badly that governments will have to give it to them.'

—Marc Pilisuk and Michael N. Nagler

NOTES

1. US Peace Registry, http://www.uspeacememorial.org/registry.
2. Bernstein et al., 1986.
3. Schell, 2003.
4. Gandhi, 1931, 48.
5. Some were, however: a "Declaration of Peace" campaign was duly launched in the United States, including the vast umbrella organization United for Peace and Justice, which coordinated civil disobedience actions.

CHAPTER 22

The West German Peace Movement

Andreas Buro Habil
Translated by Matthias Zeumer and Michael N. Nagler

According to Joachim Raschke[1] there were three phases of civil-society movements in the capitalist states: the early bourgeois movements, the labor movement, and the new social movements. The peace movement after 1945 is the first new social movement (NSM). It involves people from almost all social and religious backgrounds.

The core theme of the peace movement is the overcoming of war and the enabling of peace. Both topics are two sides of the same coin, though they use different strategies and forms of action. The first side's focus is on protesting the military and armaments; the second aims to develop and implement new forms of conflict resolution that do not involve military force and violence.

Many peace groups hold a concept of peace that embeds social justice. Time and again one encounters the slogan: "no peace without social justice." Of course, the meaning is not to fight for social justice by using violence; rather, this statement is meant to point to a *cause* of conflict that has to be overcome.

In overcoming war, the German peace movement has one significant difference from some others. In the anti-militaristic traditions, primarily originated in the labor movement, it had been considered permissible to use militaristic means to free the people from social or colonial oppression. Those struggles are often based on the expectation that this will be "the last battle," after which peace and justice will have been achieved. The true development of those struggles, however, tells a different story. The "last battle" remains always the penultimate battle. War and armament are perpetuated. The pacifistic outlook, therefore, insists on a nonmilitaristic and civic resolution of problems. The assumption here is that the means ascertain the goals, so that no permanent peace can be achieved through war.

The new social peace movement has much common ground with other social movements, since the concept of peace is connected to many facets of societal life and international structures that are the cause of wars or the preconditions for peace. In the past, during times of acute threat of war and armament races, this often led many people from other social movements to join the protests of the peace movement; however, this collaboration would last only for a period of time and they would then focus once again on their previous issues.

AFTER 1945

The political peace process for Germany after 1945 had the following characteristics:

- Germany was militarily entirely defeated and occupied. The Germans were confronted with their own history of brutal warfare and genocide. A public glorification of the German warfare was impossible. The Nuremberg Trials were an unambiguous signal. This was an important social-psychological premise for the engagement of citizens in the political peace process.
- The occupying powers assumed governance. With the unfolding of the East–West conflict the country was increasingly divided into East and West. This led inevitably to the question of Germany's reunification. This question was, due to its entanglement with militaristic confrontations, strongly related to the question of peace. This consequently led to the emergence of the so-called Nationalen Frage, *the national question*, the neutrality and permanent disarmament of Germany, and the development of the atomic arms-free zone in Middle Europe.

Up until the founding of the two German states in 1949, Germany was ruled entirely by the occupying powers and under absolute subordination. Even after 1949 the influences of the occupying powers, especially that of the United States and the Union of Soviet Socialist Republics (USSR), dominated. Consequently, demands for peace were primarily directed toward those two powers. They, however, escalated military confrontations against each other.

With existing ambitions to make the two German states military partners of East and West, the *political peace opposition* also focused on the governments of East and West.

In their own domains the occupying powers made every effort to establish their visions of the ideal social system. For that purpose they cooperated in the West with the bourgeois-capitalist forces and in the East with the socialist-communist elites. These German "partners" heavily combined their interests and destinies with the political, military, and economic interests of the respective occupying power. Peace-political approaches that infringed on the politics of the occupying powers were consequently rejected, even though they drew the right political and moral conclusions from both world wars. The basic approaches for peace movements in the West were, therefore, in direct opposition to the ruling powers. In the East they were extensively exploited for the politics of the USSR. Whoever did not integrate defaulted into the opposition.

World War II ended with the atomic bombing of Hiroshima and Nagasaki, introducing a new era of warfare and weaponry of mass destruction. War became an existential threat for people on all continents and revealed its irrational and inhumane character. Traditional thought structures of heroic battles could hardly be maintained, yet exactly these new means of mass destruction were used in the emerging arms race between East and West through doctrines of deterrence. This constellation gave the peace movement a fundamental, moral, ethical, and religious character.

Wherever there was freedom to do so, the arms-racing powers, especially the militarily leading United States, were heavily criticized. During the Cold War, which evolved exponentially after 1947, any criticism of them was represented as anti-American, freedom-opposing, and "communist" to publicly defame and isolate whatever parties were in opposition to the prevailing military course. Thus, within the German society a strong psychological barrier against participation in any peace work was created.

This tendency was amplified as both power blocs tried to present themselves ideologically as powers of peace. The peace movement, which criticized the peace-threatening reality of the arms race, was, when it could not be exploited, antagonized on its own territory, and praised and supported on the opposing side. As a consequence, the peace movement was undercut by state-supported forces. It also had to carry on a constant quarrel with such forces as depicted politics in East or West as politically motivated on the opposing side, and attempted to coerce the independent peace movement to their struggle.

The motivation in post-war society to work for peace came from very diverse traditions. This type of work after 1945 was connected to the goals of parties that operated under umbrella organizations—such as unions or churches—or organized through what we today would call civil society. Therefore, these were all heterogeneous forces that relied on very different societal environments. "The" peace movement, therefore, never existed. At the most, there were some relatively broad commonalities, especially where threats affected everyone in the same way. The reciprocal menace of atomic warfare, for example, the rearmament of West Germany, and inversely that of East Germany, stood at the beginning of the development of the peace movement in Germany.

THE PEACE MOVEMENT IN THE FEDERAL REPUBLIC OF GERMANY IN ITS HISTORICAL STAGES—OBJECTIVES, STRATEGIES, AND ACTIONS

More than half a century of peace movement in the Federal Republic of Germany cannot be described as a unity. The differences in the political situation, the objectives, organizational structures, and modes of action and participation, are simply too great. It is, therefore, necessary to describe the peace movement in its various historical stages. As follows, eight of these stages can be usefully identified:

1. Resistance against the rearmament
2. *Kampf dem Atomtod* or "Fight Atomic Death" during the second half of the 1950s
3. Easter March Movement/Campaign for Democracy and Disarmament
4. Campaign against the NATO Double-Track Decision
5. Period after the East–West conflict
6. Period during the Gulf and Balkan wars
7. The interventionist orientation of NATO states and Germany
8. Imperial wars and armament in the name of the war against suicide-terrorism (war on terrorism)

The Resistance against the Rearmament

West Germany's entry into NATO (1954) ended the "Without-Me Movement" against the rearmament.[2] It represented anti-military arguments from 1949 until 1955, ranged from conservative to liberal and religious members of society, and as far as the Left. The Federal Minister of the Interior of the Federal Republic of Germany reported in 1952, 175 organizations, research groups, and so on. Their motivational structures were exceedingly heterogeneous and ranged from aggrieved national pride, the desire for neutrality to anti-militaristic positions. Pacifist credos were represented only by a small minority.

This phase proceeds in four substeps: the Without-Me Movement, the referendum campaign, the neutrality efforts, and the St. Paul's Church movement.[3] The dominant protagonists were political parties and big organizations such as the Confederation of German Trade Unions and churches under whose roof action groups organized. Autonomous protagonists could be found in the category "endeavor for neutrality." Independent peace groupings were far away from determining the debate.

Neither goals nor subgoals were reached. The Cold War escalated and the rearmament prevailed, although, according to polls, 80 percent of the population—though driven by very different motives—militated against it. For this reason, a broad discussion was held in society about the military and armament, for the first time since the war had ended.

The "Fight the Atomic Death" Campaign

The protest against atomic weapons was organized by the Social Party of Germany (SPD), the unions, the protestant church, and several individuals within the campaign "Fight Atomic Death" in the second half of the 1950s.[4] The concentration was on the atomic threat and a broad and significant debate was achieved. The larger organizations, mainly the SPD, determined the campaign to a large extent politically, financially, and organizationally. Certainly, other independent neutrality and peace groups existed. The SPD made an about-face after the conclusion of a policy statement stemming from the party convention in Bad Godesberg in 1959, becoming a catch-all party, moving to the middle and being open to form a coalition with the conservative Christian Democratic Union (CDU). Fight Atomic Death did not fit into this new strategy and was stalled organizationally and financially by the SPD and the Confederation of German Trade Unions. The discussion over nuclear weapons led large parts of society into a confrontation about the monstrosity of military thinking and military practice (Hiroshima/Nagasaki). This caused a considerable mobilization for nuclear disarmament.

The Easter March Movement/Campaign for Democracy and Disarmament

Pacifist groups in Northern Germany organized the first Easter March in 1960, marching form Hamburg, Bremen, Hannover, and Braunschweig to the missile drill-ground Bergen-Hohne, out of which emerged the nationwide, independent, extra-parliamentary opposition.[5] At first they operated under the name "Easter March of Atomic Weapon Opponents against Atomic Weapons in East and West," which they changed in the late 1960s—the result of a social learning process—to "Campaign for Democracy and Disarmament." This campaign became a broad alliance among diverse social milieus and political camps, operated year round, was financially self-sufficient, and was independent of any political party or big organization.[6] A solid network of local groups formed. This is the first long-term new social movement (1960 to 1969) working on a broad social basis. At first, the campaign largely picked up the rallying cry of "Fight Atomic Death," but it changed over time to an anti-militaristic and pacifistic movement that would continuously incorporate more problematic areas of democratization. Since the mid-1960s Vietnam played an increasing role at public protests. It was picked up later by various student movements and intensively pursued until the withdrawal of the United States from Vietnam in 1973. In 1968 East-Bloc states marched into the Czecho-Slovak Socialist Republic (CSSR), which placed a great strain on the collaboration of the heterogeneous parts of the campaign. By the end of the 1960s the campaign was polarized in such a way—even the student movements contributed—that it dissolved itself to all intents and purposes into a pursuit of many reform projects. This ushered in the policy of détente during Willy Brandt's chancellorship. Ecological, social, developmental, and women's rights problems preoccupied people at that time more than an allegedly deactivated menace of atomic weapons and war.

The Campaign against the NATO Double-Track Decision

During the 1970s, reform-oriented social movements and citizens' initiatives formed while the topic of peace moved to the background, due to the new Ostpolitik and the hopes that it roused. The situation changed rapidly, however, when NATO decided on the Double-Track to station intermediate-range missiles with minimal lead notice. People of the versatile social movement formed peace groups all over the country and the biggest peace mobilization ever seen in Germany emerged. Civil disobedience (Committee for Basic Rights and Democracy) and nonviolent forms of action gained much currency. Moreover, during this phase an intensive discussion evolved about alternatives (1981), including alternative forms of defense that were supposed to bring an end to the policy of deterrence and disarmament.[7] The massive protest and the nonviolent blockades in Mutlangen and other places, however, made "politics" a catchword for the apprehensions of the population. The rejection of the additional armament was supported by two-thirds of the surveyed population. The German Federal Parliament nevertheless enacted the deployment of the intermediate-range missiles.

Many forms of civil protest and nonviolent resistance were tried and developed further.[8] These types of actions led to a stronger emphasis on the anti-militaristic components[9] and advanced the comprehension for pacifistic behavior patterns. The numerous litigations that arose became a forum of political disputes. Gorbachev's policy of détente and disarmament heralded a new surge of the peace movement until the end of the 1980s.

The End of the East-West Conflict

The collapse of the Soviet empire also changed the security and political landscape for the peace movement fundamentally.[10] The immediate threat was gone, and with that, alongside the fight for disarmament, the second big topic was put on the agenda: the fundamental idea that peace in Europe is not based on weapons, but rather on communication about the forms of cohabitation in the "common house."[11] Accordingly, what was called for was to pursue reconciliation between the Federal Republic, or its society, and the eastern European and former Soviet societies. The conditions for a collective pan-European peaceful future were to be nurtured. In a discussion that had already been started in 1987 the main focus evolved around the concepts of—and an accordant policy of—"positive peace" for Europe and a "pan-European general peace framework." With this re-orientation came widespread hope that a new era of equitable cooperation between East and West would arise, in which the expected peace dividend would be established to promote peace and to boost development.

THE GULF AND THE BALKAN WARS

The first Gulf War in 1991[12] destroyed such hopes and directed attention increasingly to conflicts and wars in other countries. Although the Germans were not directly threatened, the main point of focus became to support peace in former Yugoslavia.[13] The new era after the East-West conflict brought new demands on the legal instruments of the peace movement. Although it was still possible in Germany to react with protests and mass rallies with the provocative motto "No Blood for Oil" during the Gulf War, it was not possible during the wars in former Yugoslavia. That called for transborder measures, for which hardly any experience existed. Besides, the traditional structures of the peace movement, as well as its modest financial endowment and organizational capacities made possible only a limited effectiveness. The international as well as the German peace movement, nonetheless, took on this challenge. A large and multifaceted task in the sense of this newly emerging term of "civilian-based conflict" was carried out. It was barely noticed by the media, however, because they were still fixated on the old forms of protests.

The war in Croatia and Bosnia moved the people in the peace movement more than all other previous armed conflicts with the compassion and the desire to help build a great community of peace activists. The desire for a rapid end to a geographically very close inferno also divided the people of peace movements internally. The so-called warmonger/pacifist debate between the advocates and the opponents of a Western military operation in Bosnia reflected this conflict.[14] This discussion can only be understood against the background of the new unipolar global world order under the leadership of the United States, whose readiness to intervene drew Germany herself into a more aggressive "out-of-area-policy."[15]

The grand policies of the United States, the states of the European Union (EU), and NATO were not verifiably influenced by the versatile responses and transborder actions of the German and the international peace groups. In various subareas, however, they were very effective. One example is the refugee operation, provided by the Survive the War organization, which smuggled especially endangered people from Serbian-occupied regions, and housed them with families in Germany. Another effect on politics came from the systematic support of peace, human rights, and democracy groups within former Yugoslavia; groups that attempted to uphold their work under extreme political pressure and considerable danger.

The Interventionist Orientation of the NATO States and Germany

The roots of this development reach far back to the Gulf War of the 1990s and to the NATO Eastward Enlargement. The United States rested its foreign politics largely on their military potential. The Armament-Monitoring policy came rapidly to be seen as cumbersome by the United States and was damaged also by the Anti-Ballistic Missile contract. NATO took over the function of an interventionist "regulatory force" and the European NATO states, including Germany, aligned themselves with this model. This stage is significant for Germany due to its involvement in the NATO–Yugoslavia War (Kosovo War) in 1999, which was conducted without a UN mandate. The red-green government (the Social Party of Germany and the Green Party) in Berlin, which carried along the Kosovo War, instigated the "interventionist course" in its military and armament politics, unimpressed by protests of the peace movement, even though the NATO–Yugoslavia War was rejected by a large part of the population (up to 60 percent in the new and up to 40 percent in the old Federal States in reunified Germany).

Partial successes were achieved through a worldwide campaign against landmines. Time and again, successes were recorded to publicly broach the issue of arms exports such as those to Turkey. The actual limitations of arms exports were not great. The global framework, in which the German foreign as well as security politics moved, was increasingly incorporated in the analyses. The global, unipolar military system with the United States as its leading power was identified with the process of "globalization" and criticized for its "organized peacelessness"[16] and military violence.

The EU increasingly tried to build an independent military intervention capability and in addition to concentrate the European arms industry. To justify this, and in order to win the populace for this form of politics, legitimizing ideologies of a "humanitarian, military intervention" and of a "just war" were put forward, a fact that was understood by the peace movement as a dangerous fight for the minds and hearts of the population. It worked in at least three areas: the critique of militarily supported politics, the presentation of alternatives to the civil conflict-treatment, and the critique of the legitimizing ideologies.

Imperial Wars and Armament in the Name of the War on Suicide Terrorism (War on Terrorism)

The last stage to be named began in the public conscience with the attacks by suicide terrorists who flew passenger planes into the twin towers of the World Trade Center and the Pentagon on September 11, 2001. The United States received avowals of solidarity from many countries around the world. They began a war against Afghanistan to destroy training camps and structures of suicide terrorism. Many European states participated in this war as well, albeit no explicit authorization to attack Afghanistan was given by the resolutions of the UN Security Council.[17] Germany is involved through military, political, as well as economic support.

September 11 and the following military interventions, which allegedly were turned against terrorism, prompted the peace movement to increasingly deal with this term. The term *terrorism* is predominantly being applied to attacks by suicide bombers and in a criminal context, whereas warfare of the technically advanced military powers is presented as "normal" conduct. The peace movement contrasts this unilateral allocation of terrorism with "war is terror." With that it means assassination as well as state terrorism.

The Bush administration declared a global war against evil. As the only military superpower, the United States claimed for themselves the right to preemptively strike worldwide, and even to use atomic weapons against countries that do not possess such weapons themselves. International law and the charter of the UN were thus heavily damaged. In favor of the gigantic U.S. armament, arms control treaties were set aside and strategic military bases were built in key strategic parts of the world.

The U.S.- and British-led war against Iraq in 2003 took place without a UN mandate and against the will of many of the EU states and states of other continents. It was not possible to legitimize this war as a fight against terrorism.

At that stage the peace movement turned its attention to resisting the Afghanistan campaign; however, it was not able to attain mass mobilization. A mobilization of great magnitude did not succeed until this U.S.-British war of aggression against Iraq in 2003. The long negotiations of the UN Security Council, the false justifications for a war of aggression, and above all, the refusal of Germany, France, and other EU states to join a military intervention caused a huge motivation for protest in the population. In addition, there was a large international mobilization of protests in many parts of the world. The *New York Times* spoke of the public opinion, which mobilized against the war, as the second greatest world power.

Beyond the Iraq problem the peace movement focused on the critique of the EU armament and the EU constitution, as well as alternative means of prevention and civilian-based conflict management. Alongside this focus, a variety of topics were treated and campaigns advanced. An incrementally tighter collaboration developed with groups that were critical of globalization.

ORGANIZATIONS AND NETWORKS

The peace movement, as a new social movement, is composed of people and groupings of almost all segments of society with the exception of the military Right. Socialist, protestant, Catholic, atheist, pacifistic, anti-militaristic, liberal, and conservative forces work in their respective frames. The peace movement is, thus, very heterogeneous and defies efforts at unification. Its advantage lies in the multiplicity of its relationships and approaches. Commonalities have to be negotiated in each case. Cooperation and dialogue—sometimes even vigorous and controversial—instead of unification are its continuous attribute. It is open to members of political parties, unions, churches, and other large organizations; however, since 1960 it does not form alliances with such organizations, and instead is jealous of its independence, especially in relation to political parties.

The popular idea of "the" peace movement thus barely finds a counterpart on the level of organizational structures. The directory of the Network Peace Cooperative counted about 250 groups in 2004 alone. Those can be classified as local groups, organizations of different range that are affiliated with different traditions in topic-specific or campaign-oriented groups, networks/umbrella organizations, and international associations.

International cooperation always played a significant role for the peace movement, at a minimum to show that peace efforts are not only a German concern, but rather concern for many other Western countries. Moreover, the German peace movement gained much stimulus from other countries, such as the reference to Gandhi and Martin Luther King Jr., the technique of the Easter Marches, or of nonviolent resistance. In this regard, the Committee of One Hundred in England inspired much imagination. Admittedly, the demands of international cooperation oftentimes exceeded the resources of the groups.

War Resisters International had a large influence on the unfolding of the conscientious objection in Germany, as did the International Fellowship of Reconciliation. The Quakers led the San Francisco–Moscow March in 1961, in which German citizens participated. Many umbrella organizations or campaigns from European countries joined forces in the European Federation against Nuclear Arms. Peace Brigades International was launched with German cooperation in Beirut in 1962 and is working on many tasks to this day. As an answer to the World Peace Council, which was dominated by Russia, the Western European and North American peace organizations founded the International Confederation for Disarmament and Peace in Oxford in 1963. Another source of international connection was that international organizations supported various sections in Germany. That was true, for example, for the International Physicians for the Prevention of Nuclear War (IPPNW), the Fellowship of Reconciliation, and War Resisters International.

OVERALL CONCLUSION FROM THE HISTORICAL STAGES

Throughout, one has to note that governmental policy was hardly influenced by the activities of the peace movement, not even when it achieved a remarkably high mobilization. A noticeable exception is the worldwide campaign against the Vietnam War, though to be sure even to the bitter end it was not possible to change Bonn's vassalage. A second exception has to do with the Iraq intervention of 2003. If Schroeder's government had not expected a considerable anti-war attitude from the public, they would not have announced Germany's refusal to participate during the election campaign. Furthermore, we can also note some partial successes here and there, though they become questionable in the face of rapid military innovations. Clemens Ronnefeldt[18] lists the following campaigns: For the Abolition and Halt in Production of All Land Mines; Stopping of Small Arms Proliferation and of Child Soldiers; Outer Space Without Weapons and Nuclear Energy; Abolition of Atomic Weapons; Stop All Atomic Tests; Produce for Life—Stop Armament Exports.

Realizing the movement's marginal effectiveness in the area of policy brings up the whole question of the relationship between society and state. It points up a significant deficit of democratization in Germany and the autocratic tendency on the governmental and parliamentary level vis-à-vis the public.

The peace movement, however, often succeeded in making peace policy a topic in society for extended periods. Social learning processes, which were also expressed through the increasing acceptance of conscientious objection, were thus made possible.

The fact that a nationalistic-militaristic social development was avoided after 1945 until the present is arguably due, in large part, to the peace movement. The movement was also able to make a fundamental contribution to the fact that military policies were not perceived as "natural" and "without an alternative," but rather questioned critically. Furthermore, it often succeeded in thwarting and revealing to the public eye the magnitude of the menace involved in playing down and covering up various attempts at arms developments and military strategies (for example, Fulda gap). A major accomplishment, finally, is the continuous calling into question of violence as a way of dealing with conflict, with all its extensive consequences.

An important achievement of the peace movement lay in its ability to point out alternatives for peaceful solutions of conflicts and the reciprocal threats of deterrence. Although they were generally ignored by the government, they demonstrated to the public that military policies are not indispensable: peaceful alternatives do exist.

NOTES

1. Raschke, 1991.
2. Otto, 1981.
3. Rupp, 1970.
4. Ibid.
5. Buro, 1977.
6. Otto, 1977.
7. Böge and Wilke, 1984.
8. Komitee für Grundrechte und Demokratie, 1981.
9. Buro, 1997, 195.
10. Ibid.
11. Senghaas, 1992.
12. Komitee für Grundrechte und Demokratie, 1981.
13. Buro, 1997, 119.
14. Ibid., 143; Pax Christi, 1993; 1996.
15. Buro, 1997.
16. Senghaas, 1992.
17. Paech, 2001.
18. Ronnefeldt, 2004.

CHAPTER 23

PEACE IN TRANSITION: THE PEACE MOVEMENT IN SOUTH KOREA

Jujin Chung

In South Korea the peace movement has a short history. Concepts such as positive peace, nonviolence, peace building, and a culture of peace that are widely shared among organizations and people involved in peace movements around the world are not fully recognized yet by the peace movement in South Korea. There are differing ideas about the inception of the peace movement among activists; likewise, there is no shared definition of the term *peace movement*. Every year peace activists hold a workshop to share ideas and build working relationships. This open workshop brings together many people who are interested in peace issues, but they are not necessarily committed to peace. Participants' personal and organizational backgrounds show that there are different approaches to peace and diverse understandings of what constitutes a peace movement. Their interests range from reunification of the two Koreas and security in Northeast Asia, to peace education and community building. They are interested in reconfiguring their issues in terms of peace and then applying the idea of peace to their programs and activities. This practice indicates that the word "peace" has penetrated South Korean society and appealed to different actors, although many of them understand peace in abstract terms. Some of the participants admit

The author expresses special thanks to Daniel Adamski for editorial assistance.

they are involved in the peace movement, while others are less willing to acknowledge their participation in the movement.

In South Korea peace is often conflated with the reunification and security of the Korean peninsula. In this context, peace becomes political and peace activities are misunderstood as political statements connected to progressive ideas about reunification and security. The peace movement is, on the one hand, narrowly understood as a program of political campaigns aimed at confronting the government and pursuing political goals to win public support and media attention. On the other hand, the idea of peace has become popular and partly been contaminated with the change of political environment from authoritarianism to democracy, and with the disappearance of negative responses to the word "peace." Many organizations and groups—including political parties—now tend to overuse the word "peace" to appeal to the public, although they neither have programs to reflect the conceptual meaning of peace nor design activities to build peace. Peace and its conceptual meaning have become more abstract and ambiguous.

In spite of the confusing and vague ideas about peace, the peace movement has gained ground in South Korea. The issues that the peace movement deals with have been diversified and the means that the peace movement utilizes to address its concerns and appeal to the public more closely reflect the ideas of positive peace, nonviolence, peace building, and the culture of peace. The peace movement is, however, struggling with a lack of strategic approaches to long-term visions and a lack of public support that is required to sustain the movement.

INCEPTION AND SPREAD OF THE PEACE MOVEMENT

There are different ideas about the beginning of the peace movement in South Korea. Some people consider the anti-nuclear campaign in the mid-1990s (following the revelation of North Korea's nuclear program) as the beginning of the movement. Others believe the widespread anti-war campaign (before and after the South Korean government's decision to deploy troops to Iraq in 2003) contributed to the formation of the peace movement. The two campaigns are similar in terms of raising public awareness of peace and encouraging people to consider peace in relation to their daily lives. It is clear, however, that both of the campaigns challenged South Korean society and contributed to educating the people. There are also differences between the two. The anti-nuclear campaign was more inclined to pursue negative (nonwar) peace and nationalistic interests relating to the imminent danger in the Korean peninsula. By contrast, the anti–Iraq War campaign showed a more developed idea of peace, implying the meanings of positive peace and just peace building in the larger world.

It is argued that the appearance of peace movements in South Korea was mainly due to the end of the Cold War and democratization in South Korea.[1] The change of political environments inside and outside South Korea with the end of the Cold War allowed South Korean society to consider building a new relationship and seeking collaboration and reconciliation with North Korea. The democratization after 1987 encouraged and allowed civil society organizations that had focused on confronting unjust government policies to find new agendas. These organizations and social activists tried to renew social movements through bringing new agendas to the front such as human rights, the right to life, environmental concerns, and peace. The peace movement was formed as one of several social movements responding to this changed political and social environment.

The peace movement in South Korea, as with many social movements, did not appear overnight. It was built on accumulative social reflections, experiences, and resources. A variety of social movements focused on accomplishing democratization and addressing human rights violations under authoritarian governments and they contributed to training many social activists and building a strong culture of activism. The reunification movement was one of the most active social groups challenging South Korea's aggressive policies toward North Korea; it also focused on the security and military power discourses current at that time. Significantly, progressive churches tried to take a different approach and made efforts to interpret reunification issues in terms of peace. These churches, affiliated with the NCC-Korea (National Council of Churches in Korea), made clear in the early 1980s that reunification of the Korean peninsula must be peaceful. They dared to use the word "peace" in the statements on reunification under consecutive authoritarian governments. Their peace discourses started with only emphasizing peaceful reunification, but later developed by encouraging dialogues with North Korea, dealing with structural injustice in South Korea, and seeking a just peace and reconciliation between the two Koreas.[2] Their efforts to reinterpret reunification issues and emphasize the necessity of preventing war, while at the same time building just peace, were not fully absorbed by society; however, these efforts did succeed in educating many progressive church members and in training them as peace activists.[3]

It will be noteworthy to those not familiar with Korea today that while Buddhism is one of the largest religions in the country, Buddhists' involvement in social movements is not significant at all. Buddhism in South Korea, unlike many Buddhist traditions in other Asian countries, has been more of a contemplative tradition, remote from the lives of the people.

Most, if not all, Buddhist temples are located in mountainous regions and monks are trained to maintain a distance from the secular world. It was not long ago that some Buddhists, whether lay people or monks, began expressing interests in reunification and social issues, and even actively participating in social activities. But, unlike the "engaged Buddhism" of other South and East Asian traditions, their activities have been individual efforts and there has been no noticeable effort or commitment at the institutional level to engage in social issues in an active way. By contrast, Protestant and Catholic churches have been active in organizing social movements and working together with the Korean people during the rule of the authoritarian government. The public recognizes their efforts, and the church groups very often play a leading role when the country faces significant problems and challenges.

The anti–Iraq War campaign has a special meaning in the peace movement. This war provided South Korean society with an opportunity to overcome the nationalistic discourse of peace. Previously, most, if not all, peace issues were related to South Korea's political instability and the activists sought world support. In addition, peace issues were formulated in terms of the reunification and peaceful co-existence of the two Koreas. The anti–Iraq War campaign encouraged peace activists and ordinary citizens to consider world peace and review South Korea's ethical responsibility as a member of the world community. An activist who has been involved in this campaign since its beginning states that the anti–Iraq War campaign showed that peace issues beyond the Korean peninsula could appeal to citizens in South Korea.[4] This nationwide campaign against the Iraq War and South Korea's deployment of troops to Iraq was strengthened with the participation of 351 civil society organizations and the support of many ordinary citizens.[5]

The nationwide anti-war campaign contributed to the spread of the peace movement. This campaign began with opposition to the U.S. invasion of Iraq and gained momentum with the South Korean government's decision to deploy troops to Iraq. Activists emphasized that life without war and violence was one of the most fundamental human needs for everyone in the world and the effort to make and build peace was one of the most fundamental ethical responsibilities of every human being in the world. This discourse, based on a widely held understanding of peace, contributed to formulating a conception of peace that is based on a just and sustainable world for everybody. It also appealed to ordinary citizens who desire peaceful living conditions and the collective well-being of the world community. In this context, the peace movement was considered not as a radical social movement, but as a universal effort for making and building peace. One activist recalls that the anti–Iraq War campaign provided him with an opportunity to review the meanings of peace and war, and the personal and social responsibilities for waging war and making peace.[6]

Peace activists have been holding annual workshops since 2004; consequently, the peace movement has gained ground in South Korea as an important social movement. The wide spectrum of participating organizations and activists and the issues and interests they bring to the workshops show that the peace movement has broadened its scope in terms of the subjects it deals with and the approaches it takes to reach out to people. Indeed, its aims are not limited to security and reunification issues in the Korean peninsula but extend to regional peace in Northeast Asia; world peace; nonviolent resistance; and education to build a just, sustainable, and peaceful society. The approaches that peace organizations and activists take range from traditional advocacies and campaigns to street performances and peace camps in post-conflict societies. The energy and creativity of the activists are the driving forces for the spread and improvement of the peace movement.

TRANSITION OF PEACE ISSUES

The peace movement has shown a remarkable change in terms of the issues it deals with. As noted above, the peace movement was initially preoccupied with reunification, security, and anti-war issues. In dealing with these issues the peace movement was more inclined to focus on negative peace rather than on positive peace. Peace activists were not able to overcome the narrow concept of peace without war and violence, and South Korea was not stable enough politically and economically to encourage them to broaden the movement's scope.

In the mid-2000s, peace issues were diversified, and the number of groups and organizations dealing with peace issues increased. One of the most significant changes was the emergence of the concept of positive peace and the enhanced understanding of nonviolence and a culture of peace. Peace activists began to differentiate negative peace from positive peace and emphasized the importance of peaceful means for building peace. They relied more on the wider understanding of peace and peace movements. Peace organizations and activists developed an enhanced understanding of peace and their interest in nonviolence and a culture of peace brought two main changes to the movement: new interpretations of conventional reunification and security issues in terms of positive peace and new discussions on the practice of nonviolence and the use of peaceful means to achieve their goals.

One of the leading civil society organizations initiated a new interpretation of peace and security, and also of South Korea's role in building peace in the Korean peninsula and Northeast Asia. This organization's new approach to peace and security argues that South Korea must be a "peace state" to overcome security dilemmas escalated by the vicious cycle of the arms race in the Korean peninsula and Northeast Asia. The proposed "peace state" is an effort to replace security discourses with peace discourses, including long-term visions to build a just and sustainable peace in the Korean peninsula and Northeast Asia. This idea presents three principles to transform South Korea into a peace state: (1) the initiation of arms cuts, allowing a minimum level of military defense, (2) peaceful and ethical diplomacy, and (3) the pursuit of sustainable development and the transformation of unjust political and economic conditions.[7] Unfortunately, many specialists in conventional studies of security and international relations have criticized this idea as too idealistic. But this idea of a "peace state" is meaningful in terms of challenging the conventional understanding of peace and security at the national level and at the same time, is realistic in terms of addressing the challenges South Korea is facing, while also presenting the strategies this politically unstable, small country can consider for survival.

There is also an effort to reinterpret humanitarian assistance to North Korea based on the idea of positive peace. This effort creates links between humanitarian assistance to and development of North Korea and peace building in the Korean peninsula. Paying careful attention to conflict between the two Koreas and conflict inside South Korea over the assistance to North Korea, it views humanitarian assistance to North Korea as an essential component of any effort to build a sustainable peace in the Korean peninsula and seeks substantial ways to change attitudes toward North Korea and the understanding of peace. In this context, this effort puts a special emphasis on building people's capacity through designing training programs and discussions on conflict resolution and peace education to equip people with the knowledge and tools to understand peace and deal with conflict.[8]

With the spread of the peace movement some groups became more interested in nonviolent resistance and peace education. South Korea has a long history of activism. Activists often used violent tactics to counter violence or to employ violence strategically. Political resistance was not necessarily nonviolent, and violence was justified as a means to confront illegitimate authoritarian governments. But with the progress of democracy, violence can be neither supported by the public nor justified as a necessary means any longer. People's understanding of nonviolent resistance has been improved and at the same time, the number of groups and organizations relying on pacifism or nonviolence has increased. These groups and organizations provide training workshops on nonviolent resistance and programs on peace education to encourage activists and citizens to develop principles and strategies of nonviolence in their daily lives and social movements.

Theories and skills of conflict resolution were introduced to South Korea in the early 2000s. A small group of people who had participated in training or degree programs of conflict resolution organized workshops. Their programs emphasized win-win solutions, dialogues, and communication skills for the peaceful resolution of conflict. Although their number is small, there are now more groups conducting project-based conflict resolution programs and facilitating training programs and workshops. There is now an effort to deepen the understanding of conflict resolution and overcome its technical and instrumental role. This effort emphasizes transformative approaches to conflict resolution and practical applications of peace building ideas to educate citizens.

In general, however, South Korea's social movements have been independent since its beginnings. In the past, under authoritarian governments, social movements focusing on democratization and human rights relied significantly on outside financial support, but their activities were not influenced by that outside support. South Koreans had total ownership of their activities. Now, every organization is independent, mostly relying on membership fees and donations, and sometimes on government support for projects. In terms of formulating their principles and issues, South Korea's social movements have been independent as well. There may be exchanges of ideas with outsiders and outsiders may inspire activists. But outsider influence is not noticeable because outsiders' input is regarded as simple information sharing. Activists in South Korea are very knowledgeable, strong, and professional because of their tradition of formulating activism to protest dictatorships and constant ideological attacks by dictators. As to the peace movement, there has not been any one person of note who has had a great influence on it. Peace organizations invite some international figures to speak to them but activists do not rely on outsiders' ideas. Outsiders' input is regarded as the introduction to useful information and knowledge. In fact, one of the reasons the peace movement is still struggling with theoretical concepts and action principles is partly because of activists' prudent attitudes to outside interpretations of peace issues, activities, and cognitive approaches to issues.

The anti-war campaign against the wars in Iraq and Afghanistan played an important role in forming and spreading the peace movement. In fact, there were similar anti-war discussions relating to peace and reunification in the Korean peninsula in the 1980s and 1990s, but these discussions were limited to opposing armed conflict in the Korean peninsula and did not reflect the idea of positive peace. The anti-war campaign against the unjust wars in Iraq and Afghanistan provided South Koreans with an opportunity to consider their responsibility and role as world citizens. This campaign considered the universal value of positive peace, nonviolent resistance, and

peace building in formulating discourses, designing activities, and understanding the survival issues of people in Iraq and Afghanistan. This campaign has been monitoring the situations in Iraq and Afghanistan and
working to raise awareness of just peace and unjust war, and the importance
of long-term peace building efforts.

Conscientious objection became part of social movements and at the same
time, part of the peace movement in the early 2000s. Until the late 1990s,
conscientious objection was considered an individual matter based on religious beliefs in most cases and as political protest in some cases. In the early
2000s, with the progress of democracy, conscientious objection was reviewed
in terms of human rights and state violence against citizens. Some peace
activists considered conscientious objection an important subject for the
peace movement. They raised questions about state violence against conscientious objectors and interpreted the issue in terms of the problem of militarism.[9] The conscientious objection movement continually questions the
problem of state violence and militarism in terms of the human rights of the
objectors. This movement relies on nonviolent resistance in advocating its
issues with deep insights into the ideas of positive peace.

One of the issues shaping the picture of the peace movement is the peaceful life. People who are interested in practicing and maintaining peace in
their daily lives have transformed their individual interests into a social
movement. They are interested in healthy and peaceful living with others
through building communities, enhancing mutual understanding, respect
for other creatures, and respect for nature. Their concerns are not limited
to their local communities and South Korea but extend to all suffering creatures in the world.[10] They have been taking active nonviolent actions to
protest against large development projects and wars. In particular, they
marched across the country using their nonviolent resistance program of
"three steps and one kneeling bow" to show an extreme form of nonviolent
resistance and to appeal to citizens and activists.

There are many groups and organizations that are interested in the new
approaches and resources that the peace movement provides. They are
involved in the issues of reunification, relief and development, education,
the environment, and human rights. Strictly speaking, they do not belong
to the peace movement. They do not deal with peace issues or design peace
programs. And they do not necessarily support nonviolent resistance, nor
are they familiar with the concept of positive peace. But they want to gain
inspiration and find resources from the peace movement to renew or reform
their own approaches to social issues. These groups want to learn to use
the tools and skills of peaceful actions for the purpose of developing their
own activities. They also want to build working relationships with peace

organizations and activists, and use them as resources. They neither want to change their political positions and worldviews, nor fully support the ideas and approaches that the peace movement emphasizes. They are casually associated with or dissociated from the peace movement according to the issues they currently work on. However, their interest in and tacit support for the peace movement and its peaceful means to accomplish particular goals show the penetration of the peace movement and its ideas into South Korean society. This clearly indicates the growth of the movement's influence on diverse social movements and actors.

Transition of Approaches

With the change of issues that the peace movement deals with there have also been methodological changes in advocating for peace issues, reaching out to the public, and building working relationships among groups and individuals involved in the peace movement. The movement has developed its sensitivity to violence and improved peaceful means of advocating peace issues. In appealing to and working with the public, the peace movement has become more open and inclusive. Peace groups and activists have built collaborative relationships among themselves. These changes have enabled the peace movement to strengthen its foundation and cultivate human resources.

One of the most significant changes in campaigning for peace causes is the reliance on nonviolent action. South Koreans had to confront authoritarian governments for a long time. Oppressive political environments contributed to the growth of social movements and the formation of a strong activist culture. Activists would rely on violent means of protesting to achieve strategic ends, although those violent means were always vulnerable to government manipulation of public opinion and, as a result, the setback of campaigns. However, these violent means were justified by most activists as effective, strategic choices showing their determination to fight against unjust, oppressive governments. But with the introduction of democracy and the progress that followed, the strategic use of violence has lost its public appeal. Furthermore, the spread of the peace movement and the increasing interest of peace activists in nonviolent action contributed to discouraging some activists' consideration of violent means. Education programs on conflict resolution, the culture of peace, and nonviolent direct action have helped activists deepen their understanding of violence and contributed to developing peaceful ways of protesting against political, social, and economic injustice. These activists do not target the underdogs of unjust structures and institutions at the front but try to help them become inspired by nonviolent action that peace activists take to counter violence. They believe that using violence to confront violence, whether it is physical or structural, cannot be justified.

One of the most symbolic nonviolent actions was a lying-down action organized by more than 100 activists to confront the suppression of peaceful demonstrators by the police in June 2008. Citizens were holding nationwide candlelit vigils every night for more than two months to protest against the government's decision to import U.S. beef that was considered unsafe due to the potential of contamination from BSE (bovine spongiform encephalopathy), or mad cow disease. The activists organized a lying-down campaign to protest the brutal suppression by the police that occurred during previous vigils. They prostrated themselves on the street when the riot police started to arrest citizens and bore all the police footsteps on their bodies. Their campaign could not block the police operation of arresting citizens, but it made a great impression on citizens and peace activists.

More peace campaigns rely on nonviolent actions now. Anti-war campaigns organize nonviolent actions and conscientious objectors design nonviolent campaigns to appeal to the public with their causes. Some peace activists joined the vigils against the import of U.S. beef last year; they intervened in confrontations between citizens and the police, checking violent actions of both citizens and the police. Some activists actively advocated the strategic superiority of nonviolence over violence through reaching out to the media and the public. These efforts have accumulated as social capital and contributed to enhancing people's understanding of peace and violence, and the spread of a culture of peace.

The movement for peace now seeks more open and inclusive ways to encourage citizens to participate in peace campaigns and activities. Social movements and civil society organizations in South Korea have been criticized for a lack of inclusiveness in designing action plans and carrying out campaigns. Peace activists make efforts to interpret peace issues in nonpolitical and nonideological ways, and design activities that can easily appeal to ordinary citizens. They are sensitive to the rights of citizens to know the issues related to their peaceful living, while at the same time, they strive to be open to citizen feedback and input. They organize campaigns, performances, and activities on the street with citizens. In particular, many young activists who are familiar with inclusive activities design participatory programs using their individual creativity and skills. Peace activists also make efforts to know and listen to people in war zones through reaching out to them or inviting them to South Korea. This open and inclusive approach appeals to the public and encourages greater public participation.

One of the most significant characteristics of the peace movement is the development of collaborative working relationships among organizations and activists. This collaboration cannot be easily found in other social movements. The peace movement has built networks of organizations and activists, as well as collaborative working relationships. Civil society organizations working in the same sectors often compete with one another in South Korea. They collaborate with one another when there are strategic needs, yet the collaboration is often superficial and limited to announcements, expressing political positions, and organizing joint campaigns. The collaboration of peace activists is more concrete and active. They build and utilize networks to gather ideas, share information, design activities, and encourage the contribution of all organizations and activists to programs and activities under way. Their inclusiveness and collaboration have contributed to building a culture of peace within the peace movement that respects diversity and creativeness.

The collaborative and inclusive way of designing and implementing programs and actions provides many activists with opportunities of mutual teaching, learning, inspiring, and respecting. It also allows them to have new experiences of working together with equal and full participation regardless of age, position, or professionalized knowledge. This kind of working culture—based on openness, respect, and equality that are still not widespread in South Korea—draws many people to the peace movement. As one activist says, "The peace movement does not have the hierarchical culture that is commonly found in other sectors of society and restricts the free participation and contribution of all members."[11] This atmosphere plays a crucial role in building the capacity of activists to spread the peace movement. Many social activists joining the annual workshops organized by peace activists are impressed by the workshops' open and inclusive atmosphere. They have opportunities to interact with activists and to learn ways of practicing peace in daily life. This provides a more powerful message about the peace movement and its commitment to peace and effectively contributes to spreading the peace movement.

CHALLENGES

The peace movement has many issues and challenges to deal with and overcome if it is to establish a firm, sustainable foundation. The peace movement has gained ground in South Korea in spite of its short history; however, most, if not all, citizens do not yet find much difference between the peace movement and other social movements. The international peace movement generally finds its inspiration in the ideas of positive peace, nonviolence, peace building, and the culture of peace. This conceptual foundation provides the peace movement with the rationale for setting practical, desirable goals and finding realistically ideal means. However, the peace movement in South Korea is still confused with those ideas and not yet fully determined to take them as its philosophical guidelines. This ambiguity and lack of determination project the impression that the foundation of the peace movement in South Korea is not strong enough. Consequently, a major task of the peace movement is to establish a conceptual foundation that can differentiate the peace movement from other social movements.

Another serious challenge the peace movement is facing is South Korea's political environment. This country occupies half of the divided Korean peninsula and faces its major enemy in the north. Unfortunately, it is still preoccupied with ideological debates. It is not easy in South Korea to neutralize controversial social issues such as the division and security of the Korean peninsula, humanitarian assistance to North Korea, conscientious objection, peace education, and peaceful conflict resolution, or to reinterpret them in terms of positive peace and holistic peace building. Social issues are easily changed to political debates and often misunderstood as ideological struggles. The peace movement has not yet developed a legitimate conceptual framework that can transform such destructive political and ideological debates into constructive, collective discussions. Peace and reunification issues are still framed within the boundary of security debates and the peace movement is not yet able to redirect the issues to building a just, sustainable peace for all Koreans. The peace movement must, therefore, develop new methods to address South Korea's issues, and to reframe them in terms of the ideas of positive peace and sustainable peace building.

The peace movement in South Korea is based on the activism culture that definitely contributed to democratization and the progress of democracy, as well as the development of strategic social movements. But this activism culture has been criticized for lacking direct interaction with citizens and openness to citizen participation and input. This closed pattern of activism grew out of the intolerant political environment and the constant manipulation of public opinion under authoritarian governments. Ever-changing and complicated political situations made activists become analytical, strategic, and prudent in dealing with social issues and advocating their causes. Social movements have become professionalized and more distant from ordinary citizens due to their insensitivity to public sentiment and concerns. The peace movement built on this activism culture also lacks direct interaction with citizens, although it understands the essential need of public participation and support. Most peace organizations, like other civil society organizations, still employ unilateral strategies and campaigns rather than participatory programs to interact with citizens and, as a result, empower them.

A lack of human resources is not easily recognized but is a significant challenge that must not be ignored if the peace movement is to be sustained. This shortage of human resources is partly attributed to a lack of educational programs for peace activists. One activist points out that there are needs for education programs on theories and practices of peace movements and peace studies for activists.[12] As mentioned above, a peace movement based on the concepts of positive peace, peace building, nonviolence, and a culture of peace is new in South Korea. Activists find resources in studies of violence in Western cultures. But there are not many educated academics and trained activists in South Korea who are familiar with those sources, nor do they have direct access to those who can share their knowledge and experience with Korean activists. And so, peace activists are left struggling to find resources and educate themselves. The unmet needs for education and training therefore challenge the sustainability of the peace movement.

The spread of the peace movement is attributed to activists' enthusiasm. Activists have been working hard to formulate peace issues in relation to the South Korean situation, reinterpret peace issues to appeal to citizens, develop peaceful campaigns, build networks and working relationships, and find resources for the peace movement inside and outside South Korea. Their working conditions are poor and most of them receive minimum wages. They have to work long hours and do not have enough time to take care of themselves. What keeps them going is their commitment to peace. The movement is built on their sacrifices. But the peace movement must seriously consider the activists' poor working and living conditions and find ways to meet their basic needs so that activists have the time, energy, and resources to secure the present and future of the peace movement.

CONCLUSION: HEADING FORWARD

Social movements in South Korea have been mostly dealing with political agendas, and have been interested in changing society through transforming systems and institutions. Activists have been confronting unjust governments, policies, and actors benefiting from the corrupt systems and institutions. Their strategies mostly focus on fighting against those at the top rather than on communicating with those at the bottom and conceptualizing structural problems through the eyes of the stakeholders. Their ultimate goal is to establish a society where the rights of no one are violated and where Koreans pay more attention to decision makers than to ordinary citizens. They are somehow accustomed to this contradiction, although this does not mean that they are indifferent to the issues ordinary citizens have to deal with every day.

The peace movement is sensitive to the inclusiveness and openness of programs. Peace activists have been utilizing this sensitivity within the peace movement to change working relationships from competition to collaboration, and to design inclusive processes that invite greater participation in the peace movement. However, this sensitivity has not yet been fully activated to reach out to ordinary citizens and consider them not as objects of but as resources for the peace movement. This is an important matter that can determine the future of the movement and whether it remains a typical social movement focusing on advocacies and campaigns, or one that works closely with citizens and develops programs and activities that can empower and cultivate citizens.

Peace activists have been evaluating the peace movement and addressing its challenges and visions at their annual workshops. According to the workshop reports, activists' passion, devotion, beliefs, and willingness are some of the most significant resources of the movement. In addition, the reports indicate communication problems among peace organizations and activists and between the peace movement and citizens are challenges they have to overcome to sustain the peace movement.[13]

In spite of all the problems and challenges they face, peace activists hold on to their hopes. They believe that they can pluck their hopes from their frustrations and draw solutions from their problems. They make efforts to overcome communication problems through increasing opportunities to interact with other activists and by developing programs to work together with citizens at the grassroots level. They design peace education programs to provide both activists and citizens with opportunities to conceptualize peace and violence, and to view and analyze political and social issues on the basis of positive peace. They consider that building networks of organizations and activists is important to respect diversity, build capacity, and sustain the peace movement. However their efforts to build networks have not yet been extended to other sectors of society, especially those sectors that do not share the movement's ideas and philosophies about social changes.

The peace movement has a lot of potential to contribute to changing South Korean society, a society that is still struggling with political and ideological divides, and being challenged by an ever-changing political environment and instability. South Korea is still technically at war with North Korea and ideological discourses still have a great influence on many issues. This country does not provide an ideal environment for the growth of the peace movement. The ideas and approaches that the peace movement presents are often questioned and considered as naïve and unrealistic. On the other hand, this environment inevitably needs a peace movement that can help citizens develop visions for a desirable society where political divides and ideological confrontations can be transformed into resources for peaceful co-existence.

There are two main things the peace movement has to consider to change society and at the same time realize its ideas. First, the peace movement that understands the importance and power of networking and relationship building has to engage in web-making efforts. Author John Paul Lederach suggests that web-making helps groups discover resources and sustain efforts for peace building. This web-making is an effort to overcome vertical and horizontal divisions in society and build capacities to change society holistically.[14] The peace movement can engage in a web-making that covers the entire society to overcome political and ideological divisions and build a strong social foundation for change. Secondly, the peace movement has to develop long-term visions that can be shared with citizens and other social movements to build a desirable future for all. As one activist notes: "Ever-changing environments inside and outside South Korea make the peace movement frustrated from time to time."[15] This observation provides the peace movement with a rationale to develop long-term visions that can achieve resilience and flexibility, and hold on to hopes while facing ever-changing conditions.

NOTES

1. Koo, 2007, 195–209.

2. See National Council of Churches in Korea, 2000. This publication compiles all the statements on peace and reunification of the Korean peninsula announced by the National Council of Churches in Korea (NCC–Korea) and world churches in the 1980s and 1990s. NCC-Korea played a leading role in the peace and reunification movement in the 1980s and 1990s.

3. It is not deniable that many peace activists have a religious background. In particular, Christians are in the majority in the peace movement. This fact does not necessarily mean that the peace movement is inclined to reflect particular religions or their ideas.

4. One of the activists the writer met for this chapter mentions this. This activist says that South Korean society is interested in peace issues now and it is a big change. She also points out that it is still not easy to draw citizens' attention to world peace issues because those issues are not directly related to South Korea.

5. Park, 2008, 293–306.

6. An activist who has been involved in conscientious objection movement mentions that the anti–Iraq War campaign gave him an opportunity to think about the meaning of peace and violence, the unjust deployment of troops, and the killing of innocent people. According to him, the campaign was one of the important events that encouraged him to be involved in the peace movement.

7. Koo, 2008,13–28.

8. A person involved in humanitarian assistance to North Korea and policy development related to North Korea explains the reason why his organization is

interested in conflict resolution. He mentions that citizens' capacity must be built to deal with conflict between the two Koreas and also conflict over ideologies in South Korea. Also see Korean Sharing Movement Center for Peace and Sharing, 2007.

9. Lim, 2009.

10. Dobup, 2007.

11. An activist mentions that the absence of a hierarchical culture in the peace movement is one of its distinctions. She says that it makes her continue working with peace activists and engaging in the peace movement.

12. This activist mentions that the peace movement does not have a strong theoretical foundation and this lack of foundation makes it difficult for the peace movement to overcome ideological debates over peace issues and to develop new agendas.

13. See the Peace Activists Workshop Preparation Committee, 2006 and 2008.

14. Lederach, 2003.

15. This activist involved in humanitarian assistance to North Korea mentions the overwhelming political situation that rapidly changes and discourages organizations to develop long-term plans and agendas for improving the working relationship with North Korea and building peace in the Korean peninsula.

CHAPTER 24

LIFE IN PEACE: THE EMERGENCE OF THE INDIAN PEACE MOVEMENT

Ramu Manivannan

Peace movements represent the highest ethical and humanist struggle to establish a humane world. The role and objectives of peace movements can no longer be restricted to the problems of wars, the arms race, and nuclear weapons. They are, in fact, equally concerned about the problems of direct and indirect violence caused within the state and social systems. In the process they are also redefining the traditional notion of peace and security. The basic challenge facing peace movements today is not about war or weapons but the system. The challenge cannot simply be dealt with by the withdrawal of consent of the civil society to the state or dissolution of the nation-state system. The institution of the state is indispensable at least for the foreseeable future. Then how do we achieve this fundamental transformation of the state and also society? The search for a solution has to be sought in the peace movements. They represent a new hope for the civil society because they are beginning to redefine what politics is.

The peace movement in India represents an integral or holistic approach to the concept of peace. The meaning of peace in this context can be viewed as a basic condition of life. The peace movement is, in fact, an integral response to the nature of threats faced by the state and society. There is a growing linkage between the various social movements in India. The interconnections are still emerging. Some questions can be pertinent here. How does one explain the sources of interaction between the various social movements and examine their contribution to the emergence of a peace movement in India? And, how can the peace movement be mobilized to a role of gradual nonviolent transformation of the state and society?

There are four basic issues involved in the rise and role of the peace movement in India. They are as follows:

1. Creation of a humane society involving nonviolent struggle against militarization (involving both military and nonmilitary threats to peace).
2. Emphasis on political, social, cultural, economic, and other survival issues involved in the development policies of the government.
3. Struggle of the victims to take positive and constructive steps to resist the state and system and to develop an alternative perspective of development and defense.
4. Ushering in of a nonexploitative, decentralized economic and political system based on Gandhian model of state, society, and development.

MEANING OF PEACE

The peace movement in India arises from an entirely different perspective from movements elsewhere, particularly in the West. The problems that confront the Indian people have been quite different from those (the fear of nuclear war) that gave rise to peace movements in the northern hemisphere. Peace for the common people of India includes far more than the mere absence of war. To be meaningful in the everyday life of people, peace must mean freedom from social, economic, and political oppression, access to resources for survival, cultural autonomy, and freedom from violence by the state as well as the powerful. Security for them is not so much security of the state as people's security. Of course, none of the movements (anti-nuclear; human rights; ecological; cultural survival; movements of the landless, tribal people, and the diverse working classes; women's movements; and movements against inappropriate development) focuses on all these issues at once as well as on peace. But they are gradually realizing that these issues are interlinked and the issue of peace gets reflected as part of this linkage. In fact, they do not even describe themselves as peace movements. But all these seemingly diverse issues add up to a "life in peace" and the search for peace emanates from the characteristics of the new social movements. This classification is based on the fact that in recent years, many people's movements in India have started emphasizing the sociopolitical and economic aspects of militarization.

NEW SOCIAL MOVEMENTS AND THE SEARCH FOR PEACE AS A CONDITION OF LIFE

In India multiple forms of social movements have been the agents of social resistance and transformation throughout history. The struggle for freedom was accompanied by the integration of movements with a common objective. They were, however, struggling in response to economic, social, cultural, environmental, and political conditions. These struggles had converged around one very basic purpose, namely, India's independence. Since 1947 there have been a number of social movements. There has been a renewed resurgence of social movements in the country for over a period of three decades. They may be recognized as new social movements since they qualitatively differ from the old movements. They are considered to be new because they have a participatory, nonhierarchical pattern of organization. More importantly, their activities are in the process of developing a far-reaching critique of the existing political, economic, and social order. They also strive to change social values as well as public policy. The new social movements collectively focus on the quality of human life, that is, life in peace. More crucially it is this framework, which locates these movements as part of the process of social transformation, that is new.[1] They are anti-war, anti-nuclear movements, ecological movements, human rights movements, movements of indigenous peoples, and other survival-related movements.

The main issue in the fight against militarization is not that it is directly linked to armaments but rather to the central aspect of the survival of people and the societies. It can be appropriate only in the sense that militarization is analyzed in a broader context of underlying conflicts. The prime issues are of people and ecosphere, displacement and degradation of social groups, abuse of human rights, and ultimately the displacement and reduction of socioeconomic persons from native cultivation and production processes to the conditions of degraded human labor in the urban development process.[2] There has been a growing concern among people regarding the issues of militarization, cost and consequences of nuclear energy, displacement and dismemberment of the social groups, dislocation and reduction of human capital, and the steady expropriation of cultivable land.

Ramachandra Guha writes that these movements work simultaneously at two levels. He states:

> At one [level], they are defensive, seeking to protect civil society from the tentacles of the centralizing state; at another, they are assertive, seeking to change civil society from within and in the process putting forward a conception of the good life somewhat different from that articulated by any of

the established political parties. Considered individually, these movements are small and scattered; taken collectively, and keeping in mind the convergence of interests and ideologies and the growing networks of coordination and co-operation, they are an increasingly visible part of the Indian social scene. These are then the new social movements.[3]

They may remain, in physical and organizational sense, fragmented and scattered. But they are no longer restricted to specific situations or particular places. They provide, in fact, continuity over time and connection from region to region. They are beginning to share and learn from the experiences of other situations. The growing integration of diverse movements struggling in response to political, economic, ecological, social, and military conditions is derived from the common concern for a future that is seen as threatening. Though seemingly diverse, the issues raised by these movements add up to the meaning of peace, and together defined in wholly indigenous and holistic terms, they constitute a people's movement for peace.

PEACE TRADITIONS IN INDIA

There is a clear sense of history of peace traditions in India as well as the conscious beginning of the Indian peace movement that can be attributed to India's nonviolent movement for freedom itself. Gandhi, who successfully guided India in his nonviolent struggle against the British, firmly believed in the possibility of the abolition of war through establishing nonviolent, unarmed relations between peoples and groups as well as individuals. In Gandhi's view, this is not a mere utopian vision based on nonviolence or nonresistance as an ethical principle but as an ultimately practical basis of order.[4] A crucial element in this belief is the need for social and structural change. Gandhi responded by saying that the idea of nonviolence is as old as the hills when asked whether the principle of nonviolence was his contribution to the means of the Indian freedom struggle.

There are a number of peace traditions (ethical, religious, and social) that continue to influence social thought in India. The religious and other social movements that have appeared in the Indian social arena, have had concepts of peace as part of their doctrines, but they were not recognized as part of an active peace movement. In India there is no such thing as a single peace movement, but a variety of peace traditions: religious pacifism, the Gandhian nonviolent movement for freedom, unilateral nuclear pacifism or parts of the nuclear disarmament movement, the ecologically inspired movements of the 1970s, the tribal movements and the issues of cultural survival, the civil liberties movement, and the women's movement. Each one of them has made a contribution, sometimes as separate entities or subgroups. The peace movement that has arisen in India is more than the sum total of these traditions or the organizations that represent them.

In 1939, Gandhi proposed that nonviolent means of political struggle should be used as a defense policy of free India instead of military means. Gandhi believed that war is the natural expression of the spirit of violence. He was convinced that the only way of avoiding disaster was extension of *Satyagraha* (truth force) to the field of national defense. He had long believed that India had a special responsibility and duty in the development of a nonviolent alternative means of struggle that would make possible the abolition of war.[5] Gandhi said:

> I am not pleading for India to practice nonviolence because she is weak. I want her to practice nonviolence being conscious of her strength and power. No training in arms is required for realization of her strength. We seem to need it, because we seem to think that we are but a lump of flesh. I want India to recognize that she has a soul that cannot perish and that can rise triumphant above every physical weakness and defy the physical combination of whole world. . . . I believe absolutely that she has a mission for the world.[6]

Three major dimensions have prominently influenced different social groups in India. First, the nonviolent struggle for freedom; second, peace and anti-nuclear movements beginning in the late 1970s (these groups attached greater significance to problems of nuclear energy than to the threat of mass destruction); and, third, the crisis in the relationship between human beings and nature—the nature of development and its consequences to the survival of sociocultural groups. These three dimensions foster an intimate relationship that allows productive alliance and coalitions among them. The high point of the Indian peace movement in terms of mass base occurred only during the late 1980s, when the movement against the Narmada Sagar River Project and the Sardar Sarovar Dam Project became a mass movement. It also took more than a decade for the anti-nuclear groups and peace activists in the country to come together and draw up a common program and strategy for the future. The Harsud Rally held on September 28, 1989, brought together for the first time the organizational skills of the peace and survival network within the country. It was a culmination of activists and others to oppose the various "destructive development" plans all over the country, like the Narmada Valley River Project, the Kaiga Nuclear Plant, the Baliapal Missile Test Range, and so on.[7]

SOCIAL BASE OF THE PEACE MOVEMENT

The new social movements in India are essentially results of mobilization by the people and, in fact, the synthesis emerges from below. The most dominant feature of the new social movements in India is their social and grassroots impulses. These movements share a very broad and diverse "constituency," autonomy vis-à-vis political parties, and a certain mode of action and organization.[8] The new social movements also enjoy practical neutrality with an activist and nongovernmental base. Their plans can be linked to a grassroots upsurge of protest and pressure. There is a considerable sympathy enjoyed by these movements among the public in India.

The social composition of the peace movement cannot be taken as that of a middle class. The issues taken up by it have gone beyond the narrow confines of a class boundary. The most realistic assessment of the social composition of the peace movement must include both the victims themselves (fearing for physical, economic, and cultural survival) and the urban-based, middle-class activists who articulate the demands of the former and lend logistical support for the cause. These activists are now increasingly shifting to the sites of struggle leaving the tasks of coordination and networking to be accomplished through their urban centers. Therefore, the social base of the peace movement includes the agricultural population living in Narora, Baliapal, and Bhogarai, Koodankulam, and the Narmada River Valley; the tribals and the dispossessed in Chotanagpur, Bastar, Kakrapar, and Gandhamardhan hills; the role and participation of women activists in the Chipko Movement in the Garhwal region of the Himalayas, Baliapal, Chotanagpur, and Santhal Parganas; the role of civil rights activists in providing legal and logistical support to the various struggles including the anti-Narmada Dam movement, the Tehri Dam, Doon Valley, Kaiga, and Baliapal; and the role and active participation of students, teachers, lawyers, journalists, and doctors (especially on nuclear issues and other survival-related concerns), which is common in all the struggles of the peace and ecological movements in the country.

In the lengthy struggles such as the anti-Narmada Dam movement, anti-Tehri Dam Project, Chipko movement in the Garhwal region, and anti-nuclear movements in the country (Kaiga, Kakrapar, and Narora), there has grown a special interest among the university students and the younger generation. They are beginning to spend their summer vacation in these camps/sites trying to understand the cause and nature of the movement. They soon become informal spokespersons for the movement in the urban areas. In the past two decades, these social movements have shown their capacity to resist the model of Indian development. They question the ultimate aim of the development strategy that dispossesses people of their sociocultural identities, leads to economic exploitation, and causes disruption of the ecological stability, and the delicate balance between people, nature, and social needs. In the past few years, their mobilization has taken an undeniable national dimension in their effects (social, political, and economic impact), and particularly in giving rise to a new mode of thinking on development nationwide.

MOBILIZATIONAL APPROACH

The new social movements in India combine two types of action. The first is aimed at informing people and mobilizing public opinion on issues such as ecological degradation, displacement of people, survival of indigenous people, and problems of nuclear energy and human rights. This is achieved through multiple-issue campaigns aimed at maximizing the impact of the movement. The purpose of this action is to gain, on the one hand, the support of the maximum number of people and, on the other, to create pressure on the government through massive and well-timed protests. There is a close interaction between the visionary approach of the intelligentsia and the down- to-earth pragmatism of the grassroots. This is achieved through the second type of action that seeks to involve informed people through a "basic" and nonhierarchical mode of organization, although the diversified, yet related, segment of this expert knowledge is crucial in coordinating the flow of information and actions at the grassroots.

These struggles are seemingly local but their reverberations have national and global significance. Their mass protests are accompanied by a central coordinating committee, a diverse citizens' forum, and activist groups. There are many activist groups (on environmental protection, ecological stability, nuclear energy, women, and civil liberties) that have come up in the social arena since the beginning of the 1970s. They are coordinated through an immense and informal system of multiple and multiform networks, both non-hierarchical and diversified. These groups share knowledge and the experience of their respective struggles, both at the level of organization and at the level of action and collective reflection. Though their struggles are organized around precise and limited objectives, they reflect collectively on the long-term vision of fundamental transformation of state and society. A more basic and immediate challenge is the nature and model of development and its consequences impinging on the future generations and on the survival of cultures and societies. Their indispensable precondition for any development policy is that it must be responsible to both the present and the future generations.

The rise of new social movements since the beginning of the 1970s can be linked with the emerging concern for a strongly felt situation of injustice or deprivation caused by the nature of development in India. The people were beginning to feel that this model of development had only raised false hopes of improvement and in fact led to the deterioration of the actual situation. They were soon deeply concerned with the excessive threat to their own lives (health and occupational hazards, the fear of displacement, the loss of forests and traditional sustenance to life, threats to sociocultural identities, and the blatant disruption of ecological balance) for the sake of development and national security. The effects of this, clearly felt, motivated the new movements (anti-nuclear, tribal, ecological, and anti-dams). The emergence of these movements can be related to the demands that correspond to the most strongly felt grievances and needs of the local people.

The Indian state, instead of responding positively to these demands, tried to block the growing movements through its coercive mechanism, as, for example, the Baliapal movement against an anti-missile test range; tribal movements in the Bastar, Chotanagpur, and Santhal Pargana areas; anti-dam movements in Andhra Pradesh, Maharashtra, Gujarat, Madhya Pradesh, Bihar, and Tehri (UP); and ecological and other survival-related movements. The successive governments have virtually remained indifferent to the struggles of these people that are strongly felt as representing justified demands. The state has also lost its legitimacy in the eyes of these movements by violently oppressing them.

The people and the activists involved in these struggles are not discouraged because of the lack of positive results from the government. They are deeply aware that such struggles take considerable time and energy, especially in a condition of violence and indifference demonstrated by the state. They strongly believe that they can more or less successfully resist against the state and its development policies that threaten their survival. The new social movements have started emphasizing their focus beyond the symptoms to tracing the causes in the nature and model of development. These movements are also deeply aware that there are no global solutions to global problems. The only redemption that may still be available to resolution is local solution to global problems, which requires a far more intense and determined struggle at the grassroots.

THE IDEOLOGICAL BACKGROUND

The success of the Indian peace movement is dependent on the type of struggle it will forge ahead, its capacity for mass mobilization, and more importantly, of its insight into social and political power. The ideological inspiration for the peace movement comes chiefly from the nonviolent approach toward an alternative notion of peace and development belonging to the Gandhian school of thought and action.

Another important source of ideological inspiration comes from the autonomous peace initiatives. The roots of this movement lie in different but overlapping areas: students, teachers, lawyers, journalists, artists, environmental activists, women's groups, and civil rights activists. They reflect Gandhian, liberal, and radical political orientations. But they all show preparedness to talk to, and learn from, each other. They identify their common purpose and cause that draws them closer to the struggle of the victims. In overall terms, the entire movement is based on the general technique of "nonviolent action."

The peace movement in India is influenced by the Gandhian philosophy of nonviolent resistance. Gandhi, in fact, avowedly based his philosophy of nonviolent action on a theory of social power. He believed that the principle of nonviolent action is itself an instrument in the struggle for justice. It is a permanent revolution and therefore it is dynamic.[9] This nonviolent movement consists of people determined to devote their lives to the most fundamental issues of peace and survival. The method of protest in anti-nuclear movements (Kothamangalam, Narora, Kakrapar, Kaiga, Baliapal, Koodankulam, Alwaye, and Kuthiraimozhi), in ecological and anti-dam movements (Chipko, Appiko, the Tehri Dam Project, the Narmada River Valley Development Project, and the Inchampalli-Bhopalpatnam Dams), and in tribal movements (Jharkhand and Bastar) range between nonviolent demonstrations to militant nonviolence. These movements also show great inclination for direct action. This has increasingly been demonstrated in the anti-Narmada Dam Project, anti-Tehri Dam Project, Chipko and Appiko movements, and Kaiga and the Kakrapar anti-nuclear movements.

The application of nonviolent techniques has significantly increased the strength of the new social movements and that of their supporters. These movements are now gaining support and active involvement of people other than the victims and activists. They have also been successful in convincing the government of their purpose and even among the third parties, as, for example, the proposal for the withdrawal of the World Bank from the Narmada River Valley Development Project. This has enabled the movements to influence the government and at times regulate its activities. The National Debate on nuclear energy (December 10 and 11, 1988) in Bangalore sponsored by the government of Karnataka brought together for the first time the nuclear scientists and the anti-nuclear advocates. This was no mean achievement in view of the extent of secrecy under which the nuclear establishment functions in all countries. The success can be attributed to the continuous persuasion and protests organized by the anti-nuclear activists in the country insisting on an open dialogue with the country's nuclear scientists. The anti-Narmada Dam activists continue in their struggle to persuade the government to develop an appropriate policy on rehabilitation and to reduce the height of dam.

EMERGENCE OF PEACE POLITICS

There are major sociopolitical developments taking place in India today. They promise to hold long-term implications for the Indian polity. A more crucial aspect of this development is that it is taking place from the base of the political structure, that is, at the grassroots.[10] In other words, this is happening at the level of the common people. This development is directly related to the rise of new social movements as a response to the nature of state, society, and development in the post-independence period. In a deeper political sense, they are the voices of the civil society.

The activists are deeply committed to the fundamental transformation of the state and society. The process of transition has already begun. The rise and role of new social movements since 1970s signify the beginning of this transition. They are deeply aware that their struggle is a permanent one. At the outset, it may seem that they are working on specific issues and are confined to specific geographical situations. In a real sense, many of them share a common perspective of the future. Each one of them can be understood in relation to other movements and in relation to the holistic notion of peace. They are, in fact, different manifestations of the same concern, that is, peace. Each one of them is an integral and interacting part of the peace movement and can be understood in relation to the meaning of peace in which they are embedded.

In view of the Indian situation, the meaning of peace can best be understood as a basic condition of life. Therefore, the rise and role of the peace movement in India can themselves be seen as responses to the problems of peace, such as military and nonmilitary threats to peace. There is indeed a close relationship between peace and development, peace and ecology, peace and social policy, peace and human rights, and peace and survival-related issues such as wars, weapons, and threat to indigenous people and cultures. The problems of poverty, underdevelopment, income inequity, regional disparity, and social injustice are as important as other concerns of the peace movement such as wars, arms race, nuclear weapons, ecological degradation, abuse of human rights, and dignity. The new social movements have not only recognized the linkages between the military and nonmilitary threats to peace but have also identified the causes and consequences of the problems mentioned above that are mainly due to the state-centered notion of society, security, development, and politics.

The new social movements have at least been successful in giving a new thrust/dimension to politics. They are more concerned about the challenge of conscientization and people's empowerment than capturing state power, because they consider that the capturing of state power is not a precondition for the fundamental transformation of the state and society. The foremost challenge today is the empowerment of people. Though the new social movements are nonparty political entities, there is something deeply political about them. They are raising their concerns about issues and/or problems that have long been neglected by the political parties. The traditional political parties continue to believe that it will result in a major predicament for the state if they talk about the exploitation of the poor, tribal people, natural resources, and other negative consequences of the development strategy, let alone the performance and consequences of nuclear power plants in the country. The debate on nuclear weapons policy is almost non-existent among the political parties. If any, it is mainly state-centric and covered with ambiguity.

The rise of new social movements reflects gradual transitions that have been taking place at the grassroots level. In other words, this development can be described as the growth of a new kind of politics—the politics of social action. In the process they have given rise to a new political consciousness and attention given to the local and national levels. They are gradually beginning to occupy the new political space at the local level in areas and/or regions that are now widely known as movement areas. This development directly corresponds to the steady transition in the nature of the party system in India: The gradual transition from a single-party dominant system to a multi-party system is taking place at the national level. More importantly, the plural basis of the Indian political system has slowly gained eminence due to the rise of regional entities as a major determinant in national politics. There are changes taking place at the regional and local levels, too. The traditional political parties, including the left, have shown little concern with the demands raised by the new social movements. Though they have not yet organized themselves as an alternative party-oriented front, they are certainly emerging as a common (alternative) political front. The emergence of the National Alliance of People's Movements (NAPM) in 1992 was another clear indication of the efforts toward building a common platform and (political) formation, with a minimum common ideological unity and common strategy that will give rise to a strong socio-political force and a national peoples' movement for peace and just development. The logical end of the political transition at the level of the party system is likely to touch the grassroots. But the response to the transition is unlikely to be the same at the local level as it is at the regional and national levels since the people and the movement groups at the local level are more concerned about the fundamental transition of the state and society. At present they are more anxious about giving rise to a new politics in India than a new party. This development, however, is very likely to give rise to a creative conflict situation challenging the traditional political constellation and the nature of the party system itself.

One of the most outstanding characteristics of the peace movement in India is its social and grassroots impulses and orientations. It believes in the transformation of power from below. It seeks nonviolent transformation of state and society and the establishment of direct grassroots democracy. It shares with the global Green Movement the need to act locally and think globally. In a traditional sense the new social movements are nonparty political formations. The sociocultural economic aspects of development are crucial considerations for the role, nature, and mobilization strategies of the new social movements in India. Although it may seem that these struggles are fought with an immediate objective of policy change, the movements are deeply aware that their struggle is in fact a part of a larger transitional process.

CONCLUSION

Can the peace movement in India emerge as an alternative to the traditional parties like the Green parties in the West? Those parties grew out of a coalition of alternative groups and movements. Though the signs of emergence of the Green movement in India can now be seen, its potential to transform itself as an alternative to the traditional political party is not yet clear. It is most unlikely that the peace movement in India under the present circumstances can become institutionalized as a political party in the near future. The main reason is the demands and expectations that are associated with the traditional party system. It would require considerable time and skill for political mobilization. It would also require exploring new options, if any. Given the political environment and mobilization strategies involved in the politics of India, the movement interests may be represented by the concerned political parties that are prepared to modify their political and economic agenda. It is necessary to examine in the case of India why the traditional political parties including the Left have remained more or less indifferent to the issues and demands raised by the new social movements. The concerns raised by the local politicians in the case of a few movements were not even reflected at the state and central levels of the party structure.

In the light of the developments that have taken place over the past decade or so, there is little reason to believe that the new social movements will disappear from the social scene. If the political parties continue to remain silent or indifferent to the demands raised by the new social movements, there could be more direct pressure on these parties. This may come true in the Uttarkhand and the Jharkhand areas, and also in Madhya Pradesh, Gujarat, and Maharashtra, involving people opposed to the Sardar Sarovar Dam Project. This may also develop in areas where the anti-nuclear movements are active. The potential role and influence of the Chipko movement in the Garhwal region of the Himalayas and the anti-nuclear movement in north Karnataka and Koodankulam in Tamil Nadu cannot be underestimated. It is well within the interest of the political parties to respond to the demands of the new social movements. If the established parties do not show adequate response in the near future, this would result in a decline of their electoral appeal and support at least in the movement areas. Besides, this would gradually lead to the issue-based political mobilization by the new social movements. This development is most likely to bring about greater cohesiveness among the movements and their various entities. The inevitable question that arises at this stage is related to the future of the peace movement itself.

The basic dilemma facing the peace movements in the world today is related to the task of achieving compatibility between the aspirations for a broad social change and the achievement—mass mobilization for a specific goal. The pressing problem is the choice between being pragmatically successful (in broadening the popular base through adjustment and compromises) and being true to their fundamental beliefs. This is an insoluble predicament. Green parties that have been successful for a long time, including the Greens in Germany, are facing several existential choices and changes. The struggle to preserve the Green identity is continuing. There are also circumstances that the Greens, originally intending to transform power from below, have meanwhile become victims of power from above. The biggest challenge that the Green movement faces in the course of its transition into a movement party is the very survival of its utopia. It also must continue to remain an active movement, since a political organization that lacks ideological and sociocultural identity is most unlikely to survive into the future. A movement bereft of its ideological content and parties delinked from its movement character are not likely to succeed as political entities for long. This is a real challenge. This not only requires greater cohesion and coordination among the various social movements but also the development of a more comprehensive philosophy of peace politics.

NOTES

1. On the issue of convergence of objectives of the social movements, see Walker and Mendlovitz, 1987; Dalton and Kuechler, 1990; Wignaraja, 1993.

2. For understanding the specific Indian situation with reference to the rise of new social movements, see "New Social Movements: A Symposium on a Growing Response to the Crisis in Society," *Seminar* no. 355 (March 1989).

3. Guha, 1989, 12–15.

4. Young, 1987, 1.

5. For a detailed discussion, see Sharp, 1979, 131–169.

6. *Young India*, August 11, 1920, cited in Sharp, 1979, 160.

7. For a detailed discussion on the rise of new social movements, see *The Great Concern* (Special Issue on People's Movements) (1990): Vol. I.

8. Sheth, 1993, 275–287.

9. On Gandhi's view of social power, see Mathur and Sharma, 1977.

10. For a detailed discussion on the grassroots movements in India, see Kothari, 1989, Vol. II.

CHAPTER 25

PEACE PSYCHOLOGY IN ASIA

Cristina Jayme Montiel

ASIAN CONTEXT OF VIOLENCE AND PEACE

Johan Galtung provides a useful lens for a broad understanding of violence and peace through the concepts of direct and structural violence.[1] *Direct violence* refers to observable harmfulness, traceable to persons who carry out the damaging acts. On the other hand, *structural violence* means harmful conditions traceable to unequal social systems that prevent a group of people from satisfying their basic human needs. In real situations, direct and structural violence intertwine with each other. Systemic inequalities erupt into armed social conflicts and vice versa.

Foreign invasions, authoritarian regimes, and colonial occupations mark the histories of Asia in the past 500 years.[2] Except for the Maldives in South Asia, all other Asian countries have been occupied by at least one foreign country. Most Asian societies have had multicolonial invasions. For example, the Philippines was subjugated by Spain for almost 400 years, then colonized by the United States for around 50 years, and then ruled by Japan for three years. Up until the past 100 years, anti-foreign wars, mostly against colonial rule, were waged in Asia, killing a high number of local freedom fighters and traumatizing civilian populations.

A longer version of this article appeared in Cristina Jayme Montiel, "Peace Psychology in Asia," *Peace and Conflict: Journal of Peace Psychology,* 9, no. 3 (2003): 195–218.

After World War II, Asian societies gained independence from their colonial rulers. However, the rise of Cold War politics brought about Asian authoritarian regimes, many of which were supported by either the United States or the Communist Bloc. Today, most of Asia lies in a state of chronic poverty. Economic data show chronic Asian poverty and suggest that political and social inequality is a source of Asian structural violence. However, the question of economic inequality may point more to differences between Asia and developed nations, rather than internal wealth inequalities within Asian societies. Although within-country wealth inequalities need to be addressed by Asian peace advocates, the larger global issue lies in the disparities of wealth between Asia and developed societies represented by the G-9.

Asia plays host to diverse cultures that have flourished in their respective territories over centuries. Nonmigrant cultural groups and asymmetric power relations mark cultural heterogeneity in the region. The cultural diversity in Asia is unlike multiculturalism in melting-pot countries in North America, Europe, and Australia–New Zealand. Migrant cultures in developed societies tend to assimilate with the dominant host culture over time. In Asia, however, the cultural fabric is nonmigratory.

The most widespread religions in Asia are Islam and Buddhism, plus Hinduism in highly populated India. Intra-country language or dialect variations are strikingly high. Except for the Maldives, all other Asian countries claim multiple mother tongues, with India having 93, China with 49, and the Philippines with 40 languages or dialects. Intergroup cultural variations in Asia are not only different but also unequal. There is usually one dominant ethnic group and a number of minority groups that are significantly smaller in comparison to the dominant group.[3] For example, China has around 20 ethnic groups, but the Hans comprise 92 percent of the population. Afghanistan is composed of five major groups, with the Pashtuns claiming 38 percent of the population, and the Tajiks claiming 25 percent. Vietnam has 87 percent Vietnamese, plus seven other ethnic groups. Because cultural differences date back to centuries-old family lineages, aggressive territorial contestations emerge in conditions of cultural heterogeneity. Such intercultural antagonisms tend to be asymmetric in power structure, with one ethnic group having access to more material and natural resources, and imposing cultural scripts on marginalized groups.

PSYCHOLOGICAL ASPECTS OF VIOLENCE AND PEACE IN ASIA

Asian peace psychology is the study of human behaviors and processes involved in eradicating direct and structural violence, and strengthening social peace in Asia. The study and application of Asian peace psychology are embedded in regional conditions of colonial histories, authoritarian regimes, chronic poverty, and intergroup cultural variations. Although I use a structural view, I do not take the traditional Marxist stance that economic structures determine political and cultural arrangements. I assume that economics, politics, and culture are equally important, and interact with each other. Framing peace psychology in a structural context juxtaposes psychology with social structure, and shows how psychological knowledge and skills can contribute to structural peace building. I make a few claims. First, unjust social configurations produce large-scale social violence in Asia. Second, social structures, rigid as they are, can be transformed by human agency. Third, human agency falls in the realm of psychology. Hence, psychological interventions can have a direct and multiplicative impact on widescale structural transformation.

As a response to Asian politico-historical conditions, psychologists can contribute to peace building by (1) examining the meaning of peace in Asian contexts, (2) building democratic space through active nonviolence, and (3) healing traumas caused by protracted wars. To counter chronic poverty in Asian economic systems, psychologists can seek ways to build beliefs and value systems for economic democratization. To mitigate structural violence arising from unequal or unjust cultural heterogeneity, peace psychologists can attend to (1) claiming social identity and voice, (2) culture-sensitive peacemaking, and (3) peace building by crafting new political arrangements with increased intergroup fairness.

Revisiting the meanings of "peace" is important in the development of Asian peace psychology. Embedded in politico-historical contexts of foreign occupations and local dictatorships, the term *peace* takes on negative meanings associated with the imposition of colonial and authoritarian regimes. One historical view sees colonial governments dominating Asia by pacifying the natives. The Philippine experience elucidates this point. At the start of the 16th century, in the name of peace, the Spanish colonial forces promised to bring the natives' souls to heaven through Christian baptisms. The Spanish embarked on a colonization program to pacify the natives by a crafty combination of the cross and sword. Authoritarian rulers likewise abused notions of peace to maintain their state apparatus. For example, during the Philippines' martial rule from 1972 to 1986, the military used its armed force to eradicate opposition and restore peace and order. Widespread tortures, massacres, political kidnapping, and intelligence surveillance became instruments of peace and order. At that time, a whispered joke among us pro-democracy workers was, "Yes we have peace in the Philippines. We are as peaceful as a cemetery."

Building peace psychology in Asia may involve probing the subjective meanings of social peace among Asians. Peace psychologists should examine social discourses and representations in different Asian settings, recognizing the possibility that the meaning of peace is context sensitive, may take on different meanings from those that have emerged in Western settings, and may not always denote a positive evaluation.

CRAFTING A PSYCHOLOGY OF ACTIVE NONVIOLENCE IN POLITICAL DEMOCRATIZATION

Active Nonviolence (ANV) refers to strategies for changing systemic violence in a manner that refrains from using direct violence. ANV strategies can be used to dismantle politically repressive conditions and economically exploitative systems. The challenge of active nonviolence lies in its simultaneous requirements to be forceful enough to change embedded social structures, without the conventional confrontational tools of social force that rely on heavy capital and militarized aggressions using bullets, bombs, torture, and imprisonment.

ANV takes on characteristics seldom associated with conventional notions of peace. For example, ANV actions produce tensions and awareness, as social movements challenge the political status quo. Second, ANV is partisan instead of neutral, taking the side of the oppressed and exploited sectors in the social system. Third, ANV relies on collective action and is rarely an individualistic act. Its social force emanates from huge numbers of people gathered together with a shared goal of dismantling one social system and building an alternative one. Effective ANV requires streetwise skills such as networking, mobilizing, and conscientizing—psycho-organizational abilities that produce a singularly powerful yet peaceful social force.

In the past 20 years, ANV phenomena transformed the political configuration of societies that have carried the yoke of oppression and exploitation. In the Asian region, ANV forces jolted the political terrains of the Philippines in 1986 and 2001, China in 1989, Burma in the 1990s, Taiwan in 1986, South Korea in 1980, Indonesia in 1998 to 1999, and East Timor in 1999.[4] The ongoing struggle for Tibet's autonomy from China likewise demonstrates ANV at work.[5]

Religions play a major role in Asian ANV. In the Philippines' People Power and East Timor's independence struggle, the Catholic Church led and called on the local population to continue the peaceful struggle for liberation against ruthlessly oppressive conditions. Spirituality has likewise fused with pragmatic social movements, injecting Asian ANV with a particularly Buddhist orientation. Along the lines of what is referred to as engaged Buddhism, contemporary ANV movements have been inspired and led by Vietnamese monk Thich Nhat Hanh, Cambodian monk Maha Gosananda, Thai activist-intellectual

Sulak Sivaraksa,[6] and Tibetan monk His Holiness the Dalai Lama.[7] Asian ANV demonstrates how religions can play a public and positive role in the struggle for structural peace.

Student uprisings also have contributed to the transformation of political systems in Asia. For example, in South Korea from 1980 to 1988, widespread student demonstrations against martial law virtually shut down the country, and eventually produced a more open democratic system in this country.[8] Although the 1989 Tian An'men Square uprising in China did not bring about a new form of government, it nevertheless focused world attention on dedicated attempts of Chinese dissidents to create sweeping social transformation through peaceful force.[9]

Unfortunately, ANV has rarely dented the discourses of social sciences in general and psychology in particular. However, peace psychologists can contribute to ANV in Asia and other parts of the world. On theoretical and practical levels, social psychologists can attend to subjective dimensions of forceful collective action, such as the spiritual inspirations of ANV, emotional stages of an ANV build-up, psychological aspects of confronting the militarized enemy without hitting or running away, and organizational dynamics and leadership styles of ANV.

Psychologists may likewise offer emotional, intellectual, and material support to ANV participants. For example, clinical help may come in the form of healing burned-out activists and providing shelter and therapy for those who may have been tortured or physically harmed during the ANV struggle. Organizational psychologists could address internal organizational systems, impromptu street operations, and inter-organizational conflicts that arise in the course of mobilizing large numbers of people for mass actions.

HEALING TRAUMAS IN ASYMMETRIC PROTRACTED CONFLICTS UNDER UNSAFE AND IMPOVERISHED CONDITIONS

Political trauma refers to the shattering and extremely stressful effects of state-sponsored or military violence on individuals. In relation to political trauma, psychologists have studied the effects of war on children,[10] psychological effects of torture,[11] and the harmful effects of war on American combat soldiers related to posttraumatic stress disorders.[12]

A number of idiosyncratic contextual conditions influence the nature of political trauma in Asia. First, because social conflicts in Asia are usually intergroup and asymmetric, one group in the violent contestation holds more power over the other group. Although individuals on both sides of a conflict turn simultaneous victims and transgressors, members of the less powerful group may suffer more trauma because they tend to be politically less potent, militarily weaker, and economically poorer. Consequently, I believe psychological healing efforts should prioritize trauma treatment to the less powerful group in the conflict.

Second, Asian violent conflicts are usually protracted in nature. A protracted conflict extends over long time periods, waxing and waning through the years.[13] A number of such wars in developing regions like Asia can be traced back to colonial periods and Cold War power plays.[14]

Due to the prolonged nature of conflicts, traumas such as torture and combat duties are not only highly intense but also episodic. Psychological duress likewise results from low-intensity but longer-lasting systemic conditions of fear and powerlessness. Subtle yet powerful distress seeps into the psychological structures of civilian communities that have lived under protracted-war conditions for decades. Peace psychologists should explore trauma-healing therapies that address mental harmfulness of a low-intensity, long-duration conflict.

Unlike posttraumatic healings that take place in Western contexts, trauma survivors in Asia deal with recovery under conditions that are politically unsafe and impoverished. Even as individuals and entire communities grapple with trauma healing, they continue to live in unpredictably volatile conditions where violence may erupt again. Furthermore, survivors need to contend with their daily physical survival under impoverished conditions. The viability of trauma-healing projects in Asia will increase if steps are taken to address the contextual sources of violence and provisions of material needs to survivors.

CREATING BELIEFS AND VALUE SYSTEMS THAT SUPPORT ECONOMIC DEMOCRATIZATION

How one views the causes of poverty may relate to one's behaviors vis-à-vis social change. Hine and Montiel showed that people explain poverty in at least five ways: exploitation, characterological weaknesses of the poor, instability and conflicts, nature-related causes, and Third World governments.[15] Individuals who blame exploitation engage in more activist endeavors, whereas persons who attribute poverty to the character of the poor and internal conflicts participate less in social change actions.

Christie and Montiel pointed out that dominant culture could be used to rigidify economic structural violence.[16] Dominant cultural scripts that make economic inequalities look and feel right elucidate culture-structure interaction. Examples of widely unquestioned narratives are the capitalist ethos,[17] Protestant ethic,[18] just-world thinking,[19] meritocratic ideology,[20] and victim blaming.[21]

Peace psychology in Asia can examine alternative cultural scripts that support systemic equalities in economic systems. For example, attributing poverty to exploitation encourages a closer look at global structural inequities. Furthermore, peace psychologists may want to look at Asian beliefs about communal life and shared resources. Among indigenous highland communities in the Philippines, for example, the concept of land ownership is communal and not individual. Can peace psychology in Asia help identify and strengthen mental scripts favoring wealth sharing? Pushing the question further, can these alternative scripts counter the onslaught of dominant global scripts that rigidify the international and local economic structures related to Asian poverty?

CLAIMING SOCIAL IDENTITY AND VOICE

Galtung warned against the structural violence of cultural oppression. The power of culture lies in its ability to provide the symbolic, subjective basis for saying what is right and what is wrong in matters of direct violence and politicoeconomic configurations.[22] Cultural violence arises when dominant cultures provide popularly accepted scripts that support the righteousness of direct and structural violence. Cultural domination and the imposition of nonlocal cultural scripts create collective resentments over the loss of social identity.

In Asia, peace and violence issues arise over variations in cultural scripts, whether such scripts are related to religion,[23] language,[24] or deeply held symbolisms.[25] Cultural heterogeneity is likewise linked to territorial conflicts, with different cultural groups contesting legitimized boundaries constituted during colonial periods.

In addition to identity issues, a second cultural concern relates to issues of voice. Cultural inequalities may propagate cultures of silence among minority ethnic groups. Freire described a culture of silence as cultural conditions that arise when alienated and oppressed people are not heard by dominant members of society.[26] The low-power groups internalize negative images of themselves created by the dominant group. A culture of silence does not imply nonresponse, but rather a response that remains muted and uncritical of the cultural scripts that legitimize political and economic domination.

On theoretical and practical levels, Asian peace psychologists should build social identity and voice, especially among the culturally marginalized vis-à-vis the more dominant cultural groups.[27] Psychology's contribution to the mitigation of cultural violence in Asia is vital, not only because of the psychological factors involved in cultural empowerment, but also because the very nature of culture is subjective.[28] This places cultural issues smack

in the realm of psychology and cultural violence as an issue of direct importance to peace psychologists.

IDENTIFYING CULTURE-EMBEDDED ASIAN WAYS OF POLITICAL PEACEMAKING

Peacemaking pertains to methods employed to handle direct political violence.[29] Non-Asian intermediaries from developed nations frequently manage peacemaking efforts in Asia. For example, one can cite the United
Nations (UN) peacekeeping troops in Cambodia's 1993 strife;[30] East Tim-
or's post-independence government;[31] the U.S. and Russian participation
attempts to diffuse tension during the North Korean nuclear pile-up;[32] and
peacemaking attempts of China, Britain, United States, and Russia during
the India–Pakistan conflict over Kashmir in 2002.[33]

The intrusion of non-Asians, even in the name of peace, mirror the centuries-old patterns of Western colonization over Asia. I propose intrastate
or regional peacemaking instead. Asia-based peacemaking endeavors will
not only break historical patterns of foreign intrusions but will also bring
to the conflict arena peacemakers culturally attuned to local sensitivities.
Two cultural characteristics of Asian-style political peacemaking are worth
pointing out: (1) personalized trustworthiness of the intermediary and (2)
monarchic or spiritual political authority.

Perceived trustworthiness between conflicting parties increases the prob-
ability of successful negotiations.[34] When antagonists mistrust each other,
intermediaries can step into the picture as the mutually trusted third party.
The nature of trustworthiness differs between Asians and Westerners.

In Western societies, the notion is associated with a universalistic,
abstract trust, which is contingent on social attributes of the perceived.[35] In
most Asian societies, however, trust is particularistic and based on personal
knowledge of and affection toward the other person. Descriptions of political cultures in Thailand, India, Malaysia, and the Philippines assert that
social interactions and loyalties are based primarily on family ties, physical
proximity in a village, and personal patronage.[36] In Asian militaries, particularistic trust thrives among members of the same graduating class. Intense
trust and loyalty among classmates from military academies in Thailand,
Indonesia, and the Philippines can partly explain cooperation during militarized political interventions such as coup attempts.[37]

Among American troops, similar patterns of intense personal loyalties
thrive within one's unit and in relation to the commander. However, the
symbol of the American flag, and not family ties, glues troop loyalties together. In addition to personalized trust, Asian-style spiritual or monarchic

authority may come into play during peacemaking. Asians tend to bow to authority and power,[38] and Asian political peacemaking is marked by a fusion of spiritual and secular power. In Thai political language, the term *greng jai* (deference) portrays an attitude that produces passive receptivity to direction from above.[39] In a study of Indonesia's Javanese mythology, Anderson noted how secular authority anchors on a god-king concept, as temporal rulers represent incarnations of divine power.[40]

A Malay worldview recognizes hierarchical relationships not only among individuals but, more important, between a person and the supernatural.[41]

India's Mohandas K. Gandhi, guru of active-nonviolence proponents, exemplified how spirituality fuses with pragmatic political strategies to produce social transformation.[42] He showed how a powerful colonial force like Britain can be outmaneuvered by himself and ascetically disciplined masses of people ready to sacrifice themselves nonviolently to obtain political goals. Gandhi's anticolonial struggle was guided by the spiritual principles of *satya* (truth), *ahimsa* (nonviolence), and *tapasya* (self-suffering).[43]

In more recent times, spiritual leaders have led peacemaking efforts in Southeast Asian internal conflicts. For example, Cambodian Buddhist monk Venerable Maha Ghosananda guided the Dhammayietra (Buddhist walk of peace) during his country's May 1993 elections.[44] During Philippine coup attempts, catholic priests and nuns negotiated for the release of captured civilians caught in the crossfire. In one failed antistate rebellion, paramilitary coup forces refused to yield until a priest joined the government's negotiating party.[45] In Thailand politics, the monarchy is the repository of charismatic political power.

The King has the most *barami* (charisma); he is associated with Buddha. The monarch's power emanates from his being well loved and respected by most Thai people.[46] King Bhumipol Adulyadev's intervention in the October 1973 Thammasat University student protests protected hundreds of thousands of young rallyists from military onslaught.[47] Again, in May 1992, King Bhumipol halted street violence by calling to his palace antagonistic military leaders Suchinda and Noonpakdi on the one hand against the popular Chamlong on the other side.[48]

CRAFTING NEW POLITICO-PSYCHOLOGICAL SYSTEMS THAT ADDRESS INTERGROUP FAIRNESS AMONG ETHNIC AND RELIGIOUS GROUPS

The *Armed Conflict Dataset Codebook*[49] classifies contested incompatible issues into two types: governmental and territorial. Incompatibilities over governmental issues are usually ideological and are about the political system, government legitimacy, and change in the composition of state administration.

Government issues pertain to intrastate conflicts covering an entire country. In East Asia, geopolitical conflicts about government have resulted in new political systems and pragmatic administrative agreements between contending societies. The two Koreas formed separate states with contrary political systems. China, on the other hand, created special administrative arrangements with Hong Kong to maintain economic stability in the region and to demonstrate to Taiwan the feasibility of peaceful reunification between societies with contrasting sociopolitical systems.[50]

Territorial incompatibility concerns a geographical segment of a country and includes interstate issues of territorial control (for example, the India–Pakistan conflict over Kashmir from 1947 to present); secession (for example, the Philippine government versus the Moro Islamic Liberation Front); and autonomy (such as East Timor against Indonesia, 1975 to 1999). A few leaders in Asian countries plagued by intrastate territorial armed conflicts are considering federalizing as a structural approach to long-term conflict transformation.

Federalism, as a decentralized social structure, is a political system of government founded on a territorial distribution of authority. It recognizes geographically defined authority to manage matters of territorial importance. Duchacek posited the viability of federalism as a resolution to conflicts that are expressed in territorial terms, and may hence be resolved with new distributions of geographical powers satisfactory to the conflicting groups.[51]

In the Philippines, the ongoing drive for federalizing is posited on a peace agenda that aims to address the centuries-old Mindanao war.[52] A Bangsamoro federal state will enable the autonomous region of Muslim Mindanao to promote its own identity and culture and to dictate its own pace of development without seceding from the republic. As a Filipino peace advocate, I have looked into the political psychology of transitioning from a unitary form to a federalized form of government. My tentative findings include the following politico-psychological insights, in the context of the Mindanao territorial conflict:

1. A federal constitution provides the "script" of power distribution. But in developing societies, formal legislative scripts rarely create the "play" in everyday political life. To prevent post-federation uprisings, there has to be widespread local political and cultural support for the political restructuring. What is important are the conditions of national and local leadership, political culture, interplay of personal and group interests and fears, and informal diplomacies.

2. Contemporary global and regional geopolitical configurations and collective memories of past colonial abuses will influence the Philippine federation process in Mindanao. As of this writing, U.S. troops are currently deployed in Mindanao allegedly to aid in fighting the Abu Sayyaf, a Muslim group associated with Al Qaeda. Mindanaoans have raised public protests against U.S. troops, citing their collective memories of anti-Muslim massacres during the American colonial era in the Philippines.

3. Institutionalized religion and religious power—both Christian and Islam—can play a positive role in the transition stage to a Philippine federal state.

Sri Lanka is a second Asian country that is considering federalizing to resolve intrastate territorial conflict. Antagonistic parties in the bloody Sri Lankan conflict are looking at federalism as a structural solution to power sharing between Tamils and Sinhalese. Since 1983, the Liberation Tigers of Tamil Eelam (LTTE) have been fighting for a separate state for the 3.2 million minority Tamils. The Sri Lankan conflict took center stage when Indian Prime Minister Rajiv Gandhi was assassinated in 1991, allegedly by a Tamil suicide bomber.[53] At peace talks in Norway held in December 2002, the government of Sri Lanka and the LTTE agreed to explore a solution based on Tamil self-determination in areas of historical habitation of Tamil-speaking peoples, and based also on a federal structure within a united Sri Lanka.[54] Although federalism is a political concept, the process of federalizing includes social and psychological overtones as well.

CONCLUDING REMARKS

The kind of peace psychology that will emerge in Asia will be substantively and methodologically different from variants of the discipline developing in North America and Europe. Because Asian armed conflicts are intrastate and intermediate-sized, I suggest that future researchers discover new conceptual and pragmatic handles for peace psychology, in a discipline that has traditionally attended to interstate clashes of global giants. I also recommend that a peace psychology embedded in Asia recognize the pivotal role unjust global structures play in Asian scripts of peace and violence.

The nature of peace in Asia involves not only the cessation of intrastate-armed conflicts but also more fundamentally, a steady restructuring of unjust political, economic, and cultural structural arrangements. To find relevance in this tumultuous region that holds half of the world's population, peace psychology in Asia should be sensitized to domestic and global social-justice thrusts. Ideas generated by peace psychologists in Asia should avoid inaccurate and individualistic notions of peace that support new forms of foreign intrusions, authoritarian rules, insensitivities to chronic poverty, and cultural dominations.

My suggestions point to the development of Asian peace psychology along the lines of (1) re-examining the social meaning of peace, (2) active nonviolent political transformations, (3) trauma healing in protracted conflicts, (4) belief and value systems supporting economic democratization, (5) strengthening social identity and voice among the culturally marginalized, (6) cultural ways of political peacemaking, and (7) psychological requirements of federalizing political structures for inter-group fairness.

Allow me to end by echoing prayers borrowed from Cambodian villagers in the 1993 Buddhist peace march.[55] Together with them, other Filipinos, Asians, and citizens of the world, I ask that one day soon, may we sleep above the ground, may we just stop fearing the night.

NOTES

1. Galtung, 1996.
2. Microsoft Encarta, 1995, 95; Microsoft Encarta Encyclopedia, 2000.
3. Hoiberg, 2002.
4. Deats, 2001; Remarks, 2001; The Unknown, n.d.
5. Herzer, 2009.
6. Deats, 2001.
7. Herzer, 2009.
8. South Korea, n.d.
9. Nathan, 2001.
10. Cairns, 1996; Wessells and Monteiro, 2000; Westermeyer and Wahmanholm, 1996.
11. Agger and Jensen, 1996; Lavik, Nygard, Sveaass, and Fannemel, 1994; Suedfeld, 1990.
12. Kelly, 1985; Kulka et al, 1990; Sonnenberg, Blank, and Talbott, 1985.
13. Azar, 1990; Fisher, 1990; Mao, 1938; 1960.
14. Godement, 1997; Hale and Kienle, 1997; Iriye, 1974; Sturgill, 1994; Szayna et al, 1995; Winnefeld et al, 1995.
15. Hine and Montiel, 1999.
16. Christie and Montiel, 1997.
17. Falk, 1979.
18. Weber, 1948.
19. Lerner, 1980.
20. Deutsch, 1985.
21. Ryan, 1971.
22. Galtung 1996.
23. "Religious violence," 2002.
24. Andaya and Andaya, 2001.

25. Konglang, 2003.
26. Freire, 1970.
27. Heaney, 1995.
28. Triandis, 1994.
29. Wagner, 2001.
30. Um, 1994.
31. Strohmeyer, 2001.
32. Mazarr, 1995; Chronology, 2000.
33. Tomar, 2002.
34. Deutsch, 1973; Pruitt, 1981.
35. Deutsch, 1973.
36. Mabbett, 1985; Montiel, 1995b; Morell and Samudavanija, 1981; Osman, 1985; Pye, 1985.
37. Handley, 1992; The Fact Finding Commission, 1990.
38. Mabbett, 1985; Montiel, 1995b.
39. Morell and Samudavanija, 1981.
40. Anderson, 1996.
41. Osman, 1985.
42. Sharp, 1979.
43. Mayton, 2001.
44. Appleby, n.d.
45. Nebres, 1990.
46. Morell and Samudavanija, 1981.
47. Kambhu, 1973.
48. Handley, 1992.
49. Gleditsch et al, 2002.
50. Leung and Stephan, 2000.
51. Duchacek, 1970.
52. Pimentel, 2002.
53. Jeffrey, 2002.
54. Chandrasekharan, 2002.
55. Maat, 1993.

CHAPTER 26

ACTIVE NONVIOLENCE: A CREATIVE POWER FOR PEACEMAKING AND HEALING

Hildegard Goss-Mayr

To respect more authentically human life and the whole of creation, we need to remind ourselves of the inspiration and driving force of this commitment: the power of nonviolence as it is revealed to us in the Bible and particularly in Jesus Christ. We see it in action as a liberating, healing, and peacemaking force in the life of people and nations.

We are living in the age of globalization. The process of globalization contains both negative and positive aspects.

NEGATIVE CHALLENGES

Since the end of communism in the early 1990s, liberal capitalism, a materialistic economic system, has gained global influence and domination. Many millions of people suffer from the consequences of this ideology and economic system. Its aim is profit and power. Mankind must serve it. In the hard competition the small ones fall by the wayside. The weak and under-qualified are marginalized, subsisting in poverty or even misery. Worldwide

Remarks at Peace Day, Catholic University, Leuven, Belgium (February 20, 2003), printed in Richard Deats, *Marked for Life, The Story of Hildegard Goss-Mayr* (New City Press, 2009): 123–34.

economic domination is also secured by military force. This holds particularly true for the developing countries. To point out just one example: the Democratic Republic of Congo suffered the loss of over 2 million people in the recent war over its resources of gold, diamonds, and coltan, needed for space engines and cellphones. This war was supported by seven African nations and transnational enterprises of the North. Or we should remind ourselves of the recent wars over the access to reserves of oil in the Sudan, in Afghanistan or Iraq? The resources of the earth and its environment are exploited to the point of provoking a global ecological collapse (for example, the pollution of water and air, dramatic climatic changes, deforestation, advance of the deserts, etc.). Hunger, illiteracy, mass unemployment, migration, and also terrorism are consequences of this situation.

This dramatic reality forces us to search for a new vision of the relationship between humankind, God, and all of creation, that is to say, a Shalom vision.

POSITIVE CHALLENGES OF GLOBALIZATION

To me it is fundamental to recognize and welcome this development toward global unity. Never before have there existed technical instruments like the Internet that permit people all over the world to establish contacts, communicate information, exchange discoveries, and provide knowledge and insights. Relief programs in case of accidents and catastrophes can be quickly organized. Sports, art, and particularly music from all continents and cultures converge and can help to build a global human family. The increasing importance of international nongovernment organizations (NGOs) and of organizations of the United Nations like UNESCO, WHO, and UNICEF provides powerful support to regions in need, and there has been progress made in the development and application of international law. Also the peace movement is profiting from modern means of communication to build global networks and give support to endangered groups. It is the project of God, the Creator, for humanity to move toward what Teilhard de Chardin calls the Omega point—the point when the whole creation will be united in love. There is a deep desire for this unity in mankind: it finds expression in the concepts of Shalom (Judaism), of Umma (Islam), of Harmony (Asian religions and philosophies), of a world society without classes and poverty (Marxism), in the concept of self-giving love and brotherhood (Christianity). We are called on to work actively for this end.

UNIVERSAL ETHICS PROMOTED BY WORLD RELIGIONS

World religions can help to lead the way to the acceptance of ethics based on universally affirmed values, in spite of the fact of their being presently abused in a scandalous way by fundamentalist concepts for power politics, violence, terrorism, and war in all of the world religions. In order to fulfill this task, however, world religions have to return to their deepest roots to rediscover and affirm those values that are required for humane togetherness. These values include, in particular, the absolute respect for human life; commitment for justice and human rights; the use of nonviolent means of overcoming injustices and violence; forgiveness; and the search for reconciliation. Let me quote from the experience of a seminar on nonviolence in Bangladesh organized by the nonviolent movement *Dipshika* with Moslems, Hindus, Buddhists, and Christians:

> Our Muslim friends pointed out:
> When God created humanity to be vice-regents on earth, his Spirit entered every man, woman and child, for He says: "When I have fashioned him and breathed into him My Spirit, fall you down in obeisance to him" (Surate 15/29). In this sense humanity is one. Human life is sacred. "And if anyone saves a life, it would be as if he saved the life of the whole people" (5/35).

> Our Hindu friends pointed out:
> Swami Vivekananda said: "In this world the human body is the supreme body and man is the highest creature. Nobody is beyond man." He reminded us of their offerings to the Supreme and of the renunciation of the will to destroy or to hurt others. Gandhi's Ahimsa seeks not only to overcome the practice of violence but even the intention to do harm to others.

> Buddhist participants explained that they are deeply committed to liberation of the powers that cause suffering and deprive people of their value; that their faith is based on unconditioned respect for any living being and insisted on these words from the Buddha: "In those who harbour thoughts of vengeance toward others, hatred will never cease. . . . For hatred is never appeased by hatred. It is appeased by love. This is an eternal law. . . . Let one's thoughts of boundless love pervade the whole world . . . without any obstruction, without any hatred or enmity."

> Rabbis for Human Rights in Israel would add: "What is hateful to you, do not do to others" (Hillel); "When a stranger resides with you in your land he shall be to you as one of your citizens" (Lev. 19:33)—"We beat our swords into plows" (Isaiah 2).

But those of us who are Christians are challenged in particular to be pathfinders for these convictions and this commitment. If we do not return to the Sermon on the Mount and place ourselves clearly and consistently on the side of the poor and if we do not demand their rights to be respected in politics and economy, if we do not become bearers of nonviolent attitudes and conflict resolution, if we do not stand up for disarmament, strengthen trust, practice love of the enemy, and commit ourselves to forgiveness, reconciliation, and peace, we shall decline into insignificance.

NONVIOLENT PEACEMAKING IN THE OLD AND NEW TESTAMENTS

In the Bible we can discover a pedagogy of peace building that reveals, step-by-step, a growing insight into the way to deal with and overcome violence through the power of truth, justice, and love. It leads up to the revelation of universal love through self-giving nonviolence in Jesus. Let us look at the most important steps of this pedagogy.

Roots in the Old Testament

The human being is created in the image of God. It is important to remember the vision of humanity that is given us in Genesis 1:27: We have been created in the image of God, in the image of the Holy Trinity. To say God-in-Trinity is to say God-in-community: three divine persons, equal in dignity, who are in permanent relation with truth, justice, creativity, joy, and peace, united in an infinite love which gives itself. To be created in His image therefore means to be created as a community of men and women, tribes, nations, peoples in perfect equality. God wants to share with us all the aspects of his being God-in-community; He wants the human family to live in this very relationship of Love: human beings among themselves, in relation to creation and to God.

However, we have broken and are constantly breaking this relationship of love, replacing it by the desire to possess the qualities and values of others, to dominate. This rupture with the relationship of love leads to all forms of injustice, sin, exploitation, violence, greed, and killing that dominate our societies.

The response of God, however, to this revolt by humanity is not counter-violence. On the contrary, He replies with an act of nonviolence and love: with his project of liberation and reconciliation. This project shows for us the way toward the original vision of unity in love.

Israel, a Small People Chosen to Witness in Its History the Way of Liberation and Peacemaking

Israel is called to introduce into human history a substantially new vision, a new social concept and project, differing from the surrounding great nations. This was a demanding task for a small migrant people. To be able to assume this mission, God sends witnesses and prophets to guide the people and He reveals himself as Emmanuel (meaning God with the people). He promises his strength and unshakable fidelity. A profound relationship of confidence is established between Israel and Yahweh.

Violence in Israel

In contrast to the surrounding big nations, violence is no longer considered as mythical or blind destiny, but it becomes part of human responsibility. It is considered as a destructive force, but there is not yet a clear answer of how to conquer it in its roots. It is important to understand, however, that the law of Talion, "an eye for an eye" (Lev. 24:20), means progress of civilization over the prevailing attitude of revenge. It permits retaliation, but limits it to the same kind and degree as the injury, forbidding destruction of the adversary.

To achieve Shalom inside the people of Israel, several demands have to be fulfilled. The most important of these are:

- You must adore only the unique God, the God of Justice and Love. This contrasts to the attitude of the powerful neighbouring nations who adored gods of power, of riches, of military strength, and attributed divine adoration to their political leaders. There should be no submission to kings and dictators. Who are the gods WE adore?
- Life is sacred: You shall not kill: to shed human blood is the gravest sin. While the surrounding pagan nations sacrificed infants to win the favour of their gods, David, for example, was not allowed to build the temple because he had shed blood. When God renews the Covenant with Noah, he stresses only this command: life is sacred. But, as we have seen before, this law is limited to the people of Israel. We can, however, find examples in the Old Testament that go beyond the law of Talion in the direction of universal love, for example, the four chants of the Suffering Servant of Isaiah, who resists oppression by taking on himself all the violence to liberate both the people of Israel and the oppressor.
- Respect of human rights: a firm and permanent commitment to human rights is required. God manifests himself as God of the weak, the poor, of widows, orphans, strangers, and slaves. They must be cared for and be able to live in dignity. This is also a precondition for peace in our own societies!
- Economic and social justice: the earth is the Lord's and He wishes it to serve all, not just a few. The Year of Jubilee, to be celebrated once in a generation (every 50 years), was meant to give thanks to God through reciprocal pardon, reconciliation, and redistribution of the goods so that

everyone can live in dignity. To jubilate signifies to thank God through the acceptance of economic and social justice and reconciliation.

We find these commands in the books of Exodus and Leviticus. To sum up, we can say that life in the spirit of Shalom requires that the nation lives truly the love of the neighbor: It is the first level of the revelation of the Love of God. In Jesus further dimensions of the pedagogy of peacebuilding will be revealed.

Jesus's Message of Peace

Jesus enters into human history at a moment of great violence and intense suffering for the people of Israel: Roman occupation (taxes, clashes for religious reasons, etc.); a politico-religious leadership, partly compromised with the Romans, exploiting the people with taxes and oppressive rules; an armed resistance movement, mainly in Galilee.

It is in this context Jesus will implant the liberating, saving, healing force of universal love of the Father and reveal through his teaching, life, death, and resurrection how to overcome violence, injustice; all evil at its root in the conscience and heart of humans as well as in the structures of society.

- He insists on the absolute respect of every human person for being created by God (Jesus's parable of the good Samaritan).
- He takes the side of the downtrodden, the suffering, invigorating their own faith in order to be healed.
- He breaks through taboos: speaks to women in public, makes them the messengers of the good news; he puts the care for the human person above laws (healing on the Sabbath).
- He speaks the Truth and confronts injustice freely and accepts fully the consequences of doing so (encounters with Pharisees and Sadducees; the question of the purity of the temple). He faithfully gives witness to the divine love of the Father to the very last, to the gift of his life.

The Sermon on the Mount (see Matthew 5) sums up the essence of Jesus's teaching. Going beyond the love of the neighbor, extending the pedagogy of peacemaking, Jesus reveals two further dimensions of love required for reconciling humanity in brotherhood:

1. The love of enemies (Mt. 5. 44): "Love your enemies, and pray for those who persecute you" has two radical, revolutionary implications:
   —Humanity is ONE: the division between the good ones and the evil ones is over; all human life is sacred, has to be respected.

—Use nonviolent combat to overcome evil: Jesus cuts the spiral of
violence by resisting aggression and by overcoming evil with the
power of truth, justice, and love. He illustrates this by taking scenes
out of the life of the people: when you are slapped in the face, turn
the other cheek; if they take your shirt, let them have your coat as
well. This means that you should not reply to violence with
violence, but resist; do not accept injustice; do not remain passive;
take a position and stand up and fight with the power of truth and
justice by attacking the roots of evil in the conscience of the
aggressor nonviolently with respect and love. Believe and affirm
that the adversary has a conscience that can be reached, can open,
can be changed. This nonviolent combat aims at overcoming the
injustice and liberating the aggressor as well as the victim. Such
combat can obtain greater justice and opens the possibility of
reconciliation.

2. Self-giving love of God. Resistance with the power of truth and love
has consequences: Jesus takes freely on himself the violence of his
adversaries, all the violence of humanity to absorb it, to overcome it
with the power of Love. This leads to his gift of life on the cross, but
also to resurrection. He reveals to us the only way to overcome evil
at its source is in the conscience of humans and humanity by taking
on us the consequences of nonviolent actions. Thus we can create a
new, reconciled relationship.

Nonviolent combat is the realistic transforming and liberating power in
human history. In the resurrection of Jesus, the Shalom, the renewed human
person, the seed of the Kingdom of God has been implanted in our world
and it continues to transform, to heal, to avoid hatred and bloodshed, to forgive, and reconcile. People baptized in the name of Jesus Christ have the
responsibility to work out of this perspective in their own life and in society.

ACTIVE NONVIOLENCE APPLIED BY CHRISTIANS IN OUR TIMES: METHODS AND STRATEGIES

We shall now, by way of examples, see how Christians apply this peace
building and liberating power of nonviolence in the present time:

Empowering the Weak and Oppressed

The Women of Medellin

In a poverty-stricken barrio of Medellin, Colombia, poor people adhering to Christian-based communities by reading the Bible discover their

own dignity and their responsibility to struggle against the inhumane conditions. God wants life in fullness for all. Through seminars in nonviolence they discover for themselves this power of transformation, revealed by Jesus. This helps them to overcome fear that paralyzed their energies. A process of inner and outward liberation can start. In a nonviolent campaign to obtain drinking water necessary to save the lives of their children, a group of illiterate women succeeds in touching the conscience of well-to-do women, even building solidarity with them. With this experience of their power of justice and truth, they continue the process of urbanization, liberation, and empowerment among rich and poor.

The Peasant Women of the Larzac, France

A military base in the French Larzac region is to be enlarged and 110 farmers will have to give up their land. The nonviolent leader Lanza del Vasto makes a two weeks' fast and analyzes the situation with the peasants: should they sell their land for the military preparation of wars or resist nonviolently to preserve the soil for its original destination to produce food, to nourish people? The peasants unite and decide for nonviolent resistance, developing slowly their strategy that makes them change from conservative, politically noncommitted persons to persevering, peaceworkers, who defend their soil successfully during 10 years of hard nonviolent combat (1972 to 1981).

In 1973 the first mass demonstration with 60,000 participants from trade unions, peasant movements, intellectuals, church people, and students takes place in the Larzac to say NO to militarization, YES to the production of food for the hungry of the world. A peasant woman, mother of six children, with little formal education gives the main speech. The nonviolent combat has freed her from fear, liberated her hidden force of Truth, and helped her to fully develop her human and spiritual potential.

Defying Dictatorship

Madagascar 1991 and 2001

The Philippine people power movement of 1986 had considerable impact on countries with similar situations of oppression, such as Madagascar where the 12 years' reign of the dictator Didier Ratsiraka pushed the country into utmost poverty. In 1990, inspired by the example of the Philippines and helped by the ecumenical Justice and Peace Commission with training in nonviolence, the opposition opted for nonviolent resistance. Very well-organized weekly mass demonstrations accompanied a six months' general strike that was very costly for the poverty-stricken population.

FFKM, the Council of Churches, comprising all Christian Churches of the island, was accepted as mediator. It obtained a transition government, a new Constitution, and elections. However, after a few years the dictator returned. When he was defeated by the elections of 2001, he refused to resign. Several months of hard, costly nonviolent resistance and, finally, international support succeeded in bringing about the definite victory of the democratic forces. The dictator went into exile. Now the poverty-stricken country needs many years of moral and material rebuilding.

Nonviolence: Force of Healing and Pardoning

Burundi: Emphatic Listening between Hutus and Tutsis

In regions of civil war or ethnic strife, such as in Burundi, Church organizations are promoting emphatic listening—deep listening with mind and heart—between small groups of Hutus and Tutsis, who have been in war over so many years.

The objective is:

- to become able to express one's suffering
- to listen to the suffering of the adversary
- to overcome a one-sided view
- to find common ground in the same experience of suffering
- to become able to accept, to pardon, the other
- to begin to act together to overcome the origin of existing violence and injustice.

Inter-Religious Witness to the Sacredness of Life

Lubumbashi, Democratic Republic of Congo

Lubumbashi is the center of the copper-mining region of Katanga. Because of possibilities for work there was a considerable influx from surrounding provinces with differing ethnic populations. In the 1990s, under the dictatorship of President Mobutu, the mining industry broke down. The governor decided to get rid of the immigrants.

Ethnic hatred followed and, after unrest at the university, ethnic massacres were threatening. The nonviolent movement GANVE (founded in 1989 by Jean Goss) approached Christian and Muslim religious leaders. A public inter-religious peace prayer with thousands of participants was organized during which the religious authorities affirmed together: God, Allah, is the creator of all human beings, He protects all of them and demands safeguard and dignity for each person. Encouraged by this moral support, a nonviolent action was started. People of both ethnic groups, suffering from starvation because of the unemployment, began together to plant vegetables in empty spaces near the city. Through this life-supporting work they discovered their common needs as human beings. Hatred was overcome through solidarity and new reconciled relationships could evolve.

Similar large-scale public prayer and fasting of Christians and Muslims with their leaders recently took place in Ivory Coast to avoid the atrocities of a civil war.

The efforts for a peaceful solution of the Iraq crisis are presently strongly supported by Christians, their Churches, and religious bodies in particular in the United States, Europe, and the Vatican, the Orthodox, and the World Council of Churches.

Finally all depends on our own conversion to believe in the transforming power of nonviolence as God's way to peace and that we apply it in our own life and acting. Whether or not we see an immediate result, we should remember that nothing is ever lost that is done out of the power of love. It will bear fruit one day.

CHAPTER 27

Nonviolent Skills versus Repressive Conditions: The Iranian Women's Movement and Codepink: Women for Peace

Cynthia Boaz

Woman is more fitted than man to make exploration and take bolder action in nonviolence.

—Gandhi[1]

A victory for women paves the way for democracy in Iran.

—Shirin Ebadi

Since the beginning of the 20th century, nonviolent social movements have played a key role in helping to establish more peaceful and more democratic societies in places as diverse as India, Chile, and South Africa. As students of social justice, if peace and justice are the objectives we seek, then we—as scholars, citizens, and human beings—have an obligation to pay close

The author would like to acknowledge the following individuals for their valuable insights into the Iranian Women's Movement and the dynamics of nonviolent action in the Iranian context: Elham Gheytanchi, Shaazka Beyerle, Nazanin Afshin-Jam, Ivan Marovic, Sam Sedaei, Jack DuVall, and Stephen Zunes.

attention to the means by which transitions from unjust systems or regimes take place. In any given society, the manner in which conflicts over rights and freedoms are waged has everything to do with the civic culture that subsequently emerges. Put another way, the strategically skilled activist understands that the context in which a battle takes place cannot be separated from its results. Since there is no distinction between means and ends in a society that attempts to promote or create peace and justice, it follows that a peaceful, just society can only emerge from civil resistance to the underlying oppression. Democracy can only emerge through democratic means. Because of this, whenever mass nonviolent resistance confronts injustice anywhere around the world, proponents of peace cultures have a responsibility to take an interest.

As observers relying on others' accounts of nonviolent struggles, we face a number of challenges in obtaining a nuanced understanding of the dynamics underlying resistance. This is largely because most nonviolent democracy or rights movements are frequently confronted by a tenacious conventional wisdom that can hinder an audience's perception of a movement's salience. In the field of nonviolent action (a natural home for peace scholars and advocates), it is frequently assumed that although nonviolent movements are capable of extraordinary things, there are also a number of structural conditions that must be met in order for a movement to succeed. Factors such as favorable economic conditions, ethnic and/or religious homogeneity, a history of democratic institutions, and a thriving civic culture with a good degree of political space are all widely considered by most observers of nonviolent movements to be key, if not necessary, to success.

Additionally, there is another unfortunate but equally well-established assumption regarding the repressiveness of the opponent (usually a regime) arguing for a tipping point of violence beyond which a movement can no longer be effective. This prevailing mythology—which we might appropriately call "The Tiananmen Principle" because of the extent to which it is still being used to explain the failure of the uprising in China in 1989—presumes that there is a corresponding and inverse relationship between the degree of repression used by the opponent and the ability of a movement to achieve its objectives. It's a very simple equation: as violent repression increases during a struggle, a movement's likelihood of success decreases accordingly. Typically, media coverage of a struggle at this stage will reinforce the conventional wisdom by reporting on the use of violence as an effort by the repressor to "establish normalcy" or "generate stability," as opposed to widening the lens and acknowledging both the underlying reasons for resistance and that resistance perseveres despite the violence. Together, these phenomena run the risk of undermining the morale of members of a movement and diminishing the enthusiasm behind shows of solidarity. In other words, misconceptions about the effectiveness of violence can lead to a self-fulfilling prophecy in the context of a struggle.

Correspondingly, the role of nonviolent skills—the ability of a movement and its activists to organize, create, and disseminate a message; strategize, train, and promote nonviolent discipline; and select and implement tactics— is frequently downplayed in our collective understanding of nonviolent resistance. Even today, half a century after the U.S. Civil Rights Movement, the roles that strategy and discipline played in that struggle are generally regarded as less significant than the contributions of key U.S. opinion leaders and institutions that helped usher in political change. Most American history books emphasize the roles of *Brown vs. Board of Education* (1954) and the Civil Rights Acts as the key turning points in the struggle, rather than focusing on the significant contributions of skilled, disciplined students and activists from Nashville to Montgomery to Selma. Perhaps the biggest danger of this conventional wisdom is that it presupposes that power (and therefore change) comes from the top down. But if any wisdom can be gleaned from the cases of India, Poland, South Africa, Serbia, the Philippines, and other 20th-century examples, it is that power is most accurately understood as a bottom-up phenomenon and that even in the most repressive circumstances, a nonviolent victory is possible. In every one of the cases mentioned above, observers of the struggle from both the inside and outside initially predicted failure due to unfavorable conditions. For example, conditions of extreme structural racism in South Africa and a lack of civil society in Poland prompted many to proclaim: "It could never happen here."

Their reasoning is understandable. Every group of people living under a repressive and violent set of conditions believes their situation to be unique, and in many respects they are correct. However, opponents and victims of repressive regimes also have one important thing in common, which can (and this author would argue, should) be used by movements against their opponents: Violence, as an instrument of control, has a very simple and predictable dynamic. Violence, according to Hannah Arendt, is simply a tool of control (not a force in itself) and thus only works when people obey: when security forces—or those whose job it is to carry out the orders of a repressive regime—agree to use violence against other human beings. However, as Arendt argued: "where commands are no longer obeyed, the means of violence are of no use."[2] Therefore, if a movement is skilled enough to both reduce fear on the part of its members and simultaneously transform the perspective of those responsible for using the violence against the people, the opponent will quickly discover that violence is no longer an effective means of control.

The cases above, as well as the cases that are the focus of this essay, tell us that if structural conditions were the only—or even the most important—variables in a movement's ability to achieve its goals, we would have no way to explain the success of many contemporaneous movements other than to consider those successes (as media often do) to be "accidents of history." To frame those victories as such, however, is not only inaccurate, it is irresponsible to the larger goal of advancing knowledge. A sophisticated understanding of strategy is critical to a movement's success. Unfortunately, without some understanding of the explicit links between nonviolent skills and outcomes, this knowledge is likely to be underappreciated by everyone from activists to journalists to academics.

An important counter-example to the conventional wisdom regarding this question is the case of the Iranian Women's Movement generally, and the One Million Signatures campaign specifically. If repressive structural conditions were the determining factor, the Iranian Women's Movement would never have been formed, much less have celebrated any victories. Although the movement is operating in conditions of extreme repression and a very limited amount of political space, its relative success, in comparison to other contemporary and former movements in more democratic societies, is both remarkable and instructive. In this chapter, I will give background information on both the women's movement in Iran and the U.S.-based group Codepink: Women for Peace and describe the parameters of the "skills versus conditions" debate on nonviolent action. I will then compare the strategic and tactical successes and failures of the Iranian Women's Movement to Codepink to assess whether structural conditions or nonviolent skills are the bigger contributors to the success or failure of a movement struggling for freedom or rights.

DOES REPRESSION "WORK" IN IRAN?

Over the past decade, Iran is one of several Islamic countries that has been the subject of a persistent stream of cultural stereotyping and media attention from the West.[3] Hence, it is necessary to identify and dismantle the specific misconceptions about nonviolent action in Iran to understand the movement's pervasiveness.

First, a widely held belief exists regarding tyrannies in general, and Iran in particular, that violent repression on the part of the regime is indicative of strength. However, in Iran, as with other regimes engaged in ongoing conflict with a widespread civil resistance, the use of violence should be taken as a sign of desperation.[4] When an oppressor finds itself resorting to draconian measures to suppress the voice of its own people, even as an international audience watches in horror, it is a sign that the regime believes it is facing an opponent of potentially enormous power. Violence is a last resort, even for a tyrant, because the cost of using it can be devastating to a regime's legitimacy. Hannah Arendt wrote: "In a head-on clash between violence (a state-sponsored military) and power (mass civil resistance), the outcome is hardly in doubt." But, she continues, although violence can temporarily disable the momentum of power, "it is utterly incapable of creating it."[5] Since violence is purely a destructive force, while mass civil resistance has the potential to be a creative force, each use of violence by the Islamic regime against the movement erodes the political authority of the regime, thereby strengthening the case for an alternative source of power. When martyrs are created (for example, "Neda," whose death transformed her into the face of the Green Revolution and the significance of women to that struggle), internal or external parties, previously on the sidelines, are often galvanized to action. Potentially, each time the regime represses, it undermines its own power while it simultaneously helps to recruit new members to the resistance.

A related misconception is that because we can't see the movement, it is presumed the movement no longer exists. However, to the contrary, the leadership of a strategic movement understands that mass protests and rallies are only one, albeit the most visible, tactic among a menu of options available to a nonviolent civil resistance campaign. Successful movements are able to anticipate and prepare for the inevitable brutality of a regime like the Iranian Islamic Republic. These skilled leaders adopt lower-risk actions that take individuals out of harm's way but still allow the movement to sustain both their morale and momentum. Violence itself becomes a victim of the rule of diminishing marginal returns.

NONVIOLENT SKILLS VERSUS STRUCTURAL CONDITIONS: WHICH FACTORS DETERMINE SUCCESS?

As mentioned above, an emerging theme in the literature on nonviolent action is the identification of the factors most helpful for the long-term success of a movement. These factors are typically divided into two categories: structural conditions and nonviolent skills. Structural conditions are those that potentially hinder a movement's traction (for example, ethnic divisions, cultural passivity, economic hardship) and those that promote it (such as existence of a civil society, economic stability, recent history of democracy).

According to Peter Ackerman, there are three categories of "skills" common to nonviolent movements: those that contribute to the creation and maintenance of a sustained resistance to oppressive rule, those that contribute to the movement's ability to marshal resources to engage in the widest possible menu of nonviolent tactics, and those that maximize disruption of an unjust order while maintaining nonviolent discipline.[6] In a paper for the

Oxford Conference on Civil Resistance in 2007, Ackerman emphasized the importance of understanding the role of nonviolent skills to the success or failure of a struggle. He wrote:

> I come out clearly but not exclusively in favor of the importance of skills over conditions. While this violates the conventional wisdom, I hold this view more strongly today than at any previous time during my 30 years of studying civil resistance. As the pace of change accelerates in a world with fewer boundaries on the movement of people and ideas, every form of human endeavor must adapt or falter. Those waging civil resistance are not exempt from the necessity of mastering the best practices in the form of conflict they have chosen. And regimes do not get a free pass: they too must improve their game, or they will lose.[7]

Although an emphasis on skills demands more from the observer, not to mention the activist, it also, as Ackerman noted, has the potential to shift the balance of power, actual and perceived, in a nonviolent struggle, both from the lens of the movement and the opponent. Focusing on the characteristics and "best practices" of a movement rather than exogenous conditions that cannot be altered by the movement also provides a more nuanced and precise understanding of the dynamics involved in the interactions between those doing the repressing and those resisting it.

BACKGROUND ON THE IRANIAN WOMEN'S MOVEMENT AND CODEPINK: WOMEN FOR PEACE

These two cases were chosen for their comparability in that they are both large-scale movements by women against the unjust policies of their own governments. Both groups attempt to mobilize and gain the sympathy of the general population in their societies and both claim to use only nonviolent means to achieve their ends.[8]

It is somewhat imprecise to talk about "the" Iranian Women's Movement because in fact women's rights activists and Iranian women who are human or civil rights activists are found across a number of groups and organizations that vary in their objectives, tactics, and ideology. For example, there are women-led groups in Iran that exclusively work to promote workers' rights and others that focus solely on repealing the law that calls for compulsory veiling. But although some variance is characteristic of their objectives, the groups and activists are united by one overarching goal: to achieve greater gender equality in Iran.

There is some disagreement as to the specific genesis of the contemporary Women's Movement, but it is widely understood that demands for gender equality in Iran have a rich history that stretches back at least to the Constitutional Revolution of 1910. Conventional wisdom now seems to accept that the 1979 Revolution marked a turning point in the mobilization of women for equal rights in Iran. On March 8, 1979,[9] there was a violent crackdown against nonviolent protests against both the compulsory wearing of the *hajib* and other facets of Islamic law that were widely viewed as intolerably oppressive to women, namely, the practices of polygamy and stoning. It was in the early 1980s that martyrs' wives began vocally demanding equal rights from the Islamic state. After a relative quiet among women's rights activists in the 1990s, there was a rebirth of activism in the early 2000s that was animated by several simultaneous forces: the return of international human rights activist and Nobel Peace Prize laureate Shirin Ebadi to the country (a moment that was widely seen by activists and reformers as a catalyst for potential change), growing frustration of several years of "reform" without genuine results, a widespread crackdown against student activists during which women were largely ignored, increasing contact with the international community that allowed for the emergence of a transnational dimension to the women's rights movement, and a surge of nonviolent activities and tactics being implemented by eager members of the movement that subsequently helped to embolden others on the sidelines.

Between 2005 and 2007, in response to the recent surge of activism, the women's movement came under attack by the regime. Many activists were arrested, a number were reportedly tortured, and rumors of rape by security forces were widespread. Independent media outlets were shut down for their complicity with the movement. Within the official institutions, 121 defenders of women's rights (including one male MP) were arrested and received a combined sentence of nine years for their role in supporting the movement. Additionally, more than 16,000 women were arrested by the regime for "immodest" dressing, and a new quota program was instituted to reduce the ratio of female university students to male students (women currently make up more than 60% of university students in Iran).

The result of this wave of repression targeted at women and women's rights defenders was the birth of the One Million Signatures campaign. The campaign stands out among other women-led campaigns for several reasons, including the breadth of its appeal and its longevity. One Million Signatures was started in mid-2006 as an effort to acquire a million signatures on a petition to the Iranian Islamic Republic demanding that it acknowledge the equal status of women under the law. In the more than three years since its birth, numerous activists linked, or in some cases, simply rumored to be linked, to the One Million Signatures campaign, including Esha Momeni, a graduate student at the University of Southern California, have been arrested, detained, jailed, lashed, and otherwise persecuted for their connection to the campaign. The campaign is known to be active in at least 16 of Iran's 30 provinces. Its advocates include Iranians from all demographics including men and, in a few cases, prominent clerics such as reformist Ayatollah Yousaf Sanei.

The campaign's demands are very straightforward. Although activists have parsed the message into more specific aims such as "identifying women's needs and priorities" and "promoting democratic action," the overriding demand is gender equality for women.[10] In the context of the Iranian Islamic Republic, this demand resonates across virtually all of the social demographics because of the inherent implication that *fiqh* and *Shia* law struggle with internal contradictions over the issue of women's rights. Those sources of law make public claims to promote the rights and needs of women, yet engage in policies and practices that diminish the equality and quality of life under the law in Iran. The One Million Signatures campaign is explicitly clear that their demands are not in opposition to Islam but, to the contrary, are an attempt to force the regime to close the gap between the Islamic ideal and the reality.

On the other side of the world exists another women-initiated and women-led social justice organization named Codepink: Women for Peace. Codepink was formed in the United States in late 2002 in response to the Bush/Cheney administration's War on Terrorism and resulting policies. The original objective of the group was to stop the invasion of Iraq. When that goal was not manifested, the group reorganized its mission from a relatively specific anti-war message to a much broader spectrum of social justice issues. The name "Codepink" is a somewhat tongue-in-cheek reference to the Bush administration's color-coded terror alert system, and members of the organization often reference the group's desire to "wage pink for peace." Codepink activists are well known for the implementation of creative, high-visibility, and occasionally outrageous tactics, many of which draw on the sexuality of the dominant membership.[11] Although Codepink has chapters in approximately a dozen countries, the bulk of its activities are concentrated in the United States. As of this writing, the group's national Web site is listing 15 priority campaigns that include a diverse array of issue areas such as Gaza, women's rights in Afghanistan, economic recovery and health care, and environmental concerns. Additionally at the local level, chapters are encouraged to create campaigns around community issues, which means that the actual number of Codepink campaigns being implemented at any given time is virtually unknowable.

A glance at the regimes and larger cultural contexts in which these two movements in Iran and the United States respectively operate is instructive in understanding the assumptions made by the structural conditions argument. Because of the relative degree of political space, economic stability,

and overall wealth; secularism (a reasonable proxy for ethnic/religious homogeneity); a thriving civil society; and a long history of experience with
democracy in the United States, reliance on the predictive capacity of structural conditions would produce an expectation of few, if any, victories for
the women's movement in Iran on the one hand and significant potential
for victories by Codepink in the United States on the other. This hypothesis
deserves closer examination.

CONDITIONS AND SKILLS IN IRAN AND THE UNITED STATES

To effectively evaluate the relative successes of the One Million Signatures campaign versus Codepink: Women for Peace, I will consider the two
areas of analysis—structural conditions and nonviolent skills—as collec-
tions of variables. The structural conditions category is comprised of several factors including a society's economic situation, the degree of the
society's ethnic, racial, and religious homogeneity, the prevalent cultural
norms, and to what degree there exists a healthy, vibrant civil society
allowing political space for individuals and groups. The repressiveness of
the opponent is also considered a structural condition.

The nonviolent skills category is likewise comprised of several factors,
including the degree of unity among both the movement's leadership and of
its stated goals, the capacity of the movement to marshal resources, the ability of the movement to identify and target its opponent's weaknesses, and
the degree to which the movement is able to maintain nonviolent discipline.

On the question of cultural conditions, in Iran, there are a number of political, social, economic, and legal constraints on the ability of citizens to engage
openly in civil society activities. These constraints apply to women particularly. For example, women are prohibited from engaging in social activities
such as attending soccer games and singing in public. In courts of law, wom-
en's testimony is valued as half of men's. For example, it takes two women
witnesses to counter the testimony of one male witness. Additionally, women
are compelled to seek and receive permission from males (husbands, fathers,
or brothers) for a number of activities, including marriage. There is also
structural inequality in that there is no sanction prohibiting institutional
gender discrimination. Chillingly, some still tolerate honor killings, domestic
violence, and even the occasional stoning of women who've been accused of
crimes such as adultery. And politically, while Iran appears to be relatively
progressive among Islamic theocracies, in that women have the right to vote,
a reasonably high literacy rate at 70 percent, and make up the majority of
university students at more than 60 percent, it is forbidden for women to

serve as regime president, as Supreme Leader, on the assembly of experts, or even as a judge.

In contrast, the structural conditions in the United States are closer to the ideal. There is an open, thriving civil society with a significant degree of political space in which groups may operate. Cultural norms (in spirit, if not always in practice) reflect a strong emphasis on values such as participation, dialogue, and political tolerance. Also, the relative wealth and economic stability of the United States and the presence of a rule of law[12] help moderate public passion and opinion and make the act of engaging in nonviolent resistance against authorities less risky. In principle, democratic society generally, and American democracy specifically, is characterized by a series of institutional mechanisms through which citizens can process grievances and actualize the notion of democracy as people power. Additionally, from the lens of a women's rights organization, Codepink also has the advantage of functioning in an environment where there is legal and political equality between the sexes. One could argue that there is no place where systemic changes are potentially more responsive to the strategies of nonviolent struggle than the United States.

In terms of results, however, Codepink in the United States has seen far fewer successes (in both the relative and absolute senses) than the Iranian Women's Movement. Although they have been in existence for nearly seven years, there are very few campaigns over which Codepink has been able to claim victory.

One explanation for the difference is tactical. The women's movement in Iran has been clever about using "dilemma actions" against the regime. A dilemma action puts the opponent in the unwelcome position of having to choose between two bad options, either of which the movement can claim as a victory. For example, during a 2006 World Cup qualifying match at Tehran University, a large group of women staged a sit-in at the stadium (recall that women are forbidden under *fiqh* law from attending public events). A few of the women actually managed to break through the stadium barricades and get into the bleachers, where they were captured on film by the BBC and other international media. This put the regime into the position of having to choose between forcibly removing the women, which would diminish the regime's political legitimacy in the eyes of the international audience, or allowing them to stay, which would diminish the regime's moral authority in the eyes of its own more devout citizens. Ultimately, Ahmadinejad had the women removed, but also subsequently had the policy changed. Although his public justification was sexist, as he argued that the presence of women at the stadiums would keep the matches cleaner and more civil, it was also a clear-cut victory for the women of Iran.[13]

Additionally, the movement has shown skill and tactical innovation in its use of blogging, international coalition-building, and their ability to come up with low-risk, low-visibility, but high-impact actions such as asking women to push the *hajib* a few inches back on their head as a statement against the regime's policy. The tactic is effective because it is very low-risk in that it comes with a high degree of plausible deniability, but when applied *en masse*, has a powerful symbolic effect, especially in emboldening members of the movement itself. The movement has also been strategic in publicly claiming each victory and keeping their Web site and network updated with stories of those successes.

Repression and violence are only effective when people fear them. As the events of the Green Revolution and since have demonstrated, the Iranian regime should no longer assume that the threat of violence will permit them to "restore normalcy" in a context where people have collectively withdrawn their consent for the ruling elite and where resistance goes on despite the threat of brutal repression. In fact, Iranian Nobel Laureate and international human rights advocate Shirin Ebadi asserts, each act of repression now serves as a recruitment tool for the movement in Iran. "I do not agree that repression can lead to the death of the movement," says Ebadi. "For every woman arrested, 10 more replace them. If the foundations [of a strategic movement] are laid correctly," argues Ebadi, "repression makes a movement stronger."[14]

In contrast, the leadership of Codepink has been arguably less strategic in their choice of tactics. Although they generally implement high-visibility actions (such as staging a loud protest during a congressional hearing in the hope of disrupting the proceedings), the tactics of Codepink tend to alienate, rather than win the sympathy of, the larger audience. Even the most politically progressive public officials have reached their saturation point with Codepink's tactics. The following is excerpted from an article that appeared on *Salon.com* in March 2009 in reference to the events at the congressional hearings for AIG, which at the time was under investigation for fraud and misuse of stockholder funds:

> By now, the anti-war group's ritual appearances [at congressional hearings] have evolved into a fairly predictable—and, frankly, fairly boring—cycle. They show up (dressed in pink, natch), make some noise for a bit, then get kicked out. There are sitcoms that are more spontaneous.
>
> [Rep. Barney Frank, arguably the most liberal member of the House of Representatives] was forced to stop Geithner's opening statement to address the protesters, and he made it clear how he felt. "Will you please act your age back there? Stop playing with that sign. If you have no greater powers of concentration, then you leave the room," the congressman said. "We're trying to have a serious discussion which will

include, as you understand, a lot of criticism. We really need people to grow up."

Finally, the congressman offered Codepink members a solid bit of political wisdom: "I do not know how you think you advance any cause to which you might be attached by this kind of silliness."[15]

Representative Frank's comments seem to reflect a larger reality about the inability of Codepink's leadership to strategically adapt their tactics to maximize the structural conditions in which they operate. In contrast to the relative successes in Iran, where the One Million Signatures campaign has achieved transnational status and the Women's Movement has effectively forced the hand of the regime on many issues (and who was—not insignificantly—a major component of the Green Revolution uprising in the summer of 2009), Codepink appears strategically and tactically unimpressive.

In terms of specific strategic and tactical weaknesses that reflect a less refined set of skills, Codepink is relatively incoherent in their messaging and demands. With dozens of campaigns ongoing, it is not clear to the membership where to focus their energy and attention. Additionally, while the actions are provocative, they appear to be short-term and mostly *ad hoc*, rather than systematic parts of a long-term strategic plan. There is also arguably a failure to adapt by Codepink. After the 2006 congressional elections in which the Democratic Party won back the majorities in both the Senate and the House of Representatives, there was an opportunity for social justice groups like Codepink to engage in a more strategic targeting of Democrats in power; however, the overwhelming majority of their actions continued to focus on the Bush/Cheney presidential administration.[16]

Most significantly perhaps is Codepink's general lack of unity over multiple areas of organization and content. For example, regarding membership, there is still disagreement between key members of the group's leadership as to whether and to what degree men are permitted to participate in the group. On the questions of objectives and vision, there is no set of clear, precise demands, but rather a long list of somewhat vague goals embedded in broad symbolic messages. Taking the view of a policy maker, it is unclear precisely what Codepink would like to see happen on any particular issue or policy. In terms of media and communications, there is (in stark contrast to the One Million Signatures campaign, which has demonstrated exceptional adeptness in this category) a lack of message coordination between the various chapters' leadership and the national leadership as to the group's major priorities. From the lens of media messaging, the group's messages appear to be often disjointed and even inconsistent. And perhaps most disturbingly, Codepink has been unable (or perhaps unwilling) to maintain strict nonviolent discipline in the implementation of its tactics. The use of psychologically violent images and slogans and frequent use of intimidating tactics is concerning from both a principled and pragmatic nonviolence standpoint. Strategically, it would seem that the women of Codepink have some things to learn from the women of the One Million Signatures campaign.

CONCLUSIONS

In Iran, although there has been significant repression and backlash against the Women's Movement since 2005, there is also evidence of its efficacy. The movement's strategy of responding to repression by adapting a more defensive and strength-building approach has resulted in more legitimacy for the movement and its objectives.

For Codepink, in the United States, the structural conditions could hardly be more ideal, but these conditions do not guarantee the success of a movement or its campaigns. Codepink's tactics are creative, and the group has shown enormous cleverness in coming up with symbols and slogans (and by extension, a recognizable brand), but there are simply too many campaigns going on simultaneously. Furthermore, Codepink lacks a unifying message and unity among the leadership on several organizational issues, including of whom the membership demographic should consist. The preceding shortcomings have resulted in fatigue on the part of the members and redundancy in the campaigns and tactics, which has the consequence of undermining the legitimacy of both the group and its objectives.

These two cases highlight the critical nature of long-term strategy and planning and the cultivation of nonviolent skills and capacities to the success of a movement, and demonstrate that, even under ideal conditions, failure is still an option. Seen side by side, the cases of Iran and Codepink provide support for the hypothesis that there are no structural conditions that themselves are sufficient to produce success, and conversely, that even under conditions of severe repression, there can be successes. This suggests support for the corollary hypothesis that there are no structural conditions—even severe repression—that are themselves prohibitive to the success of a nonviolent movement.

Recently, Stephan and Chenoweth produced a study that provided powerful empirical support for the argument that violent movements are significantly less likely to achieve their objectives than strategic nonviolent movements.[17] So not only is the continued under-emphasis on nonviolent skills by scholars, activists, and journalists less precise and more likely to produce erroneous conclusions, but in practice—as scholars and advocates of nonviolence and peace cultures—we have a demonstrated incentive to refine and evolve our knowledge of strategic nonviolent action and the skills that accompany it.

NOTES

1. Joshi, 1998.

2. Arendt, 1969.

3. Although this unfortunate trend did not begin with George W. Bush's identification of Iran as a member of the "axis of evil" in his State of the Union address in 2002, that speech undoubtedly served to consolidate the already pervasive misconceptions held by Western publics.

4. For an earlier version of these observations, see Boaz, 2009.

5. Arendt.

6. Ackerman, 2007.

7. Ackerman, 3.

8. This author has some reservations about the claim that Codepink is strictly a nonviolent movement. Several of the commonly used actions, including what is known as a "die-in," are intended to apply a form of psychological violence to the target (and by extension, the general audience) in the hopes of provoking a response. Of course, Codepink is hardly the only social justice group to use psychologically violent tactics, and the approach (and assumption that this category of violence is somehow less violent) is also frequently seen on the right. Anti-abortion protestors who force images of aborted fetuses on passers-by is another example.

9. March 8th is now celebrated globally as International Women's Day.

10. Change for Equality.

11. For example, it was common to see Codepink members at anti-war rallies between 2003 and 2006 wearing a provocative women's garment (such as a slip) with phrases written across them in bold lettering. One seen at the September 2005 rally and march in Washington, D.C., pronounced "NO PEACE, NO PU**Y!"

12. I recognize that this is a contentious statement in the context of the post-Bush/Cheney environment and in the era of the Patriot Act and other policies that both restricted individual rights in the United States and created new and more profound political divisions. That being said, despite the arguably profound regression of democracy during the presidency of George W. Bush, the United States is still significantly more free and open than Iran in every category where structural conditions are thought to matter.

13. Unsurprisingly, the Guardian Council later overruled this decision, but it is still considered a victory by the movement.

14. Personal communication. Author's interview with Shirin Ebadi, Naropa University, Boulder, CO, October 9, 2009.

15. Koppelman, 2009.

16. Codepink did target a few individual Democrats, namely, Senator Hillary Clinton, during this time, but it was not part of a coordinated strategy.

17. Stephan and Chenoweth, 2008.

CHAPTER 28

THE 1991 GULF WAR AND AFTERMATH

Stephen Zunes

A little more than a decade prior to the massive mobilization against the U.S. invasion of Iraq, an anti-war movement struggled to prevent the first war against Iraq. This relatively brief and decisive war, launched in January 1991, was far more popular among the American public than the invasion and occupation begun in 2003, and it seemed to marginalize the anti-war movement, thereby making it difficult during the subsequent years to stop the United States from launching two wars in the greater Middle East in the aftermath of the 9/11 tragedy.

There were a number of factors that made the peace movement appear weak and lacking popular support at the time of the Gulf War—a highly effective propaganda barrage by the first Bush administration, the censorship of the press at the war front, the deliberate falsification of reports from the battlefield to exaggerate military successes and underestimate civilian casualties, the low number of American casualties, the short duration of the war, and the nefarious nature of the Iraqi regime. Many Americans were uncomfortable opposing the government in wartime. In addition, the media

This article is an updated revision of an earlier article by the same author that appeared in *Arab Studies Quarterly*.

played largely a cheerleading role, with opponents of the war—including Middle Eastern experts—largely ignored as analysts and notably absent from network talk shows. Pro-war sentiment was stage-managed from the highest level and was no match for an underfunded grassroots movement.

WEAKNESSES OF THE ANTI-WAR MOVEMENT

There were also some serious errors that cost the peace movement some support: One was the fact that peace activists largely shared with most Americans a profound ignorance of the Middle East, Islam, and the Arab world. For example, during the months preceding the outbreak of hostilities, *Time* observed that "The public response resembles a massive cram session, as earnest people try to understand the complex forces at work and calculate the potential costs, human and material, of going to war."[1]

One result was a series of tactical errors: for example, many anti-war activists focused on the precedent of Vietnam, despite great differences in the two situations. As with the old adage about generals, anti-war activists also tend to fight the last war, often ignoring the unique aspects of an unfolding crisis. For example, Vietnam did not have the capability of threatening large populations beyond their borders, as did Iraq; thereby the Bush Administration could raise a more credible—though still questionable—specter of further aggression.[2] In Vietnam, the United States fought a popular nationalist struggle utilizing guerrilla warfare in a mountainous jungle terrain. The ground offensive by U.S. forces in the Gulf War was in a flat desert area against a conventional army in a territory that was either uninhabited or inhabited by an occupied population supportive of their liberation by U.S. forces. Another error came in emphasizing the potential of large American casualties in an era when the high-tech equipment of American forces allowed for "kill ratios" so favorable to allied forces. Indeed, the lack of American casualties proved the movement's undoing. Historically, what has traditionally turned Americans against wars have been high U.S. casualties, particularly with no victory in sight. Total U.S. combat deaths in the Gulf War were less than 150 and there was little question that the war would be over within weeks.

Still another problem came with the peace movement's late start in opposing the preparation for war. The initial deployment of troops to Saudi Arabia, which began in August 1990 soon after the Iraqi invasion and occupation of Kuwait, involved the pre-positioning of hundreds of thousands of U.S. forces in preparation for an offensive military operation. However, this deployment—labeled Operation Desert Shield—was portrayed as a defensive operation against possible further Iraqi aggression. Though some critics raised questions regarding the apparent absence of any real Iraqi threat to

Saudi Arabia, and how the buildup of foreign troops on Iraq's border resulted in hardening the position of Iraqi dictator Saddam Hussein, the deployment received near-universal support from the Democratic-controlled Congress as well as from such progressive political figures as the Reverends Jesse Jackson and William Sloane Coffin, leftist intellectual Todd Gitlin, and socialist Congressman Bernie Sanders. Outside of some traditional pacifist groups, such as the Fellowship of Reconciliation, the anti-war movement did not respond, in large part, until November, when the Bush Administration went public with its intention to launch a war.

Many peace activists also fell into unfairly stereotyping the Kuwaitis as primarily a group of oil-rich sheiks not worthy of concern. Actually, most rich Kuwaitis fled south the day of the invasion. Those who suffered the most under the Iraqi occupation were the less well-off Kuwaitis who stayed behind as well as the large numbers of Palestinian and other foreign workers. Peace activists also tended to ignore the fact that, though the Sabah dynasty had many faults, Kuwait had made more advances toward political pluralism than any other country in the Gulf region and that the human rights situation under the Iraqi occupation was qualitatively worse than what was experienced under the monarchy. Some peace activists blithely accepted the Baghdad government's myth that Kuwait was historically part of Iraq. Indeed, given the propensity of the U.S. government in the preceding years to mislead the American public regarding the nature of the Sandinista government of Nicaragua and other Third World adversaries of the U.S. government, many peace activists were understandably skeptical about the reports of atrocities by the Iraqi government or of its totalitarian nature. In this case, however, despite occasional hyperbole,[3] most of these reports were true.

There were also some cases of Israel-bashing, with some war opponents even going as far as insisting that Israel was the cause of the conflict and that it was the pro-Israel lobby that led to the U.S. decision to launch the war. Though many criticisms of Israeli government policies and U.S. support for the Israeli occupation were and are valid, the United States had its own reasons for fighting the Gulf War, regardless of what Israel's right-wing leadership saw as being to their benefit. American interests in the region's oil and the establishment of a permanent military presence predate the establishment of modern Israel. And the decision to go to war in this case was far beyond the reach of any single lobbying group, no matter how influential. The U.S. refusal to consider Iraqi demands to link Kuwait's freedom from Iraqi occupation to Palestine's freedom from Israeli occupation came not as a result of Israeli pressure, but because the United States has traditionally supported allies such as Morocco, Indonesia, or Israel in their occupation and suppression of weaker neighbors if they feared independence by the captive nation could be potentially destabilizing to the region. The U.S. refusal to consider Iraq's offer for the establishment of a nuclear weapons-free zone in the Middle East was not because of Israel's unwillingness to eliminate its nuclear arsenal and thereby forfeit its nuclear monopoly, but because the United States has generally opposed the establishment of nuclear-free zones anywhere. It is also noteworthy that the majority of Jewish members of Congress voted against the war, which is more than can be said for its Christian members.

Some far-right groups, including the Liberty Lobby, the John Birch Society, followers of Lyndon LaRouche, and independent rightists known for paranoid conspiracy theories joined in with anti-war efforts, and were at times allowed into coalition efforts by those unaware of their anti-Semitic and far-right ideologies. (The LaRouche Movement had actually developed close ties with the Iraq's Ba'ath party, with which it shares an essentially fascist ideology.)[4] Not surprisingly, such alliances harmed the credibility of the peace movement.

There were also serious divisions within the left. Some prominent figures of the American left actually supported the war.[5] More seriously, however, were divisions within the anti-war movement itself. Two coalitions organized separate national demonstrations in Washington, D.C., on two separate dates in late January 1991, after the war was under way. The primary differences revolved around the preferred date of the rally as well as on the question as to whether to condemn Iraq's invasion and occupation of Kuwait along with the U.S-led war. Arguing that Iraqi aggression was not the cause, but the excuse, for U.S. intervention, the more radical of the two coalitions, which organized the January 19 rally, argued that any denunciation of Iraq would confuse the issue. Supporters of the January 26 rally, led by a coalition of over 400 more moderate progressive organizations, pacifist and other peace groups, and church-related organizations stressed the importance of taking a principled—as well as more politically acceptable— position condemning both Iraqi and American actions.

Despite these problems, however, the anti-war movement showed some real strengths as well.

STRENGTHS OF THE ANTI-WAR MOVEMENT

One interesting aspect of the anti-war movement was its popular appeal in areas not usually known as strongholds of dissident politics in recent decades.[6] Some of the most widespread opposition was in the West and Midwest, where anti-war sentiment was strongest prior to the Cold War in the first half of the 20th century. Unlike during the Vietnam War, it was not hippies versus hardhats or one generation against another; indeed, the strongest anti-war sentiment was among the elderly and a far lesser proportion of the movement was made up of students. In addition, intellectuals were behind, rather than ahead, of public opinion regarding opposition to the war. Since the armed forces had a disproportionate number of people from lower-income backgrounds, students at the less prestigious universities were more likely to know someone at risk and thus more likely to oppose the conflict. One reason that the national media coverage understated the strength of anti-war sentiment was that they tended to look primarily at elite campuses and leftist white male intellectuals, and concluded that opposition was weak. Yet a decentralized populist movement organized at the grassroots, often spontaneous and improvised without sophisticated media outreach efforts, was in evidence throughout the country.

Despite President George Bush's claim that there was "no anti-war movement" opposing the Gulf War, hundreds of thousands of people mobilized across the country in the three months before and during the war in opposition, more than during the first three years of major U.S. combat in Vietnam. The movement was overwhelmingly nonviolent and practiced an impressive degree of internal democracy. Unlike a tiny and irresponsible fringe of the anti-Vietnam War movement, anger was reserved for the policy makers, not the individual soldiers. Unlike any previous American wars, large-scale opposition began prior to the first shot being fired. The movement was inter-generational, with new activists on the campuses joining those who had fought for peace and social justice for decades. The large gap in attitudes toward the war between men and women detected in public opinion polls stimulated a growing understanding of the role of patriarchy in war making and encouraged more leadership by women in the movement.

Although it was less visible in the national demonstrations, there was impressive anti-war organizing among minority communities in both urban areas and in the rural South. Virtually all African American denominations came out against the war, in contrast to the noted lack of support among much of the black leadership of Martin Luther King's outspoken opposition to the Vietnam War. A weak economy meant that the economic consequences of the war were more apparent to those who bore the brunt of its effects, leading to greater participation and leadership by people of color, who were particularly disturbed at the disproportionate representation of minorities on the front lines.

Unlike movements concerned with Central America and Vietnam—where there was some sympathy for the other side among many peace activists—there was no sympathy for Saddam Hussein or his aggression against Kuwait. This resulted in perhaps the most genuinely anti-war movement the country had seen up to that time; there was no ideological agenda inspiring the protests. There was no draft, so people did not oppose the war out of concern over the prospects of being forced to participate in the fighting. There was a lot of popular support for the war, so it was certainly not fashionable to oppose it. The movement represented a very deep sense that, on both pragmatic and moral grounds, there were reasons to question war as the answer.

In a dramatic shift from the 1960s, the peace movement had support immediately prior to the war from key segments of organized labor. Nine major unions, representing 6 million workers, announced their opposition in early January, prior to the outbreak of the war, a major departure from the widespread support by union leaders of the war in Vietnam.[7] Hundreds of district offices from other unions also announced their opposition, often citing the disproportionate number of children of the working class in uniform.[8]

The opposition to the war by the majority of major Christian denominations was significant. Citing "just war" teachings, religious leaders observed how the Gulf War did not meet the criteria of "last resort" or "proportionality." Every major mainline religious denomination in the country went on record opposing the war as morally unjustifiable and supported continuing sanctions. An overwhelming majority of the 300 bishops at the National Conference of Catholic Bishops supported a resolution against the war as morally wrong; by contrast, the Catholic leadership did not publicly oppose the Vietnam War until 1971.[9] Eighteen prominent church leaders issued an anti-war statement that appeared in the *New York Times* in early January.[10] Churches in several cities declared themselves sanctuaries for war resisters. The great division in public opinion prior to the war was all the more remarkable given that, while there were certainly strong arguments against the use of massive military force against Iraq, the case for the war was stronger than any U.S. intervention since World War II (the U.S. government was responding to a clear-cut case of aggression by a ruthless dictator in a region where the United States had vital interests, the United States had the support of the United Nations Security Council to use force in liberating Kuwait, the president had received an effective declaration of war by Congress, and there was little risk of a nuclear exchange).

The censorship of media reports from the battle area, the threats and harassment against activists, and the enormous propaganda machinery mobilized to support U.S. policy were all predictable responses to a serious popular challenge to the war-making power of the U.S. government. If the peace movement had not posed a serious challenge to U.S. policy, the Bush Administration and its supporters would not have gone to such extraordinary efforts to counter it. As a result, there are many reasons to believe that anti-war sentiment was seen by those in positions of political power as a force with which to be reckoned.

THE DEFEAT OF THE PEACE MOVEMENT

Public opinion polls indicated that support of the war was "a mile wide and an inch deep"—people wanted to believe the government was right, even if on further reflection of the facts, many came out in opposition. Such further reflection was difficult, however, since they received only heavily censored news from the war front and a propaganda barrage from the government and media. Meanwhile, in Washington, even liberal Democrats went along with the policy once the war started, showing the same moral cowardice they did during much of the Vietnam War and would subsequently in supporting the U.S. invasion of Iraq. The fact that the war was successful militarily made it all the more difficult to question whether it was right.

Todd Gitlin, a University of California sociologist and former leader of Students for a Democratic Society, has observed that there are three conditions necessary for dissent to have an effective impact:

> Number 1, the elites have to divide. Number 2, people have to feel there's a politically convincing alternative. Number 3, people have to feel the war is going badly on its own terms. Because Americans love a winner. And, by the same token, are squeamish about a loser.

The first two conditions existed between President Bush's November 8 announcement of a buildup for offensive military action and the start of the bombing on January 16. But once the war began, Gitlin observed, "these two conditions evaporated overnight. The choice wasn't no war or war anymore. . . . The elites lined up for the war."[11] Americans tend to be notoriously impatient with U.S. military intervention. Wars that drag on with no end in sight, such as Vietnam, Lebanon, Somalia, or the current wars in Iraq and Afghanistan, become unpopular. Those that are quick and decisive, such as the 1989 invasion of Panama, the 1983 invasion of Grenada, the bombings of Libya during the intervening years, and the Gulf War, receive overwhelming popular support.

After the large demonstrations in Washington, the anti-war movement focused on teach-ins and other community education efforts. However, by this time, most Americans were either enthused at or resigned to the fact that the U.S. government would prosecute the war as it saw fit regardless of public opinion. The February 21 campus days of protests were widespread but sparsely attended, reflecting the burn-out and frustration of war opponents. The widespread civil disobedience in the initial days of the war became seen increasingly as excessive and inappropriate. Saddam Hussein's public announcements praising the anti-war movement further harmed its credibility. By the end of the second week of the war, a *Wall Street Journal*/NBC poll asked respondents "Have you gained respect for anti-war demonstrators, lost respect, or is your opinion unchanged?" Sixty percent said they had lost respect, while only 11 percent said they had gained respect.[12]

POST-WAR ISSUES

Though the traditional pacifist groups, such as the Fellowship of Reconciliation and the American Friends Service Committee, continued to address the situation in Iraq—particularly the devastating humanitarian crises resulting from the war and the ongoing sanctions—such efforts failed to mobilize much popular support. The leftist group International ANSWER also played a major leadership role opposing U.S. policy during the interwar period, but the effective control of the organization by the Trotskyist Workers World Party limited the scope of its appeal.

While the initial popular outcry against the slaughter of Iraqi Kurds by the Baghdad regime in response to the post-war uprising in March of 1991 resulted in the U.S.-led humanitarian effort known as Operation Provide Comfort and the establishment of UN-sponsored safe areas, there was little opposition to the open U.S. backing of subsequent Turkish repression of its own Kurdish minority or incursions into the UN safe areas. Similarly, periodic bombing raids by the U.S. air force in Iraq in the dozen years leading up to the 2003 invasion met with little organized opposition. Opposition to the Clinton administration's preparation for a major bombing campaign against Iraq in 1998 did lead to some protests, such as the nationally televised disruption of a "town hall meeting" at Ohio State University in which Secretary of State Madeleine Albright and other administration officials tried to make the case for resuming military action. Despite this, there was widespread congressional support for the four-day bombing campaign in December of that year known as Operation Desert Fox. With a Democratic president facing off against impeachment efforts of dubious merit by right-wing Republicans, many liberal activists were reluctant to denounce President Bill Clinton for this illegal and counterproductive act of aggression.

The Gulf War highlighted other problems with U.S. Middle East policy and the failure of the peace movement to address them.

Although peace and human rights activists had made U.S. support of undemocratic governments in Latin America and Southeast Asia more difficult politically, there had been little domestic opposition to U.S. support of similar rulers in the Middle East outside of concern over these countries' (often exaggerated) potential threat to Israel. The United States has provided well over $120 billion in arms to the Middle East since the Gulf War, a full 80 percent of the arms going into the region, and virtually all of it going to regimes that engaged in gross and systematic human rights violations. Public opinion polls in the United States have long indicated widespread and growing opposition to the high levels of arms transfers to the Middle East, yet this continued to be a low priority for peace activists.

The Clinton administration, which came into office less than two years after the Gulf War, continued pursuing the militaristic policies of previous administrations, including arms transfers and other support to repressive Arab regimes and unconditional support for the Israeli occupation. Such policies, along with the egregious humanitarian consequences of ongoing sanctions against Iraq and the permanent stationing of U.S. forces in the Gulf region, were among the grievances cited by Osama bin Laden and other Al-Qaeda leaders at the time of the 9/11 attacks.

Despite the moral bankruptcy and counterproductive strategic value of such policies in the aftermath of the Gulf War, there were no demonstrations with tens of thousands of people in Washington, no major sit-ins at congressional offices, few folk singers and other cultural workers who addressed the issue, and few other activities indicative of a popular mobilization. There was nothing comparable to protests waged against the U.S. policies toward Central America or Southern Africa during the previous decade. Had the peace movement continued to be engaged in the months and years following the Gulf War addressing these issues to a sufficient degree to change U.S. policy, the 9/11 tragedy and subsequent wars might have been prevented.

The failure to do so was not just a reflection of the moribund state of the peace movement in the post–Gulf War and post–Cold War period. Even during peak periods of the peace movement in the 1980s, when the Reagan administration was supporting such controversial Israeli actions as the invasion of Lebanon and suppression of the first intifada, the peace movement failed to launch major mobilizations. Nor was there much activity in opposition to U.S. support of Morocco's conquest and occupation of Western Sahara and the dramatic increase in military aid to the autocratic Gulf monarchies. Such a reaction, or lack thereof, was indicative of some larger problems that the American peace movement has had historically in addressing Middle Eastern issues.

At the root of the confusion of the American peace movement on the Middle East has been the issue of Israel and Palestine.

ADDRESSING ISRAEL/PALESTINE

Though the Israeli-Palestinian conflict never affected American peace activists with the same sense of urgency that came with direct large-scale U.S. military involvement as in the Gulf War, it has long been recognized that the

United States has played a direct role in exacerbating the conflict though its contradictory role as chief mediator and the principal military, economic, and diplomatic supporter of the occupying power. Despite this, up through the 1990s, the peace movement had done little to challenge U.S. policy.

As with the major peace issues of the 1980s—the nuclear freeze and U.S. intervention in Central America—the peace movement's support of an end of the Israeli occupation and the establishment of a Palestinian state alongside Israel has been backed by a majority of Americans, including most American Jews. Opinion polls showed considerable support for a two-state solution long before the U.S. government formally adopted such a position in 2004. Sizable majorities also supported linking U.S. military and economic aid to both Israel and Arab states to human rights concerns. Very few prominent American political figures supported such progressive positions at the time of the Gulf War, however.

The first major peace group to directly address the Arab-Israeli conflict was the American Friends Service Committee, beginning in the early 1970s, which emphasized the need for an end to the Israeli occupation and the recognition of both Israeli and Palestinian national rights, a position soon embraced by other pacifist groups, such as the War Resisters League and the Fellowship of Reconciliation. By the 1980s, a wider array of peace groups, such as SANE/Freeze and the Mobilization for Survival, were adopting similar positions, though the AFSC was the only organization to make the Middle East a major focus of its program work. A number of smaller organizations, focused specifically on the Middle East but allied in their approach with the broader peace movement, came into being during this period. Several liberal Christian, Jewish, and Arab-American groups also began to advocate positions that similarly supported the national rights of both Palestinians and Israelis to self-determination and for direct negotiations between the major parties to the conflict.

During the late 1980s, activist groups placed popular referenda on the ballot in several jurisdictions calling for the recognition of a Palestinian state alongside Israel. These were part of the use of voter initiatives during this period to mobilize support for other progressive causes, such as the nuclear freeze, reductions in military spending, an end to U.S. intervention in Central America, and sanctions against South Africa. To a greater degree than these other efforts, however, the organized opposition was stronger, better financed, and received the backing of a broad spectrum of elected officials. As a result, most of these initiatives failed, even in progressive urban areas as San Francisco. Across the bay in the university town of Berkeley— which had established sister city relationships with a black South African township, a Nicaraguan city, and a town in a guerrilla-controlled section of

El Salvador—an initiative to establish a similar relationship with a Palestinian refugee camp was soundly defeated.

Another effort involved efforts to influence the Democratic Party platform. At the 1988 Democratic convention, a minority plank was proposed calling for a two-state solution, with the language taken directly from a 1985 *New York Times* ad by dozens of prominent liberal Jews, but Democratic party leaders refused to allow it to even come for a vote. There were a series of battles at several state conventions in subsequent years, some of which were successful, but all of which were eventually overturned as a result of efforts by party leaders and powerful special interest groups.

Despite this increased concern over Middle Eastern issues, some peace groups, particularly those involved in the electoral arena, continued to refuse to support pro-peace positions. For example, from its founding in 1973 until its demise in 1988, the Coalition for a New Foreign Policy was the peace movement's leading lobbying group on Capitol Hill. However, they consistently refused to address the issues of Palestinian rights or U.S. aid to Israel. A 1981 Coalition statement re-affirmed the group's support of the "sovereignty, territorial integrity, and political independence" of Middle Eastern states, but explicitly stated that this principle "does not necessarily apply" to lands seized by Israel in the 1967 war. The Coalition also refused to include Israel in their normally strict standards of linking human rights and nuclear non-proliferation issues with U.S. military aid.[13]

Similarly, Gretchen Eick, a former Coalition leader who became leader of National Impact, a progressive lobbying coalition that claimed to provide "leadership of peace and justice issues," declared soon after the group's founding that they also considered the Israeli-Palestinian conflict "off limits."[14] The Human Rights Political Action Committee, which raised funds for candidates based on their support of a human rights agenda in U.S. foreign policy, also made an exception regarding Israel.

A number of former peace activists who subsequently held electoral office became outspoken defenders of Israeli militarism, even supporting Israel's devastating 1982 invasion of Lebanon. As hundreds of thousands of Israelis demonstrated against the war, California State Assemblyman and former anti-Vietnam War leader Tom Hayden toured Israeli-occupied sections of Lebanon with his wife, actress/activist Jane Fonda, and both praised the massive Israeli assault.[15] Similarly, Washington Mayor Marion Barry, a former leader in the Student Nonviolent Coordinating Committee, spoke at a rally sponsored by the city's right-wing Jewish groups in support of the invasion.

In return for getting Arab support for the Gulf War, President Bush organized a peace conference in Madrid in the fall of 1991, yet opposition to Palestinian statehood and the refusal to demand a withdrawal of Israeli occupation forces from Arab lands continued. Separate talks in Norway led to the signing of the Oslo Accords two years later, but the United States, as guarantor of the talks, was still unwilling to push Israel to make the necessary compromises for peace, and the peace movement was not strong enough or focused enough on this issue to press for a change in U.S. policy. Indeed, in the 1992 Democratic presidential primaries, much of the peace movement supported the campaign of Iowa Senator Tom Harkin who, while one of the more progressive challengers on many issues, was the most right wing on Israel and Palestine, even to the point of criticizing the Bush administration for not being anti-Palestine enough. In subsequent years, the peace move ment has been challenged not just by anti-Arab sentiments among its erstwhile supporters, but from anti-Israel elements as well. Many on the left wing of the peace movement adopted a strong anti-Zionist position, calling for the dissolution of Israel as a Jewish state. Others went as far as adopting anti-Semitic positions that included grossly exaggerating alleged Jewish political and economic control of the United States. Although American peace activists have had no trouble attributing U.S. support of Indonesia's occupation of East Timor or Morocco's occupation of Western Sahara to the exigencies of American imperialism, U.S. support of Israeli occupation forces, by contrast, has often attributed to the "Jewish lobby," effectively blaming a small and historically oppressed minority group—rather than the powerful vested interests that normally dictate the direction of U.S. foreign policy— for the policies of Congress, the Pentagon, the State Department, and the president. This created a reluctance on the part of many peace activists to address U.S. policy toward Israel/Palestine for fear that it might unwittingly encourage anti-Semitism or that they themselves would be so accused.

This polarization between these two extremes in the peace movement created problems: in popular movements concerned with Central America, Southern Africa, and the arms race, there was general agreement from across the broadly progressive political spectrum on what was wrong with U.S. policy and how it needed to change. On the Middle East, however, such unity was hard to find. Indeed, many peace groups demonstrated a profound reluctance to address the Middle East at all for fear of the divisiveness that could result from taking even a highly principled position. With the exception of the period surrounding the Gulf War, it was progressive Jewish and Arab-American groups that provided the most visible peace activism on the Middle East, not the mainstream peace groups, which resulted in the Israeli-Palestinian conflict remaining on the fringes of popular consciousness within the peace movement.

One problem facing peace activists was the perception that—because U.S. policy has always been perceived to be pro-Israel—criticism of U.S.

policy was made to appear as criticism of Israel itself. Many on the Israeli left, however, have argued that U.S. policy is ultimately anti-Israel, since it discourages the Israeli government from making necessary compromises that would ensure peace, isolates Israel further from its Arab neighbors and the international community, and increasingly militarizes its economy at the expense of sustainable economic development.

Just as the 2003 U.S. invasion of Iraq served to remobilize the American peace movement overall, the Israeli-Palestinian conflict has finally become a major focus as well. The recognition is dawning that just as one can oppose the U.S. occupation of Iraq and not be anti-American, one can oppose the Israeli occupation and not be anti-Israel. Though the peace movement has yet to have a major impact in changing U.S. policy toward Israel and Palestine, it is indicative that in now being willing to address the conflict as a peace issue, the American peace activists movement is finally at a place where U.S. policy throughout the region can be challenged, allowing for a consistent anti-war message that had eluded the movement in previous decades.

NOTES

1. Gibbs et al., 1990.

2. Vietnam did invade Cambodia in 1979, but this move was largely supported by the Cambodians suffering under the brutally repressive Khmer Rouge regime. While this initial welcoming eventually faded, Iraq's neighbors have never welcomed Baghdad's military intervention.

3. One prominent case of exaggerating the perfidy of the Iraqi regime was the false testimony before Congress of Iraqi soldiers throwing babies out of cribs in the intensive care unit of a Kuwaiti hospital.

4. Chip Bertlet, Political Research Associates, Dec. 23, 1990, unpublished manuscript "Right Woos Left Over War Issue."

5. These included Patrick Lacefield, a former staff member of the radical pacifist magazine *Win*, a leader in the Democratic Socialists of America, and editor of a popular anti-war anthology on Central America; Fred Halliday, a Marxist scholar of the Middle East and an editor of *New Left Review*; and, John Judis, a senior writer and editor of *Socialist Revolution* and *In These Times*.

6. For example, in late November, more than 1,000 people rallied in Missoula, Montana. In Kannapolis, N.C., a company town, a group called the Piedmont Peace Project was organized consisting of more than 500 mill workers, farmers, truck drivers, and others. There were 59 vigils seven days a week in New Hampshire, a conservative state. Organized opposition to the war was nothing like that during Vietnam.

7. The statement was issued by nine union presidents that appeared in the *Washington Post*. Two others added their names after the ad appeared in the January 10 edition.

8. Hinds, 1991.

9. Ibid.

10. It is rather noteworthy that with the presiding bishop of his own denomination, Episcopal Bishop Edmond Browning, advising him against war, Bush turned to fundamentalist Southern Baptist preacher Billy Graham, a supporter of the Vietnam War and confidant of President Nixon.

11. Harris, 1991.

12. Cited in Shirbman, 1991.

13. Middle East Policy Statement, Coalition for a New Foreign Policy, Spring 1981.

14. Interview, May 1989.

15. Both Hayden and Fonda have subsequently adopted more progressive positions regarding the Israeli-Palestinian conflict more consistent with that of American and Israeli peace groups.

A FINAL WORD

Marc Pilisuk and Michael N. Nagler

Like the surface of the earth itself, the prevailing war system is a relatively thin and unstable layer that effectively conceals intense energies of greater fluidity beneath its surface—energies that occasionally burst forth. Our journey through the manifold energies and projects that are represented in the chapters of these three volumes did not reveal a single, unified world peace movement but it certainly did reveal wellsprings of activity, more intense, more creative, and more widespread than one would imagine. The bubbling energies appear as contributions to a gigantic wave surging against the barriers that societies have entrenched into laws and ideologies that make inequality, exploitation, and violence appear inevitable. Slowly but with increasing likelihood, individuals and groups of individuals, facing incredibly diverse manifestations of that age-old inhumanity, are finding courage, as people have done through history, to rise up against it. But in this generation many more of us are also identifying the existing exploitative system underlying diverse violence and recognizing that this system is failing. And some are daring to view the movements toward peace, justice, and sustainability as a yet unrealized but potentially unstoppable movement. This emergence is all the more amazing as it comes on the heels of a century in which control over human identity has become all-pervasive and quite often malicious; when the war propaganda is based, ironically enough, on adaptations of Sigmund

Freud's theories about the power of appealing to basic needs and fears; when such propaganda hurled masses of humanity into paroxysms of anti-Semitic hatred, among other examples of targeted dehumanization; and when the self-image of human beings as "happiness machines that have become the key to economic progress" (to paraphrase President Hoover) came to predominate.[1] The power of such manipulation and control is slowly yielding to a culture in which the better natures of people can assert themselves.

One cannot review the efforts described in these volumes, and the many more that we could not include, without realizing that the wave is powerful and has not yet reached its crest. The power and impact of these healthier alternatives are evident and they are springing up everywhere. They remain seriously under-reported by the mainstream media that instead deliver a constant stream of tragedies, local and national, as though they were singular occurrences rather than looking deeply into the failures of unfettered corporate expansion and the war system. It is an ironically hopeful sign that the failures of that system are becoming apparent to people the world over, despite the impressive capacity of a powerful elite to "spin" the coverage. Some former powerful players of that system, some of whom appear in these pages, have recognized the failure of an unbridled quest for development and an unending search for enemies.

A more heartening sign is that the activists described in the final chapter of Volume 3 do not wait for powerful officials to lead them. In ways small and large, people are devoting their creativity, their energy, their dreams, and their quest for a meaningful life to make peace a reality. One cannot come away from the story of these efforts without being heartened by the fact that so many others have stepped forward. We are resourceful and caring custodians of the force of life. The peace movement worldwide is an inchoate but irresistible force. It grows because it must prevail. And if we nurture it, it will.

NOTE

1. See the BBC documentary, *Happiness Machines.*

BIBLIOGRAPHY

"A Human Security Doctrine for Europe." The Barcelona Report of the Study Group on Europe's Security Capabilities Barcelona, 2004.

Ackerman, Peter. "Skills or Conditions: What Key Factors Shape the Success or Failure of Civil Resistance?" Paper presented to the Conference on Civil Resistance and Power Politics, University of Oxford, March 15–18, 2007.

Ackerman, Peter, and Jack DuVall. "The Right to Rise Up: People Power and the Virtues of Civic Disruption." *Fletcher Forum of World Affairs* 30, no. 2 (2006): 33–42.

Ackerman, Peter, and Jack DuVall. *A Force More Powerful: A Century of Nonviolent Conflict.* New York: Palgrave, 2000.

Action History, http://www.soaw.org/article.php?id=171&cat=18.

Addams, Jane. *Jane Addams: A Centennial Reader.* Edited by E.C. Johnson. New York: Macmillan, 1960.

Advent Conspiracy. www.adventconspiracy.com.

Agger, Inger and Jensen, Søren Buus. *Trauma and Healing Under State Terrorism.* London: Zed books, 1996.

Akiba, Tadatoshi. *Cities are Not Targets.* 2020 Vision Campaign. 2009. http://www.2020visioncampaign.org/.

Allen, Jon G. *Traumatic Relationships and Serious Mental Disorders.* West Sussex: John Wiley & Sons, 2001.

Alpher, Joseph, and Khalil Shikaki, with the participation of the additional members of the Joint Working Group on Israeli-Palestinian Relations, "The Palestinian Refugee Problem and the Right of Return" (Weatherhead Center for International Affairs Working Paper No. 98–7). Cambridge, MA: Harvard University, 1998. (Reprinted in *Middle East Policy* 6, no. 3 (February 1999): 167–189.)

Alternatives Action and Communication Network for International Development. "Untold Suffering in the Congo." http://www.alternatives.ca/article2396.html.

American Psychiatric Association. *Diagnostic and Statistical Manual of Mental Disorders.* 4th ed. Washington, DC: Author, 1994.

American Psychological Association Presidential Task Force Report on Psychological Ethics and National Security. (The PENS Report). http://www.apa.org/releases/PENSTaskForceReportFinal.pdf and www.clarku.edu/peacepsychology/PENScall.pdf.

Amnesty International. "Killer facts: The Impact of the Irresponsible Arms Trade On Lives, Rights and Livelihoods." May 6, 2010. http://www.amnesty.org/en/library/info/ACT30/005/2010/en.

Andaya, Barbara Watson, and Leonard Y. Andaya. *A History of Malaysia,* 2nd ed. Hampshire, UK: Palgrave, 2001.

Anderson, Benedict. *Mythology and the Tolerance of the Javanese,* 2nd ed. Ithaca, NY: Cornell Modern Indonesia Project, 1996.

Appleby, R. Scott. "Militants for Peace," http://muse.jhu.edu/journals/sais_review/v018/18.2appleby.html.

Arendt, Hannah. "Reflections on Violence." *New York Review of Books,* 1969.

Arieff, Irwin. "UN Seeks New Treaty Restricting Global Arms Sales." *Reuters,* December 6, 2006. http://www.alertnet.org/thenews/newsdesk/N06439629.htm/.

Arkless, David. Keynote address covering the corporate responsibility correlation with ending modern slavery, 2009 Global Forum on Human Trafficking, San Diego, CA, October 8–9, 2009.

Arms Control Association. "The Strategic Offensive Reductions Treaty (SORT) At a Glance." 2002. http://www.armscontrol.org/factsheets/sort-glance.

Arms Trade Treaty: A Nobel Peace Laureates' Initiative. http://www.armstradetreaty.com/.

Arnold, Martin. Gütekraft: Zur Wirkungsweise erfolgreicher gewaltfreier Konfliktaustragung bei Hildegard Goss-Mayr, Mohandas K. Gandhi und Bart de Ligt. Vergleich und Synthese der Auffassungen von ProtagonistInnen der Gewaltfreiheit aus unterschiedlichen weltanschaulichen Traditionen. Forthcoming dissertation, 2011.

Arrigo, J. M., and R. Wagner, "Torture Is for Amateurs: Report on the 2006 Seminar for Civilian Psychologists and Army Interrogators." *Journal of Peace and Conflict* 13, no. 4 (2007): 393–398.

Asian Development Bank. "Selected Poverty and Related Indicators: Updated April 10, 2001," http://www.adb.org/documents/edrc/statistics/poverty/spi.pdf.

Azar, Edward. *The Management of Protracted Social Conflict.* Hampshire, UK: Dartmouth, 1990.

Bales, Kevin. *Disposable People.* Berkeley and Los Angeles: University of California Press, 2004.

Bales, Kevin. *Ending Slavery.* Berkeley and Los Angeles: University of California Press, 2007.

Balkwill, Jack. "Prison for a Peacemaker: An Interview with Kathy Kelly, Part One." *Online Journal,* April 11, 2007.

Balkwill, Jack. "A Vietnam Vet Interviews Kathy Kelly: Prison for a Peacemaker," *Counterpunch*, April 10, 2004.

Bandura, Albert, Claudio Barbanelli, Gian Vittorio Caprara, and Concetta Pastorelli. "Mechanisms of Moral Disengagement in the Exercise of Moral Agency." *Journal of Personality and Social Psychology* 71 (1996): 364–374.

Bar-Tal, Daniel. "Collective Memory of Physical Violence: Its Contribution to the Culture of Violence." In *Memories in Conflict*, edited by Ed Cairns and Michael D. Roe, 77–93. London: Macmillan, 2002.

Barnaby, Wendy. *The Plague Makers: The Secret World of Biological Warfare*. London: Vision, 1999.

Batstone, David. *Not For Sale: The Return of the Global Slave Trade and How We Can Fight It*. New York: HarperCollins, 2007.

Baue, William. "New French Law Mandates Corporate Social and Environmental Reporting." *Social Funds* (March 14, 2002). http://www.socialfunds.com/news/article.cgi/798.html.

Beales, A. C. F. The History of Peace: *A Short Account of the Organized Movements for International Peace*. New York: Garland, 1971, 1931.

Bechtel. "Sustainability and Environment." http://www.bechtel.com/sustainability_envt.html.

Beeston, Richard. "Six Arab states join rush to go nuclear." *Sunday Times*, London. November 4, 2006. http://www.timesonline.co.uk/tol/news/w.

Begg, Moazzam. *Enemy Combatant: My Imprisonment at Guantanamo, Bagram, and Kandahar*. London: Free Press, 2006.

Bennett, W. Lance. *News: The Politics of Illusion*. New York: Longman, 2004.

Bernstein, Elizabeth, Robert Elias, Randall Forsberg, Matthew Goodman, Deborah Mapes, and Peter M. Steven. *Peace Resource Book*. Cambridge, MA: Ballinger Publishing Co., 1986.

Bertell, Rosalie. "Avoidable Tragedy Post-Chernobyl: A Critical Analysis." *Journal of Humanitarian Medicine*, 2, no. 3, (2004): 21-28.

Bertell, Rosalie. *Health and Environmental Costs of Militarism*. Presented in Barcelona, June 24, 2004.

Betts, Richard K., and Samuel P. Huntington. "Dead Dictators and Rioting Mobs: Does The Demise of Authoritarian Rulers Lead To Political Instability?" *International Security* 10 (1985): 112–46.

Blair, David. "Congo Rebel Arrest Offers a Glimmer of Hope." *Telegraph UK*, January 23, 2009. http://www.telegraph.co.uk/news/worldnews/africaandindianocean/congo/4325048/Congo-rebel-arrest-offers-a-glimmer-of-hope.html.

Blass, Thomas. *Obedience to Authority: Current Perspectives on the Milgram Paradigm*. Mahwah, NJ: Lawrence Erlbaum, 2000.

Blum, William. *U.S. Military and CIA Interventions Since World War II*. Monroe, ME: Common Courage Press, 2004.

Boaz, Cynthia. "Framing the Green Revolution in Red: Iran through a Lethal Media Scope." *Truthout.org*, June 16, 2009.

Boaz, Cynthia. "The Iranian Crackdown: Who's Really Afraid of Whom?" *The Huffington Post*, June 24, 2009.

Böge, Volker, and Peter Wilke. *Sicherheitspolitische Alternativen*. Baden-Baden: Nomos, 1984.

Bolivia Says No! http://www.soaw.org/presente/index.php?option=com_content &task=view&id=103&Itemid=74.

Boly, William. "Behind the Nuclear Curtain." *Public Citizen*, 9(1) (1989): 12–16.

Boly, William. "Downwind." *In Health* (July/August, 1990): 58–69.

Bonanno, George, Jennie Noll, Frank Putnam, Michelle O'Neill, and Penelope K. Trickett. "Predicting the Willingness to Disclose Childhood Sexual Abuse from Measures of Repressive Coping and Dissociative Tendencies." *Child Maltreatment* 8 (2003): 302–318.

Bond, Trudy. "How Psychologists Became the Pentagon's Bitches, Shrinks, Lies, and Torture. April 14/15, 2007, http://www.counterpunch.org/bond 04142007.html.

Boothe, Ivan and Smithey, Lee A. "Privilege, Empowerment, and Nonviolent Intervention." *Peace & Change 32*, no. 1 (January 2000): 39–61.

Bourgeois, Fr., Roy. Conversation with Jill Latonick-Flores, telephone, September 15, 2009.

Bracken, Patrick, and Celia Petty, eds. *Rethinking the Trauma of War*. London: Free Association Books, 1998: 38–59.

Brennan, William. *Dehumanizing the Vulnerable: When Word Games Take Lives*. Chicago: Loyola University Press, 1995.

Brett, Rachel, and Irma Specht. *Young Soldiers: Why They Choose to Fight*. Boulder, CO: Lynne Rienner, 2004.

Broad, William J. and David E. Sanger. "U.N. Inspectors Report Evidence That Iran Itself Made Fuel That Could Be Used for A-Bombs." *New York Times*, February 25, 2004. http://www.nytimes.com/2004/02/25/world/un-inspectors -report-evidence-that-ira.

Broneus, K. *Reconciliation: Theory and Practice for Development Cooperation*. Stockholm: Swedish International Development Cooperation Agency (SIDA), 2003.

Bronfenbrenner, Urie. *The Ecology of Human Development: Experiments by Nature and Design*. Cambridge, MA: Harvard University Press, 1979.

Buncombe, Anthony. "Infant Mortality in Iraq Soars As Young Pay the Price for War." *The Independent*, May 8, 2007.

Buro, Andreas. "Die Entstehung der Ostermarsch-Bewegung als Beispiel für die Entfaltung von Massenlernprozessen," in *Friedensanalysen. Für Theorie und Praxis 4, Schwerpunkt: Friedensbewegung*. Frankfurt: Edition Suhrkamp, 1977.

Burton, John W. *Conflict: Resolution and Prevention*. New York: St. Martin's Press, 1990.

Burton, John W. *Conflict and Communication: The Use of Controlled Communication in International Relations*. London: Macmillan, 1969.

Burton, John W. *Deviance, Terrorism and War: The Process of Solving Unsolved Social and Political Problems*. New York: St. Martin's Press, 1979.

Burton, John W. *Global Conflict: The Domestic Sources of International Crisis*. Brighton, UK: Wheatsheaf, 1984.

Butler, Katherine. "Lipstick Revolution: Iran's Women Are Taking on the Mullahs." *The Independent UK*, February 26, 2009.

Butler, Smedley. *War Is a Racket.* New York: Round Table Press, 1935.

Butler, Smedley. *War Is a Racket: The Antiwar Classic by America's Most Decorated General.* Los Angeles: Feral House, 2003.

Büttner, Christian W. *Friedensbrigaden: Zivile Konfliktbearbeitung mit gewaltfreien.* Methoden, Münster: Lit Verlag, 1995.

Cabasso, Jacqueline. "StratCom in Context: The Hidden Architecture of U.S. Militarism." April 23, 2008. http://afterdowningstreet.org/militarism.

Cairns, Ed. *Children and Political Violence.* Oxford, UK: Blackwell, 1996.

Cairns, Ed, and John Darby. "Conflict in Northern Ireland." *American Psychologist* 53 (1998): 754–776.

Cairns, Ed, and Michael D. Roe. *Memories in Conflict.* London: Macmillan, 2002.

Calvert Investments. "SRI Issue Brief: Weapons." http://www.calvertgroup.com/sri-weapons.html.

Candidates for APA President: Dr. Steven J. Reisner http://www.apa.org/monitor/2008/06/reisner.html *Monitor on Psychology* 39, no. 6 (June 2008) (retrieved November 8, 2008).

Carey, Benedict. Psychologists Clash on Aiding Interrogations http://www.nytimes.com/2008/08/16/washington/16psych.html?_r=2&pagewanted=all&oref=slogin.

Carroll, James. "Preventing an Arms Race in Outer Space." Originally appeared in the *Boston Globe*, May 12, 2008. Retrieved from Nuclear Age Peace Foundation. http://www.wagingpeace.org/articles/2008/05/12_carroll_paros.php 1/10/09.

Cave, Rosy. "Disarmament as Humanitarian Action? Comparing Negotiations on Anti-Personnel Mines and Explosive Remnants of War." In *Disarmament as Humanitarian Action: From Perspective to Practice*, edited by John Borrie and Vanessa Martin Randin. Geneva: UNIDIR, 2006.

Chandrasekharan, S. "Sri Lanka: Third Round of Talks Brings a Surprise: Update 40." South Asia Analysis Group, Note No. 169 (December 12, 2002). http://www.saag.org/common/uploaded_files/note176.html.

Change for Equality. http://www.we-change.org/english/.

"Changes in Guantanamo Bay SOP Manual" (2003–2004), from Wikileaks, Julian Assange and Daniel Mathews with Emi Maclean, Marc Falkoff, Rebecca Dick and Beth Gilson (habeas counsel). Tuesday, December 3, 2007.

Chasnoff, Debra, (director). "Deadly Deception: General Electric, Nuclear Weapons and Our Environment." New Day Films, 1991.

Chatfield, Charles and Robert Kleidman. *The American Peace Movement: Ideals and Activism.* New York: Maxwell Macmillan International, 1992.

Chatfield, Charles. *Peace Movements in America.* New York: Schocken Books, 1973.

Chatterjee, Pratap. "Bechtel Wins Iraq War Contracts." *CorpWatch: Holding Corporations Accountable.* http://www.corpwatch.org/article.php?id=6532 .

Chatterjee, Pratap. "Bechtel's Water Wars." *CorpWatch: Holding Corporations Accountable.* http://www.corpwatch.org/article.php?id=6670.

Chomsky, Noam. *Hegemony or Survival: Americas' Quest for Global Dominance.* New York: Holt and Co., 2004.

Chorbajian, Levon, and George Shirinian. *Studies in Comparative Genocide.* New York: St. Martin's Press, 1999.

Christie, Daniel J. "A Conceptual Framework for Peace Psychology." Paper presented at the Seventh International Symposium on the Contributions of Psychology to Peace, International Union of Psychological Science, Manila, Philippines, June, 2001.

Christie, Daniel J., and Montiel, Cristina Jayme. "Cultural and Structural Peace-building." Paper presented at the Fifth International Symposium on the Contributions of Psychology to Peace, University of Melbourne, July 1997.

CleanUpGE.org, "GE Misdeed," http://www.cleanupge.org/gemisdeeds.html.

Coalition to Stop the Use of Child Soldiers. *Child Soldiers Global Report 2008*. London: Author, 2008.

Cohn, Carol. "Sex and Death in the Rational World of the Defense Intellectuals." *Journal of Women in Culture and Society* 12 (1987): 687–718.

"Cold War Relics or Tomorrow's Family Life-Savers?" November 28, 2005. http://www.radshelters4u.com/.

Corporate Accountability International. "Infant Formula Campaign." http://www.corpwatch.org/article.php?id=6670.

Corporate Accountability International. "Our Victories." http://www.stopcorporateabuse.org/nuclear-weapon-makers-campaign.

CorpWatch.org. "About CorpWatch." http://www.corpwatch.org/article.php?id=11314.

Cortright, David. *Soldiers in Revolt: GI Resistance During the Vietnam War*. Boston: Haymarket Books, 2005.

Cossa, Ralph A., and Eun Jung Cahill Che (Eds.). "Chronology of Key Events: Regional Overview, July–September 2000." *Comparative Connections: A Quarterly E-Journal on East Asian Bilateral Relations*. Vol 2(3). 2000. http://csis.org/files/media/csis/pubs/0003q.pdf

Council of Europe Committee on Legal Affairs and Human Rights (2007). http://www.coe.int/dgh/default_en.aso.

Coy, Patrick G. "Protecting Human Rights: The Dynamics of International Nonviolent Accompaniment by Peace Brigades International in Sri Lanka." PhD dissertation, Syracuse University, 1997.

Cray, Charlie. "General Electric." CorpWatch: *Holding Corporations Accountable*. http://www.corpwatch.org/section.php?id=16.

CTBTO Preparatory Commission for the Comprehensive Nuclear Test Ban Treaty. Article IV: Entry Into Force. http://www.fas.org/nuke/control/ctbt/review99/conference_report.htm.

Daejung, Kim. Remarks by President Daejung on the 20th Anniversary of the May 18 Kwangju Democratization Movement (August 17, 2001). http://www.Ahrchk.Net/Hrsolid/Mainfile.Php/2000vol10no07/589/.

Dalton, Russell J., and Manfred Kuechler, eds. *Challenging the Political Order: New Social and Political Movements in Western Democracies*. Cambridge: Polity Press, 1990.

Daniel, Sharan L. "Radiologist Contributed to Landmark Study Showing Even Low Levels of Radiation Are Unsafe." *Stanford Report*, October 24, 2005. http://cisac.stanford.edu/news/611/.

Danner, Mark. *The Massacre at El Mozote: A Parable of the Cold War*. New York: Vintage Books, 1994.

Dawes, Andrew. "Psychologies for Liberation: Views from Elsewhere." In *Peace, Conflict, and Violence: Peace Psychology for the 21st Century,* edited by Daniel J. Christie, Richard V. Wagner, and Deborah D. Winter, 295–306. Upper Saddle River, NJ: Prentice Hall, 2001.

Dawes, Andrew, and David Donald. "Improving Children's Chances." In *Addressing Childhood Adversity,* edited by David Donald, Andrew Dawes, and Johann Louw, 1–25. Cape Town: David Philip, 2000.

De la Rey, Cheryl. "Reconciliation in Divided Societies." In *Peace, Conflict, and Violence: Peace Psychology for the 21st Century,* edited by Daniel J. Christie, Richard V. Wagner, and Deborah D. Winter, 251–261. Upper Saddle River, NJ: Prentice Hall, 2001.

Deats, Richard. *The Global Spread of Active Nonviolence.* 2001. http://www.forusa.org/nonviolence/0900_73deats.html.

Deats, Richard. *Marked for Life, The Story of Hildegard Goss-Mayr.* Hyde Park, NY: New City Press, 2009.

Defense Intelligence Agency, "Iraq Water Treatment Vulnerabililties," Filename: 511, rept. 91, January 18, 1991.

"Der Widerstand gegen die Wiederbewaffnung der Bundesrepublik." In "Unsere Bundeswehr? Zum 25-jährigen Bestehen einer umstrittenen Institution." Reiner Steinweg (Hg.). *Friedensanalysen 14,* Frankfurt/M: Edition Suhrkamp, 1981.

Des Forges, Alison. *Leave None to Tell the Story: Genocide in Rwanda.* New York: Human Rights Watch, 1999.

Deutsch, Morton. "Cooperation and Competition." In *The Handbook of Conflict Resolution,* edited by Morton Deutsch and Peter T. Coleman, 21–40. San Francisco: Jossey-Bass, 2000.

Deutsch, Morton. *Distributive Justice: A Social Psychological Perspective.* New Haven, CT: Yale University Press, 1985.

Deutsch, Morton. *The Resolution of Conflict.* New Haven, CT: Yale University Press, 1973.

Dillon, Justin (Director). *Call+Response.* United States: Fair Trade Pictures Production, 2008.

Dobup. "Life and Peace and Sustainable Society." Paper presented at Kangwon Conference on Sustainable Development, Kangwon, South Korea, September 2007.

Du Boff, Richard B. Rogue Nation. Znet Daily Commentaries, December 21, 2001. http://www.zmag.org/roguenation.htm.

Duchacek, Ivo. *Comparative Federalism: The Territorial Dimension of Politics.* New York: Holt, Rinehart, and Winston, 1970.

"Duck and Cover: Original 1950 Airing." http://www.youtube.com/watch?v=ixy5FBLnh7o.

Ebert, Theodor. *Gewaltfreier Aufstand. Alternative zum Bürgerkrieg.* Waldkirchen: Waldkircher Verlagsgesellschaft, 1981.

Edwards, Rob. "US May Overturn Nuclear Fuel Reprocessing Ban." *New Scientist,* 18, no. 27, (January 26, 2006). http://www.newscientist.com/article/dn8639-us-may-overturn.

Eguren, Enrique. Protection Manual for Human Rights Defenders. Front Line — The International Foundation for the Protection of Human Rights Defenders. 2005. http://www.frontlinedefenders.org/manuals.

Einstein, Albert, Bertrand Russell et al. "Notice to the World. . . Renounce War or Perish! . . . World Peace or Universal Death!" 1955. http://www.discogs .com/Albert-Einstein-Bertrand-Russell-Notice-To-The-World-Renounce-War-Or -Perish-World-Peace-Or-Universal/release/1813226.

Eisenhower, Dwight D. "Farewell Address." January 17, 1961. http://www.independent .org/issues/article.asp?id=1133.

El Baradei, Mohamed. AFP, Feb. 23, 2005. http://www.wise-uranium.org/ eproj.html.

Electronic Iraq. www.electroniciraq.net.

Engelhardt, Tom. "Bases, Bases Everywhere: It's a Pentagon World and Welcome to It." http://www.commondreams.org/views05/0602-28.htm.

Ephron, Dan. "The Biscuit Breaker," Newsweek 27 (October 2008). http:// www.newsweek.com/id/164497 (retrieved November 8, 2008);

Epictetus. Discourses I. Internet Journal of Philosophy. http://www.iep.utm.edu/ epictetu/.

Esterling, Brian A., Luciano L'Abate, Edward J. Murray, and James W. Pennebaker. "Empirical Foundations for Writing in Prevention and Psychotherapy: Mental and Physical Health Outcomes." Clinical Psychology Review 19 (1999): 79–96.

Etzioni, Amitai. "The Kennedy Experiment." Western Political Quarterly 20 (1967): 361–380.

Everett, Paul, Tennyson Williams, and Mary Myers. Evaluation of Search for Common Ground Activities in Sierra Leone. Washington, DC: Search for Common Ground, 2004.

Eurosif. SRI News 2008. http://www.eurosif.org/publications/newsletter/2008/ january_february_2008_eurosif_newsletter/sri_news.

The Fact Finding Commission. The Final Report. Philippines: Bookmark, 1990.

Falk, Richard. "Comparative Protection of Human Rights in Capitalist and Socialist Third World Countries." Universal Human Rights 1 (1979): 3–29.

Farsetta, Diane. "Meet the Nuclear Power Lobby." Center for Media and Democracy, July 1, 2008. http://www.prwatch.org/node/7506.

Ferraro, Kathleen J. "The Culture of Social Problems: Observations of the Third Reich, the Cold War, and Vietnam." Social Problems 52, no. 1 (2005): 1–14.

Fisher, Richard. The Social Psychology of Intergroup and International Conflict. New York: Springer-Verlag, 1990.

Fisher, William. The Worst of the Worst. http://www.truthout.org/article/william-fisher-the-worst-worst (retrieved October 15, 2009).

Foa, Edna B., Terrence M. Keane, and Matthew J. Friedman, eds. Effective Treatments for PTSD: Practice Guidelines from the International Society for Traumatic Stress Studies. New York: Guilford Press, 2000.

Food and Water Watch. "Bechtel." http://www.foodandwaterwatch.org/water/ private-vs-public/corporations/Bechtel.

Foster, Major Luke. Paper presented to the Conference, Monitoring Peace in Bougainville. Australia National University, September 1999. http://rspas.anu.edu.au/ melanesia/documents/bougainville/PDF/foster.pdf.

Freire, Paulo. Pedagogy of the Oppressed. Translated by Myra B. Ramos. New York: Herder & Herder, 1970.

Friedman, Milton. "The Social Responsibility of Business is to Increase Its Profits." *The New York Times Magazine*, September 13, 1970.

Froomkin, Dan. "Cheney's 'Dark Side' Is Showing," http://www.washingtonpost .com/wp-dyn/content/blog/2005/11/07/BL2005110700793.html; Special to washingtonpost.com. November 7, 2005.

Furnari, Ellen. "The Nonviolent Peaceforce in Sri Lanka: Methods and Impact (September 2003–January 2006)." *Intervention* 4, no. 3 (2006): 260–268.

Gabel, Medard. *What the World Wants and How to Pay for It.* Philadelphia: World Game Institute, 1997.

Galbraith, Kate "Texas Mulls More Nuclear Reactors." *The Texas Tribune*, Saturday, October 9, 2010. http://www.texastribune.org/texas-energy/energy/ texas-mulls-more-nuclear-reactors/

Galtung, Johan. "Three Approaches to Peace: Peacekeeping, Peacemaking and Peacebuilding." In *Peace, War, and Defense: Essays in Peace Research*, vol. II, edited by Johan Galtung, 282–304. Copenhagen: Christian Ejlers, 1976.

Galtung, Johan. *Peace by Peaceful Means: Peace and Conflict, Development and Civilization.* London: Sage, 1996.

Gandhi, Mahatma. *Collected Works of Mahatma Gandhi*, Vol. 54: November 5, 1931.

Gaston, E. L. "Taking the Gloves off of Homeland Security: Rethinking the Federalism Framework for Responding to National Emergencies," http:// www.hlpronline.com/vol1no2/gaston.pdf (retrieved November 8, 2009).

Gates, Robert. "Nuclear Weapons and Deterrence in the 21st Century." October 28, 2008. http://www.carnegieendowment.org/events/?fa=eventDetail&id= 1202.

"Geneva Accords Quaint and Obsolete, Legal Aide Told Bush from Roland Watson in Washington—President Bush's News Conference" (Published: September 15, 2006), http://www.nytimes.com/2006/09/15/washington/15bush_ transcript.html?pagewanted=6.

Gibbs, Nancy, Christine Gormann, and Gavin Scott. "Giving Peace a Chance." *Time*, November 26, 1990: 33.

Gibson, James L. *Overcoming Apartheid: Can Truth Reconcile a Divided Nation?* New York: Russell Sage Foundation, 2004.

Gleditsch, Nils Petter, Håvard Strand, and Lars Wilhelmsen. "Armed Conflict Dataset Codebook: Version 1.1," September 9, 2002. http://www.prio.no/ CSCW/Datasets/Armed-Conflict/UCDP-PRIO/.

Gleditsch, Nils Petter, Peter Wallensteen, Mikael Eriksson, Margareta Sollenberg, and Håvard Strand. "Armed Conflict 1946–2001: A New Dataset." *Journal of Peace Research* 39, no. 5 (2002): 615–637.

Global Zero. April, 2010. http://www.globalzero.org/sign-declaration.

Godement, Francois. *The New Asian Renaissance: From Colonialism to the Post-Cold War.* Translated by Elizabeth J. Parcell. London: Routledge, 1997.

Goodman, Amy. "APA Interrogation Task Force Member Dr. Jean Maria Arrigo Exposes Group's Ties to Military," http://www.democracynow.org/2007/8/ 20/apa_interrogation_task_force_member_dr

Goodman, Amy. "APA Members Hold Fiery Town Hall Meeting on Interrogation, Torture," August 20, 2007 (retrieved October 15, 2009). http://www.democracynow.org/2007/8/20/apa_members_hold_fiery_town_hall.

Goodman, Amy. "Dissident Voices: Ex-Task Force Member Dr. Michael Wessells Speaks Out on Psychologists and Torture," August 20, 2007, http://www.democracynow.org/2007/8/20/dissident_voices_ex_task_force_member

Goodman, Amy. "Psychologists in Denial about Torture." www.democracynow.org/.../psychologists_in_denial_about_torture (retrieved November 15, 2008).

Goodman, Amy. "Renowned Psychologist Author Returns APA Award." http://www.democracynow.org/2007/8/28/renowned_psychologist_author_returns_apa_award (retrieved November 8, 2008).

Goodman, Amy and David Goodman. "Why Media Ownership Matters." CommonDreams.og. 2005. http://www.commondreams.org/views05/0403-25.htm.

Goodstein, Laura. "Sibling Nuns Will Go to Prison for Protesting US Military School." New York Times. June 24, 2001: http://www.nytimes.com/2001/06/24/us/sibling-nuns-will-go-to-prison-for-protesting-at-us-military-school.html.

Goose, Stephen, and Jody Williams. "The Campaign to Ban Antipersonnel Landmines: Potential Lessons." In Landmines and Human Security: International Politics and War's Hidden Legacy, edited by Richard Matthew, Bryan McDonald, and Kenneth Rutherford, 239–250. Albany: State University of New York Press, 2004.

Gowing, Peter G. Mandate in Moroland: The American Government of Muslim Filipinos, 1899–1920. Diliman, Quezon City: Philippine Center for Advanced Studies, 1977.

Greenpeace International. "Chernobyl Death Toll Grossly Underestimated. April 18, 2006. http://www.greenpeace.org/international/en/news/features/chernobyl-deaths-180406/.

Greider, William. Fortress America: The American Military and the Consequences of Peace. New York: Public Affairs, 1998.

Grene, Sophia. "Managers Embrace Sustainability Principles." Financial Times, June 21, 2009.

Griffin-Nolan, Ed. "Witness for Peace." In Nonviolent Intervention across Borders. A Recurrent Vision, edited by Yeshua Moser-Puangsuwan and Thomas Weber, 279–304. Honolulu: Spark M. Matsunaga Institute for Peace, 2000.

Grossman, Dave. On Killing: The Psychological Cost of Learning to Kill in War and Society. Boston: Little, Brown, 1995.

Grossman, Lt. Col. Dave. On Killing: The Psychological Cost of Learning to Kill in War and Society. Back Bay Books, Boston: 1996.

Grossman, Lt. Col. Dave. Let's Stop Teaching Our Kids to Kill. New York: Crown Publishers, 1999.

Grossman, Zolton. "Over a Century of U.S. Military Intervention" (1999). http://www.redrat.net/thoughts/criminal_behavior/interventions/.

"Guantanamo Bay Use of Psychologists for Interrogations 2006–2008," from Wikileaks (released August 20, 2008), http://wikileaks.org/wiki/Guantanamo_Bay_use_of_psychologists_for_interrogations_2006–2008.

Guantanamo Voices. "Iguana Rights vs. Human Rights." January 17, 2009. http://guantanamovoices.wordpress.com/2009/01/17/iguana-rights-vs-human-rights/

Guha, Ramachandra. "The Problem." *Seminar* 355 (March 1989): 12–15.

Gusterson, Hugh. *Nuclear Rites: A Weapons Laboratory at the End of the Cold War.* Berkeley, CA: University of California Press. 1998.

Gusterson, H. *Rituals of Renewal among Nuclear Weapons Scientists.* Washington D.C. American Association for the Advancement of Science. 1991.

Hale, William, and Eberhard Kienle, eds. *After the Cold War: Security and Democracy in Africa and Asia.* London: Tauris Academic Studies, 1997.

Handley, Paul. "Counting the Cost." *Far Eastern Economic Review* 155 (June 4, 1992): 10–13.

Happiness Machines. BBC documentary. http://freedocumentaries.org/theatre _mcd.php?filmID1/4140.

Harris, Scott. "Anti-War Activists Regroup." *Los Angeles Times* (March 26, 1991): A22.

Harvey, Mary R. "An Ecological View of Psychological Trauma and Trauma Recovery." *Journal of Traumatic Stress* 9 (1996): 3–23.

Hatte die Friedensbewegung nicht doch Recht? Hintergründe, Fakten und Zusammenhänge zum Golfkrieg. Sensbachtal: Komitee-Eigenverlag, 1991.

Hauff, Edvard. "The Phenomenology of Torture." In *Pain and Survival: Human Rights Violations and Mental Health,* edited by Nils Johan Lavik, Mette Nygard, Nora Sveaass, and Eva Fannemel, 19–28. Oslo, Norway: Scandinavian University Press, 1994.

Haugen, Gary. *Terrify No More: Young Girls Held Captive and the Daring Undercover Operation to Win Their Freedom.* Downers Grove, IL: InterVarsity Press, 2005.

Hayes, Ken. Conversation with Jill Latonick-Flores, telephone, September 22, 2009.

Hayes, Ken. School of the Americas Watch Development Working Group, telephone conversation with Jill Latonick-Flores, September 22, 2009.

Heaney, Tom. "Issues in Freirean Pedagogy" (1995), http://www1.nl.edu/academics/ cas/ace/facultypapers/ThomasHeaney_Freirean.cfm.

Helmick, Raymond G., and Rodney L. Petersen, eds. *Forgiveness and Reconciliation: Religion, Public Policy and Conflict Transformation.* West Conshohocken, PA: Templeton Foundation Press, 2002.

Herman, Judith L. *Trauma and Recovery: The Aftermath of Violence from Domestic Abuse to Political Terror.* New York: Basic Books, 1992.

Hersey, John. *Hiroshima.* New York: Alfred A. Knopf, 1946.

Herzer, Eva. "Tibet: An Evolving Democracy in Exile." (2001). http://www.tibet justice.org/ press/01.12.06-herzer.html.

Hinds, Michael de Courcy. "Drawing on Vietnam Legacy, Antiwar Effort Buds Quickly." *New York Times,* January 11, 1991: A1.

Hine, Donald W., and Cristina Jayme Montiel. "Poverty in Developing Nations: A Cross-Cultural Attributional Analysis." *European Journal of Social Psychology* 29 (1999): 943–959.

Hoiberg, Dale, ed. *Encyclopedia Britannica 2002. Deluxe Edition CD–ROM.* Chicago: Britannica.com, 2002.

Honeyman, Catherine, Shakirah Hudami, Alfa Tiruneh, Justina Hierta, Leila Chirayath. Andrew Iliff, and Jens Meierhenrich. "Establishing Collective Norms: Potentials for Participatory Justice in Rwanda." *Peace and Conflict: Journal of Peace Psychology* 10 (2004): 1–24.

Honwana, Alcinda. *Child Soldiers in Africa.* Philadelphia: University of Pennsylvania Press, 2006.

Hoodfar, Homa. "Against All Odds: The Building of a Women's Movement in the Islamic Republic of Iran." Report Published by the Communication Initiative Network, January 1, 2009.

Hoschild, Adam. *Bury the Chains: Prophets and Rebels in the Fight to Free an Empire's Slaves.* New York: Houghton Mifflin, 2005.

Hovannisian, Richard, ed. *Looking Backward, Moving Forward.* New Brunswick, NJ: Transaction Publishers, 2003.

Huband, Mark. "Rwanda." *Crimes of War 2.0.* http://www.crimesofwar.org/.

Hubert, Don. "The Landmine Ban: A Case Study in Humanitarian Advocacy," Thomas J. Watson, Jr. Institute for International Studies, Occasional Paper # 42, (2000): 41–44.

Human Rights Watch. "Landmine Monitor Report: August 2003." http://www.icbl.org/lm/2003/.

Human Rights Watch. *Sowing Terror.* New York: Author, 1998.

Human Security Now. Commission on Human Security, New York, 2003.

Human Security Report, 2005. http://www.humansecurityreport.info/.

Hyde, Harlow A. *Scraps of Paper: The Disarmament Treaties between the World Wars,* 1st ed. Lincoln, NE: Media Publisher, 1988.

Indian Embassy. Press Release on India's position on nuclear issues/CTBT. October 14, 1999. http://www.indianembassy.org/prdetail1294/-press-release-on-india's-position-on-nuclear-issues-ctbt.

INFACT. "Chicago INFACT Newsletter." Nov., 1986.

INFACT. "INFACT Newsletter: Nuclear Weaponmakers Campaign Update." Fall, 1989.

INFACT. "INFACT Newsletter: Nuclear Weaponmakers Campaign Update." Fall, 1990.

INFACT. "INFACT Newsletter: Nuclear Weaponmakers Campaign Update." Winter/Spring, 1991.

INFACT. "Twin Cities INFACT Campaign Center Newsletter: GE Boycott Update." Nov. 1986.

Information Clearing House. "Report of the International Committee of the Red Cross (ICRC) on the Treatment by the Coalition Forces of Prisoners of War and Other Protected Persons by the Geneva Conventions in Iraq During Arrest, Internment and Interrogation." n.d. http://www.informationclearinghouse.info/article6170.htm.

Inger, Agger, and Søren Buus Jensen. *Trauma and Healing under State Terrorism.* London: Zed Books. 1996.

Institute for Defense and Disarmament Studies (2005). http://www.sourcewatch.org/index.php?title=Institute_for_Defense_and_Disarmament_Studies.

Institute for Defense and Disarmament Studies. 2005. http://www.idds.org/disarm//Institute//for//Defense&Disarmament//Studies.html.

Institute for Southern Studies. "Honduran Coup Shines Spotlight on Controversial U.S. Military Training School." http://www.southernstudies.org/2009/06/honduran-coup-shines-spotlight-on-controversial-us-training-school-in-georgia.html.

International Association of Lawyers Against Nuclear Arms, International Network of Engineers and Scientists Against Proliferation, and International Physicians for the Prevention of Nuclear. *Securing Our Survival (SOS): The Case for a Nuclear Weapons Convention.* Massachusetts: Authors, 2007. http://www.icanw.org/securing-our-survival.

International Baby Food Action Network. "Information to Consumers." http://www.ibfan.org/consumers.html.

International Commission on Intervention and State Sovereignty Department of Foreign Affairs and International Trade. *The Responsibility to Protect—Report of the International Commission on Intervention and State Sovereignty.* Department of Foreign Affairs and International Trade, Canada, 2001.

International Committee to Ban Landmines. http://www.icbl.org/treaty (September 11, 20).

International Committee to Ban Landmines. http://www.icbl.org/problem/what.

International Committee to Ban Landmines. "Landmine Monitor Report 2003: Toward a Mine-Free World." http://www.icbl.org/lm/2003/findings.html.

International Panel on Fissile Materials. *Global Fissile Materials Report.* 2007 http://www.fissilematerials.org/ipfm/site_down/gfmr07.pdf.

International Renewable Energy Agency (IRENA) Act of 2008. http://thomas.loc.gov/cgi-bin/bdquery/z?d110:h.r.05529.

Interrogations and Ethics. "2008 APA Petition Resolution Ballot." 2008. http://www.apa.org/news/press/statements/index.aspx.

Invisible Children: www.invisiblechildren.com.

Iriye, Akira. *The Cold War in Asia: A Historical Introduction.* Englewood Cliffs, NJ: Prentice Hall, 1974.

Isikoff, Michael, and Stuart Taylor, Jr. "The Gitmo Fallout: The Fight Over the Hamdan Ruling Heats Up—As Fears about Its Reach Escalate." *Newsweek*; July 17, 2006. http://www.democraticunderground.com/discuss/duboard.php?az=view_all&address=364x1600061.

Jeffrey, Simon. "Sri Lanka Peace Talks." *Guardian Unlimited.* September 16, 2002. http://www.guardian.co.uk/international/story/0,3604,793294,00.html.

Johnson, Chalmers. *The Sorrows of Empire: Militarism, Secrecy, and the End of the Republic.* New York: Metropolitan Books, 2004.

Joint Working Group on Israeli-Palestinian Relations. "General Principles for the Final Israeli-Palestinian Agreement." PICAR Working Paper, Cambridge, MA: Harvard University, 1998. Reprinted in *Middle East Journal 53*, no. 1 (Winter 1999): 170–175.

Joint Working Group on Israeli-Palestinian Relations. "The Future Israeli-Palestinian Relationship" Weatherhead Center for International Affairs Working Paper No. 99–12. Cambridge, MA: Harvard University, 1999. Reprinted in *Middle East Policy* 7, no. 2 (February 2000): 90–112.

Jordan, Judith V., Maureen Walker, and Linda M. Hartling, eds. *The Complexity of Connection: Writings from the Jean Baker Miller Training Institute.* New York: Guilford Publications, 2004.

Joshi, Pushpa. *Gandhi on Women.* Ahmedabad, India: Navajivan Publishing, 1998.

Kambhu, J. "Thailand: Death of a Regime." *Far Eastern Economic Review* 82 (October 22, 1973): 13–17.

Kanzer, Adam. *Finance for a Better World: The Shift toward Sustainability.* Edited by Henri-Claude de Bettignies and Francois Lépineux. Hampshire, UK: Palgrave Macmillan, 2009.

Kassai, Susan C. "An Evaluation of Possible Transmission of Holocaust-Related Trauma to the Third Generation." PsyD diss., Hofstra University, 2005. http://www.proquest.com.

Kaye, Jeff. "How APA Made a Pact with DOD and CIA Over Torture." *Firedoglake.com*, April 28, 2009. http://firedoglake.com/2009/04/28/how-apa-made-a-pact-with-dod-cia-over-torture-interrogations/.

Kelly, Kathy. "The Children of Iraq, 1990–1997." *The Link* 30, no. 1 (Jan–Mar 1997): 3.

Kelly, William, ed. *Post-Traumatic Stress Disorder and the War Veteran Patient.* New York: Brunner/Mazel, 1985.

Kelman, Herbert C. "Applying a Human Needs Perspective to the Practice of Conflict Resolution: The Israeli-Palestinian Case." In *Conflict: Human Needs Theory*, edited by John Burton. New York: St. Martin's Press, 1990.

Kelman, Herbert C. "Coalitions across Conflict Lines: The Interplay of Conflicts within and between the Israeli and Palestinian Communities." In *Conflict between People and Groups*, edited by Stephen Worchel and Jeffry Simpson. Chicago: Nelson-Hall, 1993.

Kelman, Herbert C. "Contributions of an Unofficial Conflict Resolution Effort to the Israeli-Palestinian Breakthrough." *Negotiation Journal* 11 (1995): 19–27.

Kelman, Herbert C. "Group Processes in the Resolution of International Conflicts: Experiences from the Israeli-Palestinian Case." *American Psychologist* 52 (1997): 212–220.

Kelman, Herbert C. "Interactive Problem Solving in the Israeli-Palestinian Case: Past Contributions and Present Challenges." In *Paving the Way: Contributions of Interactive Conflict Resolution to Peacemaking*, edited by Ronald J. Fisher. Lanham, MD: Lexington Books, 2005.

Kelman, Herbert C. "Interactive Problem Solving: Informal Mediation by the Scholar-Practitioner." In *Studies in International Mediation: Essays in Honor of Jeffrey Z. Rubin*, edited by Jacob Bercovitch. New York: Palgrave Macmillan, 2002.

Kelman, Herbert C. "Negotiation as Interactive Problem Solving." *International Negotiation: A Journal of Theory and Practice* 1 (1996): 99–123.

Kelman, Herbert C. "The Role of National Identity in Conflict Resolution: Experiences from Israeli-Palestinian Problem-Solving Workshops." In *Social Identity, Intergroup Conflict, and Conflict Reduction*, edited by Richard D. Ashmore, Lee Jussim, and David Wilder. Oxford, UK and New York: Oxford University Press, 2001.

Kelman, Herbert C. and Roger J. Fisher. "Conflict Analysis and Resolution." In *Oxford Handbook of Political Psychology*, edited by D.O. Sears, L. Huddy, and R. Jervis. 315–353. Oxford, England: Oxford University Press, 2003.

Khamisa, Azim. *From Forgiveness to Fulfillment.* ANK Publishing, 2007.

Ki-Moon, Ban. "Five Steps to a Nuclear-free World." *Guardian*. November 23, 2008. http://www.guardian.co.uk/commentisfree/2008/nov/23/nuclear-disarmament -united-nations.

Kinane, Ed. "Cry for Justice in Haiti, Fall 1993." In Moser-Puangsuwan/Weber (pp. 207-232). 2000.

Kinder, Peter, Steven D. Lydenberg, and Amy L. Domini, *The Social Investment Almanac: A Comprehensive Guide to Socially Responsible Investing.* New York: Henry Holt and Company, 1992.

Kinder, Peter, *Investing for Good: Making Money While Being Socially Responsible.* New York: HarperBusiness, 1993.

Kjos, Berit. Toying with Death. March 2004. http://www.crossroad.to/articles2/ 04/toying-with-death.htm.

Komitee für Grundrechte und Demokratie (Hg.). *Frieden mit anderen Waffen.* Reinbek: Rororo, 1981.

Konglang, A. "Thailand Evacuates Nationals as Protests Rock Cambodia." *Philippine Daily Inquirer,* January 31, 2003, A13.

Koo, Kab-Woo. "Peace State: A New Political Entity That Pursues Peace with Peaceful Means." In *2008 White Paper on Peace: Citizens Speak about Security.* Edited by PSPD Center for Peace and Disarmament. Seoul: Arche, 2008.

Koo, Kab-Woo. *Critical studies of Peace and the Korean Peninsula.* Humanitas, 2007, 195–209.

Koppelman, Alex. "Frank to Code Pink Protestors: Grow Up." *Salon.com,* March 24, 2009.

Korean Sharing Movement Center for Peace and Sharing. *2007 Resource Book on Programs on South-North Unity and Conflict Resolution.* Seoul: Korean Sharing Movement Center for Peace and Sharing, 2007.

Korten, David. C. *Globalizing Civil Society.* New York: Seven Stories Press, 1998.

Kostelny, Kathleen. "What about the Girls?" *Cornell International Law Journal* 37, no. 3 (2004): 505–512.

Kothari, Rajni. *Politics and the People: In Search of a Humane India,* vol. II. Delhi: Ajanta Publications, 1989.

Krieger, David. "Troubling Questions About Missile Defense Counterpunch." http:// www.counterpunch.org/krieger09122006.html (accessed September 12, 2006).

Kriesberg, Louis. "Coexistence and the Reconciliation of Communal Conflicts." In *The Handbook of Interethnic Coexistence,* edited by Eugene Weiner, 182–198. New York: Continuum, 1998.

Kristensen, Hans M. "U.S. Nuclear Weapons Withdrawn From the United Kingdom." *Federation of American Scientists Security Blog,* June 26, 2009. http:// www.fas.org.

Kritz, Neal J ed. *Transitional Justice: How Emerging Democracies Reckon with Former Regimes. General Considerations,* Vol. I. Washington, DC: U.S. Institute of Peace, 1995.

Kropp, Robert. "2008 Sees Increases in CSR Reporting and Adherence to GRI Guidelines." *Social Funds* (April 20, 2009). http://www.socialfunds.com/news/ article.cgi/article2677.html.

KUBARK Counterintelligence Interrogation, July 1963. http://www.mindcontrol forums.com/kubark.htm (retrieved October 15, 2008).

Kulka, Richard A., William E. Schlenger, John A. Fairbank, Richard L. Hough, B. Kathleen Jordan, Charles R. Marmar, and Daniel S. Weiss. *Trauma and the Vietnam War Generation: Report on the Findings from the National Vietnam Veterans Readjustment Study.* New York: Brunner/Mazel, 1990.

Kurtz, Lester and Jennifer Turpin, eds. *Encyclopedia of Violence, Peace, and Conflict.* San Diego: Academic Press, 1999.

Lagouranis, Tony, and Allen Mikaelian. *Fear Up Harsh: An Army Interrogator's Journey through Iraq.* New York: New American Library, 2007.

Lavik, Nils Johan, Mette Nygard, Nora Sveaass, and Eva Fannemel, eds. *Pain and Survival: Human Rights Violations and Mental Health.* Oslo, Norway: Scandinavian University Press, 1994.

Lazlo, Ervin and John Yoo, eds. *World Encyclopedia of Peace.* Oxford: Pergamon Press, 1986.

Le Compte, Eric. Interviewed by Jill Latonick-Flores, telephone, September 15, 2009.

Lederach, John Paul. *Building Peace. Sustainable Reconciliation in Divided Societies.* Washington, DC: United States Institute of Peace Press, 1997.

Lederach, John Paul. *The Little Book of Conflict Transformation.* Intercourse, PA: Good Books, 2003.

Legislative Action Index. http://www.soaw.org/article.php?id=96.

Lerner, Michael. J. *The Belief in a Just World: A Fundamental Delusion.* New York: Plenum, 1980.

Leung, Kwok, and W.G. Stephan. "Conflict and Injustice in Intercultural Relations: Insights from the Arab–Israeli and Sino–British Disputes." In *Political Psychology: Cultural and Crosscultural Perspectives*, edited by Stanley Renshon and John Duckitt, 128–143. London: Macmillan, 2000.

Lewis, Neil A. "Red Cross Finds Detainee Abuse in Guantánamo" (November 30, 2004). http://www.nytimes.com/2004/11/30/politics/30gitmo.html?oref=login& adxnnl=1&oref=login&adxnnlx=1101831750- (retrieved 4 March 2008).

Lifsher, Marc. "Unocal Settles Human Rights Lawsuit over Alleged Abuses at Myanmar Pipeline." *Los Angeles Times*, March 22, 2005 (Home edition).

Lifton, Robert Jay. "The Post War War." *Journal of Social Issues* 31, no. 4 (1975).

Lifton, Robert Jay, and Greg Mitchell. *Hiroshima in America: Fifty Years of Denial.* New York: HarperPerennial, 1995.

Lim, J.S. "The Conscientious Objection Movement in South Korea as a Peace Movement: Tensions between Freedom of Conscience and Anti-Militarism." MA thesis, Seoul National University, 2009.

Louche, Celine, and Steven D. Lydenberg. *Companion to Financial Ethics.* Edited by John R. Boatright. Hoboken, NJ: John Wiley 2009.

Maat, Bob. "A Moment of Peace, a Glimmer of Hope." Mimeographed article, 1993.

Mabbett, Ian W., ed. *Patterns of Kingship and Authority in Traditional Asia.* London: Croom Helm, 1985.

Mack, Andrew, and Zoe Nielsen, eds. "Human Security Report." Human Security Centre, Liu Institute for Global Issues at the University of British Columbia. www.humansecuritycentre.org (accessed October 20, 2005).

MacNair, Rachel M. *Perpetration-Induced Traumatic Stress: The Psychological Conse-quences of Killing*. Westport, CT: Praeger/Greenwood Publishing Group, 2002.

Mahony, Liam, and Luis Enrique Eguren. *Unarmed Bodyguards. International Accompani-ment for the Protection of Human Rights*. West Hartford, CT: Kumarian Press, 1997.

Mahony, Liam. "Side by Side. Protecting and Encouraging Threatened Activists with Unarmed International Accompaniment." Edited by the Center for Vic-tims of Torture, Minneapolis, MN, 2004.

Mahony, Liam. "Proactive Presence: Field Strategies for Civilian Protection." *HD Center for Humanitarian Dialogue*, 2006. http://www.hdcentre.org/publications?filter0=45.

Makower, Joel. *Beyond the Bottom Line: Putting Social Responsibility to Work for Your Business and the World*. New York: Simon & Schuster, 1994.

Mamdani, Mahmood. *When Victims Become Killers*. Princeton, NJ: Princeton Uni-versity Press, 2002.

Manoff, Robert. "The Mass Media and Social Violence: Is There a Role for the Media in Preventing and Moderating Ethnic, National, and Religious Conflict?" Unpublished manuscript for the Center for War, Peace, and News Media, Depart-ment of Journalism and Mass Communication, New York University, 1996.

Mao, Tse-Tung. *On The Protracted War* (trans.). Peking, China: Foreign Languages Press, 1960 (original work published in 1938).

Markusen, Ann, and Joel Yukden. *Dismantling the War Economy*. New York: Basic Books, 1992.

Martín-Baró, Ignacio. *Writings for a Liberation Psychology*. Cambridge, MA: Har-vard University Press, 1994.

Massie, Robert K. *Loosing the Bonds: The United States and South Africa in the Apartheid Years*. New York: Doubleday, 1997.

Mathur, J.S., and P.C. Sharma, eds. *Non-Violence and Social Change*. Ahmedabad: Navajivan Publishing House, 1977.

Maurer, John H. *Reader's Companion to Military History*. New York: Houghton Mif-flin College Division, 2005. file:///history/readerscomp/mil/html/mh_000101_publicationd.htm.

Mayer, Jane. *The Dark Side: The Inside Story of How the War on Terror Turned into a War on American Ideals*. New York: Doubleday, 2008.

Mayer, Jane. Outsourcing Torture: The Secret History of America's Extraordinary Rendition Program, Feb. 14, 2005, http://www.newyorker.com/archive/2005/02/14/050214fa_fact6.

Mayton, Daniel. "Gandhi as Peacebuilder: The Social Psychology of Satyagraha." In *Peace, Conflict and Violence: Peace Psychology for the 21st Century*, edited by Daniel J. Christie, Richard V. Wagner, and Deborah D. Winter, 307–313. Upper Saddle River, NJ: Prentice Hall, 2001.

Mazarr, Michael. "Going Just a Little Nuclear: Nonproliferation Lessons from North Korea." *International Security* 20 (1995): 92–122.

McCann, I. Lisa, and Laurie A. Pearlman. *Psychological Trauma and the Adult Survivor: Theory, Therapy, and Transformation*. New York: Brunner/Mazel, 1990.

McCoy, Alfred. *A Question of Torture: CIA Interrogation from the Cold War to the War on Terror*. New York: Metropolitan Books, 2006.

McGovern, Ray. "McCain's Defining Moment," http://www.tompaine.com/print/mccains_defining_moment.php (retrieved November 8, 2008).

McKay, Susan, and Dyan Mazurana. *Where Are the Girls? Girls in Fighting Forces in Northern Uganda, Sierra Leone, and Mozambique: Their Lives during and after War.* Montreal: International Centre for Human Rights and Democratic Development, 2004.

McNamara, Robert S. "Apocalypse Soon." *Foreign Policy Magazine* (May/June 2005). http://www.foreignpolicy.com/story/cms.php?story_id=2829.

Mechanic, Michael. "Torture Hits Home: Voluntary Confinement." March/April 2008. http://www.motherjones.com/politics/2008/03/voluntary-confinement (retrieved October 8, 2009).

Meltzer, Milton. *Slavery: A World History.* New York: De Capo Press, 1993.

Microsoft Encarta Encyclopedia 1995 [CD–ROM]. Redmond, WA: Microsoft Corporation, 1995.

Microsoft Encarta Encyclopedia 2000 [CD–ROM]. Redmond, WA: Microsoft Corporation, 2000.

Miles, Steven. "Medical Ethics and the Interrogation of Guantanamo 063," *The American Journal of Bioethics* 7, no. 4 (2007): 5, http://ajobonline.com/journal/j_articles.php?aid=1140.

Military Industrial Complex. "Contractor/Contract Detail." http://www.militaryindustrialcomplex.com/contract_detail.asp?contract_id=8032.

Missile defense and the ABM Treaty. 2002. http://www.bits.de/NRANEU/BMD/ABM.htm.

Montague, Dena. "War Profiteers, in Africa, as Well As Iraq." *CommonDreams.org,* 2003. http://www.commondreams.org/views03/0422-09.htm.

Montiel, Cristina Jayme. "Bargaining for Peaceful Termination of Unsuccessful Coup Attempts in the Philippines." *The Journal of Contingencies and Crisis Management* 3 (1995a): 215–227.

Montiel, Cristina Jayme. "Social Psychological Dimensions of Political Conflict Resolution in the Philippines." *Peace and Conflict: Journal of Peace Psychology* 1 (1995b): 149–159.

Montiel, Cristina J. "Social Representations of Democratic Transition: Was the Philippine People Power One a Nonviolent Power-Shift or a Military Coup?" *Asian Journal of Social Psychology,* 13, no. 3 (2010b): 173–184.

Montville, Joseph V. "The Healing Function in Political Conflict Resolution." In *Conflict Resolution Theory and Practice: Integration and Application,* edited by Dennis J. Sandole and Hugo Van der Merwe. Manchester, UK: Manchester University Press, 1993.

"More than 40 Hutus Killed in Rwanda-Congo Air Raid." *Telegraph UK* (February 13, 2009). http://www.telegraph.co.uk.

Morrell, David, and Chai-anan Samudavanija. *Political Conflict in Thailand.* Cambridge, MA: Oelgeschlager, Gunn, & Hain, 1981.

Moser-Puangsuwan, Yeshua, and Thomas, Weber, eds. *Nonviolent Intervention across Borders. A Recurrent Vision.* Honolulu: Spark M. Matsunaga Institute for Peace, 2000.

Müller, Barbara. "Alkan Peace Team 1994–2001. Mit Freiwilligenteams im gewaltfreien Einsatz in Krisenregionen." Bildungsvereinigung Arbeit und Leben Niedersachsen: Braunschweig, 2004.

Muller, Jean-Marie. *Principes et methodes de l'intervention civile.* 1995.

Multilateral Arms Regulation and Disarmament Agreements, 2005. http://dis armament.un.org/TreatyStatus.nsf.

Myrdal, Alva R. *The Game of Disarmament: How the United States & Russia Run the Arms Race.* Rev. ed. New York: Pantheon Books, 1982.

Nadler, Arie, Thomas E. Malloy, and Jeffery D. Fisher, eds. *The Social Psychology of Intergroup Reconciliation.* New York: Oxford University Press, 2008.

Nadler, Arie. "Moving from Violent Confrontation to Peaceful Coexistence." Opening comments presented at the conference on Social Psychology of Reconciliation. University of Connecticut, Storrs, 2003.

Nagler, Michael N. *The Search for a Nonviolent Future. A Promise of Peace for Ourselves, Our Families, and Our World.* San Francisco: Inner Ocean, 2004.

Nathan, Andrew J. "The Tiananmen Papers." http://www.foreignaffairs.org/20010101faessay4257/andrew-j-nathan/the-tiananmen-papers.html.

National Council of Churches in Korea. *Resource Book on Korean Churches' Peace and Reunification Movement 1980–2000.* National Council of Churches in Korea, Chunji Moonwha, 2000.

Nebres, Bienvenido. *Personal Notes on Noble's Popular Uprising.* Mimeographed article, 1990.

Nonviolent Peaceforce. "Sri Lanka Quarterly Report 1, no 5," 2006. www.nonviolentpeaceforce.org.

NTI. *Why Highly Enriched Uranium is a Threat.* September, 2009. http://www.nti.org/db/heu/index.html.

Obama, Barack. April 5, 2008. http://www.whitehouse.gov/the_press_office/Remarks-By-President-Barack-Obama-In-Prague-As-Delivered/.

O'Dwyer, Gerard. "Defense Stocks and Ethics: Norwegian Pension Fund Objects to Cluster Bombs." *Defense News,* March 2, 2009. http://www.defensenews.com/story.php?i=3969088.

OPCW. "2005 Associate Programme Commences." The Organisation for the Prohibition of Chemical Weapons (OPCW) Sixth Associate Programme on 22 July 2005 at the OPCW headquarters in The Hague, the Netherlands. http://www.opcw.org/ (December 2, 2005).

OpenSecrets.org. "Bechtel Group." http://www.opensecrets.org/pacs/lookup2.php?strID=C00103697.

OpenSecrets.org. "General Electric." http://www.opensecrets.org/orgs/summary.php?cycle=A&type=P&id=D000000125.

Opotow, Susan. "Social Injustice." In *Peace, Conflict and Violence: Peace Psychology for the 21st Century,* edited by Daniel J. Christie, Richard V. Wagner, and Deborah D. Winter, 102–109. Upper Saddle River, NJ: Prentice Hall, 2001.

Organization for the Prohibition of Chemical Weapons (OPCW). "Chemical Weapons." http://www.opcw.org/.

Orlitzky, Marc, Frank L. Schmidth, and Sara L. Rynes. "Corporate Social and Financial Performance: A Meta-Analysis." *Organization Studies* 24 (2003): 403–441.

Osgood, Charles. *An Alternative to War or Surrender.* Urbana, IL: University of Illinois Press, 1962.

Osman, T. "The Traditional Malay Socio-Political World View." In *Malaysian World View*, edited by Taib Osman, 46–75. Singapore: Institute of Southeast Asian Studies, 1985.

OTTO, 1981: Der Widerstand gegen die Wiederbewaffnung der Bundesrepublik, in: Reiner Steinweg (Red.), Unsere Bundeswehr? Zum 25-jährigen Bestehen einer umstrittenen Institution (= Friedensanalysen 14), 52-105, Frankfurt/M., edition suhrkamp 1056

Otto, Karl A. *Vom Ostermarsch zur APO.* Frankfurt am Main/New York: Campus, 1977.

Paddock, Richard C. "Protest Disrupts UC Board Meeting. Hunger Strikers and Their Backers Protest the University's Involvement in the Development of Nuclear Weapons. Thirteen Are Arrested," May 18, 2007. http://articles.latimes .com/keyword/university-of-california-board-of-regents.

Paech, Norman. "Die Aufforderung der Bundesregierung ist falsch." *Blatt Für Deutsche und Internationale Politik,* December 2001.

Paluck, Elizabeth L. "Reducing Intergroup Prejudice and Conflict Using the Media: A field experiment in Rwanda." *Journal of Personality and Social Psychology* 96, (2009): 574–587.

Paluck, Elizabeth L., Donald P. Green, Ervin Staub, and Laurie Pearlman. "The Impact of Musekeweya: Changes in Knowledge, Attitudes, and Behaviors" (article in preparation).

Pan, Esther and Jayshree Bajoria. "The U.S.-India Nuclear Deal." *Washington Post,* September 4, 2008. http://www.washingtonpost.com/wp-dyn/content/article/ AR2008090401614.html.

Park, J.E. "Iraq and Afghanistan, and South Korea's Anti-War Movement." In *2008 White Paper on Peace: Citizens Speak about Security,* edited by PSPD Center for Peace and Disarmament. Seoul: Arche, 2008.

Pax Christi (Hg.). "Ultima Ratio?! Die Friedensbewegung im Streit um Militäreinsätze." In *Probleme des Friedens* Heft 3, Idstein, KOMZI.

Pax World Fund Investments. 2010. http://www.paxworld.com/about/welcome-from-the-president/pax-history/

Peace Action. http://www.peaceaction.org/Peace%20Action%20Military%20Spending %20Primer.pdf.

Peace Activists Workshop Preparation Committee. *Resource Book on 2006 Peace Activists Workshop.* Seoul: Peace Activists Workshop Preparation Committee, 2007.

Peace Activists Workshop Preparation Committee. *Resource Book on 2008 Peace Activists Workshop.* Seoul: Peace Activists Workshop Preparation Committee, 2009.

Peace Pledge Union. "War and Peace: What's It All About?" (2005). http://www .ppu.org.uk/war/war_peace-modernwar.html.

Pearlman, Laurie A. *Trauma and Attachment Belief Scale Manual.* Los Angeles: Western Psychological Services, 2003.

Pearlman, Laurie A. and Karen W. Saakvitne. *Trauma and the Therapist: Countertransference and Vicarious Traumatization in the Treatment of Incest Survivors.* New York: W.W. Norton, 1995.

Pedersen, Paul. "The Cultural Context of Peacemaking." In *Peace, Conflict and Violence: Peace Psychology for the 21st Century,* edited by Daniel J. Christie, Richard V. Wagner, and Deborah D. Winter, 183–192. Upper Saddle River, NJ: Prentice Hall, 2001.

Penal Reform International (PRI). "Research Report on the Gacaca VI. From Camp to Hill, the Reintegration of Released Prisoners." PRI Rwanda. BP 370. Kigali, Rwanda, May 2004.

Pennebaker, James W. "The Effects of Traumatic Disclosure on Physical and Mental Health: The Values of Writing and Talking about Upsetting Events." In *Posttraumatic Stress Intervention,* edited by J.M. Violanti, D. Paton, and C. Dunning. Springfield, IL: Charles C Thomas, 2000.

"Petition the APA," http://www.ipetitions.com/petition/apademocracy/faq.html (retrieved November 7, 2008).

Pettigrew, Thomas F., and Linda R. Tropp. "A Meta-analytic Test of Intergroup Contact Theory." *Journal of Personality and Social Psychology* 90 (2006): 751–781.

Pettigrew, Thomas F., and Linda R. Tropp, and Linda R. Tropp. "Does Intergroup Contact Reduce Prejudice? Recent Meta-Analytic Findings." In *Reducing Prejudice and Discrimination,* edited by Stuart Oskamp. London: Lawrence Erlbaum Associates, 2000.

Pilger, John. "Breaking the Silence: Truth and Lies in the War on Terror," 2003. http://www.bullfrogfilms.com/catalog/break.html.

Pilisuk, Marc. "Addictive Rewards in Nuclear Weapons Development." *Peace Review* 11, no. 4 (1999): 597–602.

Pilisuk, Marc. "Experimenting with the Arms Race." *Journal of Conflict Resolution* 28, no. 2 (1984): 296–315.

Pilisuk, Marc. "Globalism and Structural Violence." In *Peace, Conflict, and Violence: Peace Psychology for the 21st Century,* edited by Daniel J. Christie, Richard Wagner, and Deborah Winter, 149–160. Englewood Cliffs, NJ: Prentice Hall, 2001.

Pilisuk, Marc and Paul Skolnick. "Inducing Trust: A Test of the Osgood Proposal." *Journal of Personality and Social Psychology,* 8, no. 2 (1968): 121–133.

Pilisuk, Marc, Joanne Zazzi. "Toward a Psychosocial Theory of Military and Economic Violence in the Era of Globalization." *Journal of Social Issues* 62, no. 1 (2006): 41–62.

Pilisuk, Marc, with Jennifer Achord Rountree. *Who Benefits from Global Violence and War: Uncovering a Destructive System.* Westport, CT: Praeger Security International, 2008.

Pimentel, Aquilino. *Federalization: An Idea Whose Time Has Come,* 2002. http://www.Nenepimentel.Org/Speeches/20020725094213fed.Html.

Piven, Francis F. *The War at Home: The Domestic Costs of Bush's Militarism.* New York: The New Press, 2004.

Potyarkin, Ye, and Sergi Kortunov. *The USSR Proposes Disarmament, 1920s-1980s* [translated from Russian]. Moscow: Progress Publishers, 1986.

Powell, Jeffery H. "Amnesty, Reintegration, and Reconciliation in Rwanda." *Military Review* 88, no. 5 (September/October 2008): 84–90. http://www.dtic.mil/cgibin/GetTRDoc?AD=ADA485563&Location=U2&doc=GetTRDoc.pdf.

Power Reactor Information System, (PRIS). "Number of Reactors in Operation Worldwide." October 6, 2010. http://www.iaea.org/cgi-bin/db.page.pl/pris.oprconst.htm.

Powers, Roger and William Vogele, eds. *Protest, Power, and Change: An Encyclopedia of Nonviolence from ACT-UP to Women's Suffrage.* New York: Garland, 1997.

Priest, Dana. "U.S. Instructed Latins on Executions, Torture." *Washington Post,* September 21, 1996: A1.

Proceedings of Stockholm International Forum on Truth, Justice and Reconciliation, 2002.

Pruitt, Dean G. *Negotiation Behavior.* New York: Academic Press, 1981.

Prunier, Gerard. *Africa's world war: Congo, the Rwandan genocide, and the making of a continental catastrophe* . New York : Oxford University Press. 2009.

Public Citizen. "World Health Organization Ignored Hazards of Irradiated Foods, Declared Them Safe." Oct. 8, 2002. http://www.citizen.org/pressroom/pressroomredirect.cfm?ID=1236.

Pye, Lucian W. *Asian Power and Politics.* Cambridge, MA: Belknap Press, 1985.

Rabinowitch, Eugene. "War Papers." *New York Times,* June 28, 1971, Opinion section.

Radiation and Public Health Project (RPHP). "Tooth Fairy Project," 2003. http://www.radiation.org/projects/tooth_fairy.html.

Rapoport, Anatol. "Chicken a la Kahn." *Virginia Quarterly Review* 41 (1965): 370–389.

Rapoport, Anatol. *Fights, Games, and Debates.* Ann Arbor: University of Michigan Press, 1960.

Raschke, Joachim. "Zum Begriff der sozialen Bewegungen," in *Neue soziale Bewegungen in der Bundesrepublik Deutschland,* 2. Aufl., by R. Roth/D. Rucht (Hg. (Bonn: 1991), 32.

Reaching Critical Will. "Bechtel Corporation." http://www.reachingcriticalwill.org/corporate/dd/bechtel2.html.

Reaching Critical Will. "The Environment and the Nuclear Age." http://www.reachingcriticalwill.org/technical/factsheets/environmental.html.

"Religious Violence Worsens in Western India." http://www.Cnn.com. (accessed April 26, 2002).

Renner, Michael. "Curbing the Proliferation of Small Arms." In *State of the World 1998,* edited by Lester R. Brown, Christopher Flavin, and Hillary French, 131–148. New York: Norton, 1998.

Report of the International Committee of the Red Cross (ICRC) on the Treatment by the Coalition Forces of Prisoners of War and Other Persons Protected by the Geneva Conventions in Iraq, during Arrest, Internment and Interrogation (Feb. 2004), available at http://www.cbsnews.com/htdocs/pdf/redcrossabuse.pdf.

"Report of the American Psychological Association Presidential Task Force on Psychological Ethics and National Security." June, 2005. http://www.apa.org/pubs/info/reports/pens.pdf.

Report of the UN Truth Commission on El Salvador, April 1, 1993. http://www.derechos.org/nizkor/salvador/informes/truth.html.

"Resolution Regarding Participation by Psychologists in Interrogations inMilitary Detention Centers," http://www.earlham.edu/publicaffairs/content/press room/archive/2007/october/psychdeptresolution.php.

Resolutions Urge Psychology Assn. to Take Tougher Stand on Interrogating Prisoners," October 12, 2007, http://wiredcampus.chronicle.com/article/Resolutions-Urge-Psychology/39766/.

Rhodes, Ginger, George J. Allen, Joseph Nowinski, and Antonius Cillessen. "The Violent Socialization Scale: Development and Initial Validation." In *Violent Acts and Violentization: Assessing, Applying, and Developing Lonnie Athens' Theories*, edited by Jeffrey Ulmer and Lonnie Athens, 4 (2002): 125–144. Elsevier Science.

Richter, Robert, director. *School of Assassins*. 1994. http://richtervideos.com/SchoolofAssassins/.

Roche, Douglas. "Rethink the Unthinkable." *Globe and Mail* (Canada's "national" newspaper): March 12, 2002, A19.

Ronnefeldt, Clemens. Newsletter; "Krieg ist keine Lösung—Alternativen sind möglich.'" April 20, 2004.

Rosenbloom, Dena J., and Mary B. Williams. *Life after Trauma*. New York: Guilford, 1999.

Ross, Marc H., and Jeffrey Rothman. *Theory and Practice in Ethnic Conflict Management: Theorizing Success and Failure*. New York: Macmillan, 1999.

Rouhana, Nadim N., and Herbert C. Kelman, "Promoting Joint Thinking in International Conflicts: An Israeli-Palestinian Continuing Workshop," *Journal of Social Issues* 50 (1994): 157–178.

Rupp, Hans Karl. *Außerparlamentarische Opposition in der Ära Adenauer: Der Kampf gegen die Atombewaffnung in den fünfziger Jahren*. Koeln: Pahl-Rugenstein, 1984.

Rupp, Hans Karl 1970: Außerparlamentarische Opposition in der Ära Adenauer. Der Kampf gegen die Atombewaffnung in den 50er Jahren, Köln

Ryan, William. *Blaming the Victim*. New York: Pantheon, 1971.

Saakvitne, Karen W., Sarah G. Gamble, Laurie A. Pearlman, and Beth T. Lev. *Risking Connection: A Training Curriculum for Working with Survivors of Childhood Abuse*. Lutherville, MD: Sidran Foundation & Press, 2000.

Sands, Philippe. *Torture Team: Rumsfield's Memo and the Betrayal of American Values*. New York: Palgrave Macmillan, 2008.

Schell, Jonathan. *The Unconquerable World: Power, Nonviolence, and the Will of the People*. New York: Metropolitan Books, 2003.

Schirch, Lisa. *Keeping the Peace. Exploring Civilian Alternatives in Conflict Prevention*. Uppsala, Sweden: Life and Peace Institute, 1995.

Schock, Kurt. *Unarmed Insurrections: People Power Movements in Nondemocracies*. Minneapolis: University of Minnesota, 2005.

School of Assassins, http://richtervideos.com/SchoolofAssassins/.

Schwartz, Stephen I. (ed.). "Atomic Audit: The Costs and Consequences of U.S. Nuclear Weapons Since 1940." (Washington, DC: Brookings Institution Press, 1998). http://www.brookings.edu/projects/archive/nucweapons/contents.aspx.

Schwebel, Milton, and Daniel Christie. "Children and Structural Violence." In *Peace, Conflict, and Violence: Peace Psychology for the 21st Century,* edited by D.J. Christie, R.V. Wagner, and D.D. Winter, 120–129. Upper Saddle River, NJ: Prentice Hall, 2001.

Schweitzer, Christine. "An Experiment at Mixing Roles: The Balkan Peace Team in Croatia and Serbia/Kosovo." In *People Building Peace II*, edited by the European Centre for Conflict Prevention, 369–375. Utrecht, 2005.

Schweitzer, Christine. *Nonviolent Peaceforce—Feasibility Study.* Contributions by Donna Howard, Mareike Junge, Corey Levine, Christine Schweitzer, Carl Stieren, and Tim Wallis. Hamburg/St. Paul, September 2001. http://www.nonviolent peaceforce.org/english/resources/rstudy.asp.

Schweitzer, Christine, and Howard Clark. *Balkan Peace Team—International e.V. A Final Internal Assessment of Its Functioning and Activities*, Balkan Peace Team/ Bund für Soziale Verteidigung (eds.). Minden: Bund für Soziale Verteidigung, Hintergrund- und Diskussionspapier No. 11, 2002.

Scientists Committee for Radiation Information. "The Effect of a 20 Megaton Bomb." *New University Thought* (Spring 1962): 24–32.

Senghaas, Dieter. *Friedensprojekt Europa.* Frankfurt/M: Edition Suhrkamp, 1992.

Shanker, Thom. "Weapons Sales Worldwide Rise to Highest Level since 2000." *New York Times.* http://www.nytimes.com/2005/08/30/politics/30weapons.html. (accessed August 8, 2005).

Sharp, Gene. *Gandhi as a Political Strategist.* Boston: Porter Sargent, 1979.

Sharp, Gene. *The Politics of Nonviolent Action.* Boston: Porter Sargent, 1973.

Sharp, Gene. *Waging Nonviolent Struggle: 20th Century Practice and 21st Century Potential.* Manchester, NH: Extending Horizon Books, 2005.

Shaw, Rosalind. *Rethinking Truth and Reconciliation Commissions.* USIP Special Report 130. Washington, DC: U.S. Institute for Peace, 2005.

Sherif, Muzafer, O.J. Harvey, B. Jack White, William Hood, and Carolyn W. Sherif. *Intergroup Cooperation and Competition.* Norman, OK: University Book Exchange, 1961.

Sheth, D.L. "Politics of Social Transformation: Grassroots Movements in India." In *The Constitutional Foundations of World Peace*, edited by Richard A. Falk, Robert C. Johansen, and Samuel S. Kim, 275–287. Albany: State University of New York Press, 1993.

Shirbman, David. "Anti-War Activists, Finding They Don't Always Favor Peace, Lack Alternatives to Gulf Strategy." *Wall Street Journal,* February 1, 1991.

Shultz, George. "Remarks to the Commonwealth Club." http://wordforword .publicradio.org/programs/2008/04/11/.

Silva, J. Arturo, Dennis V. Derecho, Gregory B. Leong, Robert Weinstock, and Michelle M. Ferrari. "A Classification of Psychological Factors Leading to Violent Behavior in Posttraumatic Stress Disorder." *Journal of Forensic Sciences* 46 (2001): 309–316.

Sivard, Ruth L. *World Military and Social Expenditures.* Washington, DC: World Priorities, 1996.

Skinner, Ben. *A Crime So Monstrous: Face to Face with Modern-Day Slavery.* New York: Free Press.

Slater, Alice. "A Roadmap for US Presidential Leadership for Nuclear Disarmament." *Abolition 2000.* July 2008. HYPERLINK "http://www.abolition2000.org/?p=364" http://www.abolition20HYPERLINK "http://www.abolition2000.org/?p=364"00 .org/?p=364.

Sleek, Scott. "Older Vets Just Now Feeling Pain of War." *APA Monitor 29*, no. 1 (1998): 28.

Slim, Hugo, and Luis Enrique Eguren. *Humanitarian Protection. A Guidance Booklet.* Pilot Version, ALNAP, 2004. http://www.alnap.org/alnappubs.html.

Smith, Dan. *The Atlas of War and Peace.* London: Earthscan, 2003.

Soederberg, Susanne. "The Marketization of Social Justice: The Case of the Sudan Divestment Campaign." Paper presented at the annual meeting of the International Studies Association, New York, February 15, 2009.

Sokov, Nikolai. "START II Ratification: More Than Meets the Eye." James Martin Center for Nonproliferation Studies, April 14, 2000.

Soldz, Stephen. "Ending the Psychological Mind Games on Detainees," *Boston Globe*, August 10, 2008. http://www.boston.com/bostonglobe/editorial_ opinion/oped/articles/2008/08/10/ending_the_psychological_mind_games_on_ detainees/

Soldz, Stephen, and Brad Olson. "Psychologists, Detainee Interrogations, and Torture: Varying Perspectives on Nonparticipation." In *The Trauma of Psychological Torture*, edited by Almerindo E. Ojeda, 70–91. Westport, CT: Praeger, 2008.

Sonnenberg, Stephen M., Arthur S. Blank, and John A. Talbott. *The Trauma of War: Stress and Recovery in Viet Nam Veterans.* Washington, DC: American Psychiatric Press, 1985.

Source Watch Online. "Bechtel Group, Inc." http://www.sourcewatch.org/ index.php?title=Bechtel.

South Korea. http://www.Pbs.Org/Wgbh/Commandingheights/Lo/Countries/ Kr/Kr_Social.Html.

Sparkes, Russell. "Ethical Investment: Whose Ethics, Which Investment?" *Business Ethics: A European Review* 10, no. 3 (2001): 194–205.

Spring, Baker. "The ABM Treaty with Russia: A Treaty That Never Was." Heritage Foundation July 6, 1999. http://www.heritage.org/Research/Reports/ 1999/07/The-ABM-Treaty-with-Russia.

Stark, Lindsay. "Cleansing the Wounds of War: An Examination of Traditional Healing, Psychosocial Health and Reintegration in Sierra Leone." *Intervention: International Journal of Mental Health, Psychosocial Work and Counseling in Areas of Armed Conflict* 4, no. 3 (2006).

Stassen, Glen Harold and Lawrence Wittner, eds. "Peace Action, Past, Present, and Future." Boulder, CO: Paradigm Publishers, 2007.

Statman, Meir. "Socially Responsible Indexes: Composition, Performance and Tracking Error." *Journal of Portfolio Management* (Spring 2006). http://www

.scu.edu/business/finance/research/upload/socially_responsible_indexes_port
foliomgt_2006.pdf.

Statman, Meir, and Denys Glushkov. "The Wages of Social Responsibility." Working
paper, November 25, 2008. http://www.scu.edu/business/finance/research/
upload/Wages-112508.pdf.

Staub, Ervin. "Breaking the Cycle of Genocidal Violence: Healing and Reconciliation." In *Perspectives on Loss*, edited by John Harvey. Washington, DC: Taylor
and Francis, 1998.

Staub, Ervin. "Constructive and Destructive Forms of Forgiveness and Reconciliation after Genocide and Mass Killing." In *Handbook of Forgiveness*, edited by
Everett Worthington. New York: Brunner-Routledge, 2005a.

Staub, Ervin. "Justice, Healing and Reconciliation: How the People's Courts in
Rwanda Can Promote Them." *Peace and Conflict: The Journal of Peace Psychology*
10 (2004a): 25–31.

Staub, Ervin. *Overcoming Evil: Genocide, Violent Conflict and Terrorism*. New York:
Oxford University Press, 2011.

Staub, Ervin. "Reconciliation after Genocide, Mass Killing or Intractable Conflict:
Healing, Understanding the Roots of Violence and the Prevention of New Violence." Paper presented at Nevitt Sandford Award Address, International Society for Political Psychology Meetings. Lund, Sweden, July 2004.

Staub, Ervin. "The Cultural-Societal Roots of Violence: The Examples of Genocidal Violence and of Contemporary Youth Violence in the United States." *American Psychologist* 51 (1996): 17–132.

Staub, Ervin. "The Roots of Goodness: The Fulfillment of Basic Human Needs
and the Development of Caring, Helping and Non-aggression, Inclusive Caring,
Moral Courage, Active Bystandership, and Altruism Born of Suffering." In
Moral Motivation across the Life Span. Nebraska Symposium on Motivation,
edited by Gustav Carlo and Carolyn Edwards. Lincoln: Nebraska University
Press, 2005c.

Staub, Ervin. "Understanding the Roots of Violence, and Avenues to Its Preven-
tion and to Developing Positive Relations between the Local Ethnic Group and
Muslim Minorities in Amsterdam, in the Netherlands—and the Rest of
Europe" (unpublished manuscript, Department of Psychology, University of
Massachusetts at Amherst, 2005b).

Staub, Ervin. "Healing from a Difficult Past." In *Looking Backward, Moving Forward*, edited by Richard Hovannisian. New Brunswick, NJ: Transaction Publishers, 2003a.

Staub, Ervin. "The Origins and Prevention of Genocide, Mass Killing and Other
Collective Violence." *Peace and Conflict: Journal of Peace Psychology* 5 (1999):
303–337.

Staub, Ervin. *The Psychology of Good and Evil: Why Children, Adults and Groups Help
and Harm Others*. New York: Cambridge University Press, 2003b.

Staub, Ervin. *The Roots of Evil: The Origins of Genocide and Other Group Violence*.
New York: Cambridge University Press, 1989.

Staub, Ervin, and Laurie Pearlman. Facilitators' Summary of Observations and Recommendations from Leaders Seminar, 2002. http://www.heal-reconcile -rwanda.org.

Staub, Ervin, and Daniel Bar-Tal. "Genocide, Mass Killing and Intractable Conflict: Roots, Evolution, Prevention and Reconciliation." In *Handbook of Political Psychology*, edited by David Sears, Leonie Huddy, and Robert Jervis. New York: Oxford University Press, 2003.

Staub, Ervin, and Laurie A. Pearlman. "Healing, Reconciliation, and Forgiving after Genocide and Other Collective Violence." In *Forgiveness and Reconciliation: Religion, Public Policy and Conflict Transformation*, edited by Raymond Helmick and Rodney L. Petersen, 195–217. Radnor, PA: Templeton Foundation Press, 2001.

Staub, Ervin, and Laurie A. Pearlman. "Reducing Intergroup Prejudice and Conflict: A Commentary." *Journal of Personality and Social Psychology* 96 (2009), 588–594.

Staub, Ervin, and Laurie Pearlman. "Advancing Healing and Reconciliation." In *Psychological Interventions in Times of Crisis*, edited by Laura Barbanel and Robert Sternberg. New York: Springer-Verlag, 2006.

Staub, Ervin, Laurie A. Pearlman, Alexandra Gubin, and Athanase Hagengimana. "Healing, Reconciliation, and the Prevention of Violence after Genocide or Mass Killing: An Intervention and Its Experimental Evaluation in Rwanda." *Journal of Clinical and Social Psychology* 24 (2005): 297–334.

Stavrou, Vivi. *Breaking the Silence*. Luanda, Angola: Christian Children's Fund, 2005.

Steger, Manfred. "Peacebuilding and Nonviolence: Gandhi's Perspective on Power." In *Peace, Conflict, and Violence: Peace Psychology for the 21st Century*, edited by D.J. Christie, R.V. Wagner, and D.D. Winter, 120–129. Upper Saddle River, NJ: Prentice Hall, 2001.

Stephan, Maria J., and Erica Chenoweth. "Why Civil Resistance Works: The Strategic Logic of Nonviolent Conflict." *International Security* 33, no. 1 (2008): 7–44.

Strohmeyer, Hansjorg. "Collapse and Reconstruction of a Judicial System: The United Nations Missions in Kosovo and East Timor." *American Journal of International Law* 95 (2001): 46–63 (retrieved January 24, 2003, from JSTOR Database).

Sturgill, Claude C. *The Military History of the Third World since 1945*. Westport, CT: Greenwood Press, 1994.

Suedfeld, Peter, ed. *Psychology and Torture*. New York: Hemisphere, 1990.

Szayna, Thomas S., Graham Fuller, Robert Howe, Brian Nichiporuk, Kevin Riley, Ashley J. Tellis, et al. (1995). *Intervention in Intrastate Conflict*, Vol. 2. Santa Monica, CA: RAND.

Tajfel, Henri. "Social Psychology of Intergroup Relations." *Annual Review of Psychology* 33 (1982): 1–39.

Tausch, Nicole, Jared Kentworthy, and Miles Hewstone. "Intergroup Contact and the Improvement of Intergroup Relations." In *The Psychology of Resolving Global Conflicts: From War to Peace*, edited by Mari Fitzduff and Chris E. Stout, 2. Westport, CT: Praeger, 2006.

Tenet, George J. "The Worldwide Threat: Challenges in a Changing Global Context." Senate Select Committee on Intelligence. 24 February 2004.

The Center for Public Integrity. "Windfalls of War." 2004. http://www.publicintegrity
.org/projects/entry/297/.

The School of the Americas Watch, "Three Hundred Religious Leaders Hold Prayer
Vigil to Close the School of the Americas." http://www.soaw.org/article
.php?id=165.

The School of Americas Watch. "Action History," http://www.soaw.org/article
.php?id=321.

The School of the Americas Watch. "Bolivia Says No!" October 25, 2007. http://
www.soaw.org/presente/index.php?option=com_content&task=view&id=103
&Itemid=74.

The School of the Americas Watch. "4,408 Risk Arrest In Mass Non-Violent Civil
Disobedience Protest Of U.S. Army School Of The Americas." n.d. http://
www.soaw.org/index.php?option=com_content&view=article&id=171.

The School of the Americas Watch, "The SOA Watch Latin American Project,"
http://www.soaw.org/article.php?id=1510.

The School of the Americas Watch, "'Grave Diggers' Arrested at Pentagon for
Protest of US Army School of the Americas," http://www.soaw.org/article
.php?id=161.

The School of the Americas Watch, "SOA Watch Delegation to Mexico and Costa
Rica," http://www.soaw.org/article.php?id=1560.

The School of the Americas Watch, "2007 Direct Action at the SOA: Support the
SOA 11," http://www.soaw.org/article.php?id–1621.

The Sold Project. www.thesoldproject.com.

The Unknown Taiwan: Political Developments (n.d.). http://formosa.homelinux.com/
cwcmf/Taiwan/The_Unknown_Taiwan_TIF.pdf.

The World Bank Group Web Site, http://www.worldbank.Org.

The World Bank Group. *Dataset for David Dollar and Aart Kraay: Growth Is Good
for the Poor*, 2002 [Data File]. Available from The World Bank Group Web
Site, Http://Www.Worldbank.Org.

The World Bank Group. *GNI Per Capita 2001, Atlas Method and PPP* [Data File].
Available from World Bank Group, n.d.

Tkac, Paula. "One Proxy at a Time: Pursuing Social Change through Shareholder Proposals." *Federal Reserve Bank of Atlanta Economic Review* 91 (2006). http://www.frbat
lanta.org/invoke.cfm?objectid=D6B76A8D-5056-9F12-12D7D418FAADDABF
&method=display_body.

Tomar, Ravi. *India–Pakistan: Tensions over Kashmir* (2002, June 12). Parliament of
Australia, Department of Parliamentary Library Web Site: http://www.aph.gov
.au/library/intguide/FAD/kashmir.htm.

Torture Abolition and Survivors Support Coalition. "Film Shines Light on Torture." n.d. http://www.tassc.org/index.php.

*Totgesagte leben länger: Die Friedensbewegung. Von der Ost-West-Konfrontation zur
zivilen Konfliktbearbeitung.* Idstein: KOMZI, 1997.

Totten, Samuel, William S. Parsons, and Israel W. Charny, eds. *Century of Genocide.*
New York: Garland Publishing, 1997.

Towle, Phillip. *Enforced Disarmament: From the Napoleonic Campaigns to the Gulf
War.* Oxford: Clarendon Press; New York: Oxford University Press, 1997.

Treaty on Strategic Offensive Reductions. May 16, 2003 http://www.armscontrol
.ru/Start/sort.htm.

Triandis, Harry C. *Culture and Social Behavior.* New York: McGraw-Hill, 1994.

Trumbull, Charles P., ed. *2002 Britannica Book of the Year.* Chicago: Encyclopedia
Britannica, 2002.

Truth and Reconciliation Commission of Sierra Leone. *Truth and Reconciliation
Commission Report for the Children of Sierra Leone.* Accra, Ghana: Graphic Pack-
aging Limited, 2004.

Tullio, Francesco, ed. *Le Organizzazioni Non Governative e la trasformazione dei
conflitti. Le operazioni di pace nelle crisi internazionali. Analysi, esperienze, prospet-
tive.* Rome: Edizioni Associate Editrice Internazionale, 2002.

Tutu, Desmond M. *No Future without Forgiveness.* New York: Doubleday, 1999.

Tyler, Patrick E. "With U.S. Missile Defense, Russia Wants Less Offense." *New
York Times,* Wednesday, November 15, 2000.

Tyler, Tom R., and Heather J. Smith. "Social Justice and Social Movements." In
Handbook of Social Psychology, edited by Daniel T. Gilbert, Susan T. Fiske, and
Gardner Lindzey, 4th ed. 2: 595–629. New York: McGraw-Hill, 1998.

U.S. Defense Intelligence Agency. "Iraq Water Treatment Vulnerabilities." Jan. 1991.
http://www.gulflink.osd.mil/declassdocs/dia/19950901/950901_511rept_91.html.

Um, Khatharya. "Cambodia in 1993: Year Zero Plus One." *Asian Survey 34* (1994):
72–81.

UN Department for Disarmament Affairs. *The United Nations and Disarmament: A
Short History,* New York, 1988.

UN Department of Public Information, Media Release, "Arms Trade Treaty, 'Nu-
clear-Weapon-Free World,'" Outer Space Arms Race Among Issues, as General
Assembly adopts 54 First Committee Texts, December 6, 2006, http://www
.un.org/News/Press/docs/2006/ga10547.doc.htm/.

UNDP, United Nations Development Programme. "Human Development Report,
2007." http://hdr.undp.org/en/.

UNIDC, United Nations Institute for Disarmament Research, Geneva, Switzerland, 2005. http://disarmament.un.org/TreatyStatus.nsf.

United Nations Commission on Human Rights, "Situation of Detainees at
Guantánamo Bay," 2006, http://news.bbc.co.uk/1/shared/bsp/hi/pdfs/16_02_
06_un_guantanamo.pdf.

United Nations "Convention Against Torture and Other Cruel, Inhuman or
Degrading Treatment or Punishment." Last edited on January 25, 1997.
http://www.hrweb.org/legal/cat.html

United Nations Department for Disarmament Affairs. "Disarmament: A Short
History." New York: United Nations Institute for Disarmament Research, Geneva, Switzerland, July 22, 2005. http://disarmament.un.org/TreatyStatus.nsf.

United Nations Department of Economic and Social Affairs, Population Division.
http://www.un.org/esa/population/publications/publications.htm.

United Nations. *The United Nations and Disarmament Since 1945,* updated ed. New
York: Pantheon Books, 1996.

United States Space Command. *Vision for 2020.* http://www.fas.org/spp/military/
docops/usspac/visbook.pdf.

United States Committee for Refugees and Immigrants. "U.S. Committee for Refugees World Refugee Survey 2002–Rwanda," UNHCR Refworld. http://www.unhcr.org/refworld/docid/3d04c13b0.html.

UNODC, United Nations Office on Drugs and Crime. "Protocol to Prevent, Suppress, and Punish Trafficking in Persons." http://www.unodc.org/unodc/en/treaties/CTOC/index.html.

UNODC, United Nations Office on Drugs and Crime. "Human Trafficking FAQ's." http://www.unodc.org/unodc/en/human-trafficking/faqs.html.

US Department of State. "Trafficking Victims Protection Act." (TVPRA 2000, TVPRA 2003, TVPRA 2005, TVPRA 2009.) http://www.state.gov/documents/organization/10492.pdf. http://www.state.gov/documents/organization/28225.pdf. http://www.state.gov/documents/organization/61214.pdf. http://www.state.gov/documents/organization/87404.pdf.

US Environmental Protection Agency. "Hudson River PCBs." http://www.epa.gov/hudson/.

US Environmental Protection Agency. "Superfund Sites Where You Live." http://www.epa.gov/superfund/sites/.

US Peace Memorial. http://www.uspeacememorial.org/registry.

US Peace Registry. http://www.uspeacememorial.org/registry.

US PIRG. "America's #1 Superfund Polluter: General Electric." http://www.pirg.org/reports/enviro/super25/page3.htm.

US SIF. "2007 Report on Socially Responsible Investing Trends in US–Executive Summary." Washington: US Social Investment Forum, 2008.

Vack, Hanne, and Klaus Vack. *Politische und soziale Lernprozesse. Möglichkeiten, Chancen und Probleme.* Sensbachtal: Eigenverlag des Komitees für Grundrechte und Demokratie, 1993.

Varshney, Ashutosh. *Ethnic Conflict and Civic Life: Hindus and Muslims in India.* New Haven, CT: Yale University Press, 2002.

"Vice President Appears on Meet the Press with Tim Russert," MSNBC, transcript, September 14, 2001. http://www.msnbc.msn.com/id/3080244/.

Vitug, Marites Danguilan, and Glenda M. Gloria. *Under the Crescent Moon: Rebellion in Mindanao.* Quezon City, Philippines: Ateneo Center for Social Policy and Public Affairs and Institute for Popular Democracy, 2000.

Volkan, Vamik D. *Blood Lines: From Ethnic Pride to Ethnic Terrorism.* New York: Farrar, Straus and Giroux, 1997.

Volkan, Vamik D. "Tree Model: Psychopolitical Dialogues and the Promotion of Coexistence." In *The Handbook of Interethnic Coexistence*, edited by E. Weiner. New York: Continuum, 1998.

Wagner, Richard. "Peacemaking: Introduction." In *Peace, Conflict, and Violence: Peace Psychology for the 21st Century*, edited by D.J. Christie, R.V. Wagner, and D.D. Winter, 120–129. Upper Saddle River, NJ: Prentice Hall, 2001.

Walker, Rob B.J., and Saul H. Mendlovitz, "Peace Politics and Contemporary Social Movements." In *Towards a Just World Peace: Perspectives from Social Movements*, edited by Saul H. Mendlovitz and Rob B.J. Walker. London: Butterworths, 1987.

Washington State Department of Health. "Radionuclides in the Columbia River." http://www.doh.wa.gov/Hanford/publications/overview/columbia.html.

Watson, Roland. "Geneva Accords Quaint and Obsolete." Sunday Times of London. May 19, 2004. http://www.timesonline.co.uk/tol/news/world/iraq/article426900.ece

Weber, Max. *The Protestant Ethic and the Spirit of Capitalism.* London: Allen and Unwin, 1948.

Weber, Thomas. *Gandhi's Peace Army: The Shanti Sena and Unarmed Peacekeeping.* Syracuse, NY: Syracuse University Press, 1996.

Website of the Republic of Rwanda, "History," the Official Website of Republic of Rwanda, http://www.gov.rw/.

Weiss, Peter. "Six Reasons Why Nuclear Weapons Are More Dangerous Than Ever." http://www.wcl.american.edu/journal/ilr/22/weiss.pdf?rd=1.

Werner, Erica. "University of California, Bechtel awarded Lawrence Livermore Lab Management Contract." *Project On Government Oversight,* 2007. http://www.pogo.org/press-room/pogo-in-the-news/nuclear-security-safety/nss-livermore-20070508.html.

Wessells, Michael G. "Child Soldiers." *Bulletin of the Atomic Scientists* 53, no. 6 (1997): 32–39.

Wessells, Michael G. *Child Soldiers: From Violence to Protection.* Cambridge, MA: Harvard University Press, 2006.

Wessells, Michael G., and Carlinda Monteiro. "Healing Wounds of War in Angola: A Community-Based Approach." In *Addressing Childhood Adversity,* edited by D. Donald, A. Dawes, and J. Louw, 176–201. Cape Town: David Philip, 2000.

Wessells, Michael G., and Carlinda Monteiro. "Psychosocial Intervention and Post-War Reconstruction in Angola: Interweaving Western and Traditional Approaches." In *Peace, Conflict and Violence: Peace Psychology for the 21st Century,* edited by Daniel J. Christie, Robert V. Wagner, and Deborah D. Winter, 262–275. Upper Saddle River, NJ: Prentice Hall, 2001.

Wessells, Michael G., and Carlinda Monteiro. "Healing the Wounds following Protracted Conflict in Angola." In *Handbook of Culture, Therapy, and Healing,* edited by Uwe Peter Gielen, Jefferson M. Fish, and Juris G. Draguns, 321–341. Mahwah, NJ: Erlbaum, 2004.

Wessells, Michael G., and Kathleen Kostelny. "Youth Soldiering: An Integrated Framework for Understanding Psychosocial Impact." In *Adolescents and War: How Youth Deal with Political Violence,* edited by B. Barber, 105–122. New York: Oxford University Press, 2009.

Westermeyer, Joseph, and Karen Wahmanholm. "Refugee Children." In *Minefields in Their Hearts,* edited by Roberta Apfel and Bennett Simons, 75–103. New Haven, CT: Yale University Press, 1996.

Wette, Wolfram. "Geschichte und Frieden. Aufgaben historischer Friedensforschung." In *Lehren aus der Geschichte? Historische Friedensforschung,* edited by Reiner Steinweg. Frankfurt: Suhrkamp, 1990.

"WithholdAPADues." Some History and Information about "WithholdAPADues." http://www.ethicalapa.com/Join_Withhold.html.

White, Ralph K. *Fearful Warriors: A Psychological Profile of U.S.-Soviet Relations.* New York: Free Press, 1984.

Wignaraja, Ponna, ed. *New Social Movements.* New Delhi: Sage Publications, 1993.

Williams, Jody. "Politics Unusual: A Different Model of International Cooperation," *Harvard International Review* 22, no. 3 (Fall 2000).

Williams, Jody, Stephen D. Goose, and Mary Wareham, eds. *Banning Landmines: Disarmament, Citizen Diplomacy, and Human Security.* Lanham, MD: Rowman & Littlefield Publishers, 2008.

Willis, Frank R. *France, Germany, and the New Europe, 1945–1963.* Palo Alto, CA: Stanford University Press, 1965.

Winnefeld, James, M. Harrell, Robert Howe, Arnold Kanter, Brian Nichiporuk, Paul Steinberg, et al. *Intervention in Intrastate Conflict,* Vol. 1. Santa Monica, CA: RAND, 1995.

Wisor, Scott. "Darfur: The Economic Lifeline to Genocide." *Responsible Investor,* December 8, 2007. http://www.responsible-investor.com/home/print/darfur _the_economic_lifeline_to_genocide/.

"WithholdAPADues." Some History and Information about "WithholdAPADues." http://www.ethicalapa.com/Join_Withhold.html.

World Health Organization. *International Statistical Classification of Diseases and Related Health Problems,* 10th rev. ed. Geneva, 1992.

World Nuclear Association. "Chernobyl Accident." August 2010. http:// www.world-nuclear.org/info/chernobyl/inf07.htm.

World Nuclear Association. "Plans For New Reactors Worldwide." August 2010. http://www.world-nuclear.org/info/inf17.html.

WorldPublicOpinion.org. "American and Russian Publics Strongly Support Steps to Reduce and Eliminate Nuclear Weapons." http://www.worldpublicopinion .org/pipa/articles/international_security_bt/432.php.

Worthington, Everett L., ed. *Handbook of Forgiveness.* New York: Brunner-Routledge, 2005.

Wright, Scott. "Archbishop Oscar Romero: Easter is Now the Cry of Victory." *Signs of the Times: Oscar Romero Faith and Solidarity in the Americas.* October 15, 2008. http://www.sicsal-usa.org/2008/10/archbishop-oscar-romero-easter-is-now-the-cry-of-victory/.

York, Herbert. *The Advisors.* Berkeley: University of California Press, 1976.

Young India, August 11, 1920. Cited in Gene Sharp, *Gandhi as a Political Strategist,* 160. Boston: Porter Sargent, 1979.

Young, Nigel. "Peace Movements in History." In *Towards a Just World Peace: Perspectives from Social Movements,* edited by Saul H. Mendlovitz and Rob B.J. Walker, 137–169. London: Butterworths, 1987.

Yusuf, Huma, "Rwandan Troops Enter the Democratic Republic of Congo." *The Christian Science Monitor* (January 20, 2009). http://www.csmonitor.com/2009/ 0120/p99s01-duts.html.

Zinn, Howard. *A Power Governments Cannot Suppress.* San Francisco: City Lights Publisher, 2007.

Ziviler Ungehorsam, Traditionen, Konzepte, Erfahrungen, Perspektiven. Sensbachtal: Komitee-Eigenverlag, 1992.

Zorbas, Eugenia. "Reconciliation in Post-Genocide Rwanda." *African Journal of Legal Studies* 1 (2004): 29–52. http://www.africalawinstitute.org/ajls/vol1/ no1/zorbas.pdf.

Zunes, Stephen. "Iran's History of Civil Insurrections." *Huffington Post,* June 19, 2009.

Zunes, Stephen. "Recognizing the Power of Nonviolent Action." *Foreign Policy in Focus Report,* March 2005.

INDEX

About the Editors and Contributors

Co-editor **Marc Pilisuk** got his PhD in clinical and social psychology from the University of Michigan in 1961 and went on to teach, research, and write at several colleges, ending at the University of California and Saybrook University. His various departmental affiliations, psychology, nursing, administrative sciences, social welfare, public health, community mental health, human and community development, city and regional planning, peace and conflict studies, and human sciences, convinced him that academic disciplines could be blinders and should be crossed. He was a founder of the first Teach-in on a University Campus (Michigan) and the Psychologists for Social Responsibility, helped start SANE (now Peace Action), and is a past president of the Society for the Study of Peace Conflict and Violence. He has received several lifetime contribution awards for work for peace. Marc's books cover topics of underlying social issues, poverty, international conflict, and the nature of human interdependence. His most recent book, *Who Benefits from Global Violence and War*, uncovered information that was sufficiently shocking to motivate this new undertaking on *Peace Movements Worldwide*.

Co-editor **Michael N. Nagler** was sensitized to issues of peace and justice (the usual term is "radicalized") through folk music and various influences by the time he left his New York birthplace. After attending Cornell University and finishing his BA at New York University, he arrived in Berkeley, CA, in 1960, in time to finish a PhD in Comparative Literature before the advent of the Free Speech Movement. The successes and failures of that movement broadened his outlook such that after meeting a meditation teacher, Eknath Easwaran, late in 1966 he launched a parallel career—inward. Nonviolence, and Gandhi in particular, became a way to carve out a meaningful niche for himself within academia. At Berkeley, he went on to found the Peace and Conflict Studies Program (PACS; now probably the largest in terms of student majors in the United States) and off campus co-founded the Metta Center for Nonviolence (www.mettacenter.org). He also became chair of Peaceworkers (www.peaceworkers.org) and eventually co-chair of the Peace and Justice Studies Association (www.peacejusticestudies.org). He stopped teaching at the university in 2007 to devote his time to Metta and the Blue Mountain Center of Meditation. A frequent speaker on nonviolence and related themes around the world, his most recent recognition is the Jamnalal Bajaj International Award for Promoting Gandhian Values Outside India. His books include *The Upanishads* (with Eknath Easwaran, 1987), *Our Spiritual Crisis* (2004), and *The Search for a Nonviolent Future*, which won a 2002 American Book Award and has been translated into six languages, most recently Arabic.

Daniel J. Adamski, a native of Toledo, Ohio, and graduate of the University of Toledo, went on to earn an MA and PhD in English language and literature at the University of London. His research focused on early 20th-century periodicals and his dissertation, "Thickening the Thirties: The New English Weekly and the Discourse of Dissent," examined the literary, political, and economic networks of little magazines in Britain and America in the 1930s. Living and studying in London for nearly 10 years, he worked with homeless charities and organized student groups in efforts to combat homelessness. After teaching college English for 10 years, Daniel is now a freelance researcher. He is actively engaged in improving literacy in his local community, as well as being an ardent anti-war activist.

Melissa Anderson-Hinn is a passionate advocate and activist for all causes related to human rights and environmental protection. Her work is rooted in her belief that every human life has value, dignity, and purpose; that every story deserves to be told; and that a large part of protecting human health is protecting the health of the environment. She is particularly committed to the global efforts to end modern-day slavery and generate the social change necessary to ensure that it is no longer tolerated or perpetrated by the people of the world or the sociopolitical systems and environmental realities that exist. Balancing her roles as mother, wife, dual-doctorate student, and social entrepreneur, Melissa finds that the key to success is a fully integrated lifestyle, cultivated in community, and founded in a personal and communal commitment to the subversive values that she believes can build a sustainable, more compassionate world.

Hector Aristizábal is a native of Colombia. His commitment to the human rights work forced him to leave his country in 1989 due to death threats. Hector holds an MA in psychology from Antioquia University in Medellin, Colombia, and a degree as a marriage family therapist from Pacific Oaks College in Pasadena. Based on his own experience with torture, Hector developed a play based on his story that he uses as a springboard to invite audiences into transformative action. In recent years, Hector has developed his own techniques to awaken the imagination. These techniques are inspired by Theatre of the Oppressed and include storytelling and council circles. His work nationally and internationally has created significant changes in the lives of the different communities ranging from at risk youth centers, prisons, universities, churches, homeless shelters, health organizations combating HIV/AIDS, sex workers, and teachers. Currently, Hector is the creative director and co-founder of Imaginaction, an organization that aims to provide this kind of work globally.

Cynthia Boaz is assistant professor of political science at Sonoma State University. She is also an analyst and consultant on nonviolent action and a regular contributor to several news and commentary media outlets. Her areas of expertise include nonviolence, strategic nonviolent action, civil resistance, political development, and political communication with an emphasis on media coverage of war. Dr. Boaz is a frequent contributor to many online news and commentary sites, including Truthout, the HuffingtonPost, and Common Dreams. She is an affiliated scholar at the UNESCO Chair of Philosophy MA Program in Peace, Conflict, and Development Studies in Castellon de la Plana, Spain. Boaz also serves on the academic advisory board for the International Center on Nonviolent Conflict, and is on the board of directors of the Metta Center for Nonviolence Education and also Project Censored/Media Freedom Foundation. She also works closely with the U.S. Campaign for Burma. Her work has appeared in numerous venues including *Comparative Political Studies*, *Sojourners Magazine*, *Peace Review: A Journal of Social Justice*, and *Feminist Media Studies*.

Fr. Roy Bourgeois served as a Naval Officer for two years before entering the seminary of the Maryknoll Missionary Order. Ordained a Catholic priest in 1972, Roy went on to work with the poor of Bolivia for five years before being arrested and forced to leave the country, then under the repressive rule of dictator and School of the Americas (SOA) graduate General Hugo Banzer. In 1980 Fr. Roy became involved in issues surrounding U.S. policy in El Salvador after four U.S. churchwomen—two of them friends of his—were raped and killed by Salvadoran soldiers. Roy became an outspoken critic of U.S. foreign policy in Latin America. Since then, he has spent over four years in U.S. federal prisons for nonviolent protests against the training of Latin American soldiers at Ft. Benning, Georgia. In 1990, Roy founded the School of the Americas Watch.

Andreas Buro Habil was born in Berlin in 1928 and is a retired professor of political science and international relations at the Johann Wolfgang Goethe University in Frankfurt/Main. Cofounder of the German Easter March Movement/Campaign for Democracy and Disarmament and its longtime spokesperson for the socialist office and the Committee for Basic Rights and Democracy. Recent emphases on content include Criticism of the new military policy, concepts to support the evolvement of "civil conflict-adaptation"—in this sense political work, especially, related to the conflicts in the former Yugoslavia, Turkey, Iran, Afghanistan, and Israel/Palestine. He received the Aachener Peace Price in 2008. His most recent book publication was *Stories from the Peace Movement—Personal and Political, Committee for Basic Rights and Democracy* (2005).

Jujin Chung is a researcher, consultant, educator, and trainer working on conflict transformation and peace building issues. Dr. Chung has been engaged in building a foundation for collaborative conflict resolution and sustainable peace building programs in South Korea. She has been working with different groups of people, in particular, civil society organizations and their workers, to design programs and activities relating to peace and conflict issues to educate and empower them. She earned an MA in conflict transformation at the Eastern Mennonite University (Harrisonburg, VA) and a PhD in peace studies at the University of Bradford in the United Kingdom.

Justin C. Cliburn went to Iraq as a member of the Oklahoma Army National Guard in December 2005. During his tour, he experienced every facet of the war (socially, politically, militarily) as he and his comrades patrolled supply routes, trained Iraqi police, dealt with the political nuances of working with the Iraqis, and befriended Iraqi children. Cliburn is now a senior political science major at Cameron University and works part-time in management for a major shipping company. He hopes to go to law school.

Daniel Ellsberg spent three years (1954 to 1957) in the U.S. Marine Corps, serving as rifle platoon leader, operations officer, and rifle company commander. He earned his PhD in economics at Harvard University in 1962. His work on what has become known as the "Ellsberg Paradox," published in an article titled "Risk, Ambiguity, and the Savage Axioms" is considered a landmark in decision theory and behavioral economics. In 1959, Ellsberg became a strategic analyst at the RAND Corporation and consultant to the Defense Department and the White House, specializing in problems of the command and control of nuclear weapons, nuclear war plans, and crisis decision making. Ellsberg joined the Defense Department in 1964 as Special Assistant to Assistant Secretary of Defense (International Security Affairs) John McNaughton, working on the escalation of the war in Vietnam. He transferred to the State Department in 1965 to serve two years at the U.S. Embassy in Saigon, evaluating pacification in the field. On return to the RAND Corporation in 1967, Ellsberg worked on the top secret McNamara study of U.S. Decision-Making in Vietnam, 1945 to 1968, which later came to be known as the Pentagon Papers. In 1969, he photocopied the 7,000-page study and gave it to the Senate Foreign Relations Committee; in 1971 he gave it to the *New York Times*, the *Washington Post*, and 17 other newspapers. His trial, on 12 felony counts posing a possible sentence of 115 years, was dismissed in 1973 on grounds of governmental misconduct against him, which led to the convictions of several White House aides and figured in the impeachment proceedings against President Nixon. Ellsberg is the author of three books including *Secrets: A Memoir of Vietnam and the Pentagon Papers.* In December 2006 he was awarded the 2006 Right Livelihood Award, known as the "Alternative Nobel Prize," in Stockholm. Since the end of the Vietnam War, Ellsberg has been a lecturer, writer, and activist on the dangers of the nuclear era, wrongful U.S. interventions, and the urgent need for patriotic whistle-blowing. He is a Senior Fellow of the Nuclear Age Peace Foundation.

Inigo Gilmore is an award-winning filmmaker and journalist who has worked in more than 100 countries around the globe. He has reported from Africa, the Middle East, and Asia for *the Times of London, the Sunday Times, the Telegraph*, Sky Television, BBC, Channel 4, CNN, and PBS. Documentaries include *Nkosi's Story* (BBC 2, Correspondent, May 2001), the story of 12-year-old Nkosi Johnson, a South African child infected with HIV/AIDS; *Searching for Saddam* (BBC2 and BBC3, June 2003); *Behind the Fence* (BBC2, 2003 Correspondent). Shot over one year, *Behind the Fence* told the story of Israel's construction of its controversial security fence; it was nominated for best documentary, Amnesty International Media

Awards, 2004. In 2007 he won a Royal Television Society award for his work covering the Israel/Lebanon war.

Stephen D. Goose is executive director of the Arms Division of Human Rights Watch. He has played critical roles in securing the 1997 treaty banning antipersonnel mines, the 1995 protocol banning blinding laser weapons, and the 2003 protocol on explosive remnants of war. Goose has served as the head of delegation for the International Campaign to Ban Landmines (ICBL) to every Mine Ban Treaty meeting since 1998, and he helped create ICBL's civil society monitoring initiative, Landmine Monitor.

Hildegard Goss-Mayr is an Austrian Catholic pioneer in teaching the philosophy and practice of nonviolence amid great historical events of the past half century. During childhood and as a young person she experienced Nazism, the persecution of her family, and World War II. After graduation with a doctorate in philosophy from the University of Vienna she worked, together with her husband Jean Goss, as a staff person of the International Fellowship of Reconciliation for East-West Dialogue during the Cold War. She supported nonviolent struggles to overcome colonialism and racism (Angola, Mozambique, South Africa) and helped to build up "People Power" in the Philippines to overthrow the dictatorship of President Marcos. During the Second Vatican Council the Goss-Mayrs set up a peace lobby in Rome to promote the out-ruling of the just war concepts and the development of a theology of peacemaking built on the nonviolence of Jesus. During recent years she helped to build up nonviolent movements in francophone African countries. She published several books and numerous articles and interviews. She has been awarded several Peace prizes.

Kathy Kelly co-coordinates Voices for Creative Nonviolence (www.vcnv .org), a campaign to end U.S. military and economic warfare. As a co-founder of Voices in the Wilderness, she helped form 70 delegations from 1996 to 2003 that openly defied economic sanctions by bringing medicines to children and families in Iraq. Kathy and her companions lived in Baghdad throughout the 2003 "Shock and Awe" bombing. More recently, she has visited Gaza and Pakistan, writing eyewitness accounts of war's impact on civilians. Kathy was sentenced to one year in federal prison for planting corn on nuclear missile silo sites (1988 to 1989) and served three months in 2004, for crossing the line at Fort Benning's military training school. She and her companions at the Voices home office in

Chicago believe that nonviolence necessarily involves simplicity, service, sharing of resources, and nonviolent direct action in resistance to war and oppression. Kathy hasn't paid federal income taxes since 1980.

Herbert C. Kelman is Richard Clarke Cabot Professor of Social Ethics, Emeritus, and co-chair of the Middle East Seminar at Harvard University. He was the founding Director (1993 to 2003) of the Program on International Conflict Analysis and Resolution at Harvard's Weatherhead Center for International Affairs. A pioneer in the development of interactive problem solving—an unofficial third-party approach to the resolution of international and intercommunal conflict—he has been engaged for nearly 40 years in efforts toward the resolution of the Israeli-Palestinian conflict. His writings on interactive problem solving received the Grawemeyer Award for Ideas Improving World Order in 1997. Other awards include the Socio-Psychological Prize of the American Association for the Advancement of Science (1956), the Kurt Lewin Memorial Award (1973), the American Psychological Association's Award for Distinguished Contributions to Psychology in the Public Interest (1981), the Austrian Medal of Honor for Science and Art First Class (1998), and the Socrates Prize for Mediation (2009). His major publications include *International Behavior: A Social-Psychological Analysis* (editor and co-author, 1965), *A Time to Speak: On Human Values and Social Research* (1968), and *Crimes of Obedience: Toward a Social Psychology of Authority and Responsibility* (with V. Lee Hamilton, 1989).

Azim N. Khamisa lost his only son, Tariq, to a gang-related murder. He is a rare individual who not only speaks of powerful and life-changing concepts, but also walks his talk, having created a foundation in his son's name, the Tariq Khamisa Foundation, which is dedicated to breaking the cycle of youth violence by empowering children, saving lives, and teaching peace. Azim is also the author of three best-selling books, *Azim's Bardo—From Murder to Forgiveness: A Father's Journey, From Forgiveness to Fulfillment,* and *The Secrets of the Bulletproof Spirit.*

Jill Latonick-Flores, an advocate for peace and social justice, has supported the goals of the School of the Americas Watch for much of the past decade. Jill is a member of the Steering Committee of Psychologists for Social Responsibility. She received her Ph.D from Saybrook University in 2005. Her award winning dissertation was entitled, Awakening to the Eco-Tragedy: An Ideological and Epistemological Inquiry into the Hidden Mental Demands of Christian Environmentalism. She lives in Austin, Texas.

Diane Lefer has collaborated with Hector Aristizábal for years on such works as the stage play *Nightwind* and their book, *The Blessing Next to the Wound*. Her most recent book, *California Transit*, received the Mary McCarthy Award in Short Fiction and includes a novella that exposes abuse in immigration detention. She has volunteered with the Program for Torture Victims and teaches in the MFA Writing Program at the Vermont College of Fine Arts.

Steven D. Lydenberg is Chief Investment Officer of Domini Social Investments and Vice President of the Domini Funds. He has been active in social research since 1975. Mr. Lydenberg was a founder of KLD Research & Analytics, Inc., and served as its research director from 1990 to 2001. From 1987 to 1989, he was an associate with Franklin Research and Development Corporation (now known as Trillium Asset Management). For 12 years he worked with the Council on Economic Priorities, ultimately as director of corporate accountability research. Mr. Lydenberg has written numerous publications on issues of corporate social responsibility. He is the author of *Corporations and the Public Interest* (2005), coauthor of *Investing for Good* (1993), coeditor of *The Social Investment Almanac* (1992), and coauthor of *Rating America's Corporate Conscience* (1986). He has published articles including "Trust Building and Trust Busting: Corporations, Government, and Responsibilities" (*Journal of Corporate Citizenship*, Autumn 2003) and "Envisioning Socially Responsible Investing: A Model for 2006" (*Journal of Corporate Citizenship*, Autumn 2002). Mr. Lydenberg is a fellow with the Institute for Responsible Investment and is a member of the Boston Security Analysts Society. Mr. Lydenberg holds a BA in English from Columbia College and an MFA in theater arts from Cornell University, and holds the Chartered Financial Analyst designation.

Rachel M. MacNair is the author of the textbook *The Psychology of Peace: An Introduction* and the monograph *Perpetration-Induced Traumatic Stress: The Psychological Consequences of Killing*. She edited for an activist audience *Working for Peace: A Handbook of Practical Psychology*. She is Director of the Institute for Integrated Social Analysis, research arm of the nonprofit organization Consistent Life; she also coaches dissertation students on statistics. She graduated from Earlham College, a Quaker school, with a BA in peace and conflict studies, and got her PhD in psychology and sociology from the University of Missouri at Kansas City.

Ramu Manivannan was a former Fellow of the United Nations University. He was also a Co-Convener for the Nonviolence Commission of the

International Peace Researchers Association (IPRA) and a former Executive Member of the Nonviolent Peaceforce. He teaches political science at the University of Madras, India. He combines peace research and social activism to promote peace, democracy, and justice in South and Southeast Asia. He is an advocate for the Pro-Democracy Movement in Burma, the Free Tibet Movement, and the Just Rights of Eelam Tamils. He works among the refugee communities from Burma, Tibet, and Sri Lanka. He is a radical Gandhian who moved to the path of Non-Party Political Process following Jayaprakash Narayan. He is a trainer in nonviolence and holistic education and is socially engaged with experiments in community-based holistic education and sustainable development. He has founded the "Gandhi-King-Mandela Farm" and established within it an alternative school for the rural poor children near Vellore in Tamil Nadu. He is one of the founding members of the Nonviolent Peaceforce. He is the coordinator for the Mahatma Gandhi Centre for Peace and Conflict Resolution, University of Madras. He is an inter-faith practitioner and has led spiritual walks in the Himalayas for more than 18 years.

Cristina Jayme Montiel is a professor of peace/political psychology and has been teaching at the Ateneo de Manila University for more than 30 years. During the Marcos dictatorship, she chaired Lingap Bilanggo (Care for Prisoners), a social movement for the general amnesty of all Filipino political prisoners. She likewise coordinated nationwide grassroots seminars on Structural Change, for the PDP-LABAN (President Cory Aquino's political party). Montiel serves as editorial board member of the *Peace Psychology* Book Series by Springer Publications, and was associate editor of *Peace and Conflict: Journal of Peace Psychology.* Montiel's international experiences cover academic visits to Xiamen University (China), National University of Malaysia, University of Hawaii, Ohio State University, Georgetown University, Whitman College, Technical University of Chemnitz (Germany), and the Australian National University. Her recent journal publications include "Effects of Political Framing and Perceiver's Dominant-Group Position on Trait Attributions of a Terrorist/Freedom--Fighter" (2008) and "Social Representations of Democratic Transition: Was the Philippine People Power One a Nonviolent Power-Shift or a Military Coup?" (2010). She recently published a book on Peace Psychology in Asia, co-edited with Noraini Noor.

Gianina Pellegrini is a doctoral student at Saybrook University, pursuing a degree in psychology with a concentration in social transformation and certification in international peace and conflict resolution. While obtaining a master's degree in psychology, Gianina researched how spiritual, religious, and traditional customs in sub-Saharan Africa influenced the care and treatment of HIV-positive children. Her primary areas of interest include issues pertaining to human rights, public health, and social justice.

Tessie Petion is the lead research analyst responsible for the application of the Funds' social and environmental standards to European equities. Ms. Petion worked as an analyst and associate in Deutsche Bank's Global Institutional Services department from 2000 to 2002, and in international sales for the New York Stock Exchange from 2003 to 2004. In 2006, she worked in the Dominican Republic as a consultant for the Consejo Nacional de Competitividad and in India as a consultant for the microfinance institution Basix. Ms. Petion holds a BS in business administration and management information systems from the University at Albany, SUNY; an MA in psychology from Tufts University; and an MA in international business and development from the Fletcher School of Tufts University.

Angel Ryono is a master's degree student in the human sciences at Saybrook University. She was inspired to pursue graduate studies after working as a researcher and associate editor for Toda Institute for Global Peace and Policy Research in Honolulu, Hawaii. Currently, Angel is affiliated with the War Crimes Studies Center at University of California, Berkeley, particularly in working to support transitional justice projects in Southeast Asia. Her research focuses on the historical and structural challenges to peace building in Cambodia.

Christine Schweitzer is a social anthropologist by training and lives and works in Hamburg, Germany. She is currently working as Program Director for the international NGO Nonviolent Peaceforce (www.nonviolent peaceforce.org), an international NGO that has been founded to carry out and promote civilian peacekeeping, and a member of the German Institute for Peace Work and Nonviolent Conflict Transformation (www.ifgk.de). In the 1990s she co-founded and for some time coordinated the international Balkan Peace Team. She has published on subjects such as civilian-based defense, nonviolent conflict intervention, and peace work in general.

Alice Slater is the New York Director of the Nuclear Age Peace Foundation. She is a member of the Global Council of Abolition 2000, a global network working for a treaty to eliminate nuclear weapons, and directs the network's Sustainable Energy Working Group that produced a model statute for an International Renewable Energy Agency. She is on the

Board of the Lawyer's Committee for Nuclear Policy, is a member of the International Security Committee of the New York City Bar Association, and serves on the Executive Committee of the Middle Powers Initiative, working to create pressure on nuclear weapons states for swifter nuclear disarmament. She is a member of the Advisory Board of the Global Network Against Weapons and Nuclear Power in Space, and serves on the Steering Committee of the Indian Point Safe Energy Coalition. Ms. Slater is a UN NGO Representative and has organized numerous conferences, panels, and roundtables at the UN. She speaks frequently at meetings and conferences in the United States and abroad, contributes to the Codepink blog, Pink Tank, has written numerous articles and op-eds, and appears frequently on local and national media.

Martin Smith is a member of Iraq Veterans Against the War and has contributed to *Counterpunch* and the *International Socialist Review.* He is finishing his dissertation at the University of Illinois on troop dissent and the breakdown of the military during the Vietnam War.

Teresa Smith is an award-winning documentary filmmaker and journalist who has worked for BBC Television, the *Guardian* newspaper, Guardian-Films for www.guardian.co.uk, Channel 4 (UK), Al Jazeera International, ITN, and CNN International. She has worked extensively in the Middle East. Documentaries include *Baghdad: City of Walls* (AJI 2009); *9/11: Through Muslim Eyes* (Channel 4); *Reflections of Ground Zero* (Channel 4); *Playing to Survive* (BBC), the story of a women who played in the orchestra at Auschwitz-Birkenau; and *Cutting Up Rough* (BBC2), a profile of the British fashion designer, Alexander MacQueen. Her work has won awards from the Royal Television Society, Amnesty International, the Foreign Press Association, the Rory Peck Trust, and Mental Health in the Media (UK)

Ervin Staub is Professor Emeritus and Founding Director of the PhD program in the psychology of peace and the prevention of violence at the University of Massachusetts at Amherst. He has studied the roots of altruism, the origins of violence including genocide and mass killing, as well as prevention, and psychological recovery and reconciliation. His books include *Positive Social Behavior and Morality* (vols. 1 and 2, 1978, 1979), *The Roots of Evil: The Origins of Genocide and Other Group Violence* (1989), *The Psychology of Good and Evil: Why Children, Adults and Groups Help and Harm Others* (2003), and a number of edited volumes. A new book, *Overcoming Evil: Genocide, Violent Conflict and Terrorism,* and a collection of his past writings, *The Panorama of Mass Violence: Origins, Prevention, Reconciliation*, will be published in 2010. He is past President of the Society for the Study of Peace, Conflict, and Violence and of the International Society for Political Psychology. He has worked in schools to promote altruism and active bystandership to reduce aggression, with police to reduce the use of unnecessary force, in the Netherlands on Dutch Muslim relations, in New Orleans to promote reconciliation after Katrina, and since 1998 in Rwanda, in Burundi, and the Congo to promote psychological recovery and reconciliation and help prevent new violence through seminars, workshops, and educational radio programs. For his awards and downloads of selected articles, see his Web site (www.ervinstaub.com).

Michael Wessells, PhD, is a professor at Columbia University in the Program on Forced Migration and Health and a professor of psychology at Randolph-Macon College. He has served as President of the Division of Peace Psychology of the American Psychological Association and of Psychologists for Social Responsibility and as Co-Chair of the InterAction Protection Working Group. He is former Co-Chair of the Inter-Agency Standing Committee (IASC) (UN-NGO) Task Force on Mental Health and Psychosocial Support in Emergency Settings that developed the first inter-agency consensus guidelines for the field of mental health and psychosocial support in humanitarian crises. Currently, he is co-focal point on mental health and psychosocial support for the revision of the Sphere humanitarian standards. He has conducted extensive research on the holistic impacts of war and political violence on children, and he is author of *Child Soldiers: From Violence to Protection* (2006). He regularly advises UN agencies, governments, and donors on issues of psychosocial support. Throughout Africa and Asia he helps to develop community-based, culturally grounded programs that assist people affected by armed conflict.

Jody Williams is a Nobel Peace laureate and a founder and chair of the Nobel Women's Initiative. A distinguished visiting professor at the University of Houston's Graduate College of Social Work since 2003, she currently holds the Cele and Sam Keeper endowed professorship in peace and social justice. Williams was the founding coordinator of the International Campaign to Ban Landmines (ICBL), and she has served as an ICBL ambassador since 1998.

Howard Zinn was a historian, playwright, and peace activist, who grew up in the immigrant slums of Brooklyn where he worked in shipyards in his late teens. Eager to fight fascism, he participated in combat duty as a

U.S. Air Force bombardier in World War II. Afterward, under the G.I. Bill, he received his PhD in history from Columbia University and was a postdoctoral fellow in East Asian Studies at Harvard University. As a professor at Spelman College in Atlanta, a school for African American women, he became involved in the Civil Rights Movement, where he was an adviser to the Student Nonviolent Coordinating Committee (SNCC). He is the author of numerous books, including his epic masterpiece, *A People's History of the United States*, "a brilliant and moving history of American people from the point of view of those who have been exploited politically and economically and whose plight has been largely omitted from most histories" (*Library Journal*). He has received the Thomas Merton Award, the Eugene V. Debs Award, the Upton Sinclair Award, and the Lannan Literary Award. He was a professor emeritus of political science at Boston University and lived in Auburndale, Massachusetts, near his children and grandchildren. He died on January 27, 2010, shortly after granting permission to use his chapter in this volume.

Stephen Zunes is a professor of politics and chair of Middle Eastern Studies at the University of San Francisco. He serves as a senior analyst for the Foreign Policy in Focus project of the Institute for Policy Studies, an associate editor of *Peace Review*, and chair of the committee of academic advisors for the International Center on Nonviolent Conflict. Dr. Zunes is the author of scores of articles for scholarly and general readership on Middle Eastern politics, U.S. foreign policy, international terrorism, social movements, strategic nonviolent action, and human rights. He is the co-editor of *Nonviolent Social Movements* (1999) and *Consistently Opposing Killing* (2008), the author of the highly acclaimed *Tinderbox: U.S. Middle East Policy and the Roots of Terrorism* (2003), and the co-author, with Jacob Mundy, of *Western Sahara: Nationalism, Conflict, and International Accountability* (2009).

ABOUT THE SERIES EDITOR AND ADVISORY BOARD

SERIES EDITOR

Chris E. Stout, PsyD, MBA, is a licensed clinical psychologist and is a Clinical Full Professor at the University of Illinois College of Medicine's Department of Psychiatry. He served as an NGO Special Representative to the United Nations. He was appointed to the World Economic Forum's Global Leaders of Tomorrow and he has served as an Invited Faculty at the Annual Meeting in Davos. He is the Founding Director of the Center for Global Initiatives. Stout is a Fellow of the American Psychological Association, former President of the Illinois Psychological Association, and a Distinguished Practitioner in the National Academies of Practice. Stout has published or presented over 300 papers and 30 books and manuals on various topics in psychology. His works have been translated into six languages. He has lectured across the nation and internationally in 19 countries and has, visited 6 continents and almost 70 countries. He was noted as being "one of the most frequently cited psychologists in the scientific literature" in a study by Hartwick College. He is the recipient of the American Psychological Association's International Humanitarian Award.

ADVISORY BOARD

Bruce Bonecutter, PhD, is Director of Behavioral Services at the Elgin Community Mental Health Center, the Illinois Department of Human Services state hospital serving adults in greater Chicago. He is also a Clinical Assistant Professor of Psychology at the University of Illinois at Chicago. A clinical psychologist specializing in health, consulting, and forensic psychology, Bonecutter is also a longtime member of the American Psychological Association Taskforce on Children and the Family. He is a member of organizations including the Association for the Treatment of Sexual Abusers, International, the Alliance for the Mentally Ill, and the Mental Health Association of Illinois.

Joseph Flaherty, MD, is Chief of Psychiatry at the University of Illinois Hospital, Professor of Psychiatry at the University of Illinois College (UIC) of Medicine and a Professor of Community Health Science at the UIC College of Public Health. He is a Founding Member of the Society for the Study of Culture and Psychiatry. Dr. Flaherty has been a consultant to the World Health Organization, the National Institute of Mental Health, and also the Falk Institute in Jerusalem. He is the former Director of Undergraduate Education and Graduate Education in the Department of Psychiatry at the University of Illinois. Dr. Flaherty has also been Staff Psychiatrist and Chief of Psychiatry at Veterans Administration West Side Hospital in Chicago.

Michael Horowitz, PhD, is President and Professor of Clinical Psychology at the Chicago School of Professional Psychology, one of the nation's leading not-for-profit graduate schools of psychology. Earlier, he served as Dean and Professor of the Arizona School of Professional Psychology. A clinical psychologist practicing independently since 1987, his work has focused on psychoanalysis, intensive individual therapy, and couples therapy. He has provided Disaster Mental Health Services to the American Red Cross. Horowitz's special interests include the study of fatherhood.

Sheldon I. Miller, MD, is a Professor of Psychiatry at Northwestern University, and Director of the Stone Institute of Psychiatry at Northwestern Memorial Hospital. He is also Director of the American Board of Psychiatry and Neurology, Director of the American Board of Emergency Medicine, and Director of the Accreditation Council for Graduate Medical Education. Dr. Miller is also an Examiner for the American Board of Psychiatry and

Neurology. He is Founding Editor of the *American Journal of Addictions*, and Founding Chairman of the American Psychiatric Association's Committee on Alcoholism. Dr. Miller has also been a Lieutenant Commander in the U.S. Public Health Service, serving as psychiatric consultant to the Navajo Area Indian Health Service at Window Rock, Arizona. He is a member and Past President of the Executive Committee for the American Academy of Psychiatrists in Alcoholism and Addictions.

Dennis P. Morrison, PhD, is Chief Executive Officer at the Center for Behavioral Health in Indiana, the first behavioral health company ever to win the Joint Commission on Accreditation of Healthcare Organizations (JCAHO) Codman Award for excellence in the use of outcomes management to achieve health care quality improvement. He is President of the Board of Directors for the Community Healthcare Foundation in Bloomington, and has been a member of the Board of Directors for the American College of Sports Psychology. He has served as a consultant to agencies including the Ohio Department of Mental Health, Tennessee Association of Mental Health Organizations, Oklahoma Psychological Association, the North Carolina Council of Community Mental Health Centers, and the National Center for Heath Promotion in Michigan. Morrison served across 10 years as a Medical Service Corp Officer in the U.S. Navy.

William H. Reid, MD, is a clinical and forensic psychiatrist, and consultant to attorneys and courts throughout the United States. He is Clinical Professor of Psychiatry at the University of Texas Health Science Center. Dr. Miller is also an Adjunct Professor of Psychiatry at Texas A&M College of Medicine and Texas Tech University School of Medicine, as well as a Clinical Faculty member at the Austin Psychiatry Residency Program. He is Chairman of the Scientific Advisory Board and Medical Advisor to the Texas Depressive and Manic-Depressive Association, as well as an Examiner for the American Board of Psychiatry and Neurology. He has served as President of the American Academy of Psychiatry and the Law, as Chairman of the Research Section for an International Conference on the Psychiatric Aspects of Terrorism, and as Medical Director for the Texas Department of Mental Health and Mental Retardation. Dr. Reid earned an Exemplary Psychiatrist Award from the National Alliance for the Mentally Ill. He has been cited on the Best Doctors in America listing since 1998.

ABOUT THE SERIES

THE PRAEGER SERIES IN CONTEMPORARY PSYCHOLOGY

In this series, experts from various disciplines peer through the lens of psychology, telling us answers they see for questions of human behavior. Their topics may range from humanity's psychological ills—addictions, abuse, suicide, murder, and terrorism among them—to works focused on positive subjects, including intelligence, creativity, athleticism, and resilience. Regardless of the topic, the goal of this series remains constant—to offer innovative ideas, provocative considerations, and useful beginnings to better understand human behavior.

Series Editor
Chris E. Stout, Psy.D., MBA
Northwestern University Medical School
Illinois Chief of Psychological Services

Advisory Board
Bruce E. Bonecutter, Ph.D.
University of Illinois at Chicago
Director, Behavioral Services, Elgin Community Mental Health Center